Studies in Marxism and Social Theory

Self-ownership, freedom, and equality

In this book G. A. Cohen examines the libertarian principle of self-ownership, which says that each person belongs to himself and therefore owes no service or product to anyone else. This principle is used to defend capitalist inequality, which is said to reflect each person's freedom to do as he wishes with himself.

The author argues that self-ownership cannot deliver the freedom it promises to secure. He thereby undermines the idea that lovers of freedom should embrace capitalism and the inequality that comes with it. He goes on to show that the standard Marxist condemnation of exploitation implies an endorsement of self-ownership, since, in the Marxist conception, the employer steals from the worker what should belong to her, because she produced it. Thereby a deeply inegalitarian notion has penetrated what is in aspiration an egalitarian theory. Purging that notion from socialist thought, he argues, enables construction of a more consistent egalitarianism.

Studies in Marxism and Social Theory

Edited by G. A. COHEN, JON ELSTER AND JOHN ROEMER

The series is jointly published by the Cambridge University Press and the Editions de la Maison des Sciences de l'Homme, as part of the joint publishing agreement established in 1977 between the Fondation de la Maison des Sciences de l'Homme and the Syndics of the Cambridge University Press.

The books in the series are intended to exemplify a new paradigm in the study of Marxist social theory. They will not be dogmatic or purely exegetical in approach. Rather, they will examine and develop the theory pioneered by Marx, in the light of the intervening history, and with the tools of non-Marxist social science and philosophy. It is hoped that Marxist thought will thereby be freed from the increasingly discredited methods and presuppositions which are still widely regarded as essential to it, and that what is true and important in Marxism will be more firmly established.

Also in the series

JON ELSTER   *Making Sense of Marx*
ADAM PRZEWORSKI   *Capitalism and Social Democracy*
JOHN ROEMER (ed.)   *Analytical Marxism*
JON ELSTER AND KARL MOENE (eds.)   *Alternatives to Capitalism*
MICHAEL TAYLOR (ed.)   *Rationality and Revolution*
DONALD L. DONHAM   *History, Power, Ideology*
DAVID SCHWEICKART   *Against Capitalism*
PHILIPPE VAN PARIJS   *Marxism Recycled*
JOHN TORRANCE   *Karl Marx's Theory of Ideas*

Self-ownership, freedom, and equality

G. A. Cohen

Chichele Professor of Social and Political Theory
and Fellow of All Souls College, Oxford

Maison des Sciences de l'Homme

Published by the Press Syndicate of the University of Cambridge
The Pitt Building, Trumpington Street, Cambridge CB2 1RP
40 West 20th Street, New York, NY 10011–4211, USA
10 Stamford Road, Oakleigh, Melbourne 3166, Australia

© Maison des sciences de l'Homme and
Cambridge University Press 1995

First published 1995

A catalogue record for this book is available from the British Library

Library of Congress cataloguing in publication data
Cohen, G. A. (Gerald Allan), 1941–
Self-ownership, freedom, and equality / by G. A. Cohen.
(Studies in Marxism and social theory)
    p.   cm.
Includes bibliographical references (p.   ) and index.
ISBN 0 521 47174 5 (hardback). – ISBN 0 521 47751 4 (pbk.)
1. Equality. 2. Libertarianism. 3. Liberty. 4. Capitalism.
5. Marxian economics. I. Title.
JC575.C63 1995 323.44-dc20   94–40948 CIP

ISBN 0 521 47174 5 hardback
ISBN 0 521 47751 4 paperback
ISBN 2 7351 0684 2 hardback (France only)
ISBN 2 7351 0695 0 paperback (France only)

Transferred to digital printing 2001

WD

For Arnold Zuboff:
brilliant critic, devoted friend

Contents

Preface   *page* xi
Acknowledgements   xii

Introduction: history, ethics and Marxism   .   1

1 Robert Nozick and Wilt Chamberlain: how patterns
   preserve liberty   19

2 Justice, freedom, and market transactions   38

3 Self-ownership, world-ownership, and equality   67

4 Are freedom and equality compatible?   92

5 Self-ownership, communism, and equality: against
   the Marxist technological fix   116

6 Marxism and contemporary political philosophy,
   or: why Nozick exercises some Marxists more than
   he does any egalitarian liberals   144

7 Marx and Locke on land and labour   165

8 Exploitation in Marx: what makes it unjust?   195

9 Self-ownership: delineating the concept   209

10 Self-ownership: assessing the thesis   229

11 The future of a disillusion   245

Bibliography   266
Index of names   272
Subject index   274

Preface

Seven chapters of this book were once published as articles: they reappear here in (sometimes extensively) altered form. Four chapters, and the Introduction, are new. But the whole book represents a single intellectual journey. It displays the development of my response to the challenge posed to my once dogmatic socialist convictions by libertarian political philosophy.

In coping with that challenge, and in writing this book, my greatest debt has been to Arnold Zuboff, who convinced me to drop many misconceived ideas and who helped me to sharpen those that survived his scrutiny. I am also grateful to the members (Pranab Bardhan, Sam Bowles, Bob Brenner, John Roemer, Hillel Steiner, Robert van der Veen, Philippe Van Parijs, and Erik Wright) of the September or (as it is sometimes called) Non-Bullshit Marxism Group, who raked through early versions of most of the chapters. Daniel Attas, Ronnie Dworkin, Susan Hurley, David Miller, Derek Parfit, Alan Patten, Joseph Raz, Amartya Sen, Andrew Williams, and Bernard Williams made excellent criticisms at Oxford meetings. My former students Chris Bertram and Jo Wolff read the penultimate draft and offered penetrating observations and liberating suggestions. Dozens of friends and colleagues outside Oxford commented orally and in writing at different stages of the development of much of the material, but I have culpably failed to keep a complete running account of their contributions. Since it would be unjust to mention only those interventions of which I happen to have a record, I hope that they will forgive me for not listing them individually.

My children, and Maggie, strengthened me with their solidarity, and their wonderful kindness.

And without Michèle I would be a ship without a sail on a stormy sea, with no harbour in sight.

Acknowledgements

I thank the relevant publishers and editors for permission to draw on material in the following articles in the preparation of the indicated chapters:

1: 'Robert Nozick and Wilt Chamberlain: How Patterns Preserve Liberty', in *Erkenntnis*, 11, 1977. Copyright 1977 by *Erkenntnis*.

3: 'Self-Ownership, World-Ownership, and Equality', in Frank Lucash (ed.), *Justice and Equality Here and Now*, 1986. Copyright 1986 by Cornell University Press.

4: 'Self-Ownership, World-Ownership, and Equality: Part II', in *Social Philosophy and Policy*, 3, Issue 2 (Spring 1986). Copyright 1986 by *Social Philosophy and Policy*.

5: 'Self-Ownership, Communism, and Equality', in *Proceedings of the Aristotelian Society*, supp. vol. 64, 1990. Copyright 1990 by the Aristotelian Society.

6: 'Marxism and Contemporary Political Philosophy, or: Why Nozick Exercises Some Marxists More than He Does any Egalitarian Liberals', in *Canadian Journal of Philosophy*, supp. vol. 16, 1990. Copyright 1990 by *Canadian Journal of Philosophy*.

7: 'Marx and Locke on Land and Labour', in *Proceedings of the British Academy*, 71, *1985 Lectures and Memoirs*. Copyright 1986 by The British Academy.

11: 'The Future of a Disillusion', in Jim Hopkins and Anthony Savile (eds.), *Psychoanalysis, Mind and Art: Perspectives on Richard Wollheim*, Basil Blackwell, Oxford, 1992. Copyright 1992 by Basil Blackwell Ltd.

Introduction: history, ethics and Marxism

1. When I was a young lecturer at University College, London, I taught subjects that were not closely related to my research interests. I was hired, in 1963, to teach moral and political philosophy, but I wrote about Karl Marx's theory of history, for I passionately believed it to be true, and I wanted to defend it against criticism that was widely accepted but which I considered (and consider) to be misjudged. To be sure, I did also have views about issues in moral and political philosophy, but those views did not generate any writing. I had, in particular, strong convictions about justice and about the injustice of inequality and of capitalist exploitation, but I did not think that I had, or would come to have, anything sufficiently distinctive to say about justice, or about capitalist injustice, to be worth printing.

My conception of moral and political philosophy was, and is, a standardly academic one: they are ahistorical disciplines which use abstract philosophical reflection to study the nature and truth of normative judgements. Historical materialism (which is what Karl Marx's theory of history came to be called) is, by contrast, an empirical theory (comparable in status to, for example, nineteenth-century historical geology) about the structure of society and the dynamics of history. It is not entirely without implications for normative philosophy, but it is substantially value-free: one could believe historical materialism but regret that the career of humanity is as it describes, and, more specifically, that, as it predicts, class society will be superseded by a classless one.

Since historical materialism was, at the time in question, the only part of Marxism that I believed[1] – I no longer also believed in dialectical

---

[1] I had once believed the whole thing, as a result of having been raised inside the Canadian communist movement: see section 1 of Chapter 11 below.

materialism, which is a comprehensive philosophy about reality as such – I often said, with the complacent self-endorsement of youth, that in so far as I was a Marxist I was not a philosopher, and in so far as I was a philosopher I was not a Marxist. In further description of the separation between my philosophical and my Marxist engagements, I shall first explain why my Marxism did not control or affect my moral and political philosophy in a manner that many Marxists and anti-Marxists would have thought that it should, and then why I did not recruit to Marxist or even to socialist service the competence in political philosophy that I was developing through teaching it.

People familiar both with Marxism and with mainstream anglophone normative philosophy might expect the first to challenge the second, since, for the philosophy, normative statements are timelessly true (or false), whereas, according to Marxism, so it is supposed, either there is no such thing as normative truth or it is a truth which changes historically with economic circumstances and requirements. Now, I endorsed – I still do – the stated severely ahistorical view of normative philosophy, but, for two reasons, I was able to reconcile it with my Marxism. For, first, and as I have already indicated, I had shed, by the time I reached University College, my belief in a general Marxist philosophy (dialectical materialism) which is commonly understood to imply scepticism, or, at least, relativism, about value. And, second, I did not believe that historical materialism, in its best interpretation, reduces all values and principles to rationalizations of class interest, but, on the contrary, I believed that it looks to the end of class domination as the beginning of a society governed by 'a really human morality which stands above class antagonisms',[2] a morality which has always had some sort of historical manifestation, within the confinement of class constraint. Accordingly, my particular Marxist convictions did not disturb my view that ultimate normative truth is historically invariant, that, while historical circumstances undoubtedly affect what justice (for example) demands, they do so only because timelessly valid principles of justice have different implications at different times.

Although I thought that Marxism had little to say, in philosophical terms, about justice, I did not think that Marxists could be indifferent to justice. On the contrary: I was certain that every committed Marxist was exercised by the injustice of capitalist exploitation, and that Marxists who affected unconcern about justice, from Karl Marx down, were kidding

---

[2] Frederick Engels, *Anti-Dühring*, p. 133.

themselves. I never believed, as many Marxists professed to do, that normative principles were irrelevant to the socialist movement, that, since the movement was of oppressed people fighting for their own liberation, there was no room or need for specifically moral inspiration in it. I thought no such thing partly for the plain reason that I observed enormous selfless dedication among the active communists who surrounded me in my childhood, and partly for the more sophisticated reason that the self-interest of any oppressed producer would tell him to stay at home, rather than to risk his neck in a revolution whose success or failure would be anyhow unaffected by his participation in it. Revolutionary workers and, *a fortiori*, bourgeois fellow-travellers without a particular material interest in socialism, must perforce be morally inspired. But I thought that, while historical materialism threw light on the different historical forms of injustice (such as slavery, serfdom and the condition of being a proletarian), and on how to eliminate injustice, it had nothing to say about what justice (timelessly) is. It therefore did not control my conception of political philosophy.

Nor did I put my Marxism and my philosophy together in an opposite way, by recruiting political philosophy, as I conceived it, to socialist use. For, although I took for granted that socialism was to be preferred to capitalism for reasons of normative principle, and not, as some weirdly suggested, because historical materialism showed its advent to be inevitable, I also thought that socialism was so evidently superior to capitalism from *any* morally decent point of view, with respect to *any* attractive principle (of utility, or equality, or justice, or freedom, or democracy, or self-realization) that there was no necessity to identify the right point(s) of view from which to endorse it, no need to specify what principle(s) should guide the fight for socialism, and, therefore, no call to do normative philosophy for socialism's sake. I did not think that it was incumbent on a socialist philosopher, in his capacity as a socialist, to bother with political philosophy, because the case for socialism seemed to me to be so overwhelming that only sub-intellectual reasons, reflecting class and other prejudice, could persuade a person against it. Animating principles were of course needed by the socialist movement, and they were abundantly present in it. But political philosophy, the systematic search for the right principles, and for the structures (very generally described) that might realize them, was not required by allies, and would be unlikely to make enemies move in a socialist direction, since their resistance to socialism was not a principled one. So I did not engage in moral and political philosophy, in a creative sense. I taught it, but it was not the site of my research work, which was directed towards the clarification and defence of historical materialism.

2. I had never heard an argument against socialism for which I did not (so I thought) already have an answer in my pocket. Then one day in 1972, in my room at University College, Jerry Dworkin nudged me. He began a process that, in time, roused me from what had been my dogmatic socialist slumber. He did that by hitting me with an outline of the anti-socialist Wilt Chamberlain argument, as it was to appear in Robert Nozick's then forthcoming *Anarchy, State, and Utopia*.[3] My reaction to the argument was a mixture of irritation and anxiety. There was a would-be confidence that it depended on sleight of hand, alongside a lurking or looming fear that maybe it did not.

Then Nozick's argument appeared in full force, first in *Philosophy and Public Affairs* for Fall 1973, and, finally, in 1974, in *Anarchy* itself, and now I was vigorously engaged by it. It happened that I spent February to May of 1975 in Princeton, in the vicinity of two exceptionally sapient philosophers, namely Tom Nagel and Tim Scanlon. They were considerably to Nozick's left, but, I was both heartened and puzzled to observe, they were not disconcerted by his arguments. This was perhaps partly for the undeep reason that, unlike me, they had had years of pre-acquaintance with the author and his developing book, and, therefore, the time to form a response to it, long before it appeared; but I am sure that it was at least partly for the deeper reasons explored in Chapter 6 below, where, as its sub-title indicates, I seek to explain why Marxists like me were vulnerable to Nozick's libertarianism in a way that liberals like Nagel and Scanlon were not. Many friends and colleagues were surprised by how seriously I and some other Marxists took libertarianism. They thought that, since leftish liberals like Scanlon and Nagel could comfortably dismiss Nozick's view, then, *a fortiori*, it should not detain people like me. Conjectures which, so I believe, illuminate the unexpected contrast are offered in Chapter 6 below.

Whether or not people were right to be surprised that I regarded Nozick's challenge as very considerable, I did so regard it, and I resolved, in 1975, that, when I had completed a book that I was then writing on historical materialism, I would devote myself in the main to political

[3] The core of the Wilt Chamberlain argument is reproduced in the long excerpt from *Anarchy* which is given at Chapter 1, pp. 20–1 below. Readers who are unfamiliar with the argument may like to read that excerpt before continuing with this Introduction.

philosophy proper, and the present book is one product of that turn of engagement.

At Princeton I lectured on Nozick and I thereby developed the ideas which appear in Chapter 1 below. I shall presently review that and the other chapters of this book. But first I want to turn from the somewhat local topic of the demise of my earlier cavalier attitude to the question of the justification of socialism, to the wider neglect of questions of normative justification in the Marxist tradition. Among other things, I shall explain why some excuses for that neglect which existed in the past are no longer available.

3. Classical Marxism distinguished itself from what it regarded as the socialism of dreams by declaring a commitment to hard-headed historical and economic analysis: it was proud of what it considered to be the stoutly factual character of its central claims. The title of Engels' book, *The Development of Socialism from Utopia to Science*,[4] articulates this piece of Marxist self-interpretation. Socialism, once raised aloft by airy ideals, would henceforth rest on a firm foundation of fact.

Marxism's heroic – and possibly incoherent[5] – self-description was in part justified. For its founders and adherents did distinguish themselves from socialist forerunners like Charles Fourier and Robert Owen by forsaking the detailed depiction of imaginary perfect societies, and they did achieve a great leap forward in realistic understanding of how the social order functions. But the favoured classical Marxist self-description, whether incoherent or not, was certainly in part bravado. For values of equality, community, and human self-realization were undoubtedly integral to the Marxist belief structure. All classical Marxists believed in some kind of equality, even if many would have refused to acknowledge that they believed in it and none, perhaps, could have stated precisely what principle of equality he believed in.

Yet Marxists were not preoccupied with, and therefore never examined, principles of equality, or, indeed, any other values or principles. Instead, they devoted their intellectual energy to the hard factual carapace surrounding their values, to bold explanatory theses about history in

---

[4] The book is usually called, in English, *Socialism: Utopian and Scientific*. The version of the title given above translates the more evocative German title: *Die Entwicklung des Sozialismus von der Utopie zur Wissenschaft*.

[5] Whether it really was incoherent depends on the exact sense in which socialism was now supposed to *be*, or to *rest* on, science. That matter of interpretation is too complex for me to address here.

general and capitalism in particular, the theses which gave Marxism its commanding authority in the field of socialist doctrine, and even, indeed, its moral authority, because its heavy intellectual labour on matters of history and economic theory proved the depth of its political commitment.

And now Marxism has lost much or most of its carapace, its hard shell of supposed fact. Scarcely anybody defends it in the academy, and there are no more apparatchiki who believe that they are applying it in Party offices. To the extent that Marxism is still alive, as, for example, one may say that it (sort of) is in the work of scholars like John Roemer and Philippe Van Parijs, it presents itself as a set of values and a set of designs for realizing those values. It is therefore, now, far less different than it could once advertise itself to be from the Utopian socialism with which it so proudly contrasted itself. Its shell is cracked and crumbling, its soft underbelly is exposed.

Let me illustrate Marxism's loss of factual carapace with respect to the value of equality, which inspires this book.

Classical Marxists believed that economic equality was both historically inevitable and morally right. They believed the first entirely consciously, and they believed the second more or less consciously, and exhibited more or less evasion when asked whether they believed it. It was partly because they believed that economic equality was historically inevitable that classical Marxists did not spend much time thinking about *why* equality was morally right, about exactly what made it morally binding. Economic equality was coming, it was welcome, and it would be a waste of time to theorize about why it was welcome, rather than about how to make it come as quickly and as painlessly as possible – for the date at which economic equality would be achieved, and the cost of reaching it, were, unlike economic equality itself, not themselves inevitable.

Two supposedly irrepressible historical trends, working together, guaranteed ultimate economic equality. One was the rise of an organized working class, whose social emplacement, at the short end of inequality, directed it in favour of equality. The workers' movement would grow in numbers and in strength, until it had the power to abolish the unequal society which had nurtured its growth. And the other trend helping to ensure an eventual equality was the development of the productive forces, the continual increase in the human power to transform nature for human benefit. That growth would issue in a material abundance so great that anything that anyone needed for a richly fulfilling life could be taken from the common store at no cost to anyone. The guaranteed future abundance served as a source of rebuttal to the suggestion that inequality might re-emerge, in a new form, *after* the revolution, peaceful or bloody, legal or illegal, fast or slow, that the proletariat could and would accomplish. There would be an interim period of limited inequality, along the lines of the lower stage of communism as Marx described that in his *Gotha Programme* critique, but, when 'all the springs of social wealth [came] to flow more freely', even that limited inequality would disappear,[6] because everyone could have everything that they might want to have.

History has shredded the predictions sketched in the foregoing paragraph. The proletariat did, for a while, grow larger and stronger, but it never became 'the immense majority',[7] and it was ultimately reduced and divided by the increasing technological sophistication of the capitalist production process that had been expected to continue to expand its size and augment its power. And the development of the productive forces now runs up against a resource barrier. Technical knowledge has not stopped, and will not stop growing, but productive power, which is the capacity (all things considered) to transform nature into use-value, cannot expand *pari passu* with the growth of technical knowledge, because the planet Earth rebels: its resources turn out to be not lavish enough for continuous growth in technical knowledge to generate unceasing expansion of use-value.

It was not only my encounter with Nozick, but also my loss of confidence in the two large Marxist factual claims about the prospects for equality, which altered the direction of my professional research. Having spent (what I hope will turn out to be only) the first third of my academic career devoting myself to exploring the ground and character of the two predictions described above,[8] I find myself, at the end of the (putative) second third of my career, engaged by philosophical questions about equality that I would earlier have thought do not require investigation, from a socialist point of view. In the past, there seemed to be no need to *argue* for the desirability of an egalitarian socialist society. Now I do little else.

4. Let us look more closely at the two leading Marxist inevitabilitarian claims that were distinguished above.

The first claim is false because the proletariat is in process of disinte-

---

[6] See Chapter 5, section 3 below.
[7] *The Communist Manifesto*, p. 495.
[8] I did more work on the development of the productive forces than I did on the character and the destiny of the working class, but I had begun a project on class and class conflict, which was set aside when normative questions moved to the centre of my vision.

gration, in a sense that I try to make precise in section 5 of Chapter 6 below. The struggle for equality is consequently no longer a reflex movement on the part of an agent strategically placed within the capitalist process itself: socialist values have lost their mooring in capitalist social structure. For, however one chooses to apply the much contested label 'working class', there is now no group in advanced industrial society which unites the four characteristics of (1) being the producers on whom society depends, (2) being exploited, (3) being (with their families) the majority of society, and (4) being in dire need. There certainly still exist key producers, exploited people, and needy people, but these are not, now, as they were in the past, even roughly coincident designations, nor, still less, alternative designations of the great majority of the population. And, as a result, there is no group with both (because of its exploitation, and its neediness) a compelling interest in, and (because of its productiveness, and its numbers) a ready capacity to achieve, a socialist transformation. In confidently expecting the proletariat to become such a group, classical Marxism failed to anticipate what we now know to be the natural course of capitalist social evolution.

It is partly because there is now patently no group that has the four listed features and, therefore, the will to, and capacity for, revolution, that Marxists, or what were Marxists, are impelled into normative political philosophy. The disintegration of the characteristics produces an intellectual need to philosophize which is related to a political need to be clear as never before about values and principles, for the sake of socialist advocacy. You do not have to justify a socialist transformation as a matter of principle to people who are driven to make it by the urgencies of their situation, and in a good position to succeed. And you do not have to decide what principle justifies socialism to recommend it to all people of good will when you think that so many principles justify it that any person of good will would be moved by at least one of them. For, when the group whose plight requires the relief supplied by socialism is conceived as having the four features that I have listed, socialism will then present itself as a demand of democracy, justice, elementary human need, and even of the general happiness.[9]

But the proletariat did not, and will not, gain the unity and power

---

[9] Sometimes, when I utter the foregoing thoughts about the disintegration of the working class, someone urges that, if I widen my focus, I shall see that the four features on my list may still come together, but, now, on a global scale. I am accused of overlooking the fact that a classically featured *international* proletariat is emerging. But that, so I believe, is instructively false: see my 'Equality as Fact and as Norm', section 3.

anticipated for it in Marxist belief. Capitalism does not dig its own grave by rearing up an agency of socialist transformation.[10] Socialists must therefore settle for a less dramatic scenario, and they must engage in more moral advocacy than used to be fashionable. And I now want to discuss, in the spirit of those acknowledgements, an aspect of the present predicament which brings to the fore a basis for demanding equality which is new, relative to traditional Marxist, and also to mainstream liberal, expectations. As we shall see, that new basis is connected with the falsehood of Marxism's abundance prediction, which was the basis, in the past, not for demanding equality, but for believing it to be inevitable.

The new basis of a demand for equality relates to the ecological crisis, which is a crisis for the whole of humanity. The scale of the threat is a matter of controversy among the experts, and so is the shape of the required remedy, if, indeed, it is not too late to speak of remedies. But two propositions seem to me to be true: that our environment is already severely degraded, and that, if there is a way out of the crisis, then it must include much less aggregate material consumption than what now prevails, and, as a result, unwanted changes in life-style, for hundreds of millions of people.

Let me distinguish between what is certain and what is conjectural in that uncongenial assessment. It is beyond dispute that Western consumption, *measured in terms of use of fossil fuel energy and natural resources*, must, on average, fall, drastically, and that non-Western consumption, considered in the aggregate, will never reach current Western levels, *so measured*. But the qualification carried by the italicized phrases is important. It is certain that we cannot achieve Western-style goods and services for humanity as a whole, nor even sustain them for as large a minority as has enjoyed them, by drawing on the fuels and materials that we have hitherto used to provide them. It is less certain that the desired consumption satisfactions themselves, the goods and services considered in abstraction from the customary means of supplying them, cannot be secured, by new means, on the desired scale. But I believe that the second claim, about goods and services as such, is also true,[11] and the following remarks proceed under that assumption.

[10] See *The Communist Manifesto*, p. 496.
[11] This means that I believe, among other things, that, if a fusion gun is coming, then, relative to how parlous our situation already is, it is not coming soon enough to vitiate the remarks that follow. (It cannot be excluded that Marx's abundance prediction will be vindicated in some distant future. The present remarks perforce reflect my own assessment of likely constraints for a future sufficiently extensive to justify extreme concern, whether or not the classical prediction will one day be fulfilled.)

When aggregate wealth is increasing, the condition of those at the bottom of society, and in the world, can improve, even while the distance between them and the better off does not diminish. Where such improvement occurs (and it has occurred, on a substantial scale, for many disadvantaged groups), egalitarian justice does not cease to demand equality, but that demand can seem shrill, and even dangerous, if the worse off are steadily growing better off, even though they are not catching up with those above them. When, however, progress must give way to regress, when average material living standards must fall, then poor people and poor nations can no longer hope to approach the levels of amenity which are now enjoyed by the world's well off. Sharply falling average standards mean that settling for limitless improvement, instead of equality, ceases to be an option, and huge disparities of wealth become correspondingly more intolerable, from a moral point of view.

Notice the strong contrast between the foregoing ecologically grounded case for reduced tolerance of inequality and traditional Marxist belief. The achievement of Marxist equality ('From each according to his ability, to each according to his needs') is premised on a conviction that industrial progress brings society to a condition of such fluent abundance that it is possible to supply what everyone needs for a richly fulfilling life. There is therefore no longer any occasion for competition for precedence, either across individuals or between groups. A (supposedly) inevitable future plenty was a reason for *predicting* equality. Persisting scarcity is now a reason for *demanding* it.

 abundance no longer feasible

We can no longer sustain Marx's extravagant, pre-green, materialist optimism. At least for the foreseeable future, we have to abandon the vision of abundance. But, if I am right about the straitened choices posed by the ecological crisis, we also have to abandon, on pain of giving up socialist politics, a severe pessimism about *social* possibility which accompanied Marx's optimism about *material* possibility. For Marx thought that material abundance was not only a sufficient but also a necessary condition of equality. He thought that anything short of an abundance so complete that it removes all major conflicts of interest would guarantee continued social strife, a 'struggle for necessities . . . and all the old filthy business'.[12] *It was because he was so uncompromisingly pessimistic about the social consequences of anything less than limitless*

[12] *The German Ideology*, p. 49.

abundance that Marx needed to be so optimistic about the possibility of that abundance.[13]

And that amplifies the explanation of traditional Marxism's failure to bring questions of distributive justice into close focus. Under conditions of scarcity, so traditional Marxism maintains, class society is inescapable, its property structures settle questions of distribution, and discussion of justice is therefore futile, for a political movement whose task must be to overturn class society, rather than to decide which of the many criteria by which it comes out unjust is the right one to use to condemn it. Nor is it necessary to inquire into what, precisely, will be demanded by justice in the future condition of abundance. For communism, in which everyone has what she wants, will then supervene effortlessly, and justice will be achieved, on any conception of it, from utilitarian through egalitarian to libertarian. Devoting energy to the question 'What is the right way to distribute?' is futile with respect to the present and unnecessary with respect to the future.[14]

We can no longer believe the factual premises of those conclusions about the practical (ir)relevance of the study of norms. We cannot share Marx's optimism about material possibility, but we therefore also cannot share his pessimism about social possibility, if we wish to sustain a socialist commitment. We cannot rely on technology to fix things for us: if they can be fixed, then we have to fix them, through hard theoretical and political labour. Marxism thought that equality would be delivered to us, by abundance, but we have to seek equality for a context of scarcity, and we consequently have to be far more clear than we were about what we are seeking, why we are justified in seeking it, and how it can be

---

[13] It does not follow that his optimism on that score was entirely irrational, driven, that is, by nothing but an aversion to inequality. Whether Marx also had good reasons for believing in a future abundance cannot be judged without a closer study than I have conducted of his critique of classical political economy's pessimistic forecasts.

[14] What Marx called 'the lower stage of communism" (which, following later Marxist discourse, I shall call 'socialism') provides an objection to that statement, but not a devastating one. The objection is that socialism enforces a rule of distribution ('to each according to his contribution') which can be represented as an answer that Marxists give to the question of what is the right way to distribute. But this objection to the statement in the text is not devastating, for two reasons. First, socialism is seen as a merely transitional form, and the rule governing it is justified as appropriate to socialism's task of preparing the way for full communism, rather than as required by abstract justice. Second, Marxism considers the socialist rule to be more or less inescapable, at the given historical stage: it does not regard that rule as a choice requiring normative justification from a substantial menu of policy options. (For further discussion of the two stages of communism, see section 3 of Chapter 5 below.)

implemented, institutionally. That recognition must govern the future efforts of socialist economists and philosophers.

5. I now want to describe the chapters that lie ahead, which display the development of my response to the libertarian challenge.

The libertarian principle of self-ownership says that each person enjoys, over herself and her powers, full and exclusive rights of control and use, and therefore owes no service or product to anyone else that she has not contracted to supply. It took me several years to come to see, what I now regard as elementary, that the stated principle is the centre of libertarianism, and several years more to see that that is why libertarianism disturbs some Marxists, since, as will be explained in Chapter 6, an appeal to self-ownership is latent in the standard Marxist condemnation of exploitation, and it is therefore difficult for Marxists to reject libertarianism without putting a key position of their own into question.

Before achieving the first realization, around 1980, and thereby getting the enemy – though not yet our own (Marxist) side – into focus, I essayed a reply to libertarianism in which the idea of self-ownership is not mentioned. Chapter 1 reprints, with little change, that initial reply, which is an extended critique of Robert Nozick's Wilt Chamberlain argument: I demonstrate that the argument fails of its purpose, which is to establish that liberal and socialist principles promote injustice and unfreedom.

The article which has become Chapter 1 was my first exercise in normative political philosophy. It side-steps, sometimes expressly, a number of questions about the relationships among freedom, justice and coercion my answers to which were as yet unclear, and which I had the opportunity to confront in later work. Chapter 2 addresses two of the issues raised in Chapter 1 that need further attention. I take a close look at the Nozickian formula that 'whatever arises from a just situation by just steps is itself just', and I show that its apparent self-evidence, on which Nozick trades, is illusory. I then turn to the libertarian assimilation of private property and freedom, and I expose the conceptual chicanery on which it depends.

When I had come to see that the organizing centre of libertarianism is the principle of self-ownership, the realization set in train a research programme whose results are presented in Chapters 3 through 10 below. (Chapters 3 to 7 reprint published articles, in revised and extended form; 8 to 10 are new.)

Chapter 3 records the first stages of my struggle with the thesis of self-ownership. It looks at a common argument in which the thesis features as a premiss. The argument is that equality can be achieved only at the cost of injustice, since securing and maintaining equality requires violation of rights of self-ownership.

Now, to defeat that justification of inequality, it is necessary either to refute its self-ownership premiss or to show that the conclusion here inferred from it, that inequality is inescapable when justice is observed, does not, in fact, follow from it. I decided to train my sights on the inference, partly because I could not see how to attack the self-ownership premiss itself. I do not mean that I accepted that premiss, but rather that I could not then find a neutral standpoint from which to challenge it. Perhaps, moreover, I was obscurely aware that there was enough liaison between the Marxist doctrine of exploitation (to which I had a certain loyalty) and the principle of self-ownership to make frontal attack on the latter dangerous. In any case, the inference from self-ownership to the unavoidability of inequality was my target.

In the course of my reflection on that inference, it struck me that, while the principle of self-ownership says that each person is entirely sovereign over herself, it says, on the face of it, nothing about anyone's rights in resources other than people, and, in particular, nothing about the substances and capacities of nature, without which the things that people want cannot be produced. Why would inequality in the distribution of desired things be a necessary consequence of implementing a principle which speaks only of the ownership of people and which places each person on a par with everyone else, with respect to that ownership?

The answer seemed to be, in Nozick's case, that the self-ownership principle was thought to imply a principle which readily permits formation of unequal private property in portions of external nature: instituting such a principle would ensure extensive inequality of distribution, on any measure of the latter. I therefore thought it necessary, and I found it possible, to argue against Nozick's rules for initial appropriation of the external world, which say that it is up for grabs (subject to a very weak proviso). I demonstrated that those rules were not, in truth, derivable from self-ownership, and, independently of the matter of their derivation, that they were also bizarrely lax: they could look acceptable only to someone who had not devoted much thought to *cf* the issue of initial appropriation. I was thereby able to conclude that the *primitive accumulation* principle of self-ownership could not be shown to require inequality in the particular way that Nozick purports to show that it does. It might still have been true that it necessitated inequality for some other reason, but I thought it worthwhile to have established that Nozick had not shown that inequality was a necessary consequence of self-ownership.

The next, and somewhat more ambitious task, pursued in Chapter 4, was to prove that self-ownership and equality of condition were, in fact, compatible. With that end in view, I noted that the idea of an equalizing pooling of external resources lacked the sinister aspect which many discern in the idea of an equalizing pooling of people's powers over themselves. This prompted the speculation that one might secure, or approach, equality of ultimate condition by insisting on equality of external resources only, without, that is, touching people's rights over their own powers. If that could be achieved, then a reconciliation of equality and self-ownership would be available.

Accordingly, I entertained an alternative to Nozick's 'up for grabs' hypothesis about the external world, to wit, that it is jointly owned by everyone, with each having a veto over its prospective use. And I showed that final equality of condition is assured when that egalitarian hypothesis about ownership of external resources is conjoined with the thesis of self-ownership.

I was delighted with that result, until I noticed that it was exposed to a serious objection. Equality had indeed been derived with no breach of the rules of self-ownership, but joint ownership of the external world rendered the self-ownership of its inhabitants merely formal. They could not use their rights of self-ownership to achieve substantial control over their own lives, since anything that they might want to do would be subject to the veto of others.

On further reflection, however, a victory emerged from what had looked like the jaws of defeat. For I realized that my libertarian antagonists could not press the objection to my demonstration which is aired in the foregoing paragraph. They could not complain that joint ownership of the external world degrades self-ownership, since the pale self-ownership enjoyed by persons in a jointly owned world is at least as robust as that of self-owning propertyless proletarians, who, unlike joint world owners, have no rights at all in external resources, and who also, therefore, lack real control over their own lives. Yet libertarians defend, as a realization of self-ownership, the capitalist world in which proletarians proliferate.

I concluded that libertarians were caught in a dilemma: they could not *both* reject a jointly owned (and thoroughly egalitarian) world on the ground that it drains self-ownership of its substance *and* defend an unmodified capitalist economy, in which the self-ownership of many people is no less insubstantial. And that dilemma, within the particular polemic that I had constructed, reflected a deeper one. For libertarians had now to choose *either* self-ownership as such, that is, the purely juridical condition, which disregards the question of whether rules about resources, and material circumstances, mean that self-ownership delivers the freedom and autonomy that it promises, *or* the freedom and autonomy that self-ownership, so it turns out, does not guarantee. On the first alternative, their philosophical view loses its allure. On the second, their political position needs drastic revision.

But if the reasoning recorded in Chapter 4 succeeded in exploding the libertarian position, it also posed a problem for Marxists, as I now proceed to explain.

Whatever polemical or debating value the idea of joint ownership may have, it is not a rule that can be favoured by egalitarians who care about real freedom and autonomy. And a salient alternative attempt to secure real freedom together with equality, by combining self-ownership with an initial equal division of external resources, also fails. Implementation of that recipe, in a world of different tastes and talents, generates inequality of goods and, if differences among people are great enough, class division. And the point generalizes: no egalitarian rule regarding external resources alone will, together with self-ownership, deliver equality of outcome, except, as in the case of joint ownership, at an unacceptable sacrifice of autonomy. There is a tendency in self-ownership to produce inequality, and the only way to nullify that tendency (without formally abridging self-ownership) is through a regime over external resources which is so rigid that it excludes exercise of independent rights over oneself.

It follows that if, as I believe that they are, Marxists (and their lineal descendants) are committed both to equality and to autonomy, then they have to reject self-ownership, in some or other fashion and degree. They must, in particular, distinguish themselves more clearly than it has been their practice to do from 'left-wing libertarians', who affirm complete self-ownership but divide worldly resources in an initially equal way.[15] And that admonition is the main theme of Chapter 5. The Chapter identifies two areas in which Marxists fail to distance themselves from left-wing libertarians, as they must to be true to their basic convictions.

The first area is the Marxist critique (not of this or that stretch of capitalist history, but) of the injustice of the capitalist system as such. In

[15] Hillel Steiner's *Essay on Rights* is the most recent, and probably the most sophisticated ever, statement of left-wing libertarianism. Some of his precursors are listed at footnote 7 of Chapter 5 below.

that critique, the exploitation of workers by capitalists derives entirely from the fact that workers have been deprived of access to physical productive resources and must therefore sell their labour power to capitalists, who enjoy a class monopoly in those resources. Hence, for Marxists, the injustice of capitalism is traceable to an initial inequality with respect to the distribution of external things, and suppression of exploitation should therefore require no rejection of the thesis of self-ownership: a rectification of original resource inequality should suffice. If its diagnosis of the source of capitalist injustice were correct, then Marxism could prescribe as an antidote to it what left libertarians prescribe as a matter of principle. But no Marxist would in fact tolerate a world in which differential talent allows self-owning individuals to be class-divided into buyers and sellers of labour-power, even when that position is reached from a starting point of initial equality of external resources. The standard Marxist critique of capitalist exploitation works only against capitalisms with dirty histories. Because Marxists wish to reject capitalism as such, it is necessary for them to deny the principle of self-ownership.

The second area in which Marxists must distance themselves from left-wing libertarianism is with respect to the design of the good society. In Marx's good society, productive resources are not privately (or, for that matter, jointly) owned,[16] but the individual remains effectively sovereign over himself. He conducts himself 'just as he has a mind',[17] developing himself freely not only without blocking the free development of others, but even as a 'condition'[18] of the free development of others. Abundance renders it unnecessary to *press* the talent of the naturally better endowed into the service of the poorly endowed for the sake of establishing equality of condition, and it is therefore unnecessary to trench against or modify self-ownership, in order to achieve that equality. But if, as I insisted in section 4 above, such abundance is now out of the question, then so, too is an egalitarian society in which no one is obliged to do what she would rather not do, for the sake of others. Marxists must legislate against self-ownership, instead of avoiding the issue by celebrating the entirely untrammelled freedom for all that abundance would provide.

If Chapter 5 maintains that Marxists fail to reject self-ownership,

---

[16] One might say that they are owned in common, in the Lockean sense that all have liberty of access to them, or even that they are not owned at all, since abundance means that no rules governing their use are required.

[17] *The German Ideology*, p. 47.

[18] *The Communist Manifesto*, p. 605.

Chapter 6 mounts the stronger claim that in standard presentations of the doctrine of exploitation they more or less affirm it, as an implication of the charge that exploiting capitalists steal labour-time from workers, since the latter are therein represented as owning their labour-power. I venture that it is for this reason that those of us who have a Marxist formation are more disturbed by libertarian arguments than Rawls-like liberals are: we inherit a critique of capitalism which relies, unthinkingly, on a libertarian premiss. We are consequently both more vulnerable to libertarianism and in one way better placed than liberals are to appreciate, and therefore to defeat, the libertarian challenge.

Chapter 7 interrupts the forward course pursued across Chapters 3 to 6, since it is more concerned than they are with the history of political thought, and with conceptual and textual issues in Marx and Locke in particular. I argue, with respect to Marx, that there is a severe tension between the extreme importance imputed to the distribution of worldly resources in his diagnosis of the root cause of capitalist exploitation (see the foregoing summary of Chapter 5), and the total unimportance of worldly resources in his account of the source of value, which traces it to labour inputs alone. I then point out that the questionable (indeed, confused) idea that labour is the sole source of value can be made to serve inegalitarian ends, and that such are the ends which something *like* a labour theory of value is made to serve in certain paragraphs of Chapter 5 of Locke's *Second Treatise of Government*. I subject Locke's labour theory to destructive scrutiny, and, in closing, I contrast my interpretation of Locke with that of James Tully, who finds little defence of private property and inequality in the *Second Treatise*.

Chapter 8 addresses an apparent inconsistency in characterizations of Marxism in earlier chapters, between the suggestion (mainly in Chapter 5) that initial unequal distribution of means of production is, for Marxism, the fundamental injustice in capitalist exploitation and the seemingly contrary suggestion (mainly in Chapter 6) that Marxism considers capitalism's fundamental injustice to be the extraction of surplus product which the skewed distribution of productive resources makes possible. Reconciliation of the two claims is achieved by distinguishing between causally fundamental and normatively fundamental injustices, with unequal resource distribution being, here, the first, and surplus extraction the second. The resulting account is used to defeat a scepticism about the normative significance of exploitation which has been voiced by John Roemer.

Chapter 9 attempts a reasoned delineation of the content of the concept of self-ownership, in the face of claims (e.g. by Immanuel Kant) that it is incoherent, and (e.g. by Richard Arneson and Ronald Dworkin) that it is too vague to be of interest in political philosophy. I also argue, against David Gauthier, that the principle of self-ownership forbids taxation of returns to productive talent, and, against John Rawls, that libertarians are right when they insist that such taxation forces the productive to *help* the unproductive.

Chapter 10 concludes the systematic discussion of self-ownership. I seek to deprive the thesis of appeal by arguing that its proponents comprehensively misrepresent both the price of rejecting it and the benefits of accepting it. I show, more particularly, that forthright denial of self-ownership does not mean endorsing slavery, nullifying human autonomy, and treating people as means rather than as ends, and that affirming self-ownership threatens autonomy and provides no guarantee at all against a utilitarian use of people. The thesis of self-ownership is not thereby (strictly) refuted, but it is hard to see why anyone would remain attracted to it, once its true character has been exposed.

The final chapter opens with personal reflections on the impact on socialists of the disastrous failure of the Soviet experiment. That is followed by commentary on the standing and prospects of socialist ideals in the closing decade of the twentieth century.

1. Robert Nozick and Wilt Chamberlain: how patterns preserve liberty

Let us now suppose that I have sold the product of my own labour for money, and have used the money to hire a labourer, i.e., I have bought somebody else's labour-power. Having taken advantage of this labour-power of another, I turn out to be the owner of value which is considerably higher than the value I spent on its purchase. This, *from one point of view*, is very just, because it has already been recognized, after all, that I can use what I have secured by exchange as is best and most advantageous to myself . . . (George Plekhanov, *The Development of the Monist View of History*)

1. Robert Nozick occupies the point of view Plekhanov describes, and his *Anarchy, State, and Utopia* is in good measure an ingenious elaboration of the argument for capitalism that Plekhanov adumbrates. The capitalism Nozick advocates is more pure than the one we have today. It lacks taxation for social welfare, and it permits degrees of poverty and of inequality far greater than most apologists for contemporary bourgeois society would now countenance.

This chapter is only indirectly a critique of Nozick's defence of capitalism. Its immediate aim is to refute Nozick's major argument against a rival of capitalism, socialism. The refutation vindicates socialism against that argument, but no one opposed to socialism on other grounds should expect to be converted by what is said here.

Nozick's case against socialism can be taken in two ways. He proposes a definition of justice in terms of liberty, and on that basis he argues that what socialists[1] consider just is not in fact just. But even if his definition of justice is wrong, so that the basis of his critique, taken in this first way, is faulty, he would still press a claim against socialism, namely, that, however

---

[1] And others, such as American liberals, but my concern is with the application of the argument to socialism.

just it may or may not be, it is incompatible with *liberty*. Even if Nozick is mistaken about what justice is, he might still be right that the cost in loss of liberty imposed by what socialists regard as just is intolerably high. (Hence the title of the section of the book on which we shall focus: 'How Liberty Upsets Patterns' – patterns being distributions answering to, for example, a socialist principle of justice.) So it is not enough, in defending socialism against Nozick, to prove that he has not shown that it is unjust. It must also be proved that he has not shown that it frustrates liberty.

2. A full definition of socialism is not required for our purposes. All we need suppose is that a socialist society upholds some principle of equality in the distribution of benefits enjoyed and burdens borne by its members. The principle need not be specified further, since Nozick's argument is against the institution of *any* such principle.

Let us now imagine that such an egalitarian principle is instituted, and that it leads to a distribution of goods and bads which, following Nozick, we shall call D1. Then Nozick argues by example that D1 can be maintained only at the price of tyranny and injustice. The example concerns the best basketball player in the imagined society.

. . . suppose that Wilt Chamberlain is greatly in demand by basketball teams, being a great gate attraction . . . He signs the following sort of contract with a team: In each home game, twenty-five cents from the price of each ticket of admission goes to him . . . The season starts, and people cheerfully attend his team's games; they buy their tickets, each time dropping a separate twenty-five cents of their admission price into a special box with Chamberlain's name on it. They are excited about seeing him play; it is worth the total admission price to them. Let us suppose that in one season one million persons attend his home games, and Wilt Chamberlain winds up with $250,000, a much larger sum than the average income . . . Is he entitled to this income? Is this new distribution D2, unjust? If so, why? There is *no* question about whether each of the people was entitled to the control over the resources they held in D1; because that was the distribution . . . that (for the purposes of argument) we assumed was acceptable. Each of these persons *chose* to give twenty-five cents of their money to Chamberlain. They could have spent it on going to the movies, or on candy bars, or on copies of *Dissent* magazine, or of *Monthly Review*. But they all, at least one million of them, converged on giving it to Wilt Chamberlain in exchange for watching him play basketball. If D1 was a just distribution, and people voluntarily moved from it to D2, transferring parts of their shares they were given under D1 (what was it for if not to do something with?), isn't D2 also just? If the people were entitled to dispose of the resources to which they were entitled (under D1), didn't this include their being entitled to give it to, or exchange it with, Wilt Chamberlain? Can anyone else complain on grounds of justice? Each other person already has his legitimate share under D1. Under D1, there is nothing that anyone has that anyone else has a claim of justice against.

After someone transfers something to Wilt Chamberlain, third parties *still* have their legitimate shares; *their* shares are not changed. By what process could such a transfer among two persons give rise to a legitimate claim of distributive justice on a portion of what was transferred, by a third party who had no claim of justice on any holding of the others *before* the transfer?[2]

· According to Nozick

(1) 'Whatever arises from a just situation by just steps is itself just.'[3]

Nozick holds that *steps* are just if they are free of injustice, and that they are free of injustice if they are fully voluntary on the part of all the agents who take them. We can therefore spell (1) out as follows:

(2) Whatever arises from a just situation as a result of fully voluntary transactions on the part of all the transacting agents is itself just.

So convinced is Nozick that (2) is true that he thinks that it must be accepted by people attached to a doctrine of justice which in other respects differs from his own. That is why he feels able to rely on (2) in the Chamberlain parable, despite having granted, for the sake of argument, the justice of an initial situation patterned by an egalitarian principle.

Even if (2) is true, it does not follow that pattern D1 can be maintained only at the price of injustice, for people might simply *fail* to use their liberty in a pattern-subverting manner. But that is not an interesting possibility. A more interesting one is that they deliberately *refuse* to use their liberty subversively. Reasons for refusing will be adduced shortly. But is (2) true? Does liberty always preserve justice?

A standard way of testing the claim would be to look for states of affairs which would be accounted unjust but which might be generated by the route (2) endorses. Perhaps the strongest counter-example of this form would be slavery. We might then say: voluntary self-enslavement is possible. But slavery is unjust. Therefore (2) is false. Yet whatever may be the merits of that argument, we know that Nozick is not moved by it. For he thinks that there is no injustice in a slavery that arises out of the approved process.[4]

[2] *Anarchy, State, and Utopia*, pp. 161–2.
[3] *Anarchy*, p. 151.
[4] A putative example of justly generated slavery: *A* and *B* are identical in talents and tastes. Each would so like to own a slave that he is willing to risk becoming one in exchange for the same chance of getting one. So they toss a coin, *B* loses, and *A* clamps chains on him. (For discussion of this case, see subsection 1d of Chapter 2 below. For penetrating remarks on Nozick's toleration of slavery, see Attracta Ingram's *Political Theory of Rights*, pp. 38–9. For a reply to Ingram, see Hillel Steiner, *An Essay on Rights*, pp. 232–3.)

Though Nozick accepts slavery with an appropriate genesis, there is a restriction, derived from (2) itself, on the kind of slavery he accepts: (2) does not allow slave status to be inherited by offspring of the self-enslaved, for then a concerned party's situation would be decided for him, independently of his will. 'Some things individuals may choose for themselves no one may choose for another.'[5] Let us remember this when we come to scrutinize the Wilt Chamberlain transaction, for widespread contracting of the kind which occurs in the parable might have the effect of seriously modifying, for the worse, the situation of members of future generations.

Should we say that in Nozick's conception of justice a slave society need be no less just than one where people are free? That would be a tendentious formulation. For Nozick can claim that rational persons in an initially just situation are unlikely to contract into slavery, except, indeed, where circumstances are so special that it would be wrong to forbid them to do so. This diminishes the danger that (2) can be used to stamp approval on morally repellent social arrangements.

I attribute some such response to Nozick on the basis, *inter alia*, of this passage:

> it must be granted that were people's reasons for transferring some of their holdings to others always irrational or arbitrary, we would find this *disturbing* . . . We feel more comfortable upholding the justice of an entitlement system if most of the transfers under it are done for reasons. This does not mean necessarily that all deserve what holdings they receive. It means only that there is a purpose or point to someone's transferring a holding to one person rather than to another; that usually we can see what the transferrer thinks he's gaining, what cause he *thinks* he's serving, what goals he *thinks* he's helping to achieve, and so forth. Since in a capitalist society people often transfer holdings to others in accordance with how much they *perceive* these others benefiting them, the fabric constituted by the individual transactions and transfers is largely reasonable and intelligible.[6]

Accordingly, Nozick emphasizes the motives people have when they pay to watch Chamberlain, instead of stipulating that they do so freely and leaving us to guess why. It is important to the persuasive allure of the example that we should consider what the fans are doing not only voluntary but sensible: transactions are disturbing (even though they are entirely just?)[7] when we cannot see what the (or some of the) contracting parties *think* they are gaining by them.

---

[5] *Anarchy*, p. 331.   [6] *Anarchy*, p. 159, my emphases.
[7] Nozick does not say whether or not our finding a transaction 'disturbing' should affect our judgement of its justice.

Yet we should surely also be disturbed if we can indeed see what the agent *thinks* he is gaining, but we know that what he *will* gain is not that, but something he thinks less valuable; or that what results is not only the gain he expects but also unforeseen consequences which render negative the net value, according to his preferences and standards, of the transaction. We should not be content if what he *thinks* he is getting is good, but what he actually gets is bad, by his own lights. I shall assume that Nozick would accept this plausible extension of his concession. It is hard to see how he could resist it.

Accordingly, if we can show that Chamberlain's fans get not only the pleasure of watching him minus twenty-five cents, but also uncontemplated disbenefits of a significant order, then, even if, for Nozick, the outcome remains just, it should, even to Nozick, be disturbing. We shall need to ask whether we do not find Chamberlain's fans insufficiently reflective, when we think through, as they do not, the *full* consequences of what they are doing.

But now we can go further. For, in the light of the considerations just reviewed, (2) appears very probably false. Nozick says that a transaction is free of injustice if every transacting agent agrees to it. Perhaps that is so. But transactional justice, so characterized, is supposed – given an initially just situation – to confer justice on what results from it. (That is why (2) is supposed to follow from (1).) And that is questionable. Of each person who agrees to a transaction we may ask: *would he have agreed to it had he known what its outcome would be?* Since the answer may be negative, it is far from evident that transactional justice, as described, transmits justice to its results.

Perhaps the desired transmission occurs when the answer to the italicized question is positive. Perhaps, in other words, we can accept (3), which increases the requirements for steps to be justice-preserving:

(3) Whatever arises from a just situation as a result of fully voluntary transactions which all transacting agents would still have agreed to if they had known what the results of so transacting were to be is itself just.

(3) looks plausible, but its power to endorse market-generated states of affairs is, while not nil, very weak. Stronger[8] principles may also be

---

[8] In the sense that they endorse a larger set of market-generated states of affairs. Notice that the weaker the conditions for justice in steps are in a principle of the form of (2) and (3), the stronger, in the specified sense, that principle is.

plausible,[9] but (2), Nozick's principle, is certainly too strong to be accepted without much more defence than he provides.

3. Let us now apply this critique of Nozick's principles to the parable which is supposed to secure (or reveal) our allegiance to them.

Before describing the Chamberlain transaction, Nozick says: 'It is not clear how those holding alternative conceptions of distributive justice can reject the entitlement conception of justice in holdings.'[10] There follows the Chamberlain story, where we assume that D1 is just, and are then, supposedly, constrained to admit that D2, into which it is converted, must also be just; an admission, according to Nozick, which is tantamount to accepting the entitlement conception. But how much of it must we accept if we endorse D2 as just? At most that there is *a* role for the entitlement principle. For what the transaction subverts is the original pattern, not the principle governing it, *taken as a principle conjoinable with others to form a total theory of just or legitimate holdings*. The example, even if successful, does not defeat the initial assumption that D1 is just. Rather, it exploits that assumption to argue that D2, though it breaks D1's pattern, must also be just. The Chamberlain story, even when we take it at its face value, impugns not the original distribution, but the *exclusive* rightness of the principle mandating it.

Now Nozick is certainly right to this extent, even if we do not accept everything he says about the Chamberlain story: there must be *a* role for entitlement in determining acceptable holdings.[11] For unless the just society forbids gifts, it must allow transfers which do not answer to a patterning principle. This is compatible with placing restraints on the scope of gift, and we shall shortly see why an egalitarian society might be justified in doing so. But the present point is that assigning a certain role to unregulated transactions in the determination of holdings is compatible with using an egalitarian principle to decide the major distribution of

[9] Some might say that this is one of them, but I would disagree:

   (4) Whatever arises from a just situation as a result of fully voluntary transactions where the transacting agents know in advance the probabilities of all significantly different possible outcomes is itself just.

   I raise doubts about (4) in subsection 1e of Chapter 2 below.
[10] *Anarchy*, p. 160.
[11] For an investigation of the concept of entitlement that is deeper and more general than Nozick's own, see Robert J. van der Veen and Philippe Van Parijs, 'Entitlement Theories of Justice'. Pages 70–4 of that article are particularly instructive in the present connection: the authors show both that all theories of justice have an entitlement component and that no theory of justice is a pure entitlement theory.

goods and to limit, for example by taxation, how much more or less than what he would get under that principle alone a person may come to have in virtue of transactions which escape its writ. I think socialists do well to concede that an egalitarian principle should not be the only guide to the justice of holdings, or that, if it is, then justice should not be the only guide to policy with respect to holdings.[12]

Among the reasons for limiting how much an individual may hold, regardless of how he came to hold it, is to prevent him from acquiring, through his holdings, an unacceptable amount of power over others: the Chamberlain transaction looks less harmless when we focus on that consideration.[13]

The fans 'are excited about seeing him play; it is worth the total admission price to them'. The idea is that they see him play if and only if they pay, and seeing him play is worth more to them than anything else they can get for twenty-five cents. So it may be, but this fails to cover everything in the outcome which is relevant. For, once Chamberlain has received the payments, he is in a very special position of power in what was previously an egalitarian society. The fans' access to resources might now be prejudiced by the disproportionate access Chamberlain's wealth gives him, and the consequent power over others that he now has. *For all that Nozick shows*, a socialist may claim that this is not a bargain informed people in an egalitarian society will be apt to make: they will refrain from so contracting as to upset the equality they prize, and they will be especially averse to doing so because the resulting changes would profoundly affect their children. (This may seem an hysterical projection of the effect of the Chamberlain transaction, but I take it that we have to consider the upshot of general performance of transactions of that kind, and then the projection is entirely realistic.)

It is easy to think carelessly about the example. How we feel about people like Chamberlain getting a lot of money *as things are* is a poor index of how people would feel in the imagined situation. Among us the ranks of the rich and the powerful exist, and it can be pleasing, given that they

12 I prefer the second formulation, being persuaded that distributive justice, roughly speaking, *is* equality. (See Christopher Ake, 'Justice as Equality'.) For more on trade-off between equality (be it justice or not) and other desiderata, see section 2 of my 'On the Currency of Egalitarian Justice'.

13 My near-exclusive emphasis on this consideration in the sequel does not mean that I think that there are no other important ones, including the sheer unfairness of substantial differences in people's purchasing power. But swollen purchasing power, as such, which is not immediately the same thing as power *over* others, is less likely than the latter to worry those who are not already principled egalitarians.

do, when a figure like Chamberlain joins them. Who better and more innocently deserves to be among them? But the case before us is a society of equality in danger of losing its essential character. Reflective people would have to consider not only the joy of watching Chamberlain and its immediate money price but also the fact, which socialists say that they would deplore, that their society would be set on the road to class division. In presenting the Chamberlain fable Nozick ignores the commitment people may have to living in a society of a particular kind, and the rhetorical power of the illustration depends on that omission. At a later stage, Nozick takes up this point, but, so I argue in section 4 below, he says nothing interesting about it.

Nozick tacitly supposes that a person willing to pay twenty-five cents to watch Wilt play, is *ipso facto* a person willing to pay *Wilt* twenty-five cents to watch him play. It is no doubt true that in our society people rarely care who gets the money they forgo to obtain goods. But the tacit supposition is false, and the common unconcern is irrational. Nozick exploits our familiarity with this unconcern. Yet a person might welcome a world in which he and a million others watch Wilt play, at a cost of twenty-five cents to each, and consistently disfavour one in which, in addition, Wilt rakes in a cool quarter million.

Accordingly, if a citizen of the D1 society joins with others in paying twenty-five cents to Wilt to watch Wilt play, without thinking about the effect on Wilt's power, then the result may be deemed 'disturbing' in the sense of p. 159 of *Anarchy* (see p. 22 above). Of course a single person's paying a quarter makes no appreciable difference if the rest are anyway going to do so. But a convention might evolve not to make such payments, or, more simply, there could be a democratically authorized taxation system which maintains wealth differentials within acceptable limits. Whether Wilt would then still play is a further question on which I shall not comment, except to say that anyone who thinks it obvious that he would not play misunderstands human nature, or basketball, or both.

4. In defending the justice of the Chamberlain transaction, Nozick glances at the position of persons not directly party to it: 'After someone transfers something to Wilt Chamberlain, third parties *still* have their legitimate shares; *their* shares are not changed.'[14] That is false, in one relevant sense. For a person's effective share depends on what he can do with what he has, and that depends not only on how much he has but on what others

---

[14] *Anarchy*, p. 161.

have and on how what others have is distributed. If it is distributed equally among them he will often be better placed than if some have especially large shares. Third parties, including the as yet unborn, may therefore have an interest against the contract. It is roughly the same interest as the fans themselves may have in not making it. (But, unlike third parties, a fan gets the compensation of watching Wilt play, which – I have not ruled this out – might be worth a whole lot of inequality, as far as a particular individual fan is concerned.)

Nozick addresses this issue in a footnote:

Might not a transfer have instrumental effects on a third party, changing his feasible options? (But what if the two parties to a transfer independently had used their holdings in this fashion?)[15]

He promises further treatment of the problem later, and, although he does not say where it will come, he presumably has in mind his section on 'Voluntary Exchange', which I shall address in section 7 below. Here I respond to Nozick's parenthetical rhetorical question.

First, there are some upshots of transfers of holdings, some effects on the options of the other parties, which will not occur as effects of the unconcerted use of dispersed holdings by individuals, because those individuals could not, or would not, use them in that way. The Chamberlain fans, acting independently, are less likely than Chamberlain is to buy a set of houses and leave them unoccupied, with speculative intent. Sometimes, though, a set of fans, acting independently, could indeed bring about effects inimical to the interests of others, of just the kind one may fear Chamberlain might cause. But whoever worries about Chamberlain doing so will probably also be concerned about the case where it results from the independent action of many. The rhetorical second question in the Nozick passage should not silence those who ask the first one.[16]

As an argument about *justice*[17] the Chamberlain story is either question-begging or uncompelling. Nozick asks:

---

[15] *Anarchy*, p. 162.
[16] The purpose of the second question, so I take it, is to suggest this argument:

    1. The fans might have so used their several quarters with the same effect on third parties that one asks the first question fears Wilt's use of his quarter million might have.
    2. No one could object to the fans so using their quarters.
∴ 3. No one can object to what Wilt does with his quarter million.

    Whether or not the stated premisses imply that argument's conclusion, the present point is that an alert rejecter of its conclusion will also reject its second premiss.
[17] Recall the two ways of taking Nozick, distinguished at pp. 19–20 above.

If the people were entitled to dispose of the resources to which they were entitled (under D1), didn't this include their being entitled to give it to, or exchange it with, Wilt Chamberlain?[18]

If this interrogative is intended as a vivid way of asserting the corresponding indicative, then Nozick is telling us that the rights in shares with which people were vested are violated unless they are allowed to contract as described. If so, he begs the question. For it will be clear that their rights are violated only if the entitlement they received was of the absolute Nozickian sort, and this cannot be assumed. Whatever principles underlie D1 will generate restrictions on the use of what is distributed in accordance with them.[19]

The other way of taking the quoted question is not as an assertion but as an appeal. Nozick is then asking us whether we do not agree that any restrictions which would forbid the Chamberlain transaction must be unjustified. So construed the argument is not question-begging, but it is inconclusive. For considerations which might justify restrictions on transactions are not canvassed. It is easy to think that what happens afterwards is that Chamberlain eats lots of chocolate, sees lots of movies and buys lots of subscriptions to expensive socialist journals. But, as I have insisted, we must remember the considerable power that he can now exercise over others.[20] In general, holdings are not only sources of enjoyment but, in certain distributions, sources of power. Transfers which look unexceptionable come to seem otherwise when we bring into relief the aspect neglected in 'libertarian' apologetic.

5. Let us turn, now, from justice to liberty: is it true that a 'socialist society would have to forbid capitalist acts between consenting adults'?[21] Socialism perishes if there are too many such acts, but it does not follow that it must forbid them. In traditional socialist doctrine capitalist action wanes not primarily because it is illegal, but because the impulse behind it atrophies, or, less Utopianly, because other impulses become stronger, or because people believe that capitalistic exchange is unfair. *Such expectation rests on a conception of human nature, and so does its denial.* Nozick

[18] *Anarchy*, p. 161.
[19] Thomas Nagel construes Nozick as I do in the paragraph above, and my reply to Nozick, so construed, follows Nagel. See his 'Libertarianism Without Foundations', pp. 201–2.
[20] Once again – see p. 25 above – this assessment will seem hysterical only if we fail to take the Chamberlain transaction as we must for it to pose a serious challenge, namely as an example of something which occurs regularly, or will occur regularly in the future.
[21] *Anarchy*, p. 163.

has a different conception, for which he does not argue, one that fits many twentieth-century Americans, which is no reason for concluding that it is universally true. The people in Nozick's state of nature are intelligible only as well-socialized products of a market society. In the contrary socialist conception, human beings have and may develop further a (non-instrumental) desire for community, a relish of cooperation, and an aversion to being on either side of a master/servant relationship. No one should assume without argument, or take it on trust from the socialist tradition, that this conception is sound. But *if* it is sound, then there will be no need for incessant invigilation against 'capitalist acts', and Nozick does not *argue* that it is unsound. Hence he has not shown that socialism conflicts with freedom, even if his unargued premiss that its citizens will want to perform capitalist acts attracts the assent of the majority of his readers.

How much equality would conflict with liberty in given circumstances depends on how much people would value equality in those circumstances. If life in a cooperative commonwealth appeals to them, they do not have to sacrifice liberty to belong to it.

This banal point relates to the first of what Nozick says are the three 'unrealistic' presuppositions of the moral and practical possibility of socialism:

(5) that all will most want to maintain the [socialist] pattern
(6) that each can gather enough information about his own actions and the ongoing activities of others to discover which of his actions will upset the pattern
(7) that diverse and far-flung persons can coordinate their actions to dovetail into the pattern.[22]

Something like the first presupposition is made by socialists in the light of the idea of human nature which informs their tradition. It is, of course, controversial, but its dismissal as 'unrealistic' contributes nothing to the controversy.

Socialists presuppose only something *like* (5), because they need not think that everyone will have socialist sentiments, but only a preponderant majority, especially in the nascency of socialism. If (5) itself is unrealistic, three possibilities present themselves: very few would lack enthusiasm for socialism; very many would; some intermediate proportion would. What I mean by these magnitudes emerges immediately.

In the first possibility, there remain a few capitalistically minded

---

[22] *Anarchy*, p. 163.

persons, meaning by 'a few' that their capitalist acts would not undermine the basic socialist structure. No sane socialist should commit himself to the suppression of capitalist activity on the stated scale. (It might even be desirable to allocate to capitalistophiles a territory in which they can bargain with and hire one another.)

Suppose, though, that the disposition to perform capitalist acts is strong and widespread, so that socialism[23] is possible only with tyranny. What socialist favours socialism in such circumstances? What socialist denies that there are such circumstances? Certainly Marx insisted that it would be folly to attempt an institution of socialism except under the propitious conditions he was confident capitalism would create.[24] A socialist believes that propitious conditions are accessible. He need not proclaim the superiority of socialism regardless of circumstances.

Could a socialist society contain an amount of inclination to capitalism of such a size that unless it were coercively checked socialism would be subverted, yet sufficiently small that, in socialist judgement, socialism, with the required coercion, would still be worthwhile? Marxian socialists believe so, and that does commit them to prohibiting capitalist acts between consenting adults in certain circumstances, notably those which follow a successful revolution. But why should they flinch from that prohibition? They can defend it by reference to the social good and widened freedom that it promotes. Nozick would object that the prohibition violates moral 'side constraints': certain freedoms, for example of contract, ought never to be infringed, whatever the consequences of allowing their exercise may be. We shall look at side constraints in the next section.

But first we must treat presuppositions (6) and (7) (see p. 29 above). Unlike (5), these are red herrings. At most, they are preconditions of realizing socialist justice *perfectly*.[25] But justice is not the only virtue of

---

23 Or 'socialism': scare-quotes would be added by those who think that socialism is, by definition, incompatible with tyranny; but, contrary to what some socialists seem to think, such a definition, even if it is correct, provides no argument against those who say that the (extensively non-market) form of economy that many socialists favour required tyranny.

24 According to Marx, socialist revolution will not succeed unless and until 'capitalist production has already developed the productive forces of labour in general to a sufficiently high level' (*Theories of Surplus Value*, Vol. II, p. 580), failing which 'all the old filthy business would necessarily be restored' (*The German Ideology*, p. 49) in the aftermath of revolution. See sections (6) and (7) of Chapter VII of my *Karl Marx's Theory of History*. See also Chapter 5, section 6, below.

25 I say 'at most' because even that is probably false. Given the truth of (5), people could form a Pattern Maintenance Association and appoint experts to watch over and correct the pattern. With popular willingness to do what the experts said, and a properly sophisticated technology for detecting deviations, (6) and (7) would be unnecessary to pattern

social orders (and it is not even 'the first virtue' of socialism, for most socialists). Even if we identify justice with equality, as socialists, broadly speaking, do, we may tolerate deviations from equality consequent on perturbations caused by gift, small-scale market transactions, and so on. Considerations of privacy, acquired expectations, the moral and economic costs of surveillance, etc. declare against attempting a realization of justice in the high degree that would be possible if (6) and (7) were satisfied. We let justice remain rough, in deference to other values.

Accordingly, socialism tolerates gift-giving, and 'loving behaviour' is not 'forbidden'.[26] Gift is possible under a system which limits how much anyone may have and what he may do with it. Relatively well-endowed persons will sometimes not be fit recipients of gifts, but we are assuming a socialist psychology whose natural tendency is not to give to them that hath. And the notion that the institutions we are contemplating fetter the expression of love is too multiply bizarre to require comment.

6. Any but the most utopian socialist must be willing under certain conditions to restrict the liberty of a few for the sake of the liberty of many.[27] But, so Nozick would charge, such a socialist would thereby violate 'moral side constraints' that apply to all human action. For Nozick thinks that we may never restrict one person's freedom in order to enhance the welfare or the freedom of very many others, or even of everyone, that person included (where we know that the restriction will redound to his benefit).

If children are undernourished in our society, we are not allowed to tax millionaires in order to finance a subsidy on the price of milk to poor families, for we would be violating the rights, and the 'dignity' of the millionaires.[28] We cannot appeal that the effective liberty of the children

maintenance without coercion (unless doing what the experts say counts as a way of coordinating action, in which case (7) *is* required in the above fantasy – but it is easily satisfied).
[26] *Anarchy*, p. 167.
[27] See Chapter 2, subsection 2c, on how socialist restriction on private property rights may enhance general freedom.
[28] *Anarchy*, p. 334. ' "But isn't justice to be tempered with compassion?" Not by the guns of the state. When private persons choose to transfer resources to help others, this fits within the entitlement conception of justice' (*ibid.*, p. 348). 'Fits within' is evasive. The choice 'fits' because it is a choice, not because of its content. For Nozick there is no more justice in a millionaire's giving a five dollar bill to a starving child than in his using it to light his cigar while the child dies in front of him.
For subtle comments on Nozick's falsely exclusive and exhaustive distinction between compulsory and voluntary donation, see Nagel, 'Libertarianism Without Foundations', pp. 199–200.

(and the adults they will become) would be greatly enhanced at little expense to the millionaires' freedom, for Nozick forbids any act which restricts freedom: he does not call for its maximization. (This means that if it were true that certain exercises of freedom would lead to totalitarianism, Nozick would still protect them. Market freedom itself would be sacrificed by Nozick if the only way to preserve it were by limiting it.)[29]

If Nozick argues for this position, he does so in the section called 'Why Side Constraints?', which begins as follows:

Isn't it *irrational* to accept a side constraint C, rather than a view that directs minimizing the violations of C? . . . If nonviolation of C is so important, shouldn't that be the goal? How can a concern for the nonviolation of C lead to the refusal to violate C even when this would prevent other more extensive violations of C? What is the rationale for placing the nonviolation of rights as a side constraint upon action instead of including it solely as a goal of one's actions?

Side constraints upon action reflect the underlying Kantian principle that individuals are ends and not merely means; they may not be sacrificed or used for the achieving of other ends without their consent. Individuals are inviolable.[30]

The second paragraph is lame as a response to the questions of the first, for they obviously reassert themselves: if such sacrifice and violation are so horrendous, why should we not be concerned to minimize their occurrence?[31] There is more appearance of argument[32] in the final paragraph of the section:

Side constraints express the inviolability of other persons. But why may not one violate persons for the greater social good? Individually, we each sometimes choose to undergo some pain or sacrifice for a greater benefit or to avoid a greater harm . . . Why not, *similarly*, hold that some persons have to bear some costs that benefit other persons more, for the sake of the overall social good? But there is no *social entity* with a good that undergoes some sacrifice for its own good. There are only individual people, different individual people, with their own individual lives. Using one of these people for the benefit of others, uses him and benefits the

---

[29] It is, indeed, a reasonable conjecture that market freedom is less than it was, partly because, had the bourgeois state not imposed restrictions on it, its survival would have been jeopardized.

[30] *Anarchy*, pp. 30–1.

[31] Since 1977 (when what is substantially the text of this chapter was first published), many philosophers have offered challenging answers to this question, especially in response to Samuel Scheffler's relentless pressing of it in his *Rejection of Consequentialism*. I cannot address those answers here. (For an attempt to show that Nozick's invocation of Kant is unjustified, see section 4 of Chapter 10 below.)

[32] Note, though, that what Nozick initially contends against is *violating rights in order to reduce the violation of rights*, whereas in what follows his target is *violating rights to expand aggregate welfare*. He is unconvincing on both counts, but one who agrees with him about 'overall social good' could still press the questions in the first paragraph of the text to footnote 30.

others. Nothing more. What happens is that something is done to him for the sake of others. Talk of an overall social good covers this up . . . [33]

This passage is hard to construe. In one interpretation what is says is correct but ineffectual, in the other what is says is pertinent, but wrong, and anyone who is impressed has probably failed to spot the ambiguity. For it is unclear whether Nozick is only arguing *against* one who puts redistribution across lives on a moral par with a person's sacrificing something for his own greater benefit, or arguing *for* the moral impermissibility of redistribution. In other words, is Nozick simply rejecting argument *A*, or is he (also) propounding argument *B*?

A since   persons compose a social entity relevantly akin to the entity a single person is (*p*), redistribution across persons is morally permissible (*q*).

B since   it is false that *p*, it is false that *q*.

If Nozick is just rejecting argument *A*, then I agree with him, but side constraints remain unjustified. Unless we take Nozick to be propounding argument *B*, there is no case to answer. And then the answer is that the truth of *p* is not a necessary condition of the truth of *q*. A redistributor does not have to believe in a social entity.[34]

According to Nozick, the redistributive attitude ignores the separateness of persons. But what does it mean to say in a normative tone of voice (for it is uncontroversial, descriptively speaking) that persons are separate? Either it means that who gets what is morally relevant, or it means that it is morally forbidden to redistribute across persons. If the first (moral relevance) is what is meant, then all patterned principles (as opposed to, for example, the unpatterned end-state principle of utilitarianism)[35] embody the requirement, and even an unpatterned egalitarianism manifestly presupposes the moral separateness of persons. If the second (prohibition on redistribution) is what is meant, then the separateness of persons is no *argument* against redistribution.

Side constraints remain unjustified, and socialists need not apologize for being willing to restrict freedom in order to expand it.

---

[33] *Anarchy*, pp. 32–3.
[34] For elaboration of this point, see Nagel ('Libertarianism Without Foundations', pp. 197–8), who takes Nozick to be propounding *B*.
[35] For the differences among non-entitlement principles between ones that are and ones that are not patterned, see pp. 153ff. of *Anarchy*. (Nozick is not careful in his application of this distinction.)

7. I now examine Nozick's section on 'Voluntary Exchange', which I presumed (see p. 27 above) to be his more extended treatment of the problem of the effect of market transactions on persons not party to them, including the as yet unborn. Nozick allows that agreed exchanges between *A* and *B* may reduce *C*'s *options*, but he implies that they do not thereby reduce *C*'s *freedom*. He explicitly says that they do not render involuntary anything that *C* does. And since what *C* is forced to do he does involuntarily, it follows that, for Nozick, the actions of *A* and *B*, though reducing *C*'s options, cannot have the result that *C* is *forced* to do something that he might not otherwise have done.

The last claim entails a denial of a thesis central to the socialist critique of capitalism, which may usefully be expressed in the terms of Nozick's doctrine of natural rights, without commitment to the truth of the latter.

For Nozick, every person has a natural right not to work for any other. If one is a slave, then, unless one contracted freely into slavery (see p. 21 above), one's rights were violated, as they are in slave states, which do not confer on everyone as a matter of civil right the rights that he enjoys naturally. And natural rights would remain violated if the law permitted slaves to choose for which master they should labour, as long as it forbade them to withhold their services from all masters whatsoever.

One difference between a modern capitalist state and a slave state is that the natural right not to be subordinate in the manner of a slave is a civil right in modern capitalism. The law excludes formation of a set of persons who are legally obliged to work for other persons. That status being forbidden, everyone is entitled to work for no one. But the power matching this right[36] is differentially enjoyed. Some *can* live without subordinating themselves, but most cannot. The latter face a structure generated by a history of market transactions in which, it is reasonable to say, they are *forced* to work for some or other person or group. Their natural rights are not matched by corresponding effective powers.

This division between the powerful and the powerless with respect to the alienation of labour power is the heart of the socialist objection to claims on behalf of the justice and freedom of capitalist arrangements. The rights Nozick says we have by nature we also have civilly under capitalism, but the matching powers are widely lacking. That lack is softened in contemporary rich capitalist countries, because of a hard-won

---

[36] The concept of a *power which matches a right* is explicated in section (2) of Chapter VIII of my *Karl Marx's Theory of History*. The basic idea: power *p* matches right *r* if and only if what *X* is *de jure* able to do when *X* has *r* is what *X* is *de facto* able to do when *X* has *p*.

institutionalization of a measure of protection for working-class people. In Nozick's capitalism such institutionalization would be forbidden on the ground that it was coercive, and the lack would be greater.

But Nozick, in the course of his full reply to the problem of 'third parties', denies that even the most abject proletarian is *forced* to work for some capitalist or other. Addressing himself to 'market exchanges between workers and owners of capital', he invites us to reflect on the situation of a certain Z (so-called because he is at the bottom of the heap in a twenty-six-person economy) who is 'faced with working [for a capitalist] or starving':

the choices and actions of all other persons do not add up to providing Z with some other option. (He may have various options about what job to take.) Does Z choose to work voluntarily? . . . Z does choose voluntarily if the other individuals A through Y each acted voluntarily and within their rights . . . A person's choice among differing degrees of unpalatable alternatives is not rendered nonvoluntary by the fact that others voluntarily chose and acted within their rights in a way that did not provide him with a more palatable alternative . . . [Whether other people's option-closing actions] makes one's resulting action non-voluntary depends on whether these others had the right to act as they did.[37]

One might think that people of necessity lack the right so to act that someone ends up in Z's position, a view that I put forward later (see p. 37 below). But here we suppose, with Nozick, that all of A through Y acted as impeccably upright marketeers and therefore did nothing wrong. If so, says Nozick, Z is not *forced* to work for a capitalist. If he chooses to, the choice is voluntary.

Notice that Nozick is not saying that Z, although forced to work *or* starve, is not forced to *work*, since he may choose to starve. Rather, he would deny that Z is forced to work-or-starve, even though Z has no other alternative, and would accept that Z is indeed forced to work, if, contrary to what Nozick holds, he is forced to work or starve. For Nozick believes that

(8) if Z is forced to do A or B, and A is the only thing it would be reasonable for him to do, and Z does A for this reason, then Z is forced to do A.[38]

Nozick holds that

[37] *Anarchy*, pp. 262, 263–4.
[38] See Nozick, 'Coercion', p. 446. I derive (8) above from principle (7) of the 'Coercion' essay on the basis of Nozick's commitment to: Z is forced to do A if and only if there is a person P who forces Z to do A. See (9) in the next sentence of the text above.)

(9) Z is forced to choose between working and starving only if human actions caused his alternatives to be restricted in that way,

and that

(10) Z is forced so to choose only if the actions bringing about the restriction on his alternatives were illegitimate.

Both claims are false, but we need not discuss (9) here.[39] For we are concerned with choice restriction which Nozick himself attributes to the actions of person, *viz.*, some or all of A through Y. We need therefore only reject his claim that if someone is forced to do something, then someone acted *illegitimately*: we need to refute (10) only.

Let me once again display the text in which (10) is affirmed:

Other people's actions may place limits on one's available opportunities. Whether this makes one's resulting action non-voluntary depends upon whether these others had the right to act as they did.[40]

But there is no such dependence, as the following pair of examples shows.

Suppose farmer Fred owns a tract of land across which villager Victor has a right of way. Then, if Fred erects an insurmountable fence around the land, Victor is forced to use another route, as Nozick will agree, since Fred, in erecting the fence, acted illegitimately. Now consider farmer Giles, whose similar tract is regularly traversed by villager William, not as of right, but because Giles is a tolerant soul. But then Giles erects an insurmountable fence around his land for reasons which justify him in doing so. According to Nozick, William may not truly say that, like Victor, he is now forced to use another route. But the examples, though different, do not so contrast as to make such a statement false. William is no less forced to change his route than Victor is. (10) is false even if – what I also deny – (9) is true, and the thesis that Z is forced to place his labour power at the disposal of some or other member of the capitalist class is sustained.

8. Nozick's claim about Z is so implausible that it may seem puzzling, coming as it does from an extremely acute thinker. Can it be that he is driven to it because it occupies a strategic place in his defence of libertarian capitalism? How is libertarian capitalism *libertarian* if it erodes the liberty of a large class of people?

Still, we can imagine Nozick granting that Z is forced to work for a

---

[39] For criticism of (9), see Frankfurt, 'Coercion and Moral Responsibility', pp. 83–4.
[40] *Anarchy*, p. 262.

capitalist, and attempting to recoup his position by saying this: Z is indeed so forced, but, since what brings it about that he is forced is a sequence of legitimate transactions, there is no moral case against his being so forced, no injustice in it. (Cf. (1) and (2), at p. 21 above.)

That would be less impressive than the original claim. Nozick is in a stronger position – could he but defend it – when he holds that capitalism does not deprive workers of freedom than if he grants that the worker is forced to subordinate himself yet insists that, even so, his situation, being justly generated, is, however otherwise regrettable, unexceptionable from the standpoint of justice. For the original claim, if true, entitles Nozick to say, given his other theses, that capitalism is not only a just but also a free society; while the revised claim makes him say that capitalism is just, but not entirely free. When Z is accurately described capitalism is less attractive, whatever we may say about it from the standpoint of justice.

Turning to that standpoint, and bearing Z in mind, what should we say about Nozick's important thesis (1)? It seems reasonable to add to the constraints on just acquisition a provision that no one may so acquire goods that others suffer severe loss of liberty as a result. We might, that is, *accept* thesis (1) but extend the conditions steps must meet to be just, and thus reject capitalism.[41]

Alternatively, we might grant, in concessive spirit, that there is no transactional injustice (no unjust step) in the generation of Z's position, but *reject* (1), and contend that the generative process must be regulated, even, perhaps, at the cost of some injustice, to prevent its issuing in very unjust results. Nozick would invoke side constraints against that, but they lack authority (see section 6 above).

Whatever option we take – and there are others – it should now be clear that 'libertarian' capitalism sacrifices liberty to capitalism, a truth its advocates are able to deny only because they are prepared to abuse the language of freedom.[42]

---

[41] It is immaterial here if this yields what Nozick would call a 'gimmicky' (see *Anarchy*, p. 157) reading of (1).

[42] For an extended defence of that charge of abuse, see sections 2 and 3 of Chapter 2 below.

2. Justice, freedom, and market transactions

Whatever arises from a just situation by just steps is itself just. (Robert Nozick, *Anarchy, State and Utopia*)

In protecting property the government is doing something quite apart from merely keeping the peace. It is exerting coercion wherever that is necessary to protect each owner, not merely from violence, but also from peaceful infringement of his sole right to enjoy the thing owned. (Robert L. Hale, 'Coercion and Distribution is a Supposedly Non-Coercive State')

In this chapter, I consider more closely two topics that were introduced in Chapter 1: the relationship between justice in transactions and justice in their upshots, which is addressed afresh in section 1, and the charge that Nozick-style libertarians play fast and loose with the language of freedom, which is elaborated in sections 2 and 3. Finally, in section 4, I foreground a principle, that of self-ownership, which is, if I may be permitted the oxymoron, latently salient in the Chamberlain argument. The principle of self-ownership is at centre stage in the next eight chapters of this book.

I remarked on p. 21 of Chapter 1 that Nozick is so confident of the truth of the formula exhibited at the head of this page that he believes that he need but apply it, without arguing for it, to overturn end-state and patterned theories of justice. In Chapter 1, I was less interested in the credentials of the formula itself than in the supposed threat it poses to egalitarian conceptions of justice, and I therefore did not inspect it at leisure, in its own right. In section 1 here, I do offer a somewhat minute examination of Nozick's formula. I first argue that its apparent self-evidence is only surface-deep, and I then press a case against it which does not rest on prior affirmation of theories of justice that Nozick rejects.

The political temperature throughout section 1 is comparatively low, and readers who are impatient with minutiae may wish to proceed immediately to section 2, in which the ideological confrontation between libertarianism and egalitarianism is resumed.

1a. Let us return to Nozick's formula:

(1) Whatever arises from a just situation by just steps is itself just.

A just situation, here, is one in which everyone has all and only those holdings which they ought to have, and 'just steps', for Nozick, are human actions that are free of injustice, in the sense that no one behaves with force or fraud in the course of them. I shall follow those (not implausible) characterizations of 'just situation' and 'just steps' throughout this section, but I must here mention two difficulties attending the reference to absence of force and fraud in the explication of 'just steps'.

The first difficulty concerns the appropriate interpretation of the expression 'force'. An interpretation of 'force' will be unserviceable, in the present context, if it is fixed by norms of justice. For if lack of force is, as it is for Nozick, central to the definition of justice, and injustice is, as, once again, remarkably enough, it is for Nozick, central to the definition of force,[1] then a circularity ensues which threatens our grip on the concepts of justice and force alike. This problem is pursued in section 2 (see, especially, subsection 2j) but it will be set aside in the present section.

The second difficulty concerns 'fraud'. Consider a particularly egregious instance of it: grossly false information published by a trader about the character and/or the economic value of what she puts on offer. Such a lie is crucially unlike force in that it appears to involve no intrusion into anyone's protected sphere', and hence, arguably, no breach of the side-constraints on action raised by libertarians like Nozick, and hence, further arguably, no injustice, from a libertarian point of view. This problem[2] will not be pressed at all. I shall allow that libertarians can regard fraud as polluting the justice of a 'step'.

The rest of this section unrolls as follows. In 1b I describe (bad) reasons for thinking that formula (1) must be true. The reasons I review can be at the back of people's minds, motivating their thoughts, but, once they are brought to the forefront, they are seen to be bad reasons for affirming (1).

The antecedent prejudice in favour of (1) having thereby been dissolved, I proceed, in subsection 1c, to cast doubt on (1), first on the basis of petty counter-examples to it, and then on the basis of more substantial ones, for

---

[1] See Chapter 1, section 7 above, and subsection 2g below.
[2] Which is discussed in James Child, 'Can Libertarianism Sustain a Fraud Standard?'

which the petty ones prepare the way. The first counter-examples are petty in that relatively minimal modification of (1) will circumvent them, but they prepare the way for more substantial ones because they show that, contrary to what turns out to be a surface impression, (1) is not incontrovertible, and that raises the credibility of the stance of those of us whose disagreement with (1)-like formulations is substantial.

The focus in 1c is on 'just steps'. In 1d I shift to an inspection of 'just situation', and I expose an ambiguity in that notion, which casts further doubt on formula (1).

Next, in subsection 1e, which is semi-digressive, I argue that one can regard the unavoidable riskiness of (just) market transactions as spoiling the justice of their upshots even if one thinks that the upshots of (literal) lotteries are free of injustice.

(1) being by now, so I hope, discredited, I raise the question, in 1f, about what features steps must have, *in addition* to justice (in the agreed sense: see the first paragraph of this subsection) for steps to be (not merely just but) *justice-preserving*. I argue that plausible requisites of justice-preservingness entail that market transactions are not (in general) reliably justice-preserving.

The principal claims of this section are that (a) just steps are not justice-preserving (that is, (1) is false) and that (b) common or garden 'innocent' market transactions are not justice-preserving. If those claims are correct, then not only is (1) false, but its purpose, which is to justify the upshots of ordinary market transactions, cannot be fulfilled: neither (1) itself nor any substitute for (1) will deliver what (1) is supposed to achieve. (Note that one might believe that (1) is true, but that market transactions do not always preserve justice, because they are not always just, and that one might believe that, although (1) is false, market transactions do preserve justice, because they have features additional to justice itself which, together with justice, ensure that initial justice is transmitted to market upshots, or even because, whether or not they are just, in general or in particular cases, market transactions nevertheless have features which ensure the transmission of justice. The second of those beliefs is, unlike the first, utterly implausible, and the third belief is very wild indeed, but the mere logical possibility of the two unusual beliefs helps to show that (a) and (b) are different denials.)

I defend (a) and (b) without appeal to substantive patterned or end-state criteria of distribution. Invoking such criteria would readily ensure the truth of my claims, but doing so would also beg the central question dividing entitlement and other theories of justice. Instead of invoking the mentioned criteria, I focus on processes which are free of unjust behaviour but which may nevertheless reasonably be thought to subvert the justice of situations which form their points of departure. 'May reasonably be thought': the sum of my ambition in this section is to throw doubt on the two theses which (a) and (b) contradict and not, strictly, to refute those theses: libertarian hard-liners might be unmoved by my arguments, but I am confident that the arguments would weaken the propensity to affirm (1) of 'floating voters'.

Recall that I do not endorse a *purely* end-state theory of justice. It is evident that identical distributions of holdings can differ with respect to justice because they differ with respect to their histories.[3] But that is not to say that end-state criteria are irrelevant to justice, and it is also not to say that Nozick provides an adequate account of what constitutes a justice-preserving history.

1b. Before I mount an assault on (1), in subsection c below, I want to explain how one might come to think, as Nozick and other libertarians manifestly do, that (1) is axiomatic, or otherwise unassailable.

(1) can appear invulnerable because of a train of reasoning that goes roughly so: if we start with justice, and we add nothing but justice, and, in particular, no injustice, then how can we get any injustice as a result?

Now, that train of reasoning might be based on one or other of two more general thoughts, the first being more primitive than the second. The first, and ultra-primitive thought, is that the result of adding an f-ish thing to an f-ish thing could not possibly be a counter-f-ish thing. But that alleged impossibility occurs all the time: when, for example, two odd numbers add up to an even one, or when two combustible substances combine to form an incombustible one.

That first thought is no doubt too primitive to attribute to academic libertarians. But perhaps, in the case of some of them, a somewhat less primitive, but still unacceptably crude, thought underlies their conviction that adding justice to justice cannot produce injustice. Those who do have this less primitive thought can acknowledge (unlike those who labour under the first one) that two wrongs sometimes make a right. But, they would explain, that is because errors and defects, being negative things, can neutralize each other. How, though, so they would protest, could two rights make a *wrong*?

The relevant (non-ultra-) primitive thought is that injustice is a defect

---

[3] See Chapter 1, section 3 above.

and that a defect must come from something deficient: if a new situation arises from (nothing but) an earlier just situation and just steps, how, then, can there be any defect in it? The answer is that combining perfect things can indeed generate imperfection, when, for example, the wrong fine wine is taken with a matchless dish, or when unsurpassably beautiful but inappropriate music is played in a perfect formal garden. So we can dismiss this reason for belief in (1).

Belief in (1) could also be generated by a thought process which does not employ a primitive premiss but which is nevertheless erroneous, the error being the familiar one of equivocation, as I shall now explain.

What does it mean for steps to be just? That they are free of injustice. But what is it for steps to be free of injustice? Either, as was suggested in the first paragraph of this section, that (a) there is no injustice within them; or that (b) in addition, they ensure that no injustice ensues. If we take interpretation (a), then we cannot immediately infer, from the definition of 'just steps', that (1) is true: it remains to be shown that just steps always preserve justice in situation. If we take interpretation (b), then (1) is true, but trivial. And if we slur over the difference between the two interpretations, if we equivocate across them, then we can wrongly think (1) both non-trivial (because of interpretation (a)) and true (because of interpretation (b)).

I am not sure how much the lately described primitive thinking and the just-exposed equivocation contribute to libertarian confidence in (1). But I am certain that a third pathology of thought is among what underlies that confidence.

Let me explain. A situation is just, that is, a set of holdings is justly held, if and only if no one holds what, as a matter of justice, they ought not to hold, and everyone holds what, as a matter of justice, they ought to hold:[4] that much we have here taken to be true by definition (see p. 39 above). If, now, one also takes it to be true by definition that such a situation obtains if no injustice figures in the production of it, if, that is, a situation is accounted just if and because the process generating it is just, then (1) will indeed come out true, but only by trivializing definition of 'just situation'.[5] For (1) to be interesting, it cannot be immediately true by definition in that way, it must not be excluded, by what amounts to fiat, that a situation

---

[4] It is necessary to add the second clause to cover, e.g., the case where someone wilfully destroys an object justly held by another.

[5] This is the opposite of the equivocator's trivializing move, for he defines 'just steps' in terms of the justice of the situation that they produce, and here a 'just situation' counts as such by virtue of the justice of the steps that lead to it.

which encompasses non-rightful holding(s) should emerge from a process which involves no injustice. I believe that there is among libertarians an inclination to make (1) true by definition in the explained trivializing way, but *also* an inclination to regard (1) as an interesting conceptual truth, of the sort that could and must be tested through review of putative counter-examples to it. For (1) to be an interesting conceptual truth, counter-examples to it must be (at least) abstractly possible; it must be possible to investigate, by *Gedankenexperiment*, whether or not a wedge can be driven between just process and just upshot. An attempt to drive such a wedge begins in the next subsection.

1c. We may begin to doubt formula (1) when we note the important difference of category between the two sorts of items to which 'just' is applied in (1): on the one hand to situations, and, in particular, here, to distributions (≠ distributings) of holdings, which are states of affairs that obtain at a point in time; and, on the other, to steps, or transactions, kinds, that is, not of states of affairs, but of events or processes, which take time to occur. For, corresponding to that radical difference of category, there is, so I shall argue, a difference in the criteria that items within the two categories must satisfy to qualify as just. It is, accordingly, entirely possible that chemical-like reactions will occur when justice of the one sort is added to justice of the other sort.

Consider a partly parallel case. Suppose we (not unreasonably) define a healthy person as one who flourishes in most environments, and a healthy environment as one in which most people flourish. It might then be true that putting a healthy person in a healthy environment could destroy his health, and, therefore, that adding health to health could produce illness. And we need not think, antecedently, that things go differently with justice, once we have liberated ourselves from the primitive conceptions and trivializing manœuvres reviewed in subsection 1b above.

A *situation* is just if and only if no one holds what, as a matter of justice, they ought not to hold, and everyone holds what, as a matter of justice, they ought to hold. It follows, so I would contend, that injustice in situation (unlike injustice in a step, as we have agreed to understand that: see p. 39 above) does not presuppose *wrongdoing*, that it could result from misadventure. To get an illustration of my claim, imagine that one of my justly held rolling pins rolls out of my front door and down the hill and through your open door, without your knowledge. You innocently mistake it to be the one you mislaid, and you keep it and use it. Now, so I take it, not everything is justly held, but no one has behaved, or is behaving, unjustly. And if, to vary the example instructively, you keep the rolling pin, in full knowledge of how it reached you, then you indeed behave unjustly, but whether or not what you then do counts as carrying out an unjust *step*, what you do is unjust because you are preserving a situation that counts as unjust for *other* reasons: it is not your action of keeping the rolling pin that makes the situation unjust in the first place.

In the rolling pin example a just situation is transformed into an unjust one without any unjust step occurring. That is not in itself a refutation of (1), since (1) says that just steps are sufficient to preserve justice, not that unjust steps are necessary to subvert it. (One reason why the two formulae presented in that sentence are not equivalent is that, as the rolling pin case illustrates, steps (taken by human beings) are not the only things that can transform one distribution into another). But if unjust steps are indeed unnecessary to overturn justice, why *should* just steps suffice to preserve it? Suppose that steps occur in which no one behaves with force or fraud: why, nevertheless, may not some accompanying misadventure generate an unjust resultant situation? The misrolling in the rolling pin case could have occurred even as just steps *also* occurred: perhaps we freely exchanged a knife for a fork while the errant pin was heading towards your door.

But, against that reflection, a defender of (1) might insist that misadventure, to be relevant here, cannot merely accompany just steps, like a meteor that disarranges a transaction, or on the model of my rolling pin example: for, in such cases, the new situation is not one that arises straightforwardly '*by* (nothing but) just steps', and, therefore, no clear counter-example to (1) emerges. Here, the insistence continues, misadventure must derive from aspects of the just steps themselves, ones that do not detract from their justice, as steps, but which nevertheless generate an unjust result.

Two replies may be made to that insistence. First, stress on the phrase '*by* just steps' produces at best a Pyrrhic victory for the defender of (1). For, since transactional steps do not occur in isolation from environing contingencies, protection of the truth-status of (1) through stress on '*by*' threatens to reduce its power to vindicate the results of market transactions: and that is the political function of (1).

We can, moreover, cast a shadow on (1) even if we accede to the insistence that the original just situation be transformed by nothing but just steps. Recall that we are taking the view, favoured by Nozick, that steps qualify as just as long as no one behaves coercively or fraudulently in the course of them. Given that view, we can envisage justice-subverting misadventure of the required just-steps-inherent kind: where agents behave with extreme ignorance. I sell a diamond to you for a pittance (or I give it to you on a whim), a diamond that we both think is glass.[6] *By* that (*ex* Nozick's *hypothesi*) just step, a situation arises in which you hold a diamond. But few would think that justice is fully served if, its true character having come to light, you now hang on to it, even though no one behaved unjustly in the generating transaction. (Your hanging on to the diamond would not be part of the transaction generating what I here claim to be an unjust situation, but one possible sequel to it. If your hanging on to the diamond would be unjust, that is surely because the situation of your having it would be unjust, despite its (Nozick-) just genesis.)

Notice that use of the rolling pin and diamond incidents as counter-examples to (1) conforms to the ordinance, laid down at p. 40 above, that patterned and end-state criteria of justice in situation should not be used to impugn (1). No such criteria have been used here, since nothing has here been said about the total sets of holdings of the relevant parties, before or after the change of situation. That is why the rolling pin and diamond counter-examples to (1) are especially difficult to gainsay, even for Nozick. Still, so it must be admitted, they are correspondingly easy for him to cope with, through a weakening of (1) which would not dramatically alter his position. He need only say that just steps preserve justice provided that no (gross) accident or (gross) error attends them. But the purpose of the petty examples, here, is to open the way for substantial putative counter-examples which can get no hearing if (1) is regarded as unassailable. Once (1) is seen to be debatable, and to be (pretty well) refuted by the petty counter-examples (the rolling-pin and the diamond), then, although (1) is not thereby definitively refuted in a substantial sense, since it can be patched up, it should no longer intimidate non-libertarians who have intuitions about injustice that do conflict substantially with (1). Counter-examples which Nozick must indeed reject appear less question-begging than they might otherwise seem to be in the light of the need to reject (1) in face of the petty counter-examples.

Turning, then, to more substantial counter-examples, it seems evident that ignorance could plausibly be thought to subvert justice even when it is not, as it is in the diamond example, of the immediate upshot of a prospective exchange. If we widen our focus, away from discrete pairs of

---

[6] To forestall unhelpful objections, let us suppose that I managed to buy the diamond as a result of hard labour, forgoing (other) entertainments, etc. Later, I forgot that it was a diamond.

transacting agents to the mass of uncoordinated transactions that occurs in a market economy, then the scope for justice-subverting misadventure due to ignorance becomes large. Thus, a substantial putative counter-example to (1) would be an accident involving no injustice but which is not (like the rolling pin event) principally due to physics: an insurance company (innocently) goes bust and thereby (in the absence of state assistance to them) ruins the lives of people who could not have known that its position would come to be exposed; people who now have to sell their assets voluntarily (in the relevant libertarian sense), for a snip, to alert non-fraudulent buyers. And it is also permissible to think that a just situation could be transformed into an unjust one because of the way that a mass of uncoordinated transactions *foreseeably or otherwise* combine.[7]

The counter-examples presented in the previous paragraph would not be acknowledged as such by Nozick: he would stonewall in the face of them, and continue to affirm (1) in a lightly modified (to cater for petty counter-examples) form. Yet Nozick himself provides a substantial counter-example to (1), although he does not represent it as such, because (1) is not on the agenda at the point in his book[8] where the example appears. I have in mind his case of the person who inadvertently becomes the monopoly holder of drinking water. No injustice *generates* that situation, but Nozick thinks that it calls for rectification. So either he rejects (1) for a substantial reason,[9] or, if he protects (1) by pressing hard on '*by just steps*' – see p. 44 above – then (1) becomes less powerful polemically (see, again, p. 44). In either case, (1) loses its spell as an instrument against believers in end-state theories of justice.

Let me end this subsection with some pedantic formulations: in this domain it is easy to lose track by not being pedantic enough. Suppose that we start with a just situation, and a just transaction occurs. If there is (what Nozick thinks that there consequently could not be) any injustice in the upshot, then, *ex hypothesi*, that injustice could not be due to any injustice in the transaction itself. But it does not therefore follow that there could be no injustice in the upshot, and accidents, lack of relevant foreknowledge, and foreknown combinatorial processes may reasonably be regarded as producers of situational injustice.

[7] For a similar chain, see section 4 of John Rawls, 'The Basic Structure as Subject'. Rawls' claim is similar to, but not identical with, mine, since his relies on end-state criteria of justice, which (see p. 40 above) I have forsworn here. (Whether Rawls begs the question by employing such criteria in the context of his different discussion is an interesting question that I shall not pursue.)

[8] See *Anarchy*, p. 180.

[9] And, indeed, one which, arguably, reflects an end-state principle of justice.

1d. In this subsection, I shall expose an unexpected ambiguity in (1) which serves further to reduce the case for accepting it. The ambiguity relates to a complexity in the concept of a 'just situation', as that was fixed at p. 39 above: there are, it turns out, significantly different dimensions of justice in situation (so understood). To make this point, I return to the example of justly generated slavery, which was sketched in footnote 4 of Chapter 1. Recall that the example runs as follows: *A* and *B* are identical in talents and tastes. Each would so like to have a slave that he is willing to risk becoming one in exchange for the same chance of getting one. So they toss a coin, *B* loses, and *A* clamps chains on him.

This example raises a difficulty for Nozick. As he applies 'just' to a set of holdings, justice is what a justice-enforcing authority rightly enforces. But the slavery case shows that such enforceability is a seriously conjunctive matter. Because of the spotlessly just *genesis* of their relationship,[10] one might think that *B* has no enforceable grievance against his owner: a justice-enforcing authority might rightly hesitate if and when *B* asks to be freed. Yet, allowing that, one might nevertheless resist the idea that *A* can legitimately expect his control over *B* to be enforced. Thus, suppose that *B* breaks his chains and runs away, and *A* calls upon the selfsame authority to recapture him. Why may it not say, and consistently with its unwillingness to help *B* to liberate himself: 'Slavery is such a demeaning practice that justice could not demand that we help you to recover *B*'?

In the slavery example someone loses hugely on a perhaps unwise gamble. Because he faces a fully symmetrical opposite number, (Nozickian) transactional justice undoubtedly obtains. But the upshot might still be judged unfair, even if, in John Mackie's phrase, 'it would not . . . be fair for [the loser] to complain of the unfairness'.[11]

In the course of a subtle discussion of the conditions under which contracts confer justice on their results, Alistair MacLeod lists ways in which agreements themselves can be unfair because the parties are not 'equally competent to make use of the information available to them'. And he adds that

---

[10] It has been suggested to me that its genesis might be considered unjust on the ground that the parties behave unjustly to themselves, but, however that may be, for Nozick a step is unjust only if in the course of it someone commits an injustice against someone else, and such a charge seems impossible to sustain here: there is no trace of force or fraud in the genesis of this particular instance of slavery.

[11] Mackie, *Ethics*, p. 95. In an inquiry more nuanced than the one that I am conducting here, the difference between injustice and unfairness would need to be investigated.

although it is chiefly blameless stupidity that is at issue in [such] contexts, not the stupidity associated with careless or sloppy use of information, it seems likely . . . that the fairness of an agreement can be vitiated even by culpable stupidity.[12]

When the stupidity is culpable, Mackie's distinction operates: because of the stupidity, the upshot is unfair; because of the culpability, the agent is poorly placed to complain about its unfairness.

The distinctions made here yield further reason to be cautious about (1). Since justice in situation, conceived in Nozickian terms of legitimate enforceability, turns out to have distinguishable aspects, which call for separate judgements of justice, superficially appealing primitive thoughts (see subsection 1b above) which may help to account for (1)'s attractive power look cruder still.

1e. Critics of the justice of the market are wont to fix on the uncertainty of market outcomes as a reason for denying (1), and, more generally, for denying that market outcomes are just, whether or not (1) is true. If market agents knew what the upshot of their trading would be, the market might be just: but what they know, at most, are the probabilities of various outcomes of that trading.

Some defenders of the market bite the bullet here. Of course, they acknowledge, the market can be compared to a lottery, but, at least in favoured cases, where outcome probabilities are indeed known, lottery gamblers suffer no injustice, even when they are large-scale losers. Why, then, should comparably informed market losers have a grievance?

The principle underlying that defence of the market was introduced in footnote 9 of Chapter 1:

(4) Whatever arises from a just situation as a result of fully voluntary transactions where the transacting agents know in advance the probabilities of all significantly different possible outcomes is itself just.

I said in Chapter 1 that I had my doubts about (4), and I shall now expose them.

The transactional conditions specified in (4) are satisfied in the slavery gamble of subsection 1d. Yet, as we saw, the resulting situation is not unambiguously just. That is an initial, relatively minor, reason for doubting (4).

[12] 'Distributive Justice, Contract, and Equality', p. 711.

But suppose, now, that the slavery-creating gamble of subsection 1d was imposed on the parties, rather than chosen by them. We could then hardly regard the result as in any respect just, even though neither party had engaged in an unjust step. This reflection is a clue to why foreknowledge of the probabilities of upshots of market transactions cannot justify their results on the model of a lottery. The imposed slavery gamble does not challenge (4) itself, because of (4)'s 'fully voluntary' requirement, but it points to the unserviceability of (4) as a defence of the justice of real markets. For there is always some degree of constraint behind entry into a market 'lottery'.

Suppose we start with a just distribution and a (literal) money lottery is proposed, which persons are free both to enter and to avoid. Then, whatever may be said about third parties,[13] it is plain that no loser in the lottery has any grievance. But that comment does not apply to losers in the market lottery.

A person might want to make his living running a small shop. He is not interested in large gains: he would settle for an unvarying modest annual profit (which, let us suppose, no affordable insurance policy will secure for him) if he could. But, in a market society, he cannot run a shop without putting himself at the mercy of market contingency: he might prosper more than he aspires to do, but he might also lose his shirt. Our man might credibly say: I wish my choice whether or not to run a shop were not constituted in this way. The entrant in a literal lottery can say nothing comparable. There is nothing *to* such a lottery beyond entirely voluntary gambling. Entering a real lottery is not a way of doing *something else* (that you might prefer to do differently), but entering the market lottery is always a (possibly dispreferred) way of doing something else.

A further pertinent dissimilarity between real lotteries and markets. In the former the risk is avoidable: you simply keep your money. In the latter, there is no comparably safe option. The would-be shop owner could indeed eschew risking his (possibly borrowed) capital, but he will not then face a risk-free life. For he must then enter another's employ, and there is plenty of risk in that course.

It is unclear whether these considerations challenge (4), since it is unclear whether the quotidian constraint that features in them suffices to remove the voluntariness which (4) requires for just outcomes. But that is not important, polemically. If ordinary constraint suffices to remove

---

[13] And much, indeed, may be said, in line with what was said in section 4 of Chapter 1 regarding third parties to the Chamberlain transaction.

voluntariness, then (4) fails as a justification of the market, since the market does not satisfy its conditions. And if that constraint is deemed consistent with voluntariness, then (4) is dubious principle.

Now, the exhibited problematic nature of the market does not show that the market should be eliminated, or even that market contingency should as much as possible be reduced. We do not know how to proceed efficiently without markets, and we can compromise autonomy by reducing contingency: people cherish choices in their lives, and (sometimes) submission to contingency is inseparable from that. So the right conclusion is not that the market must go, but that the considerations which vindicate it (to whatever extent it can be vindicated) are not shown by (4) to be ones of justice, even when all probabilities are foreknown.

1f. Having cast doubt on thesis (1), that just steps preserve justice in situation, I turn to the question of what might have to be added to justice in steps for steps to be (situational-) justice-preserving. The interest of the question is great in relation to the question whether standard market steps preserve justice, which is distinct from the question of the truth of (1) (see p. 42 above).

Just steps can be thought non-justice-preserving for two general kinds of reason. The first was illustrated in subsection 1e: the structure within which agents behave without force and fraud always excludes some options and promotes others, with relevantly different effects on people's prospects. As we saw, one might then regard the steps that they take as (though just) not fully voluntary, and, consequently, as non-justice-preserving. Alternatively, one might regard the steps as voluntary, by less stringent criteria of voluntariness, but the unchosen structure within which they occur is still a potential enemy of justice in upshot. I shall henceforth set aside the problem posed by unchosen structure for the justice-preservingness of just steps.

The other principal reason, in general terms, why one may doubt that just steps are justice-preserving is that justice in steps is consistent with any degree and kind of ignorance on the part of the transacting agents. There is, however, a way of extinguishing the justice-defeating power of ignorance, which was contemplated in a principle introduced at p. 23 of Chapter 1 above:

(3) Whatever arises from a just situation as a result of fully voluntary transactions which all transacting agents would still have agreed to if they had known what the results of so transacting were to be is itself just.

Ignorance does not matter when knowledge would have induced the same steps, but, as I said in Chapter 1, the conditions imposed on justice-preservingness in (3) are so strong that they will quite widely fail to obtain, to the detriment of this mode of vindicating market justice.

Counter-examples to (1) like the diamond case of p. 45 do not touch (3), and principles with less demanding conditions, such as this one, are also immune to such counter-examples:

(5) Whatever arises from a just situation as a result of fully voluntary transactions whose agents know what the immediate upshot of the transaction will be is itself just.

The diamond case is no objection to (5), since a feature of its immediate upshot, that the buyer comes to hold a diamond, is not foreknown.

A market could work under (5)'s proviso, which is essentially a rejection of (unqualified) *caveat emptor*. But ignorance of what will occur further afield casts a shadow on the justice-preservingness of transactions which satisfy the undemanding epistemic condition laid down in (5). If radical ignorance about its immediate upshot (in terms of economic value) defeats justice in the diamond transaction, why should similar ignorance about economic values further afield have *no* effect on the power of the transaction affected by such ignorance to preserve justice?

One might have recourse to principle (4) (see subsection 1e above), which requires only knowledge of probabilities of (all future) upshots before a transaction is considered justice-preserving. But (apart from the problem of structural constraint, laid out in subsection 1e, which is consistent with knowledge of probabilities, and which I have here set aside) if a highly improbable future contingency materializes, the mere fact that its probability (say, of 0.00001) was known will do little to weaken the intuition, for those who have it, that injustice has ensued. We might both have known that there was a 1 in 10,000 chance that the number 2 bus would be rerouted, and that all the patrons of my sandwich bar would consequently switch to yours, but it is not therefore evident that the resulting failure of my bar can generate no reasonable sense in me that I have suffered an upshot injustice.

And, apart from the fact that knowledge of probabilities does not clearly suffice for justice-preservingness, such knowledge will usually be unavailable. That is because the results to which given market transactions contribute are so complex and ramifying that little beyond the probabilities of various *immediate* outcomes can ever be generally known: how could everyone, or even anyone, know, for example, what (all) future stock market prices are (so much as) *likely* to be?

The general problem, already raised in Chapter 1 (see p. 23), is that steps which satisfy conditions strong enough to make them securely justice-preserving are uncharacteristic of the market. Yet, laying aside the project of vindicating actual markets, one might try to define an ideal (from the point of view of justice) market, from which actual market processes differ in different degrees. Interestingly, however, and as I shall now argue, the more a 'market' approaches the ideal to be defined, the less it truly is a market.

The ideal is defined by the proposal that market transactions transform a just situation into a fresh just situation when each agent knows *precisely* what the effect of his transaction will be, including, therefore, its effect on how he will be able, and will want, to transact in the future. In an ideal market, so it is suggested, transactions have that full epistemic transparency.

But the stated proposal is misbegotten. For the notion of an (ongoing) market society is conceptually tied to the idea of ignorance about the future.[14] If everyone could anticipate her future transactions, there would be no need to conduct any transactions in the future: instead of a market process, there would be a grand once-and-forever multilateral contract laying out all future exchanges.

For consider. If I am to know the full effect of a mooted prospective transaction, then one thing that I must know is how I and others will transact in the future, since that will help to determine the upshot of the forthcoming transaction. But then it is pointless to wait for the future to do

---

[14] This claim holds even for (if such a thing is possible) a market without entrepreneurs. It is therefore not Israel Kirzner's claim that 'the market process depends, in fact, on the profitability of entrepreneurial trading with market participants who have at least to some extent – erred', but it does resemble Kirzner's more general claim, which is somewhat differently grounded from mine, that 'a market process without "erroneous" transactions is unthinkable' ('Entrepreneurship, Entitlement and Economic Justice', pp. 386, 388). (Kirzner countenances the deliberate exploitation of others' errors by drawing on a bizarre account of the relationship between knowledge and creation, according to which, *inter alia*, 'until a resource has been discovered, *it has not*, in the sense relevant to the rights of access and common use, *existed at all*' (*ibid.*, p. 395: see, further, Chapter 7, footnote 37 below).

Kirzner's essay is an attempt to answer those who say 'that error (which invariably characterizes market transactions) introduces an ineradicable stain of *involuntariness* into the very fabric of these transactions' (*ibid.*, p. 391). But that way of posing the challenge presented by ignorance and error is misplaced. It is not the voluntariness (or even, standardly, the justice) of a transaction that is prejudiced by error, but the justice of its upshot.

the foreseeable transacting: why would I refuse, on Tuesday, to give you a promise about what I shall do on Thursday that you and I are both absolutely certain I shall give you on Wednesday? Under ideal information, we will (in fact or in effect) all sign life contracts with one another and there will be no further transacting. Ideal information is incompatible with an economy in which trading occurs in episodes separated by stretches of time.

Accordingly, one cannot say: market transactions preserve justice except when they occur in a frame of ignorance. One cannot say that, simply because the market is always framed by ignorance (except, of course, in the case of the full-information-one-shot 'market' which is plainly impossible). But one need not conclude that the market should be rejected. What I conclude, once again (see the end of subsection 1e above), is that, if the market is to be endorsed, then that will not be because it is flawless from the point of view of justice.

2a. In section 8 of Chapter 1 I dealt briefly and bluntly with the relationship between freedom and justice in Nozick. I said that he could not claim that a society in which some are forced to sell their labour power on pain of starvation upheld the value of freedom, but I allowed that he might nevertheless claim that such a society is consistent with the idea of justice. There was a certain lack of nuance in that summation of the position. For, in Nozick's conception, freedom and justice are closely related matters. It was, therefore, a little swift to allow that Nozick might rest his case on justice despite its unsustainability on grounds of freedom. In this section further investigation of the relationship between the two concepts will occur.

2b. A proponent of D1 might respond to the Chamberlain argument by proposing a tax on his earnings. The rate of tax, and the destiny of its proceeds, would be decided by the principles underlying D1. Now, taxation for the sake of equality (or whatever D1 is) will often dampen productivity in a capitalist economy. But let us suppose, as might well be true in the Chamberlain case (see Chapter 1, p. 26), that such a tax would not act as a disincentive, so that we can focus on this distinct question: would the contemplated tax policy be unacceptable because it unjustifiably restricts freedom?

2c. Well, such a policy undoubtedly removes *certain* freedoms. With the taxing policy, Chamberlain loses the freedom to enter a contract under which he plays basketball and earns a cool quarter of a million, and the fans lose the freedom to enter a contract under which they each pay twenty-five cents and he gains the aforementioned sum. But the removal of *certain* freedoms can be in the interest of freedom itself, and before we conclude that a policy of taxing people like Chamberlain restricts freedom *tout court*, or restricts it unjustifiably, we must check to see whether its removal of *certain* freedoms might not promote other ones that also matter.

How much freedom I have depends on the number and nature of my options. And that in turn depends *both* on the rules of the game *and* on the assets of the players: it is a very important and widely neglected truth that it does not depend on the rules of the game alone.

Suppose that I am the sovereign of an island up on which, from time to time, marooned sailors are washed. At the moment, there is only one washed up sailor, sailor One, in residence. He has built himself a shelter, and, by the rules I, the sovereign, have made, he is the owner of that shelter: he need not part with it, or let anyone else use it. Others will be entitled to use it only if he agrees to let them do so, perhaps for a consideration. And now a storm washes up a second sailor, sailor Two, who, battered by the storm, will probably die unless sailor One lets him shelter, temporarily, in his hut. Under the existing rules, sailor One can legitimately demand the life-long slavery of sailor Two in exchange for letting him shelter. The existing rules permit any kind of contract, including that extreme one, and the sailors' assets and motivations might ensure that that would be the contract that occurs. But, because I am a freedom-loving sovereign, I change the rules so that they forbid slave contracts. Now, we can suppose, sailor Two will get a better deal, under which he will enjoy more freedom. Precisely as a result of the prohibition that I laid down, he now has an option superior to slavery which was unavailable when the rules of contract were more permissive.[15] More permissive rules look unambiguously freedom-promoting only when all we look at is the rules and we ignore, unjustifiably, the asset distribution in which they operate. When 'a socialist society forbids capitalist acts between consenting adults',[16] some of them will be freer than they otherwise would have been

---

[15] To be sure, sailor One loses an option which contributed to his freedom, and, *ceteris paribus*, gains no freedom by way of compensation. Suppose, then, that the (good) sense in which I am a freedom-loving sovereign is that I want the person who is least free to be as free as possible.

[16] See Chapter 1 above, p. 28.

just because of that restriction on everyone's, and, therefore, on their own, freedom.[17]

2d. Let me now relate the foregoing reflections to the less drastic case of Chamberlain and his fans. Taxing him pretty unequivocally reduces Chamberlain's freedom: to think otherwise, you have to believe an implausible story about knock-on effects, or fancy Marxist stuff about how deeply free we all really are when we are all equal together. But it is not at all obvious that preventing the fans from entering a contract whose proceeds will be free of tax reduces *their* freedom. For the prohibition creates an option which is otherwise unavailable to them, to wit, the option of paying twenty-five cents to see Wilt play *without* endowing a member of their society with enormous wealth, and at the same time regaining much of what they pay in benefits financed by a suitably constructed tax policy.

That casts doubt on whether the taxing policy, which removes certain freedoms, is, for all that, to be eschewed out of a respect for freedom. But there is another, and partly distinct, point, to be made, which is that although D1's tax rules restrict freedom, they do so because all rules do, and so, therefore, in particular do the rules which would prevail in the private property free market economy favoured by libertarians. It follows that no one can claim that D1's rules restrict freedom, *by contrast* with the rules that libertarians favour.

Nozick presents himself as a defender of unqualified private property *and* as an unswerving opponent of all restrictions on individual freedom. I claim that he cannot coherently be both, if only because no one who is not an anarchist can be the second, and I now want to drive that point home. With a view to doing so, I shall begin by exploiting a banal truth, so banal, indeed, that, as we shall see, my use of it excited a (wholly misplaced) protest from the pen of John Gray: he was unable to believe that something so banal could be polemically consequential. Having laid out the case[18] to which Gray objected, I shall respond to his complaints.

The banal truth is that, if the state prevents me from doing something that I want to do, then it places a restriction on my freedom. Suppose, then,

---

[17] For an excellent development of this point, see Thomas Pogge, *Realizing Rawls*, pp. 48–50. Pogge's important distinction between *established* and *engendered* states of affairs is closely related to the distinction made here between what happens because of the rules and what happens because of the rules *and* the asset distribution.

[18] In presenting the case, I draw on material that appeared in 'Capitalism, Freedom and the Proletariat', pp. 167–72, and, in less developed form, in *History, Labour, and Freedom*, pp. 293–6.

that I want to perform an action which involves a legally prohibited use of your property. I want, let us say, to pitch a tent in your large back garden, perhaps just in order to annoy you, or perhaps for the more substantial reason that I have nowhere to live and no land of my own, but I have got hold of a tent, legitimately or otherwise. If I now try to do this thing that I want to do, the chances are that the state will intervene on your behalf. If it does, I shall suffer a constraint on my freedom. The same goes, of course, for all unpermitted uses of a piece of private property by those who do not own it, and there are always those who do not own it, since 'private ownership by one person presupposes non-ownership on the part of other persons'.[19] But the free enterprise economy rests upon private property: in that economy you sell and buy what you respectively own and come to own. It follows that libertarians cannot complain that a socialist dispensation restricts freedom, *by contrast* with the dispensation that they themselves favour.

2e. Before proceeding further with the present critique of libertarians, I pause to point out that the banal truth pressed against them here also constitutes an objection to the way that anti-libertarian liberals of the American type often describe the modified capitalism that they favour.

According to Thomas Nagel, who is an anti-libertarian liberal of an especially perspicacious kind, 'progressive taxation' entails 'interference' with individual freedom.[20] He regards the absence of such interference as a value, but one which needs to be compromised for the sake of greater economic and social equality, as what he calls the 'formidable challenge to liberalism . . . from the left' maintains.[21] Yet it is quite unclear that social democratic checks on the sway of private property, through devices like progressive taxation and the welfare minimum, represent *any* enhancement of governmental interference with freedom. The government certainly interferes with a landowner's freedom if it establishes public

---

[19] Karl Marx, *Capital*, Vol. III, p. 812.
[20] Nagel believes that libertarians go too far towards the liberty end of a spectrum on which leftists go too far towards the equality end: 'Libertarianism . . . fastens on one of the two elements [that is, freedom and equality – GAC] of the liberal ideal and asks why its realization should be inhibited by the demands of the other. Instead of embracing the ideal of equality and the general welfare, libertarianism exalts the claim of individual freedom of action and asks why state power should be permitted even the interference represented by progressive taxation and public provision of health care, education and a minimum standard of living' ('Libertarianism Without Foundations', p. 192).
[21] *Ibid.*, p. 191.

rights of way and a right for others to pitch tents on his land. But it also interferes with the freedom of would-be walkers or tent-pitchers when it prevents them from indulging *their* 'individual inclinations'.[22] The general point is that incursions against private property which *reduce* owners' freedom by transferring rights over resources to non-owners thereby *increase* the latter's freedom. In advance of further argument, the net effect on freedom of the resource transfer is indeterminate.

Libertarians are against what they describe as an 'interventionist' policy in which the state engages in 'interference'. Nagel is not, but he agrees that such a policy 'intervenes' and 'interferes'. In my view, the use of words like 'interventionist' to designate the stated policy is an ideological distortion detrimental to clear thinking and friendly to the libertarian point of view. It is, though friendly to that point of view, consistent with rejecting it, and Nagel does reject it, vigorously. But, by acquiescing in the libertarian use of 'intervention', he casts libertarianism in a better light than it deserves. The standard use of 'intervention' esteems the private property component in the liberal or social democratic settlement too highly, by associating that component too closely with freedom.

2f. My zeal on behalf of anti-ideological clear-mindedness about 'intervention' and 'interference' prompts me to comment on a well-known sequence of political debate, which runs as follows. The Right extols the freedom enjoyed by all in a liberal capitalist society. The Left complains that the freedom in question is meagre for poor people. The Right rejoins that the Left confuses freedom with resources. 'You are free to do what no one will interfere with your doing', says the Right. 'If you cannot afford to do it, that does not mean that someone will interfere with your doing it, but just that you lack the means or ability to do it. The problem the poor face is lack of ability, not lack of freedom'. The Left may then say that ability should count for as much as freedom does. The Right can then reply, to significant political effect: so *you* may think, but our priority is freedom.

In my view, the depicted right-wing stance depends upon a reified view of money. Money is unlike intelligence or physical strength, poor endowments of which do not, indeed, prejudice freedom, where freedom is understood as absence of interference. The difference between money and those endowments implies, I shall argue, that lack of money *is* (a form of)

---

[22] *Ibid.*, p. 191.

lack of freedom, in the favoured sense of freedom, where it is taken to be absence of interference.[23]

To see this, begin by imagining a society without money, in which courses of action available to people, courses they are free to follow without interference, are laid down by the law. The law says what each sort of person, or even each particular person, may and may not do without interference, and each person is issued with a set of tickets detailing what she is allowed to do. So I may have a ticket saying that I am free to plough this piece of land, another one saying that I am free to go to that opera, or to walk across that field, while you have different tickets, with different freedoms inscribed on them.

Imagine, now, that the structure of the options written on the tickets is more complex. Each ticket lays out a disjunction of conjunctions of courses of action that I may perform. I may do A and B and C and D OR B and C and D and E OR E and F and G and A, and so on. If I try to do something not licensed by my tickets or ticket, armed force intervenes.

By hypothesis, these tickets say what my freedoms (and, consequently, my unfreedoms) are. But a sum of money is nothing but a highly generalized form of such a ticket. A sum of money is a licence to perform a disjunction of conjunctions of actions – actions, like, for example, visiting one's sister in Bristol, or taking home, and wearing, the sweater on the counter at Selfridge's.

Suppose that someone is too poor to visit her sister in Bristol. She cannot save, from week to week, enough to buy her way there. Then, as far as her freedom is concerned, this is equivalent to 'trip to Bristol' not being written on someone's ticket in the imagined non-monetary economy. The woman I have described has the capacity to go to Bristol. She can board the underground and approach the barrier which she must cross to reach the train. But she will be physically prevented from passing through it, or physically ejected from the train, or, in the other example, she will be physically stopped outside Selfridge's and the sweater will be removed. The only way that she will not be prevented from getting and using such things is by offering money for them.

To have money *is* to have freedom, and the assimilation of money to mental and bodily resources is a piece of unthinking fetishism, in the good

---

[23] Accordingly, poverty should not be bracketed with illness and lack of education and thereby treated in the manner of the Commission on Social Justice, as a restriction on 'what [people] can do with their freedom' (*The Justice Gap*, p. 8). Poverty restricts freedom itself, and social democrats needlessly accede to the Right's misrepresentation of the relationship between poverty and freedom when they make statements like the just quoted.

old Marxist sense that it misrepresents *social relations of constraint* as *things* that people lack. In a word: money is no object.

2g. Here is an objection to the banal argument presented in 2d above. In the course of that argument, I supposed that to prevent someone from doing something that he wants to do is to make him, in that respect, unfree: I am *pro tanto* unfree *whenever* someone interferes with my actions, *whether or not I have a right to perform them, and whether or not my obstructor has a right to interfere with me.* But there is a definition of freedom which informs much libertarian writing and which entails that interference is not a sufficient condition of unfreedom. On that definition, which may be called the *rights definition of freedom*, I am unfree only when someone prevents me from doing what I have a right to do, so that he, consequently, has no right to prevent me from doing it. Nozick was using the rights definition of freedom when he wrote the passage from which I had occasion to quote at p. 36 of Chapter 1 above:

Other people's actions place limits on one's available opportunities. Whether this makes one's resulting action non-voluntary depends upon whether these others had the right to act as they did.[24]

Now, if one combines this rights definition of freedom with a moral endorsement of private property, with a claim that, in standard cases, people have a moral right to the property that they legally own, then one reaches the result that the protection of (legitimate) private property cannot restrict anyone's freedom. It will follow from the moral endorsement of private property that you and the police are justified in preventing me from pitching my tent on your land, and, because of the rights definition of freedom, it will then further follow that you and the police do not thereby restrict my freedom. So, on the rights definition of freedom, which is, after all, the one that Nozick uses, private property need not, as I contend it must, restrict freedom. It does not restrict freedom if and when the formation and protection of private property proceeds congruently with people's legitimate rights.

2h. I have two replies to this manœuvre against my banal argument. The first reply is that the characterization of freedom exercised in the objection is unacceptable. It is false that, in order to determine whether actions

[24] *Anarchy*, p. 262.

which 'place limits on one's available opportunities'[25] make one (*pro tanto*) unfree, it is necessary to investigate whether the resulting limits on opportunities are wrongfully produced. A properly convicted murderer is rendered unfree when he is justly imprisoned.

That first reply to the objection in 2g invokes the ordinary use of such terms as 'free' and 'freedom'. My second reply to the objection does not rely on how language is ordinarily used.

Suppose that we overrule ordinary usage and we say, with Nozick, that *rightful* interference with someone's action does not restrict his freedom. It cannot then be argued, without further ado, that interference with private property is wrong *because* it restricts freedom. For one can no longer take for granted, what is evident on a rights-neutral ordinary language conception of freedom, that interference with private property *does* reduce freedom. On a rights account of what freedom is one must abstain from that assertion until one has shown that people have moral rights to their private property. Yet libertarians tend *both* to use a rights definition of freedom *and* to take it for granted that interference with his private property diminishes its owner's freedom. But they can take the latter for granted only on the rights *neutral* account of freedom, on which, however, it is equally obvious that the protection of private property diminishes the freedom of *non*-owners, to avoid which consequence they adopt a rights definition of the concept. And so they go, back and forth, between inconsistent definitions of freedom, not because they cannot make up their minds which one they like better, but under the propulsion of their desire to occupy what is in fact an untenable position. Libertarians want to say that interferences with people's use of their private property are unacceptable because they are, quite obviously, abridgements of freedom, *and* that the reason why protection of private property does not similarly abridge the freedom of non-owners is that owners have a right to exclude others from their property and non-owners consequently have no right to use it. But they can say both things only if they define freedom in two incompatible ways.

2i. The retreat to the rights definition lands Nozick inside a circle. On the rights definition of freedom, a person is entirely free when he is not prevented from performing any action that he has a right to perform: on the rights definition, interfering with a person interferes with his freedom only if the interfering person lacks the right to commit the given

[25] See the quotation from Nozick at p. 59 above.

interference. Accordingly, to know whether a person is free, in the rights-laden sense of the term, we have to know what his (and others') rights are. But what characterization of people's rights does Nozick provide? Either no characterization at all, or a characterization in terms of freedom, something like: people have those rights the possession of which secures their freedom.

Thereby Nozick locks himself inside a circle. For Nozick, there is justice, which is to say no violation of anyone's rights, when there is lack of coercion, which means that there is justice when there is no restriction on freedom. But freedom is then itself defined in terms of non-violation of rights, and the result is a tight definitional circle and no purchase either on the concept of freedom or on the concept of justice.

2j. Let me show how the circularity in Nozick's conceptions of freedom and justice affects principle (1):

(1) Whatever arises from a just situation by just steps is itself just.

To apply (1), we have to know what makes steps just. Nozick's answer is that they are just when voluntarily performed, or coercion-free. But, when we now ask what voluntary performance is, we are told that someone's action is voluntary, no matter how limited his opportunities were, if and only if there was no injustice in the production of the limitation on his opportunities. And that creates a circle: justice in transfer is defined in terms of voluntariness and voluntariness is defined in terms of justice. I think that the first definition is mistaken and that the second is a ridiculous deviation from ordinary language, but the present different point is that, under such ways with words, we cannot use either freedom or justice as a criterion of evaluation.

In section 4 I describe a possible way out of the circle, the principle of self-ownership, which is neither freedom nor justice and which is the real ground on which Nozick stands.

2k. Return for a moment to the insistence that the rights definition of freedom violates ordinary language. It is not equally clear that a rights definition of liberty would do so. Some might say that, although a well-enforced law against rape restricts rapists' *freedom*, it nevertheless does not restrict their *liberty*, since there is no such thing as a liberty to rape. If the suggested contrast between freedom and liberty obtains, then Nozick could say, in an unconcessive tone, that his defence is not of freedom but of liberty.

Now this would protect Nozick against the ordinary language objection, but it will not eliminate the circularity from his construction. For we would now require a characterization of liberty, and we could not now take for granted, as Nozick inconsistently does, that restrictions on freedom of contract restrict liberty. Liberty, when it is not identical with freedom, is freedom seasoned with justice. But then we do not know what liberty is until we have a freedom-independent characterization of justice, and that is something that we have not been given.

3a. I now want to respond to a broadside delivered by John Gray against (a predecessor form of) the critique of Nozick pursued in section 2 above. The discussion here will be minutely polemical, and many readers will want to proceed immediately to section 4 below.

Gray writes:

In Nozick's conception, freedom is a moral notion whose scope is given by a theory of justice. It is this conception which Cohen calls the moralized view of freedom[26] and which (for reasons that are unclear to me) he thinks to be 'false'. The falsity of Nozick's view seems to be revealed to Cohen by the fact that *justified* interferences remain interferences with freedom. In Nozick's theory, however, in which the domain of individual freedom is specified by principles of justice, justified violation of the freedoms demanded by justice remains a violation of freedom: if we violate side-constraints in order to prevent a moral catastrophe, we curtail liberty and justify doing so by reference to the broader morality within which considerations of justice are usually paramount. What Nozick's view excludes as a possibility is not, then, justified restraints on liberty, but *justicizable* restraints on liberty – that is to say, restraints justifiable in terms of justice. Justice cannot compete with liberty, but morality may *in extremis* license a violation of the liberty demanded by justice. Nozick's conception does not have the feature which Cohen thinks shows its falsity, and the only reason I can see that might otherwise give this result is the deviation of Nozick's view from the intuitions embodied in our ordinary-language deliberations. But ordinary language has no special authority here, if Nozick's conception is compelling for other reasons. If, for example, it suggests that the would-be rapist loses no freedom under laws forbidding sexual assault, because he is not entitled to subject another to forcible sexual intercourse, then I think that squares with our moral intuitions better than does the liberal view.[27] For Nozick's view disqualifies, what the liberal view necessitates, weighing in the scales the rapist's liberty against that of his victim. What is required to evaluate Nozick's conception of freedom as a moral notion is

---

[26] I now prefer to call it the *rights definition of freedom*. Some were misled by the earlier name because of a widespread tendency to identify morality with the broader realm of value in general.

[27] By which Gray (somewhat oddly) means the view, held, for example, by me, that any interference with action reduces freedom.

not servility to the supposed deliverances of ordinary language but, rather, something akin to Rawlsian reflective equilibrium, in which the claims of the larger theory of justice are matched against the whole body of our intuitions. The Nozickian conception may in the end fail, but not for any of the reasons Cohen has advanced.[28]

3b. Gray may be right to attribute to Nozick the thought (thus cast) that it is justifiable to curtail freedom in the interests of preventing moral catastrophe, and that such prevention is a justified injustice. But Gray can muster forth this attribution only on the basis of a solitary sentence at the end of a footnote,[29] a sentence that Nozick, and I following him, ignore in the main *démarche*. It is, moreover, a nice question whether Nozick intends to say that, under the circumstances envisaged in the featured sentence, one might have a *right* to engage in a justified interference with *freedom*. If he does mean that, then there is contradiction in *Anarchy*, since, by the passages quoted in section 7 of Chapter 1 above, the freedom of the agent is not abridged when others act within their rights. It is no doubt because the footnote sentence appears to contradict so much of what Nozick says elsewhere that he ignored it in the body of his book.

3c. I need not resist Gray's (cacophonous) distinction between the justifiable and the justicizable. The ordinary language claim about freedom rides through that distinction, since English (with Gray's 'justicizable' added to it) requires us to say that you are unfree to do A not only if you are justifiably but also if you are justicizably prevented from doing A. And the claim that, to avoid deliverances of ordinary language, libertarians lock themselves inside a conceptual circle is also unaffected by Gray's distinction.

3d. Gray says that 'ordinary language has no special authority here, if Nozick's conception is compelling for other reasons'. Well, one might agree that, if a conception is truly *compelling*, then nothing has authority against it. I note, however, that, within this rhetoric, there is an element of

---

[28] 'Marxian Freedom', pp. 169–70, and cf. the successor article, 'Against Cohen on Proletarian Unfreedom', p. 96. In both articles Gray also criticizes things that I have written about *collective* freedom and unfreedom. I do not confront those criticisms here, because the collective aspect of the matter does not figure in the foregoing discussion.

[29] A sentence, moreover, whose message Gray massages to achieve his attribution: 'The question of whether these side constraints [i.e., rights – GAC] are absolute, or whether they may be violated in order to avoid catastrophic moral horror . . . is one I hope largely to avoid' (*Anarchy*, p. 30). I say that Gray massages because he proceeds as though Nozick has provided an answer to the question he actually leaves up in the air.

acknowledgement that there needs to be a *reason* for so deviating from ordinary language that what you say makes no sense in ordinary terms.

Gray gives a reason, but it is not a good one. The reason he gives is embodied in what he says about rapists. He says that 'our moral intuitions' 'square better' with the revisionary mode of speech 'than with the liberal view'[30] 'that the rapist loses [a] freedom under laws forbidding sexual assault'. What Gray says confuses conceptual and moral issues.

It might be thought question-begging for me to claim (as I would) that, on the view preferred by Gray, one cannot say the reasonable thing that laws forbidding rape are justified because in their absence rapists are free to rape, and, under such laws, they rightly, indeed justly, lose that freedom. But whether or not that is a question-begging remark (because it forthrightly supposes that unrestrained rapists are free to rape, and thereby presupposes the 'liberal', or ordinary, view) an independent and sufficient response to what Gray says about rape is available. It is that the 'liberal' view, that is, the view Gray thinks ordinary language embodies, does not necessitate, as he supposes it does, that the rapist's liberty be 'weighed in the scales' against his victim's. On what Gray calls the liberal view, whether or not the rapist loses a freedom requires no judgement about moral rights nor any value judgement whatsoever, and not, in particular, the judgement that Gray here groundlessly foists, that there is some value in the rapist's freedom to rape.

3e. In the course of my disagreement with Nozick, I make an (in my view, important) point about ordinary language, but Gray is mistaken in his repeated complaint that I *rely* on ordinary language. For I leave ordinary language behind entirely when I confront the rights definition of freedom, and I show how inadequate to the purpose that non-ordinary definition is, because of the circularity that it induces.

Now, Gray completely ignores the circularity objection.[31] That is interesting, given how inconsiderable he thinks the ordinary language objection is, and in the light of his plea that we look at whole theories:[32] the circularity objection is a result of doing that.

Departures from ordinary meaning should be signalled as such. Nozick's are not clearly signalled, perhaps because, as I explained in

[30] Recall – see footnote 27 above – that Gray oddly associates the ordinary language notions of what freedom and restrictions on freedom are with liberalism.
[31] Not only in the article from which I have quoted but also in the successor article mentioned at footnote 28 above, which is entirely devoted to a critique of my views on freedom.
[32] See 'Against Cohen', section V.

subsection 2g, he sustains an ambivalent relationship to the ordinary language of freedom. He wants us to take for granted that interference with rights of private property restricts owners' freedom. But that is a judgement cast in ordinary terms, whose implications indeed depend on ordinary meanings, and those implications are not consistent with the implications of a rights definition of freedom.

Accordingly, Gray is comprehensively mistaken about the dialectical situation. I use truths about ordinary language against what Nozick tries to infer from one limited truth about ordinary language. Nowhere do I attempt what Gray accuses me of: the construction of a political philosophy on the basis of conformity to ordinary language. I never propose such a 'theory of freedom'.[33]

3f. Gray's propensity to confuse conceptual and moral issues (see 3d above) shows up in his invocation of Rawlsian reflective equilibrium. Reflective equilibrium is achieved when a theory of justice is in harmony with (possibly revised or regimented) intuitions about justice. In the exercise of reflective equilibrium, the matter of what *words* ordinarily mean is not salient. So, whether or not Gray is right that the search for reflective equilibrium is the route to truth in political philosophy, that methodological matter has no bearing on our disagreement about ordinary language.

4. I argued in subsection 2d that Nozick could not object that a practice of taxing high earners like Chamberlain restricts their freedom, since the institutions that he himself proposes (like all institutions) restrict freedom. Nor, I further argued, could he side-step this *tu quoque* response by defining freedom in terms of justice or rights. That course is unpromising for a number of reasons (see 2g–2i), one being that Nozick also wants to characterize justice in terms of freedom, so that, on the suggested course, he lands himself inside a circle. I concluded by promising to put forth a possible way out of that circle (see p. 61 above).

That possible way out is the principle of self-ownership, which says that each person is the rightful owner of his own person and powers, and therefore of what he can get from others by placing himself at their service. It is because libertarians believe that Chamberlain owns his powers that they think that what he earns through their exercise may not be taxed.[34] Now the principle of self-ownership requires argument, and the Chamberlain example does not provide any for it. Indeed, the example is the more persuasive precisely when, like me in the reading of it that generated the original article-version of Chapter 1, we do not notice that it carries us along because of an antecedent prejudice in favour of self-ownership. (Often, when a substantial premiss in an argument is unexposed, the argument convinces more than it would if that premiss were laid bare for inspection.) I now find it amazing that the idea of self-ownership was not brought to the fore in my article of 1977 (which became Chapter 1 above), or in the other early literature in criticism of *Anarchy, State, and Utopia*. It is to that idea that we now turn.

---

[34] According to David Gauthier (*Morals by Agreement*, sections 3.1–3.2), self-ownership is consistent with taxation of earnings. For criticism of Gauthier on that score, see section 4 of Chapter 9 below, and, for more general demonstration of the inconsistency between self-ownership and taxation of earnings, see pp. 215–16 of that chapter.

3. Self-ownership, world-ownership, and equality

. . . the original 'appropriation' of opportunities by private owners involves investment in exploration, in detailed investigation and appraisal by trial and error of the findings, in development work of many kinds necessary to secure and market a product – besides the cost of buying off or killing or driving off previous claimants. (Frank H. Knight, 'Some Fallacies in the Interpretation of Social Cost')

1. *Anarchy, State, and Utopia* is routinely characterized as *libertarian*, an epithet which suggests that liberty enjoys unrivalled pride of place in Nozick's political philosophy. But that suggestion is at best misleading. For the primary commitment of his philosophy is not to liberty but to the thesis of self-ownership, which says that each person is the morally rightful owner of his own person and powers, and, *consequently*, that each is free (morally speaking) to use those powers as he wishes, provided that he does not deploy them aggressively against others. 'Libertarianism' affirms not freedom as such, but freedom of a certain type, whose shape is delineated by the thesis of self-ownership.[1]

In so designating what is central and what is derivative in Nozick, I am denying that he thinks that freedom comes first and that people qualify as self-owners because lack of self-ownership means lack of freedom. For Nozick gives us no independent purchase on freedom which would enable us to derive self-ownership from it. Although he is promiscuous in his use of the rhetoric of freedom, Nozick's real view is that the scope and nature of the freedom that we should enjoy is a function of our self-ownership: self-ownership, not freedom, is the point of departure for

---

[1] For invocations of self-ownership, and disparagement of the ownership of a person by others, see *Anarchy*, pp. 172, 281–3, 286, 290. For arguments that 'libertarians' do not deserve that label, see Chapter 2, section 2 above; this chapter, sections 3 and 6; Chapter 4, section 6; and Chapter 10, section 3.

generating the rights over our bodies and our powers on which he insists.

It is because self-ownership is basic for Nozick, and freedom (independently conceived) is not, that he does not regard the apparent unfreedom of the propertyless proletarian[2] as a counter-example to his view that freedom prevails in capitalist society. For the proletarian forced daily to sell his labour power is nevertheless a self-owner, indeed must be one in order to sell it, and is, therefore, nevertheless free, in the relevant sense.

According to the thesis of self-ownership, each person possesses over himself, as a matter of moral right, all those rights that a slaveholder has over a complete chattel slave as a matter of legal right, and he is entitled, morally speaking, to dispose over himself in the way such a slaveholder is entitled, legally speaking, to dispose over his slave. A slaveholder may not direct his slave to harm other (non-slave) people, but he is not legally obliged to place him at their disposal to the slightest degree: he owes none of his slave's service to anyone else. So, analogously, if I am the moral owner of myself, and, therefore, of this right arm, then, while others are entitled, because of *their* self-ownership, to prevent it from hitting them, no one is entitled, without my consent, to press it into their own or anybody else's service, even when my failure to extend service voluntarily to others would be morally wrong.

Nozick could allow that my failure to help someone might be morally wrong, but he would deny that anyone, be it a private person or the state, would, even so, be justified in *forcing* me to help him. Notice, then, that Nozick does not encourage people not to help one another. Nor need he think that they are blameless if they never do so. What he forbids is *constrained* helping, such as is involved – or so Nozick thinks – in redistributive taxation.[3] He insists that no one enjoys an enforceable non-contractual claim on anyone else's service; or, equivalently, that any enforceable claim on another's service derives from an agreement that binds to the provision of that service. But he does not forbid, or even, Ayn Rand-like, discourage, mutual aid. The self-ownership principle says that people should be free to do as they please with themselves, not that what they are pleased to do with themselves is beyond criticism.

Note that what is owned, according to the thesis of self-ownership, is not a self, where 'self' is used to denote some particularly intimate, or essential, part of the person. The slaveholder's ownership is not restricted to the self, so construed, of the slave, and the moral self-owner is, similarly,

---

[2] See Chapter 4, section 6, below.   [3] *Anarchy*, p. 169.

possessed of himself entire, and not of his self alone. The term 'self' in the name of the thesis of self-ownership has a purely reflexive significance. It signifies that what owns and what is owned are one and the same, namely, the whole person. There is, consequently, no need to establish that my arm or my power to play basketball well is a proper part of my self, in order for me to claim sovereignty over it under the thesis of self-ownership.[4]

Nozick believes not only that people own themselves, but that they can become, with equally strong moral right, sovereign owners of indefinitely unequal amounts of such raw external resources as they can gather to themselves as a result of proper exercises of their own and/or others' self-owner personal powers. When, moreover, private property in external resources is rightly generated, its morally privileged origin insulates it against expropriation or limitation.

Now, a union of self-ownership and unequal distribution of raw resources readily leads to indefinitely great inequality of private property in material goods of all kinds, and, hence, to inequality of condition, on any view of what equality of condition is, be it equality of income, or of utility, or of well-being (if that is different from utility), or of need satisfaction (if that is different from each of those), or of something else yet again. It follows that inequality of condition is, when properly generated, morally protected, and that the attempt to reduce inequality of condition at the expense of private property is an unacceptable violation of people's rights. Removing someone's legitimately acquired private property may not be as outrageous as removing his arm, but it is an outrage in the same sense: in each case, a fundamental right is violated.

A common left-wing response to Nozick is to recoil from the inequality his view allows, to affirm some sort of equality of condition as a fundamental value, and to reject (at least unqualified) self-ownership because of the inequality of condition that it appears to generate. The left-wing conclusion is that people lack the exclusive right to their own powers that goes with self-ownership, and that force may be applied against naturally well-endowed people not only to prevent them from harming others but also to ensure that they help them, so that equality of condition (or not too much inequality of condition) will be secured.

But this line of response to Nozick, in which some sort of equality of

---

[4] It is (at least) a double confusion to suppose that, for self-ownership to be possible, 'selves' must be 'separable enough from their abilities to be in an ownership relation' (James Tully, review of Grünebaum, p. 853). For the existence of 'selves' is not required by the thesis of self-ownership, and if ownership requires separability of what owns from what is owned, then self-ownership is impossible.

condition is mandated and a denial of self-ownership is derived from it, suffers from two related disadvantages. It has, first, the polemical disadvantage that it is powerless against those who occupy Nozick's position, since they have not failed to notice that their view contradicts the fundamentalist egalitarianism here set against it. And the other disadvantage of the stated strategy is that the thesis of self-ownership has, after all, plenty of appeal, quite apart from anything that Nozick urges on its behalf. Its antecedent (that is, pre-philosophical) appeal rivals that of whatever principles of equality it is thought to contradict, even for many committed defenders of such principles: that is why *Anarchy, State, and Utopia* unsettles so many of its liberal and socialist[5] readers.

In my experience, leftists who disparage Nozick's essentially unargued affirmation of each person's rights over himself lose confidence in their unqualified denial of the thesis of self-ownership when they are asked to consider who has the right to decide what should happen, for example, to their own eyes. They do not immediately agree that, were eye transplants easy to achieve, it would then be acceptable for the state to conscribe potential eye donors into a lottery whose losers must yield an eye to beneficiaries who would otherwise be not one-eyed but blind. The fact that they do not deserve their good eyes, that they do not need two good eyes more than blind people need one, and so forth – the fact, in a word, that they are merely lucky to have good eyes – does not convince them that their claim on their own eyes is no stronger than that of some unlucky blind person.[6] But if standard leftist objections to inequality of resources, private property, and ultimate condition are taken quite literally, then the fact that it is sheer luck that these (relatively) good eyes are mine should deprive me of special privileges in them.

Now, one might infer, not that the usual objections to considerable inequality of private property in external things are without force, but that their force is due to the comparative antecedent weakness of the case for exclusive rights in external things. It is an intelligible presumption that I

---

[5] And, in particular, Marxist socialist: see Chapter 6, section 4 below.

[6] I am here trying to motivate the thesis of self-ownership, not to provide a knock-down argument for it. There are ways of resisting compulsory eye transplanting without affirming (full) self-ownership, because rights other than those of (full) self-ownership might explain that resistance. One such right would be a right to bodily integrity: one might hold that non-contractual duties to others begin only once that right is secure, and thereby reject both eye-transplanting and self-ownership. But leftists rarely reflect on examples like that of eye-transplanting, and they are therefore caught off guard, and baffled about how to resist the self-ownership thesis, when such examples are presented. (For more on my ownership of my eyes, see Chapter 10, section 5 below.)

alone am entitled to decide about the use of this arm, and to benefit from its use, simply because it is my arm. (Do not think that I am here confusing[7] the factual truth that this is my arm with the normative claim that I should have exclusive disposal over it. My contention is that the stated factual truth is a *prima facie* plausible basis for, not a logical entailer of, the stated normative claim.) But there is no comparable presumptive normative tie between any person and any part or portion of the external world. Hence one may plausibly say of external things, or, at any rate, of external things in their initial state, of raw land and natural resources (out of which all unraw external things are, be it noted, made), that no person has, at least to begin with, a greater right in them than any other does; whereas the same thought is less compelling when it is applied to human parts and powers. Jean-Jacques Rousseau described the original formation of private property as a usurpation of what should be freely accessible to all,[8] and many have found his thesis persuasive, but few would discern a comparable injustice in a person's insistence on sovereignty over his own limbs.

These reflections suggest that those who stand to the left of Nozick might consider a different reaction to him from the one that I described at p. 69 above. They might cease treating equality of condition as a premiss and rejecting self-ownership on that basis. Instead, they might relax their opposition to the idea of self-ownership, but resist its use as the foundation of an argument that proceeds, via a legitimation of inequality in ownership of external resources, to defend the inequality of condition that they oppose. They might strive, first, to undo the argument which proceeds from an affirmation of self-ownership to a justification of inequality of raw worldly resources. If they succeed in doing that, they might then try, in a second movement of argument, to defend the equality of condition they prize by combining an egalitarian approach to worldly resources with an affirmation, or, at any rate, a non-denial, of the thesis of self-ownership.

The first of those tasks is accomplished in the present chapter. In the next chapter I turn to the second task, and I seek an economic constitution which (1) upholds the principle of self-ownership but (2) enforces equality of raw worldly resources and, thereby, (3) preserves equality of final condition. I conclude, however, that no such constitutional design is available, and, therefore, that the second stage in the attractive response to

---

[7] As, perhaps, Richard Overton did: see the beginning of Chapter 9 below.
[8] See the epigraph at the beginning of Chapter 4.

Nozick projected in the previous paragraph cannot be completed. It follows that self-ownership and socialist equality are incompatible. Anyone who supports equality of condition must oppose (full) self-ownership, even in a world in which rights over external resources have been equalized. And that conclusion generates a criticism of Marxism, pursued in Chapters 5–7, for its failure to oppose the self-ownership principle. (I show how to defeat that principle in Chapter 10.)

So much by way of preview. The task of this chapter is to prove that, whatever may be said about the principle of self-ownership in its own right, and whether or not it can be combined with equality of worldly resources to yield equality of condition, affirmation of self-ownership does not warrant the strongly inegalitarian distribution of worldly resources with which Nozick associates it. This I show by means of a critique of Nozick's account of legitimate original appropriation of worldly resources.

2. Libertarians, or, to name them more accurately, entitlement theorists, maintain that the market legitimates the distribution of goods it generates. But every market-generated distribution is only a redistribution of titles that buying and selling are themselves powerless to create, and the upshot of market activity is therefore no more legitimate than the titles with which it operates.[9] How, then, do the titles that necessarily precede market activity acquire legitimacy in the first place?

On any characterization of private property, the question of what constitutes a rightful original acquisition of it enjoys a certain priority over the question of what constitutes a rightful subsequent transfer of it, since, unless private property can be formed, it cannot, *a fortiori*, be transferred. But, in virtue of the way entitlement theorists characterize private property, the priority of the question of how it may be appropriated is, for private property as they understand it, even more marked. For private property in entitlement discourse is property in what is sometimes called 'the full liberal sense'. It is decked out with all the rights that could conceivably attach to private property; and, once an original acquisition of such plenary private property is achieved, then no separate question

---

[9] As Marx and Spencer noted: 'the title itself is simply transferred, and not created by the sale. The title must exist before it can be sold, and a series of sales can no more create this title through continued repetition than a single sale can' (Karl Marx, *Capital*, Vol. III, p. 911). 'Does sale or bequest generate a right where it did not previously exist? . . . Certainly not. And if one act of transfer can give no title, can many? No: though *nothing* be multiplied for ever, it will not produce *one*' (Herbert Spencer, *Social Statics*, p. 115).

about its transfer can arise, since the full complement of private property rights includes unfettered rights of transfer and bequest. Accordingly, the topic of original appropriation is a most important crux for Nozick's defence of property, and it is therefore startling that he begins his brief discussion of it by remarking that he will now 'introduce an additional bit of complexity into the structure of the entitlement theory'.[10] That 'additional bit' is arguably the most important part of the theory on offer.

Note that even now not everything around us is privately owned, and most people would agree that what remains privately unowned, such as the atmosphere we breathe and the pavements we tread, should not be available for privatization. But the better part of what we need to live is, by now, private property. Why was its original privatization not a theft of what rightly should (have continued to) be held in common?

The question would not arise if a certain false thing that Nozick says were true, namely, that 'things come into the world already attached to people having entitlements over them'.[11] That is relevantly false, since people create nothing *ex nihilo*, and all external private property is made of something that was once no one's private property, either in fact or morally (or is made of something that was made of something that was once not private property, or is made of something that was made of something that was made of something that was once not private property, and so on).[12] In the history of anything that is now privately owned there was at least one moment at which something privately unowned was taken into private ownership. If, then, someone claims a Nozick-like right to something he legally owns, we may ask, apart from how he in particular came to own it, with what right it came to be *anyone's* private property at all.

Now it is easy to doubt that much actually existing private property was formed in what entitlement theorists could plausibly claim was a legitimating way. But let us here set aside questions about actual history. Let us ask, instead, how, if at all, full liberal private property *could* legitimately be formed.

---

[10] *Anarchy*, p. 174.
[11] *Ibid.*, p. 160.
[12] Hillel Steiner formulates the essential point as follows: 'It is a necessary truth that no object can be made from nothing, and hence that all titles to manufactured or freely transferred objects must derive from titles to natural and previously unowned objects' ('Justice and Entitlement', p. 381; cf. Steiner, 'The Natural Right to the Means of Production', p. 44.) Nozick himself recognizes the relevant truth elsewhere: 'Since as far back as we know, everything comes from something else, to find an origin is to find a relative beginning, the beginning of an entity as being of a certain kind *K*' (*Philosophical Explanations*, p. 660 n. 11).

Nozick's answer to that question is part of his total theory of justice in holdings. According to that theory, a distribution of property is to be defended or criticized not in the light of considerations of utility or human flourishing or need or reward for effort or the like, but by reference to information about the whole past history of the objects in the distribution.[13] With respect to a given item of private property, we obtain the required information when we learn whether or not its owner acquired it justly, either from nature (call such acquisition *appropriation*) or from another who held it justly, because he in turn similarly acquired it justly from nature or from another who held it justly, because he in turn . . . (and so on, as before). Just holding depends on originally just appropriation and subsequently just transfer, except where the holding is a result of redistribution justified by injustice in past acts of appropriation and/or transfer.

Nozick devotes nine densely packed pages to the topic of just appropriation. Considering how important appropriation is for his theory, and bearing in mind Nozick's powers of exposition and advocacy, the pages are remarkably unsatisfactory. I do not mean merely that it is possible to criticize Nozick's argument, though that is certainly true. I mean that the pages are wanting in two more purely expository respects. First, Nozick distinguishes awkwardly between various provisos on acquisition without noting other noteworthy provisos that belong to the same conceptual area, and, as a result, without producing agreeably exclusive and exhaustive distinctions.[14] And, second, it is not at all points clear whether he is engaged in expounding John Locke or in developing his own position. He is not utterly forthright about how satisfactory he thinks various provisos on acquisition are. It is consequently hard to know how much he thinks he achieves in these critically important pages. But what matters most, of course, is how much he in fact achieves, whatever his own appraisal of his achievement may be.

Nozick interprets Locke conventionally, as holding that an agent may appropriate what he mixes his labour with, provided that he leaves

[13] Information of the required kind is, of course, to a large extent inaccessible, and this makes it hard to derive policy implications from Nozick's theory, but it is not obvious that it weakens the theory itself, since it might belong to the nature of justice that it is typically very hard to tell whether or not an existing distribution of property is just. (Compare the argument sometimes wrongly thought to be decisive against utilitarianism, that it is impossible in practice to determine in advance – or even in arrear – the consequences for human happiness of competing courses of action.)

[14] A laborious exposition of Nozick's expository sloppiness appears as an addendum at the end of this chapter.

enough and as good for others and does not waste what he takes. He comments sceptically on the labour mixture notion, expresses puzzlement at Locke's insistence that appropriators must avoid waste, and spends most of his time discussing and refining the proviso that they must leave enough and as good for others.

I think that Nozick is right to concentrate his attention on the 'enough and as good' proviso. For resistance to an appropriation is more likely to fix on its impact on others than on the means whereby it was brought about. And if, in particular, its impact on others is (at worst) harmless, as satisfaction of Locke's proviso would seem to ensure, then it will be difficult to criticize it, regardless of how it was effected, and even, therefore, if no labour was expended in the course of it. It is, moreover, worth remarking that some of Locke's most plausible examples of legitimate appropriation cannot reasonably be said to result from labour, unless all acting on the world is regarded as labouring.[15] For, even on a reasonably broad view of what labour is, picking up a few fallen acorns and immersing one's head in a stream and swallowing some of its water are not good examples of it.[16] Or, if they are indeed labour, then they are not labour that it would be plausible to cite in defence of the relevant appropriations. If you were asked what justified your appropriation of the water from the stream, you could not credibly reply: 'Well, to begin with, the labour of dunking my head and opening my mouth.' Your powerful reply is to say that no one has any reason to complain about your appropriation of the water, since no one has been adversely affected by it.

So I agree with Nozick that 'the crucial point is whether an appropriation of an unowned object worsens the situation of others'.[17] Disagreement will come on the question of what should here count as worsening another's situation.

Nozick refines the crucial condition as follows: 'A process normally giving rise to a permanent bequeathable property right in a previously unowned thing will not do so if the position of others no longer at liberty to use the thing is thereby worsened'.[18] He makes no attempt to specify the nature of the 'normal' acquisition process, but, as I just allowed, that is not

---

[15] Para. 44 of the *Second Treatise* suggests that Locke may indeed regard all action as labour. For an argument that Locke should not have made labour a necessary condition of acquisition, see Richard Arneson, 'Lockean Self-Ownership', p. 43.

[16] See paras. 28, 29 and 33 of the *Second Treatise of Government*. (Para. 33 is given in full at p. 77 below.)

[17] *Anarchy*, p. 175.

[18] *Ibid.*, p. 178.

very important, since, whatever process is required, controversy is likely to settle on the provision just quoted. Hence, although it is not so billed,[19] the quoted statement, with Nozick's elaboration of it, *is* Nozick's doctrine of appropriation; or, speaking more cautiously, if Nozick presents any doctrine of appropriation, then the quoted statement is the controversial element in his doctrine, and therefore the element which requires close scrutiny.

Nozick's further discussion justifies the following comments on his proviso. It requires of an appropriation of an object O, which was unowned and available to all, that its withdrawal from general use does not make anyone's prospects worse than they would have been *had O remained in general use*. If no one's position is in any way made worse than it would have been had O remained unowned, then, of course, the proviso is satisfied. But it is also satisfied when someone's position is in some relevant way worsened, as long as his position is in other ways sufficiently improved to counterbalance that worsening. Hence I appropriate something legitimately if and only if no one has any reason to prefer its remaining in general use, or whoever does have some reason to prefer that gets something in the new situation which he did not have before and which is worth at least as much to him as what I have caused him to lose. To illustrate: I enclose the beach, which has been common land, declare it my own, and announce a price of one dollar per person per day for the use of it (or, if you think there could not be dollars in what sounds like a state of nature situation, then imagine that my price is a certain amount of massage of my bad back). But I so enhance the recreational value of the beach (perhaps by dyeing the sand different attractive colours, or just by picking up the litter every night) that all would-be users of it regard a dollar (or a massage) for a day's use of it as a dollar well spent: they prefer a day at the beach as it now is at the cost of a dollar to a free day at the beach as it was and as it would have remained had no one appropriated it. Hence my appropriation of the beach satisfies Nozick's proviso.

Now it might seem that appropriations satisfying Nozick's condition

---

[19] Or perhaps it is so billed. For Nozick's pages on appropriation begin, as I reported earlier, with the announcement that 'an additional bit of complexity' will now be introduced 'into the structure of the entitlement theory' and they end with an announcement that 'this completes our indication of the complication in the entitlement theory introduced by the Lockean proviso' (*ibid.*, pp. 174, 182). If the 'complexity' of p. 174 (that is, the doctrine of initial appropriation as such) is the 'complication' of p. 182 (that is, the proviso on acquisition), then the condition on appropriation stated on p. 178 *is* Nozick's theory of appropriation, in so far as he has one.

could not conceivably generate a grievance. But that is an illusion. For Nozick's proviso on acquisition is not as demanding as Locke's. To see how Locke intended his proviso, and how solicitous it is towards non-appropriators, consider paragraph 33 of the *Second Treatise*:

Nor was this appropriation of any parcel of land, by improving it, any prejudice to any other man, since there was still enough and as good left; and more than the yet unprovided could use. So that in effect there was never the less left for others because of his enclosure for himself. For he that leaves as much as another can make use of, does as good as take nothing at all. Nobody could think himself injured by the drinking of another man, though he took a good draught, who had a whole river of the same water left to quench his thirst; and the case of land and water, where there is enough of both, is perfectly the same.[20]

Note that there is no way at all in which anyone might have been or become better off had the man not drunk that water: as far as others are concerned, his drinking it leaves things exactly as they were. They would not have been better off even if he had given them the water he took, since

---

[20] The quoted passage proves that Locke's proviso does not mean what Hillel Steiner says it means when he writes that 'it imposes an egalitarian structure on individuals' appropriative entitlements, prescribing to each a quantitatively and qualitatively similar bundle of natural objects' ('The Natural Right', p. 45). For the passage plainly implies that one must leave for others enough and as good to use and/or appropriate *as they had before one appropriated*, not (merely) enough and as good to appropriate, *per capita, as one appropriates oneself*. Satisfaction of Locke's proviso entails satisfaction of the proviso Steiner misattributes to him, but the converse entailment fails, and Locke's proviso is therefore more stringent than the one Steiner states. (I grant that Locke notes, at para. 34, that legitimate appropriators satisfy what Steiner thinks is Locke's proviso, since Locke says that, in the wake of a legitimate appropriation, nonappropriators have 'as good left for [their] improvement as was already taken up'. But it does not follow that this entailment of what I say is Locke's proviso *is* his proviso, and I think it textually demonstrable that it is not.)

If an appropriator must leave for others resources as good as they had available to them before, then why add the apparently further stipulation that he leave them *enough*? 'Enough' presumably means 'enough to survive by the use of', but if resources as good as were previously available are left, then the 'enough' stipulation is unsatisfied only if others already lacked enough to live on. It is therefore difficult to see what the force of the 'enough' stipulation is. (Note that this puzzle also arises for Steiner's different interpretation of Locke's proviso.)

John Simmons (*The Lockean Theory of Rights*, p. 292) rejects my reading of the 'enough and as good proviso', and suggests that 'enough' means 'enough for similar use' (to the one made by the appropriator). Two considerations prevent me from acceding to his counter-proposal. First, it is not superior to mine by way of endowing 'enough' and 'as good' with coherent independent senses, since 'enough for similar use' must *mean* 'as good', in this context. Second, Simmons' interpretation fails to account for Locke's use of the water example as a model for legitimate appropriation of land. The example falsifies Simmons' claim that '*any* appropriation makes some others worse off in some way, if only in the loss of the opportunity to appropriate that particular thing' (*ibid.*), since losing the opportunity to appropriate that particular quantity of water is not being made worse off in any way.

the stream, we are to imagine, flowed so abundantly that, however much water they wanted, they did not need his.[21]

But whereas people cannot be made worse off than they might have been by an appropriation that satisfies Locke's proviso, the same is not true of Nozick's. People can be made seriously worse off than they would have been, even when it is fulfilled. That is because of the phrase I had occasion to italicize on p. 76: *'had O remained in general use'*. It has the upshot that, as Nozick intends his proviso, *the only counterfactual situation relevant to assessing the justice of an appropriation is one in which O would have continued to be accessible to all*.[22] I shall argue that there are other intuitively relevant counterfactuals, and that they show that Nozick's proviso is too lax, that he has arbitrarily narrowed the class of alternatives with which we are to compare what happens when an appropriation occurs with a view to determining whether anyone is harmed by it. One might agree with Nozick that the way to determine the legitimacy of an appropriation is by looking at what might or would otherwise have happened to the people concerned, but one cannot take for granted that the appropriated thing would have remained in common use: it is unjustifiable to ignore other things that could have happened to it.

---

[21] Locke's drinker satisfies a proviso even stronger than Locke's, and one that Nozick's medical researcher (*Anarchy*, p. 181), who satisfies Locke's proviso, does not satisfy. That researcher makes a much-needed drug, which no one else knows how to make, out of resources in superfluent supply, and therefore makes no one worse off than he was before by doing do. But, unlike Locke's water taker, the researcher could benefit others, namely, those who need the drug, by giving it to them or selling it to them cheaply. Locke's proviso allows one to take and transform and keep what others had no need of in its untransformed state, even if they need it once it has been transformed. A stronger proviso, satisfied by the water taker but not by the researcher, would allow one to take and transform and keep only what no one had reason to want even after it had been transformed. (Nozick's researcher, in satisfying Locke's proviso, thereby satisfies a proviso much stronger than Nozick's own. It is important to notice that, for otherwise Nozick's proviso might look more innocent than it is.)

At p. 45 of his superb article on 'Lockean Self-Ownership', Richard Arneson questions my attribution of so stringent a proviso on acquisition to Locke on the basis of para. 33. But the very words ('enough and as good') which Locke uses when he introduces (what is generally acknowledged to be) his proviso on acquisition in para. 27 reappear in 33, and that surely suffices to establish that the drinker example is intended to illustrate that proviso. Arneson is right that 'in this passage Locke is not committing himself on the more difficult issue of how to draw the line between permissible and impermissible appropriations under conditions of scarcity', but I do not say that he is, and it bears adding that Locke does not commit himself anywhere else on that issue. Whatever may be the *circumstances* (be they of scarcity, of abundance, or of both) for which Locke lays down the 'enough and as good' proviso if, as Nozick supposes, it is a proviso on acquisition, then my claim stands that that proviso is much stronger than Nozick's.

[22] At p. 181 of *Anarchy* Nozick in effect acknowledges that to consider only that counterfactual situation makes the 'baseline' above which people must be for private property to be justified very low.

Some of the possibilities that Nozick neglects will now be exposed. Our examination of them will generate a decisive case against his theory of private property formation, and a case, be it noted, which raises no challenge to the thesis of self-ownership.

3. To see how Nozick's condition operates, and to test it, imagine a world containing two self-owning persons[23] and in which everything non-human is in Lockean common ownership, a regime in which no one privately owns anything and each may use anything that no one else is currently using. Each of the self-owning persons, who are A and B, draws sustenance from the land without obstructing the sustenance-drawing activity of the other. A is able to get m from the land, and B is able to get n, where m and n are, let us say, numbers of bushels of wheat (or, if you think individual wheat production hard to manage on common land, think of m and n as numbers of gallons of cows' milk, or, better,[24] of moose milk, taken from moose that neither A nor B owns). One might say that m and n represent what A and B are able to obtain under common ownership of the external world through exercise of the personal powers each separately owns. Note that the sizes of m and n, which reflect the relative productive powers of A and B, are not specified here, since they play no role in the reasoning to follow.

Now suppose that A appropriates all the land, or -- this being the crucial amount for the purposes of the ensuing argument -- an amount that leaves B less than enough to live off. He then offers B a salary of $n + p$ ($p \geqslant 0$) bushels to work the land, which B perforce accepts. A himself gets $m + q$ under the new arrangement, and q is greater than p, so that A gains more extra bushels from the change than B does. In other words, B loses no wheat and maybe gains some, but in any case A gains more than B does. The rise in output, from $n + m$ to $n + m + p + q$, is due to the productivity of a division of labour designed by A, who is a good organiser. Let us call the situation following A's appropriation the *actual situation*. It is the situation with which we shall compare various counterfactual ones. (The relevant features of the situations to be discussed will be found in Table 1.)

Now, does A's appropriation satisfy Nozick's proviso? To see whether

---

[23] It is sometimes rash to draw general conclusions from examples of worlds with only two people in them, but everything that I shall say about this small world can be applied to more populous ones.

[24] Because, unlike cows, moose do not need regular human attention, which might be thought to require enduring tenure of land.

it does, we must compare B's condition after A's appropriation with how B would have fared had common ownership persisted, and, to keep things simple, let us suppose that B would have fared exactly as he was already faring: he would have continued to draw just n bushels of wheat. Then A's appropriation clearly satisfies Nozick's condition, *if* the way to reckon the change in B's prospects is by comparing numbers of bushels of wheat. If, however, being subject to the directives of another person is regarded as a relevant effect on B of A's appropriation, then we cannot say whether or not the latter violates Nozick's proviso, since we have not put a value on the disbenefit to B of being under A's command. In assessing the gains and losses people sustain following transformations such as the one we are examining, entitlement theorists frequently neglect the value people may place on the kind of power relations in which they stand to others,[25] a neglect that is extraordinary in supposed libertarians professedly committed to human autonomy and the overriding importance of being in charge of one's own life. I shall, however, make no further use of this point in my demonstration of the inadequacy of Nozick's position on private property formation.[26] I shall henceforth reckon benefit and disbenefit in terms of nothing but numbers of bushels of wheat.

To see that Nozick's condition on appropriation is too weak, consider that, had A not appropriated, then a different counterfactual situation might have come to obtain: not that in which common use persisted but one in which B, perhaps concerned lest A do so, would have appropriated what A appropriates in the actual situation. Suppose that B is also a good organizer, and that, had he appropriated, *he* could have got an additional q and paid A only an additional p (see II(a) in Table 1). Then although A's appropriation in the actual situation satisfies Nozick's proviso,[27] it does not seem that A has, what he does have on Nozick's view, the right to force B to accept it. For why should B be required to accept what amounts to a doctrine of 'first come, first served'? Perhaps B abstained from appropriating out of regard for A. Ought A to profit only because he is more ruthless than B? It should now be clear that Nozick's proviso is too weak.

[25] Cf. Chapter 1, sections 3 and 7 above. Nozick nods at this issue in passing at a couple of points at pp. 177–8, but he does not give it the attention it would have to get before his confident conclusion that capitalism satisfies his proviso on acquisition could be justified. If we take liberty very seriously, the state of nature baseline may not be very low (see footnote 22 above).
[26] The point is central to the further criticism of Nozick mounted in section 6 of Chapter 4 below.
[27] If, that is, B's loss of liberty is ignored: see the previous paragraph in the text.

Table 1. *Counterfactual situations*

	Actual situation (*A*'s appropriation)	I. Persistence of common ownership	II. *B*'s appropriation		
			(*a*) *B*'s talent = *A*'s talent	(*b*) *B*'s talent > *A*'s talent	(*c*) *B*'s talent < *A*'s talent
A gets	$m + q$	m	$m + p$	$m + q + r$ ·	m
B gets	$n + p$	n	$n + q$	$n + p + s$	n
	$(q > p \geqslant 0)$			$(r > 0; s > 0)$	

Other possibilities[28] make this still more clear. To take one of them, suppose that *B* is a much better organizer than *A* so that, had *B* appropriated, then each of *A* and *B* would have had more wheat than he does in the actual situation (see II(b) in Table 1). Nozick's proviso is, nevertheless, satisfied, since whether or not it is satisfied is unaffected by anything that might have happened had *B* appropriated. And this means that Nozick's condition licenses, and protects, appropriations whose upshots make each person worse off than he need be, upshots that are therefore, in one good sense, Pareto-inferior.[29] *A*, if sufficiently ignorant or irrational to do so,

---

[28] Not, that is, (entirely) different counterfactual situations, but different possible upshots of the same (generally described) counterfactual situation, in which *B* appropriates: see, again, Table 1.

Beyond the distinctions among ways of worsening a person's situation featured in the text, I need to register this modal one: *X* worsens *Y*'s situation in a (relatively) weak sense if *X* removes superior (from *Y*'s point of view) *possibilities* (that might not, in the event, have been actualized), but *X* worsens *Y*'s situation in a stronger sense if *X* prevents something that would otherwise *actually* have happened and been better for *Y*. The scenarios I press against Nozick to show that his proviso is too weak can be taken either way, as excluded possibilities, or as what would actually have happened had *A* not appropriated. I cannot say which is the right way to take them because Nozick does not say which sense of 'worsening', within the stated modal distinction, he intends.

I should respond here to Thomas Münzer's complaint that 'Cohen elides the difference . . . between an acceptable and the best possible system of property' (*A Theory of Property*, p. 271n). My point is not that *A*'s appropriation fails to generate 'the best possible system', but that if (what cannot be ruled out) particular superior (from *B*'s point of view) systems would have been possible, or would have developed, in the absence of *A*'s appropriation, then, intuitively, *B* has a grievance that throws doubt on the legitimacy of *A*'s appropriation.

(On certain views about counterfactual statements, there is nothing that counts as *the* thing that would have happened, had *A* not appropriated. One might then look at the expected value for *B* of *A*'s non-appropriation, as a function of all possible alternatives, weighted by their probabilities.)

[29] Pareto-inferiority is an ambiguous notion among economists, who tend not to distinguish between the idea that everyone would *favour* a different situation and the idea that everyone would *benefit from* a different situation (whatever they might themselves think and

would be entitled to prevent B from taking what A had appropriated, even if both would become better off if B took it.

In constructing the 'actual situation', I supposed that the productivity increase it displayed was due to A's organizational talent. But that supposition was unnecessary, and, if we suppose otherwise, then the case against Nozick is seen to be even stronger. Suppose, then, that B alone is a good organizer, and that, when A has appropriated, he proposes to B that B design an optimal division of labour and then play his role in it, for the same $n + p$ wage, and that B, preferring survival to starvation, accepts. Then A's appropriation is still justified under Nozick's proviso, even though here it is the case not merely (as in II(a) and II(b)) that B could also have engineered a productivity gain but that he actually engineers the gain, and a gain, moreover, that A is incompetent to produce. The example shows that, even when privatization generates additional value, the privatizer need not be the value adder, and, if one thinks that value adders merit reward,[30] then one should note that Nozick's condition does not ensure that they get any. To reap all the benefit from any enhancement of production that results from privatization, his just appropriators need not do anything to resources beyond making them their own.

I also supposed that the productive division of labour in force in the actual situation and in II(a) and II(b) could not have been implemented under Lockean common ownership. That seems to me to be true by definition. To be sure, A and B might have agreed to a division of labour without either of them privately appropriating the land. But then, so I would argue, they would, in effect, have appropriated it collectively. They would have instituted a form of (at least *pro tem*) socialism, which is another possibility unjustifiably neglected by Nozick, and about which I shall say more in section 5.[31]

By way of summary, we may note that Nozick transforms Locke's

hence whatever they would be inclined to favour). I am here using the Pareto notion in the second of these two ways, and what I say is false when it is taken in the first way.

Nozick himself sometimes allows (what would otherwise be?) violations of rights to secure a Pareto-improvement in the present sense, but only if communication with unconsenting but benefiting persons is impossible, or terribly expensive. (See *Anarchy*, pp. 22–3, and see Eric Mack, 'Nozick on Unproductivity', for an argument that Nozick's selective permission of 'boundary crossings' with compensation threatens to unfound his defence of the sanctity of private property.)

[30] I am not myself here affirming that they do. Note, among other things, that one need not suppose that value adders should get the value of what they add in order to regard them as exploited by those who get it just because they have power over them. See my *History, Labour, and Freedom*, p. 230 n. 37.

[31] For yet more neglected possibilities, see section 3 of Hillel Steiner, 'Capitalism, Justice, and Equal Starts'.

proviso in two ways, one legitimate and the other not. The legitimate move is to permit failure to leave enough and as good provided that sufficient compensation is forthcoming. That does not weaken Locke's proviso in a principled way: it captures its spirit and formulates it in an appropriately general fashion. But the other, unacceptable, move is to weaken the proviso by considering not what might or would have happened *tout court*, absent the appropriation, but what would have happened on the special hypothesis that the world would have remained commonly owned. This move unjustifiably relaxes the criteria for saying that *A* harms *B*.[32]

4. But now suppose that *B* lacks *A*'s organizational skills, and that, if he had appropriated the land, he could not have so directed *A* as to generate any increase over what gets produced under common ownership (see II(c) of Table 1). Under that assumption, is *A*'s appropriation legitimate?

Note that, even if we say that it is legitimate, then it is legitimate only by virtue of satisfying conditions far stronger than those Nozick lays down. And my own view is that its legitimacy is even then contestable. For to suppose otherwise is to take for granted that the land is not, from the start (that is, before anyone operates on it), jointly or collectively owned by *A* and *B*, so that the proper way to decide its fate would be by the democratic device of consensual agreement, instead of unilaterally. Why should we not regard the land, prior to *A*'s appropriation, as jointly owned, rather than, as Nozick takes for granted, owned by no one?[33]

When land is owned in common, each can use it on his own initiative, provided that he does not interfere with similar use by others: under

[32] Richard Arneson objects to my string of counter-examples to Nozick's proviso that 'if we are wondering whether your action harms me the fact that an alternative action which you might have performed would have lavished great benefit on me is not germane to the issue' ('Lockean Self-Ownership', p. 45). True enough, but the fact on which I rest my case is not the one formulated by Arneson but the fact that your action prevents me from gaining benefits that you would not be lavishing on me.

Arneson says that 'Cohen claims to be making an internal criticism of Nozick from the standpoint of self-ownership', and that, so construed, 'this criticism is wrong' (*ibid.*, p. 45 fn. 23), for the reason quoted above. But my claim is not that premisses affirmed by Nozick refute his own theory of appropriation but this weaker one, which does not count as 'an internal criticism' in the relevant strong sense of that phrase: that Nozick lacks the premisses to justify that theory, and that the self-ownership premiss, in particular, fails to justify it.

[33] Some think that, in laying down his proviso, 'Nozick vests everyone with original rights in natural resources' (Attracta Ingram, *A Political Theory of Rights*, p. 55). In my different interpretation of him, Nozick thinks that the proviso reflects no such original rights in the world, but the self-ownership right over oneself that one not be harmed: see further, p. 114 of the 'Retrospect' in Chapter 4 below.

common ownership of the land no one owns any of it. Under joint ownership, by contrast, the land *is* owned, by all together, and what each may do
with it is subject to collective decision.[34] The appropriate procedure for
reaching that decision may be hard to define, but it will certainly not be
open to any one of the joint owners to privatize all or part of the asset
unilaterally, no matter what compensation he offers to the rest. If you and
I jointly own a house, I cannot, against your will, section off a third of it
and leave you the rest, even if what I leave is worth more than your share
in the whole was. So if joint ownership rather than no ownership is,
morally speaking, the initial position, then *B* has the right to forbid *A* to
appropriate, even if *B* would benefit by what he thereby forbids. And *B*
might have good reason to exercise his right to forbid an appropriation by
A from which *B* himself would benefit. For, if he forbids *A* to appropriate,
he can then bargain with *A* about the share of output he will get if he
relents and allows *A* to appropriate. *B* is then likely to improve his take by
an amount greater than what *A* would otherwise have offered him.

So Nozick must suppose that the world's resources are, morally
speaking, nothing like jointly owned, but very much up for grabs, yet, far
from establishing that premiss, he does not even bother to state it, or show
any awareness that he needs it.

I return to the theme of joint ownership in Chapter 4. The rest of this
chapter is framed by continued acceptance of the assumption that, prior to
any appropriation of any of it, the world is unowned.

5. In the section of *Anarchy, State, and Utopia* which precedes the one in
which he states the proviso criticized above, Nozick asks and answers a
question that is germane to that proviso, although it is obscure whether or
not he has that very proviso in mind when he puts the question. The
question is whether 'the situation of persons [like our *B*] who are unable
to appropriate (there being no more accessible and useful unowned
objects) [is] worsened by a system allowing appropriation and permanent

---

[34] For a partial explication of the idea of joint ownership of the world by all of its inhabitants,
and a defence of it against what seem at first to be fatal objections, see John Exdell,
'Distributive Justice', especially pp. 147–9. The idea is more or less explicit in various
articles by Hillel Steiner; see, for example, his 'Liberty and Equality', pp. 555–69, and 'The
Rights of Future Generations', pp. 225–41. There is, of course, no *legally* constituted joint
ownership *institution* in the state of nature, but the implication of that for natural rights
with respect to raw resources is no greater than the implication for natural rights over
persons of the fact that there is no legally constituted self-ownership institution in the state
of nature.

For a friendly discussion of 'the principle that natural resources are the joint possession
of the human race as a whole', see Brian Barry, 'Humanity and Justice', p. 450 *et circa*.

property'.[35] Nozick intends thereby to ask whether such people are worse off than they would have been had such a system never developed. His question is roughly equivalent to the question whether the existence of capitalism makes non-capitalists better off than they otherwise would have been.

Nozick replies by affirming familiar empirical theses about the utility of private property, the usual claims about risks, incentives, and so forth which represent capitalism as a productive form of economic organization. But, as he points out, he does not invoke these considerations to provide a utilitarian justification of private property, for here they 'enter a Lockean theory to support the claim that appropriation of private property satisfies the intent behind the "enough and as good left over" proviso'.[36] When there is nothing left to appropriate, the situation of those who have appropriated nothing is to that extent worse than it would have been, but capitalist mechanisms of production and distribution ensure that they are more than adequately compensated for their loss of freedom of access to resources that are not privately owned.

As explained, the empirical claims about the utility of private property figure here in an argument whose major premiss is not utilitarianism. The argument is not: whatever makes people better off is a good thing, and private property makes people better off; but: anyone has the right to appropriate private property when that makes nobody worse off, and appropriation of private property in general makes everyone better off (and therefore not worse off). And Nozick's conclusion, unlike the utilitarian one, is not that a private property system, being best, should be brought into being or, if already in being, kept. It is that if a private property system exists, then the fact that some people own no or little private property in it is not a reason for removing it.

Such people, and there will be many of them in libertarian capitalist society, are, because of their propertylessness, dependent for their survival on someone wanting to buy their labour power. Their predicament might be thought dire, but Nozick denies that they have a grievance. For a propertyless person, or proletarian, has a grievance, in Nozick's view, only if his propertylessness renders him worse off than he would have been had the world remained in Lockean common ownership, without private property, and Nozick believes that proletarians are unlikely to be, in that way, worse off. He would say, of those proletarians who do manage to sell their labour power, that they will get at least as much, and

---

[35] *Anarchy*, p. 177.   [36] *Ibid.*

probably more, in exchange for it than they could have hoped to get by applying it in a rude state of nature; and, of those proletarians whose labour power is not worth buying, that, although they will therefore, in Nozick's non-welfare state, die (in the absence of charity), they would have died in a state of nature anyway.

Because his major premiss demands attention to the fate of each person, taken separately, Nozick's argument is, as I said, not a utilitarian one. Even so, because he depends on an empirical minor premiss, his defence of private property turns out to be, like the utilitarian defence of it, potentially vulnerable to empirical counterargument. His major premiss is not empirical, but neither is the major premiss of the utilitarian defence, which is that whatever makes people better off in the aggregate is a good thing. I point this out because it is often thought to be a feature of libertarian political philosophy that, through its emphasis on rights, it finesses empirical questions about consequences which are hard to answer and in which utilitarianism becomes enmired. That is an illusion, since, as we now see, theses about consequences are foundational to Nozick's defence of private property rights, and the rights he affirms therefore lack the clarity and authority he would like us to suppose they have.

Nozick's empirical claims are addressed and rebutted, one by one, by Hal Varian, who argues that 'market socialist' or 'people's capitalistic' property arrangements are more productive still than the pure capitalism Nozick favours, at any rate under certain conditions.[37]

But Varian's empirical counter-claims do not, strictly speaking, touch the case for capitalism which Nozick builds at page 177 of *Anarchy*, as Nozick intends that case. For Varian compares the regime of capitalist private property not to unstructured common ownership but to an organized non-, or semi-, capitalist property system. And if institutionally undeveloped common ownership is the only thing to which we are supposed to compare capitalism when we seek an answer to the question quoted in the first paragraph of this section, as it is indeed the only thing we are supposed to consider when testing Nozick's proviso, then Varian's remarks are, in an immediate sense, beside the point. But only in an immediate sense. For if Varian's counter-claims are irrelevant in the suggested way, then that is only because Nozick is, once again,

---

[37] See Varian, 'Distributive Justice', pp. 235, 237–8. Another theorist of appropriation who emphasizes the advantages of capitalism over the Lockean state of nature without noting that a non-capitalist system might be more advantageous still is Baruch Brody. See his 'Redistribution without Egalitarianism', especially p. 82.

unreasonably restricting the range of permissible comparison. For why should institutionally primitive common ownership be the only alternative to capitalism which is allowed to count, and not also more structured non-capitalist arrangements? Yet, if the latter are indeed allowed to count, then Nozick's confidence in his case for capitalism, and his blithe certainty that capitalism satisfies his proviso,[38] may be judged to be unfounded. When assessing *A*'s appropriation we should consider not only what would have happened had *B* appropriated, but also what would have happened had *A* and *B* cooperated under a socialist economic constitution.

Now once we broaden, in these and other ways,[39] our range of comparison, then, so it seems, a defensibly strong Lockean proviso will forbid the formation of full liberal private property. For there will always be some who would have been better off under an alternative dispensation that it would be arbitrary to exclude from consideration. (An example of an alternative dispensation that it would *not* be arbitrary to exclude is that whose rule is that everyone must slave for the tallest person in society.) And since, moreover, a defensibly strong Lockean proviso on the formation and retention of economic systems will rule that no one should be worse off in the given economic system than he would have been under some unignorable alternative, it almost certainly follows that not only capitalism but every economic system will fail to satisfy a defensibly strong Lockean proviso, and that one must therefore abandon the Lockean way of assessing the legitimacy of economic systems.

One alternative is to settle for utilitarianism. Because of its aggregative character, utilitarianism is insensitive to the fate of the individual, and it therefore has no use for Lockean provisos. But, because it aggregates, utilitarianism is consistent with monstrous violation of individual rights, and a different alternative is therefore necessary.

A further alternative to Locke-like criteria is John Rawls' difference principle, in its canonical sense, which contrasts with the way many, including, I think, Rawls, have sometimes misinterpreted it. In its canonical sense the difference principle is satisfied by a given economic system only if those who are worst off under it are not more badly off than the worst off would be under any alternative to it. But since those who are actually worst off need not be those who would be worst off in an

---

[38] Expressed at *Anarchy*, p. 181 (see footnote 22 above): that certainty depends on regarding Lockean common ownership as the only alternative with which capitalism need be compared.

[39] For we might also consider what would have happened had the land been equally divided

alternative system, the difference principle may be satisfied even if those who are actually worst off would be better off in that alternative. The difference principle is therefore not, as it may falsely appear to be, a Lockean proviso whose range is restricted to the worst off, and it can be satisfied even when such a proviso is not satisfied. But the difference principle has an intuitive power comparable to that of a Lockean proviso. For when it is satisfied one may respond[40] to the complaint of the worst-off group by pointing out that others would suffer at least as much as they do in any dispensation in which they were better off than they actually are.

Now Rawls seems sometimes to interpret the difference principle as though the worst off in an economy that satisfies it would *themselves* be no better off under any alternative.[41] He seems so to interpret it when he urges the immunity of a society that satisfies it to instability because of unrest from below, for in an economy that satisfies the difference principle in its incorrect form the worst off would indeed have no reason for unrest. But this involves a misinterpretation of the difference principle, since the latter is chosen in the original position, whose occupants must treat 'worst-off group' as a variable designator.

The misinterpreted difference principle *is* a strong Lockean proviso, with its range restricted to those who are worst off. So misinterpreted, the principle is, like unrestricted Lockean provisos, almost certainly unsatisfiable. The difference principle proper can, however, be satisfied, and it is to that extent superior to a Lockean test of economic systems, once the whole feasible set of them is brought into view.

---

[40] For a subtle version of this response, see Joshua Cohen, 'Democratic Equality', pp. 739–40.
[41] This misconstrual is manifest at p. 103 and fairly evident at p. 536 of *A Theory of Justice*. Why does Rawls commit it? An unkind speculation would be that he tacitly supposes that the worst off in any given economic system are by nature so constituted that they would be the worst off in every one. Or perhaps he conflates the truth that the worst off in an inequality that satisfies the difference principle would, necessarily, be even worse off under flat equality with the falsehood that they would, necessarily, be the worst off under any other system.
   To see the distinction between the difference principle proper and its misconstrual, suppose that a society is in state *A* and that *B* is the only feasible alternative to it:

	A	B
Jack	10	10
Jill	8	5
Mary	6	9

(The numbers represent amounts of primary goods.) The difference principle mandates retention of *A*, its misconstrual a change to *B*.

6. I have argued elsewhere that the familiar idea that private property and freedom are conceptually connected is an ideological illusion.[42] In the light of Nozick's doctrine of appropriation, I am able to provide further support for that claim.

Call an action *paternalist* if it is performed for the sake of another's benefit but against his will, and if it actually does benefit him as intended. A state that imposes a health insurance scheme on people all of whom benefit from it but some of whom are, for whatever reason, opposed to it acts paternalistically in the defined sense (if, as I am supposing, the state applies the scheme to those who do not want it for their own good, and not, for example, because the scheme is a public good and the state is against free riding). Nozick would say that the scheme is unjust, because the taxation it levies, like all taxation whose purpose is not to protect property rights, violates property rights. He would, *a fortiori*, regard as unjust a policy that taxes someone against his will and that in fact benefits him, even though it may not be intended to benefit him: we can call that an *objectively paternalist* policy. Note that the Nozickian objection to such a policy that we are considering here is not that there is a constrained transfer from one person to another, that, for example, nobody should be forced to pay for anyone else's health care. Nozick would object even if the amount of tax a person paid were strictly related to his own health prospects.

Nozick disallows objectively paternalist use of people's private property.[43] But he permits objectively paternalist treatment of people in other ways. For, since he permits appropriations that satisfy nothing but his proviso, he allows A to appropriate against B's will when B benefits as a result, or, rather, as long as B does not lose.[44]

Are Nozick's positions consistent? He would say that they are, since B's rights are not violated when A appropriates, and rights are violated when the state funds a medical plan through taxation. And that is so, *if* Nozick's theory of appropriation and property rights is correct, but it would seem question-begging to allow that theory to establish the mooted consistency

[42] See 'Illusions about Private Property and Freedom', and also Chapter 1 above, sections 3 and 7, and Chapter 2 above, section 2.
[43] The special case mentioned in footnote 29 above is not a counter-example to that statement, since what Nozick there allows is benefiting someone not against his known will but merely without his known compliance.
[44] Actually, he permits still more, since he allows B to be made worse off than he would have been, as long as he is not made worse off than he would have become under persistence of common ownership. But that point was made in section 3, and I am here setting it aside in order to focus on the present different one.

here, where we are examining Nozick's attempt to ground property rights in the first place. And whether or not the move would be question-begging, it is clear beyond doubt that an appropriation of private property can contradict an individual's will just as much as levying a tax on him can.[45] Therefore Nozick cannot claim to be inspired throughout by a desire to protect freedom, unless he means by 'freedom' what he really does mean by it: the freedom of private property owners to do as they wish with their property.

Addendum

Here is the laborious demonstration of Nozick's sloppiness promised in footnote 14 above.

At p. 176 of *Anarchy, State, and Utopia*, Nozick contrasts two ways in which 'someone may be made worse off by another's appropriation': 'first, by losing the opportunity to improve his situation by a particular appropriation or any one; and second, by no longer being able to use freely (without appropriation) what he previously could'. He then proceeds to distinguish between a 'stringent' (here called S) and a 'weaker' (W) proviso on acquisition. Call the appropriator A and any person whose position might be worsened by A's appropriation B. Then W and S may be formulated as follows:

W: A must not cause B to lose the opportunity to use freely what he previously could.

S: W, and A must not cause B to lose the opportunity to improve his situation by appropriating something, unless B is adequately compensated for any such loss of opportunity.

Now S is a conjunction, one conjunct of which is W, and the rest of which I shall call S'. Then note that S' differs from W in three independent ways. First, S' focuses on B's opportunities to appropriate things, whereas W focuses on his opportunities to use them. Second, S' requires that B not lose opportunities to *improve* his situation, whereas W does not mention possible improvements and therefore presumably forbids only making B worse off than he was, and not (also) making him worse off than he would, or might, have become. And, finally, S' contains a compensation clause ('unless . . . '), whereas W does not. (Nozick may wrongly have thought

---

[45] The point that formation of private property can contradict a person's (such as B's) will should not be confused with the point made at p. 80 above, that it can turn one person into another's subordinate.

that *B* could improve his condition only by appropriating something, and, also wrongly, that no compensation could be added to *W*; in which case the three differences between *S'* and *W* would not be independent.)

Both the second and third differences have consequences unnoticed by Nozick, but I shall here fix on the third difference only, that *S'* has and *W* lacks a compensation clause. It has the effect that *W* is weaker than *S* only because *W* is a conjunct of *S*, and not also because, as Nozick surely thought, *W* is weaker than *S'*. *W* is not weaker than *S'*, since the compensation clause in *S'* generates a way of satisfying *S'* without satisfying *W*.

I think Nozick has confused the difference between *W* and *S'* with the difference between *S'* and *S''*, *S''* being *S* shorn of both *W* and the compensation clause:

S'': *A* must not cause *B* to lose the opportunity to improve his situation by appropriating something.

Here are three reasons for thinking that Nozick has confused the *W/S'* and *S'/S''* differences:

(a) Nozick distinguishes between *S* and *W* in order to meet a regress argument which he presents at p. 176 of *Anarchy* (and to which the reader is referred: I shall not expound it here). He says that *S* generates the regress and *W* does not. But it is not true that *S* generates the regress: its compensation clause offers apropriators the possibility of compensating those who can no longer appropriate, and therefore permits the final appropriation prohibition of which is necessary to get the regress going. It is *S''*, not *S'* (or, hence, *S*), that makes the regress inescapable.

(b) On p. 178 Nozick states a proviso which I quoted at p. 75 above and which, he says, is 'similar to the weaker of the ones we have attributed to Locke'. But the p. 178 proviso resembles not *W* but *S'*, its relative weakness being due solely to the compensation clause which Nozick attaches to it (see the last full sentence in the text on p. 178).

(c) Whereas *W* indeed invalidates the regress argument, it does forbid transformation of all common land into private property, at least if some end up with no private property. But in the kind of capitalist society that Nozick thinks defensible just such privatization of all common land has occurred, and there exist propertyless people without access to anything still held in common. Therefore *W* cannot serve Nozick's polemical purposes, whereas *S'*, because of its compensation clause, can.

4. Are freedom and equality compatible?

The first man who, having enclosed a piece of land, took it into his head to say, 'This is mine', and found people simple enough to believe him, was the true founder of civil society. The human race would have been spared endless crimes, wars, murders, and horrors if someone had pulled up the stakes or filled in the ditch and cried out to his fellow men, 'Do not listen to this impostor! You are lost if you forget that the fruits of the earth belong to everyone, and the earth to no one!' (Jean-Jacques Rousseau, *Discourse on Inequality*)

I Introduction

1. Two kinds of response to Nozick were contrasted in Chapter 3. In the first, a premiss that equality of condition is morally mandatory is used to reject his starting point, the thesis of self-ownership. But this first response (so I claimed) has the defect that the idea of self-ownership enjoys an initial appeal which so swiftly derived a rejection of it will not undermine. (In Chapter 10 I hope to undermine it in the more painstaking way that I think is necessary.)

In light of the poverty of that first response, a second response was projected (see Chapter 3, p. 71), which proceeds in two stages. First, it is shown that self-ownership does not justify an inegalitarian scramble for raw worldly resources: this first stage of the second response was completed, with success, in Chapter 3. The second stage of the projected response is pursued in the present chapter. Here, once again, equality of condition is not put as a premiss, and the principle of self-ownership is not rejected, on that or any other basis. Instead, one strives to reconcile self-ownership with equality (or not too much inequality) of condition, by constructing an economic constitution which combines self-ownership with an egalitarian approach to raw worldly resources. The strategy is to concede to libertarianism its attractive thesis, which is its assertion of each person's rights over his own being and powers, while attacking its implausible one, which is its view of the original moral relationship between people and things, the moral relationship, that is, between people and things which have not as yet been acted on by people.

The desired economic constitution respects both self-ownership and equality of worldly resources. Any such constitution would be opposed both by Nozick and other entitlement theorists on the one hand, and by John Rawls and Ronald Dworkin on the other. For both ranges of theorists are unwilling to distinguish as sharply as the stated strategy does between the moral status of ownership of external resources and the moral status of ownership of persons. Nozick endows people's claims to legitimately acquired external resources with the moral quality that belongs, so he believes, to people's ownership of themselves, and Rawls and Dworkin treat people's personal powers as subject, albeit with important qualifications,[1] to the same egalitarian principles of distribution that they apply, less controversially, to external wherewithal. The suggested intermediate position, to be reflected in the desired constitution, is with Nozick and against Rawls and Dworkin in its affirmation (or at least non-denial) of self-ownership, but with Rawls and Dworkin and against Nozick in subjecting the distribution of non-human resources to egalitarian appraisal.

One conclusion of this chapter is that no constitution that is truly intermediate in the described sense is capable of ensuring equality of condition. It follows that the two-stage response to Nozick rehearsed in the second paragraph of this chapter is not, in fact, a viable one. An intermediate constitution would preserve self-ownership but equalize rights in worldly resources. The present chapter examines two ways of achieving that latter equalization. One is by placing all external resources under the joint ownership of everyone in society, with each having a veto over what is to be done with them. That regime, together with self-ownership, indeed ensures equality of condition, but the joint ownership element deprives the self-ownership with which it is combined of its intended effect, which is the provision of autonomous self-governance. For people can do (virtually) nothing without using parts of the external world. If, then, they require the leave of the community to use it, then, effectively (as opposed to formally, or juridically), they do not own themselves, since they can do

---

[1] Rawls and Dworkin assert a certain sovereignty of persons over themselves in their affirmation of political and other liberties, such as choice of career, and granting those liberties has distributive implications.

nothing without communal authorization. Accordingly, no constitution that prescribes this first way of equalizing rights in external resources is truly intermediate.

But, if the contrast between effective and merely formal self-ownership upsets the described attempt to design an intermediate constitution, it also generates a serious problem for libertarians. For the propertyless proletarian who cannot use means of production without a capitalist's leave suffers a lack of effective self-ownership. It follows, as I argue in section 6 below, that, since libertarians regard proletarianhood as consistent with all the rights that they think people have, the self-ownership that they defend is much thinner and far less attractive than it appears, at first sight, to be.

Another way of equalizing rights in external resources is by distributing an equal amount of them to each person. Then each, if self-owning, could do with his share as he pleases. This yields a truly intermediate constitution, at any rate initially, but one that, I argue, fails to secure the equality of condition that socialists prize. I conclude that socialists must reject self-ownership, and I show how to reject it in Chapter 10.

II Returns to ability and inability under joint ownership

2. In Chapter 3, I questioned Nozick's blithe assumption that 'virgin' things may be regarded as quite unowned and therefore (virtually) up for grabs; one scarcely need share that assumption even if one accepts that people are full owners of themselves. Now, a radical alternative to the view that things are, in their native state, quite unowned, is to regard them as jointly or collectively owned by all persons. In this section, I study an attempt to combine such a conception of the original moral relationship between people and things with the principle of self-ownership. I inquire into the upshot of uniting self-ownership with joint ownership of the external world, with a view to shedding some light on the distributive effect of self-ownership in a world whose parts are not open to unilateral privatization.

For the sake of simplicity, imagine a society of two people, who are called Able and Infirm, after their respective natural endowments. Each owns himself and both jointly own everything else. (It is immaterial, here, how these rules of ownership are enforced. We can imagine that a suitably powerful external authority (e.g., God) enforces them.) With suitable external resources, Able can produce life-sustaining and life-enhancing good, but Infirm has no productive power at all. We suppose that each is rational, self-interested, and mutually disinterested (devoid, that is, of spite, benevolence, and all other motivations into which the welfare of others enters essentially),[2] and we ask what scheme of production and distribution they will agree on. We thereby investigate the reward which self-owned ability would command in one kind of world without private property.

Now, what Able and Infirm get depend not only on their own powers and decisions but also on what the world is like, materially speaking. Five mutually exclusive and jointly exhaustive possible material situations, not all of which are interesting, may readily be distinguished:

i. Able cannot produce per day what is needed for one person for a day, so Able and Infirm both die.

ii. Able can produce enough or more than enough for one person, but not enough for two. Infirm lets Able produce what he can, since only spite or envy would lead him not to.[3] Able lives and Infirm dies.

iii. Able can produce just enough to sustain both himself and Infirm. So Infirm forbids him to produce unless he produces that much. Able consequently does, and both live at subsistence.

iv. If Able produces at all, then the amount he produces is determined independently of his choice, and it exceeds what is needed to sustain both Able and Infirm. They therefore bargain over the distribution of a fixed surplus. The price of failure to agree (the 'threat point') is no production, and, therefore, death for both.

v. Again, Able can produce a surplus, but now, more realistically, he can vary its size, so that Able and Infirm will bargain not only, as in (iv), over who gets how much, but also over how much will be produced.

The interesting cases are (iv) and (v), in which bargains will be struck.[4] It is a controversial question, in the relevant philosophical and economic literature, what one should expect the outcome of such bargaining to be. But it seems clear that the inputs to the bargaining process will be the utility functions of Able and Infirm, including the disutility of labour for

[2] The point of these familiar stipulations is to trace what reflects the structure of rights as such, apart from special generosity or malice.
[3] Alternatively, and on the assumption that each must eat in the evening to be alive the next day, Infirm allows Able to work for a day on condition that, at the end of it, a lottery decides who gets the food. If Infirm wins, Able dies and Infirm lives one day more than he would if Able wins (and then lives out his span).
[4] I am supposing that it is not open to Able to wait until Infirm dies in order to become the sole owner of everything: assume that he would himself die no later than Infirm does in the absence of production. (Recall that the land is jointly owned, so that production by Able requires Infirm's permission.)

Able and the disutility of infirmity for Infirm. What will matter, in other and less technical words, is their preferences, what they like and dislike, and how much. And the crucial point is that Able's talent will not, just as such, affect how much he gets. If the exercise of his talent is irksome to him, then he will indeed get additional compensation, but only because he is irked, not because it is his labour which irks him. In short, he gets nothing extra just because it is he, and not Infirm, who does the producing. Infirm controls one necessary condition of production (relaxing his veto over use of the land), and Able controls two, but that gives Able no bargaining advantage. If a good costs $101, and you have one hundred of the dollars and I only one of them, then, if we are both rational and self-interested, you will not get a greater share of the good if we buy it jointly just because you supply so much more of what is required to obtain it.

Here, then, joint world ownership prevents self-ownership from generating an inequality to which egalitarians would object. And, while the Able and Infirm story is an extremely special one in several respects, the particular point that talent as such yields no extra reward even under self-ownership where there is also joint ownership of external resources is, I believe, generalizable. (I do not say that no inequality repugnant to egalitarians can arise in the Able/Infirm situation, but only that either there will be no such inequality, or its source will not be Able's ownership of his own powers, but the influence of the parties' utility functions on the outcome of the bargaining process. One cannot guarantee that no inequality repugnant to egalitarians will arise, if only because different egalitarians favour different equalities, and it is extremely unlikely that all of them will emerge from the bargaining process.)

3. In section 4 I shall describe a seemingly fatal objection to the argument of section 2, and one from which, as I try to show in section 6, we can learn a great deal. But here, somewhat digressively, I develop a relatively minor objection to the argument, and one which is rather difficult to assess, because of controversial questions about the concept of rationality.

The objection questions the claim that self-ownership has no unequal-izing effect in a jointly owned world. The following model may be used to develop the objection.

Consider two sets of equally able farmers. Members of the first set, the Joint farmers, own all the land jointly. Members of the second set, the Mixed farmers, each own some land privately, in varying amounts, but in no case enough to live off, and they also jointly own a further tract of land. Land fertility is such that the material position for each set of farmers is a multi-person version of either (iv) or (v) of section 2: more than enough to keep everyone alive is available, if all the farmers work all the soil. If I am right in section 2, then the upshots of bargaining among Joint and among Mixed farmers should be identical whenever production possibilities are the same in the two cases, because private ownership of tracts of land insufficient to sustain life confers no more bargaining leverage than private ownership of nothing but talent alone does, where the rest of what is required for life-sustaining production is jointly owned.

The objection is that a Mixed farmer could threaten to destroy (part of) his private plot, whereas no one can threaten to destroy anything which is held jointly. If such threats would be credible, then it seems that privately well-endowed Mixed farmers could assert leverage over their privately less well-endowed cousins. And, if they could do so, then so could Able in the case, not excluded above, in which he has it in his power to let (part of) his talent decay. What is unclear, because of difficulties in the concept of rationality, is whether such a Schellingian[5] threat would be credible, and, therefore, effective, *under the assumption that everyone is rational*. If it would be, then those with greater power to produce could get more in a jointly owned world for reasons which go beyond the consideration that their labour might be irksome to them.

But this objection to the argument of section 2 is, as I said, relatively minor, even if it is sound. One reason why it is minor is that it achieves purchase only in the rather peculiar case in which Able can indeed diminish his own productive power. But a more important reason for considering the objection secondary is that no libertarian would want to defeat the Able/Infirm argument (for the consistency of equality and self-ownership) on so adventitious a basis. He would want, instead, to overcome it by pressing the more fundamental objection to which I now turn.

4. Whatever should be said about the objection of section 3, there remains a deeper and seemingly fatal objection to the lesson drawn in section 2 from the Able/Infirm story. That lesson is that, without denying self-ownership, and without affirming equality of condition as an underived principle, one may move towards a form of equality of condition by insisting on joint ownership of the external world. And the seemingly fatal objection is that to affirm joint ownership of the world is, as the story of

---

[5] See Thomas Schelling, *Strategy of Conflict*.

Able and Infirm might be thought to show, inconsistent with achieving the purpose and expected effect of self-ownership. What is the point of my owning myself if I can do nothing without the agreement of others? Do not Able and Infirm jointly own not only the world but also, in effect, each other? Would they not bargain exactly as they do if, instead of being self-owning, each was jointly owned by both? Does not joint world ownership entitle a person to prohibit another's wholly harmless use of an external resource, such as taking some water from a superabundant stream,[6] and is it not, therefore, inconsistent with the most minimal *effective* self-ownership (and independently indefensible to boot)? It looks as though the suggested form of external resource equality, namely, joint world ownership, renders nugatory the self-ownership with which we had hoped to combine it. Self-ownership is not eliminated, but it is rendered useless, rather as it is useless to own a corkscrew when you are forbidden access to bottles of wine.

There are two possible replies to the objection that self-ownership is useless when it is combined with joint ownership of the world. The first, which is explored in section 5, is to argue that joint world ownership does not, in fact, deprive self-ownership of all use, since, to put the point crudely, economics isn't everything. The second reply, which I regard as both correct and very important, and which is mounted in section 6, is to accept that joint world ownership renders self-ownership merely formal, while showing that present polemical purposes do not require it to be anything more than that.

5. The first reply says that people have vital interests in matters other than production and the distribution of its fruits, matters on which joint world ownership might have no, or only a reduced, bearing. It would then be false that joint world ownership would render individual self-ownership useless.

But this reply seems to be incompatible with the fact that all human action requires space, which is jointly owned if the world is.[7] (Even the mental activity of an immobile agent requires the space he occupies.) Or, if that is thought far-fetched, then consider, instead, that all human action requires nourishment, which requires food, which comes from the

---

[6] See Chapter 3, p. 77 above.
[7] On the importance of space as a resource, see my *Karl Marx's Theory of History*, pp. 50–2. For strong claims about the relationship between freedom and rights over space, see Hillel Steiner, 'Individual Liberty', pp. 44ff.

external world. It seems to follow that collective control over what anyone may do with the external world affects every department of life, and not just the domain of production. It looks, indeed, as though joint world ownership fully determines the entire outcome, whatever may be laid down officially about who owns whose powers.[8]

There is, perhaps, one 'action' which could be performed without the permission of others in a jointly owned world as long as there is self-ownership, and possibly not without it, namely, letting oneself die: in the absence of self-ownership one has noncontractual obligations which might forbid letting oneself die. (I speak of letting oneself die rather than of (other forms of) suicide, since active suicide might require external resources, and letting oneself die is achieved by refraining from using any.) But even this suggestion may be incorrect, since the world's joint owners might be thought to have the right to forbid one to die on the ground, for example, that one's dead body might pollute some of the world's resources.

6. But now let us recall our polemical task, which is to address Robert Nozick's contention that honouring people's self-ownership requires extending to them a freedom to live their own lives which is incompatible with the equality of condition prized by socialists. The recently suggested response to that contention was that self-ownership is, contrary to what Nozick says, compatible with equality of condition, since the inequality which Nozick defends depends on adjoining to self-ownership an inegalitarian principle of external resource distribution, which need not be accepted. When, instead, self-ownership is combined with joint ownership of the world, its tendency to generate inequality is removed.

The section 4 objection to that response was that the resource distribution under joint world ownership renders the self-ownership with which it is officially combined merely formal. *But that objection would, for immediate polemical purposes, be laid to rest, if it could be shown that the*

[8] If, that is, the joint world ownership is itself substantive rather than merely official. For consider a regime in which a person *A* owns both himself and everyone else, with all other resources being in joint ownership. Then either that joint ownership remains substantive (because *A*'s ownership of everyone is substantively consistent with the exercise of rights over things), in which case the statement in the text applies; or the joint world ownership itself lacks substance (because all 'rights' over things by owned persons belong, substantially, to the owner of those persons). I provisionally conclude, pending further possible counter-examples, that joint world ownership fully determines the outcome, rendering other provisions merely official, except for the case, if there is one, where it is itself merely official.

self-ownership defended by Nozick is itself merely formal, for he could not then maintain that self-ownership necessitates inequality of condition (since the Able/Infirm model shows that merely formal self-ownership does not do that).

To be sure, Nozick would like us to think, what he evidently himself thinks, that the self-ownership which he favours is more than merely formal. In Chapter III of *Anarchy, State, and Utopia* he pleads that each person should be free to live his own life, a *desideratum* which is supposed to be secured by the rights constituting Nozickian self-ownership.[9] But Nozick also thinks that the most abject proletarian – call him Z[10] – who must either sell his labour power to a capitalist or die, enjoys the relevant rights.[11] And if that is so, then Nozick could not object that Able's self-ownership is merely formal, since, whether or not it is indeed merely formal, it is not less consequential than Z's.

If Able and Z lack self-ownership, in an effective sense, then that is because neither can do anything without the agreement of Infirm and the capitalist, respectively. But they are, nevertheless, different from chattel slaves. For while each can do nothing without another's agreement, it is also true that there is nothing which either need do without his own agreement: neither Infirm nor the capitalist has rights of sheer command that are not grounded in a prior contract to obey. By contrast, the slave's master may unilaterally determine what the slave must do.

The resulting dilemma for Nozick is severe. Either capitalism does not confer consequential self-ownership, since Z's self-ownership is not robust enough to qualify as such; or, if it does so qualify, then genuine self-ownership allows the enforcement of equality of condition, since Able's self-ownership is at least as robust as Z's, and no inequality follows from self-ownership in the Able/Infirm world.

Notice, moreover, that both Able and Infirm are in one respect far better placed than Z is. For each of Able and Infirm must strike an agreement with the other in order to survive, and, since both are rational and self-interested, it follows that the survival of each is assured (in a world abundant enough to sustain two people on the labour of one). By contrast,

---

[9] See *Anarchy*, pp. 28–35 (on side constraints) and pp. 42–5, 48–51 (on leading one's own life).

[10] After *ibid.*, pp. 262–4.

[11] Z is abject because he owns no private property, and he will therefore contract, on adverse terms, with someone who does own some, if he can find a propertied person willing to contract with him. His predicament might be thought dire, but Nozick does not think that he has (in general) a just grievance: see Chapter 3 above, pp. 85–6.

no capitalist need strike an agreement with Z in order to survive,[12] and Z's very survival is, therefore, not guaranteed.

To put the main point differently: Nozick says that a propensity to inequality is unavoidable when people are allowed to live their own lives. Yet he must hold that, despite the constraints on his life choices, and despite his adverse power position *vis-à-vis* others, Z leads his own life. But it then follows that Nozick is wrong that, when people lead their own lives, equality of condition cannot be guaranteed, since Able and Infirm lead their own lives at least as much as Z does, and the constitution under which they live guarantees a certain equality of condition.[13]

I have said (see Chapter 3, p. 70 above) that it is a strength in Nozick's position that the thesis of self-ownership is inherently appealing. But what exactly, we should now ask, possesses appeal for us? What, in this conceptual region, do we feel moved to insist that people should enjoy? Is it (i) self-ownership as such, the bare bourgeois freedom which distinguishes the most abject proletarian from a slave; or is it (ii) the more substantive circumstance of control over one's life? If (i) is the right answer, then we win both the polemic against Nozick and the larger struggle to reconcile socialist equality with liberty. But I think that most of us believe that people should have more effective sovereignty over themselves than either Able or the proletarian enjoy. This does not, of course, rescue Nozick. On the contrary: whereas it seemed that it was a virtue in libertarianism that it affirms self-ownership, it now turns out that self-ownership as such, in the absence of further enfranchisement, has no special attraction. But it is also true, for similar reasons, that socialists should not favour joint world ownership. They must seek another way of achieving equality of condition, one that supports greater autonomy than joint world ownership allows.

We can now draw three conclusions. First, the tale of Able and Infirm shows that strict socialist equality is compatible with the freedom that defenders of capitalism boast that everyone has in capitalist society, since that freedom is nothing more than formal self-ownership, and formal self-ownership obtains in the world of Able and Infirm.

---

[12] Some would question this contrast between the capitalist and the worker. I defend it in section 13 of Chapter 13 ('The Structure of Proletarian Unfreedom') of *History, Labour and Freedom*.

[13] For a challenge to the parallel between Able and Z, see Jan Narveson, *The Libertarian Idea*, pp. 71–3. For excellent defence of it, see Grant Brown, review of Narveson's book, pp. 442–3.

Second, although it indeed turns out that the freedom of which Nozick speaks can be reconciled with equality, that is only because it is a very confined freedom, and it remains to be shown that equality can be reconciled with a freedom more worthy of the name.

Such freedom – and this is the third conclusion – is not self-ownership, but autonomy, the circumstance of genuine control over one's own life. Universal self-ownership with the world up for grabs fails to ensure autonomy, since it tends to produce proletarians, who lack it. Universal self-ownership does not, indeed, produce proletarians when it is conjoined with joint ownership of external resources, but the latter breaches autonomy in a different way. I shall argue, later, that the right conclusion is that, for real freedom, or autonomy, to prevail, there have to be restrictions on self-ownership,[14] and that is ironical, since it is autonomy that attracts us to self-ownership, through a disastrous misidentification. The very thing that makes the self-ownership thesis attractive should actually make us spurn self-ownership. But I now proceed to expound, and reject, a different attempt to secure equality of condition, which combines self-ownership with an egalitarian dispensation over external resources of a kind other than joint ownership.

III The Steiner constitution

7. A third economic constitution, different from both Nozick's and the one described in section 2 above, combines self-ownership with private ownership of initially equal parts of the world's resources. Unlike joint ownership, which forbids a Nozickian formation of unequal private property by placing all resources under collective control, the new proposal, which I shall call the Steiner constitution,[15] institutes private property from the start, but it forbids the inegalitarian Nozickian scramble by privatizing resources in an initially equal division. The Steiner constitution is not Ronald Dworkin's well-known economic constitution, which Dworkin calls 'Equality of Resources', since Steiner equalizes external resources only, whereas Dworkin also favours an equalizing

---

[14] See Chapter 10, section 3 below.
[15] I so name it because it is Hillel Steiner's solution to the problem of justice in distribution when the issue of successive generations, which I do not address here, is set aside. See Steiner's 'The Natural Right to the Means of Production', pp. 48–9, and his superb 'Capitalism, Justice and Equal Starts', *passim*. The latter article is particularly relevant to and against Ronald Dworkin's claim – see part IV below – that the Steiner constitution lacks coherent motivation.

compensation for inequality of personal talent.[16] In fact, and as we shall see in section 9, Dworkin contends, in my view unsuccessfully, that a constitution of the Steiner type is incapable of consistent justification.

At first blush, joint ownership and equal division look to be equally egalitarian ways of treating external resources, but, whether or not they really are both egalitarian, and equally so, their outcomes are utterly different. Consider, again, Infirm and Able. Suppose that Steiner is in force, so that each owns an equal amount of land. Suppose, further, that Able could work both plots of land and thereby produce more than enough to sustain both himself and Infirm, and that Able can also produce at least enough to sustain himself by working his own land only. Then Able's precontractual 'threat-point' would be much higher than Infirm's: Infirm's would be death, but Able's would be whatever standard of living he could achieve by working his own land only. If, then, Able contracts to support Infirm in return for some of the product of working Infirm's land, he is likely to supply Infirm with his subsistence only, since he has Infirm over a barrel. And if the product Able could keep for himself after tilling Infirm's land is not, in his view, worth the additional labour he must spend to get it, then Able will let Infirm die.[17] So in this case, and, no doubt, generally, joint ownership is kinder than equal division to the less able. Note, further, that Infirm would fare even worse under Lockean common ownership.[18] Common ownership would allow Able to till as much land as he wished without giving Infirm anything, and, unlike the Steiner constitution, it would endow Infirm with nothing to offer Able in return for Able's support.

Notice that, under many circumstances, equal division will generate capitalism. If people's talent and/or luck are sufficiently unequal, relatively high fliers may so transform their original shares that they can profitably hire others to work on them at wages superior to what those others could glean from working their own resources. Low fliers will then have reason to sell their shares to their more fortunate brethren and

---

[16] I do not know whether Dworkin thinks that the equalizing compensation ought, if possible, to be complete. The following pages of 'Equality of Resources' suggest more than one answer to that question: pp. 299, 301, 327, 337.

[17] I suppose, once again (see footnote 4 above), that Able may not wait until Inform dies in order to pick up his share. (Perhaps Infirm forestalls that by designating his land as his burial plot.)

[18] At least if we ignore the *First Treatise of Government* (see especially paras. 41, 42), which can be interpreted as laying a duty on Able to support Infirm. For more on that, see the critique of James Tully at Chapter 7, section 11 below.

become their wage labourers.[19] By contrast, joint ownership turns into capitalism only if every joint owner agrees that it should, or agrees to an equal (or other) division out of which capitalism develops. And capitalist societies which develop out of an initially equal division will tend to display more inequality (or display the same inequality sooner) than those capitalist arrangements with joint ownership in their prehistory, even if both sorts will also tend to display less inequality than those growing out of Nozickian appropriation.

Unlike joint ownership, equal division does not guarantee subsistence for Infirm, even when that is materially possible,[20] and it therefore contradicts a basic welfare state principle. Equal division under self-ownership must therefore be unacceptable to anyone who believes in even a minimally demanding principle of equality of condition, and it might therefore be argued that equal division does not, in fact, respect the egalitarian intuition about external resources.[21] But, however that may be, self-ownership together with equal division will not yield the equality of condition prized by socialists. And, since joint ownership, which might yield that equality, rules out the substantive personal rights definitive of effective self-ownership, a constitution of the sort I described in section 1, combining self-ownership (in something more than name) with equality

[19] There is less tendency to such an upshot when the greater talent of more productive people cannot be developed, and/or exercised to differentially productive effect, except as a result of a division of labour in which less productive people are essential participants. But socialists and left-wing liberals are inclined to exaggerate the extent to which that is likely to be so.

For a set of statements urging some such dependence of the more on the less productive, see William Galston, *Justice and the Human Good,* pp. 207, 211–12; and two authors he quotes: David Miller, *Social Justice,* pp. 105–6; and Leonard Hobhouse, *The Elements of Social Justice,* pp. 140–1. Part of the claim is nicely put by Bishop Latour in Willa Cather's *Death Comes for the Archbishop.* Latour says to his friend, the excellent cook, Father Joseph Vaillant: 'I am not deprecating your individual talent, Joseph . . . but, when one thinks of it, a soup like this is not the work of one man. It is the result of a constantly refined tradition. There are nearly one thousand years of history in this soup' (p. 39). For a persuasive attempt to block inferences which socialists might wish to draw from Bishop Latour's observation, see Nozick, *Anarchy,* p. 95.

[20] As it is in scenarios iii–v (but not i and ii) in section 2 above.

[21] For an implicit claim to that effect, see the axiomatization of self-ownership with external resource equality offered by John Roemer in his 'Public Ownership'. I must emphasize 'might' in the text because I do not believe that Roemer demonstrates that external resources are unequally distributed in the Steiner constitution. They patently *are* equally distributed, and some (at least) of Roemer's axioms therefore lack generality, as conditions on self-ownership and external resource equality, even if they are true of particular ways of achieving that conjunction. In an unpublished paper which I will send to anyone who asks for it, I show that axioms 3, 5 and 6 (Land Monotonicity, Technological Monotonicity and Self-Ownership of Skill, respectively: see, further, footnote 25 below) lack the stated generality. I distinguish in that paper respects in which Roemer's construction is successful from the particular respect, mentioned here, in which it fails.

of worldly resources and securing equality of condition, has not been discovered here.

I believe, moreover, that no such constitution is to be discovered: no egalitarian rule regarding external resources alone will, together with self-ownership, deliver equality of outcome, except, as in the case of joint ownership, at an unacceptable sacrifice of autonomy. There is a tendency in self-ownership to produce inequality, and the only way to nullify that tendency (without expressly abridging self-ownership) is through a regime over external resources which is so rigid that it excludes exercise of independent rights over oneself.

8. A comparative examination of the convertibility into one another of equal division (ED) and joint ownership (JO) constitutions supports the view that, *if* self-ownership is to be maintained, then ED is the preferable form of external resource equality. What follows is not intended as a case for ED over JO *tout court*, though some of it might also be so viewed, but only for ED over JO *given* that people are regarded as sovereign over their own powers.

Where there is unanimous preference for the other constitution, either of JO and ED may readily be converted into the other. If everyone under JO wants ED, they will simply divide the jointly owned resources. And if everyone under ED wants JO, they will simply pool what they separately own. Neither system has a convertibility advantage over the other under unanimous preference for the alternative system, when transaction costs are ignored (as they surely should be at the present level of reflection). But what if some but not all under ED want JO, or some but not all under JO want ED?

Under ED the some who want JO will not get it. They will not, that is, get full joint ownership of everything by everybody, since some will keep their separate shares. But those who want JO could join with all those who want to join with them in a less than comprehensive joint ownership: call it VJO (V for voluntary). Now, not all of those who want JO will want VJO as much as they do JO, or even at all. Do they therefore have a grievance against the ED starting point? Can they say that those who want ED get what they want but those who want JO do not? No, for the proper parallel to someone who wants comprehensive JO is someone who wants comprehensive ED, and he is not guaranteed what he wants under ED either (since ED makes VJO possible). If those who want JO go into VJO, then neither they nor those who want comprehensive ED get what they want. But both groups fail to get what they want because others make choices which a believer in self-ownership must endorse their right to make.

If, on the other hand, there is JO at the beginning, then it persists as long as just one person wants it to, and that seems inconsistent with regarding the others as self-owners, in an effective sense. One could, of course, begin with a JO under which any of the n joint owners would be entitled to leave with 1/nth of total external resources. But, when transaction costs are ignored, to add such an entitlement to JO is to assimilate it to ED: JO with the right to contract out is, for practical purposes, equivalent to ED (since ED permits each to contract into JO or VJO).

The conclusion seems to be that, if one begins with a commitment to both self-ownership and equality of external resources, and one has to choose between JO and ED, then the natural way to realize external resources equality is through ED rather than through JO. To go for JO would probably reflect a belief, prejudicial to self-ownership, that people should be endowed with rights which enable them to benefit from (the fruits of) the personal powers of others.

IV Dworkin on Steiner

9. The Steiner constitution unites self-ownership with an equal division of external resources (only), and therefore implements what Ronald Dworkin calls 'the starting gate theory of justice', which he wrongly supposes may readily be dismissed.[22]

Before I address Dworkin's case against the starting gate theory, it will be useful to relate the concerns of the present chapter to those of his magisterial diptych on the theme of equality.[23] The Dworkin articles define a distinction between equality of welfare, which Dworkin rejects, and equality of resources, which he favours. That distinction is orthogonal to the one which has exercised me here, which is between personal and worldly endowments. An egalitarian view of wordly resources may be attached to an egalitarian view of personal powers, or, instead, as in Steiner, to a view which represents them as self-owned. If one takes, as Dworkin does, a doubly egalitarian view, then one may, as he shows, develop that view either as an egalitarianism of welfare or as an egalitarianism of (all) resources. Whichever way one develops the comprehensively egalitarian view, no one owns anything as of basic moral right, and relations among things and persons are arranged so that either

---

[22] See Dworkin, 'Equality of Resources', pp. 309–10.
[23] I refer to the two-part essay which appeared in *Philosophy and Public Affairs* for 1981.

welfare or share in total resources is equalized. But if, like Steiner, one restricts one's egalitarianism to worldly resources, then, too, one might develop the egalitarian component either as an egalitarianism of resources or as an egalitarianism of welfare. The first alternative is to divide the external resources themselves equally[24] and then let people do what they want with them. The second alternative, to wit, welfare egalitarianism with respect to external resources only, might seem incoherent (since external resources produce no – or only a negligible – stream of utility dissociable from the result of applying talent to them), but John Roemer has provided an arresting axiomatic sketch of it.[25]

Thus, Dworkin's distinction between welfare and resources egalitarianism, and my distinction between comprehensive egalitarianism and egalitarianism with respect to external resources only, generate, when they are put together, the following four-fold classification of views:

	Welfare egalitarianism	*Resources egalitarianism*
with respect to all resources	comprehensive welfare egalitarianism (e.g., as described by Dworkin)	comprehensive resources egalitarianism (e.g., as espoused by Dworkin)
with respect to external resources only	partial welfare egalitarianism (e.g., as axiomatized by Roemer)	partial resources egalitarianism (e.g., as espoused by Steiner)

Dworkin emphasizes the distinction separating the columns of the above table, but he gives short shrift to the distinction which separates its rows. He does not bring the bottom row into clear focus, and he therefore does not deal successfully with its right-hand side, which is tantamount to what he calls the 'starting gate theory', a theory whose fairly obvious rationale eludes him. The starting gate theory 'holds that justice requires equal initial resources' and 'laissez-faire thereafter'. It says that 'if people start in the same circumstances and do not cheat or steal from one another, then it is fair that people keep what they gain through their own skill'. This, says Dworkin, is 'hardly a coherent political theory at all'. It is 'an

---

[24] For example, by means of the auction described by Dworkin at pp. 286–90 of 'Equality of Resources'.

[25] See footnote 21 above. Two of Roemer's axioms are (1) Land Monotonicity: nobody's welfare declines if all retain the same skill as before and the amount of land increases and (2) Self-Ownership of Skill: if *A* has at least as much skill as *B*, then he has at least as much welfare as *B*.

indefensible combination of very different theories of justice': for Dworkin, an initial equality is justifiable if and only if it is justifiable to preserve equality throughout.

But Dworkin misunderstands the motivation for the starting gate theory. He is wrong that the laissez-faire component depends on 'some version of the Lockean theory that people acquire property by mixing their labour with goods or something of that sort', and that a similar approach should, therefore, apply at the beginning, that consistency requires Lockean or Nozickian acquisition then, rather than an equal division of resources. It is, I shall argue, false that 'the moment when the immigrants first land is . . . an arbitrary point in their lives at which to locate any one-shot requirement that they each have an equal share of any available resources'.[26]

The laissez-faire component in the starting gate theory cannot be grounded in Locke's theory that people acquire property by mixing their labour with things, since starting gate's laissez-faire begins only once all external resources have been distributed, and it is then too late to acquire title in something by mixing one's labour with it. Labour mixture secures title, for Locke, only in what is not yet owned, and there is nothing unowned with which to mix one's labour once the initial equal division of external resources has been effected.

Dworkin represents Locke as holding that labour secures title because it joins what the labourer works on to something he already owns, to wit, his labour. I think that is a correct exegesis of Locke. But some think that, for Locke, labouring on something makes it one's own not (only) for the stated reason, but when and because, by labouring on it, one thereby enhances its value. And *some* such consideration might indeed be used to justify the laissez-faire component in the starting gate theory. But one who drew upon it would not, I shall argue, be thereby committed against an initial equal division.

Note that what I shall call the 'value argument' is truly different from the argument from labour mixture, even though many (and sometimes, perhaps, Locke) are prone to confuse the two. If the justification of your ownership of what you have laboured on is that your labour is in it, then you do not own it because you have enhanced its value, even if what deserves to be called 'labour' necessarily creates value. And, for the value argument, it is the conferring of value itself, not the labour by which it is conferred, which is essential: if you magically enhanced something's value

---

[26] All quotations in the foregoing two paragraphs are from 'Equality of Resources', p. 309.

without labouring, but, say, by wishing that it was more valuable, then, on the value argument, you would be entitled to whatever that argument justifies you in having.

Locke's principal labour mixture paragraphs do not, in my view, invoke the consideration that labour enhances the value of that to which it is applied. And Karl Olivecrona may be right that when, in later paragraphs, Locke does bring value enhancement to the fore, he is not trying to justify the initial appropriation of private property.[27] According to Olivecrona, Locke is there, instead, justifying the extensive inequality of goods that comes to obtain long after original appropriation has ceased. Locke's justification of it is that almost all of the value of what is now so unequally distributed is due not to any unequal initial appropriating but to the labour which followed long after initial appropriation.[28]

So construed – not, that is, as a justification for original appropriation – the value argument might indeed be used to justify the inequality generated by laissez-faire, the justification of it being that labour is responsible for (almost all of) the value difference in which that inequality inheres. But it is perfectly consistent to propound that defence of laissez-faire inequality while yet insisting on an equal division at the outset of the resources for whose value no one's labour is responsible. Indeed, if labour's value-creating power is the basic justification of the inequality brought about by laissez-faire, then an initial equal division of external resources is not merely consistent with, but also a natural prelude to, laissez-faire, since no one creates the value of raw natural resources.

To conclude: if what matters about labour is that it annexes something already owned to something unowned, then labour plays no part in justifying the laissez-faire component in the starting gate theory, since, on that theory, everything is already owned once laissez-faire begins. And if what matters about labour is that it adds value, then that might indeed justify the laissez-faire component, but without having inegalitarian implications for the distribution of raw resources. To be sure, one *might* contrive a (not very good) argument for original appropriation by reference to labour's value-creating power,[29] but one is not *committed* to endorsing such an argument when one justifies inequalities which arise *after* appropriation by arguing that labour brought them about. It is, then, false that

---

[27] See his 'Locke's Theory of Appropriation', pp. 231–3.
[28] For more on Locke on labour's value-creating power, see Chapter 7, sections 6–10 below.
[29] See, Chapter 7, footnote 37, below.

the theory of Lockean acquisition (or whatever other theory of justice in acquisition is supposed to justify the laissez-faire component in a starting gate theory) can have no less force in governing the initial distribution than it has in justifying title through talent.[30]

Now, the true foundation of the starting gate theory is the contrast between persons and worldly resources as possible objects of rights and egalitarian dispensation. It is reasonable to think, with respect to external resources that have not been acted upon by anyone, that no one has more right to them than anyone else does, and that equal rights in them should therefore be instituted. But it is not so evidently reasonable to suppose, similarly, that no one has, to begin with, more right than anyone else over the powers of given people. And if you also think that each individual has the right to decide what to do with his own powers, and you (surely not inconsistently) combine that thought with external resources egalitarianism, then the upshot is the 'starting gate theory'.

The fundamental distinction for the starting gate theory is not between what is appropriate at the beginning and what is appropriate later. The theory gets framed that way only on the supposition that all external resources are to hand at the outset. If that is false, and some of them come forward later, by rising out of the sea, or as a consequence of exploration, then the so-called (and essentially misnamed) starting gate theory requires a supplementary equal division rather than a Nozickian free-for-all. 'The moment when the immigrants first land' is not, therefore, 'an arbitrary point' at which to insist on equality. It is unarbitrary in virtue of the auxiliary assumption that all the external resources that will ever exist are already available.

The combination of initial equality and subsequent unequalizing competition which, Dworkin claims, 'cannot hold together a political theory', makes sense, he thinks, in the game of Monopoly, 'whose point is to allow luck and skill a highly circumscribed and, in the last analysis, arbitrary role'.[31] Now, whatever Dworkin means (I find the statement baffling) when he says that part of the point of Monopoly is to allow skill to play an arbitrary role, consider instead a different game, which models the 'starting gate theory' rather more accurately, and indeed gives it its name, to wit, some sort of track race. One may find a political theory which takes that as a suitable model for distributive justice repugnant. One may think that the Coes and Ovetts and Chamberlains in the game of life

---

[30] Dworkin, 'Equality of Resources', p. 309.   [31] *Ibid.*, p. 310.

should not receive high rewards because of their God- or nature-given talents. But then one must contend with intelligible qualms about people's rights over their own powers, which Dworkin ignores. The normative stance of the left would be easier to sustain if the starting gate theory were simply incoherent. But it is not.[32]

V Conclusion

10. It is a familiar right-wing claim that freedom and equality are conflicting ideals, and that, to the extent that they conflict, freedom should be preferred to equality. Some rightists regret that, as they suppose, equality has to be rejected, whereas other see no harm in that.

Most leftists reply either that there is no real conflict between equality and freedom, when both are properly conceived, or that, to the extent that there indeed is one, freedom should give way to equality, since justice demands equality, and justice comes before all other political values.

This chapter has been about equality and freedom, and its author is one kind of leftist. But I have not tried to show that there is no conflict between equality and freedom for leftists to worry about: that large question has gone unaddressed here. What I have shown, instead, is that there is no conflict between equality and what the libertarian Right *calls* freedom. For, under joint ownership of the world's resources, everyone has the rights constituting self-ownership – which is the libertarian Right's conception of freedom – without prejudice to the maintenance of equality of condition.

---

[32] It is curious that Dworkin should object to the starting gate theory on the ground that it distinguishes an initial just distribution from later distributions justified as voluntary transformations of that initial one, since his own theory of justice, equality of resources, has the same structure. Readers familiar with the 'Equality of Resources' article will understand that if people do not differ in their intangible personal resources, then what follows the auction's equal division of external resources is, precisely, laissez-faire. Nor does Dworkin's theory articulate itself in that two-stage starting-gate-like way only in the special case in which intangible resources are equal. A structurally identical dichotomous articulation also holds in the more general case in which a redistributive tax scheme (modelled on a scheme insuring against low talent endowment) precedes pure market process. So Dworkin's privileged starting point is no less (and no more) arbitrary than Steiner's. What divides their theories is nothing to do with temporal structure, but the content of the initial quality. Dworkin characterizes the starting gate theory as urging that (this was quoted at p. 107 above) 'if people start in the same circumstances, and do not cheat or steal from one another, then it is fair that people keep what they gain through their own skill' ('Equality of Resources', p. 309). But if we read 'circumstances' in the extended fashion (which includes internal resources) in which Dworkin uses that term (see *ibid.*, p. 302), then he himself affirms the quoted statement.

VI Retrospect

I now offer a summary of the pair of chapters that come to an end here, which some readers may find useful.

One way of doing philosophy well is to assemble premisses which even opponents will not want to deny, and by dint of skill at inference, to derive results which opponents will indeed want to deny but which, having granted the premisses, they will be hard pressed to deny. The trick is to go from widely accepted premisses to controversial conclusions. It is, of course, no trick at all to go from premisses which are themselves controversial to controversial conclusions.

Now some critics of Robert Nozick dismiss his work as belonging to the second category just distinguished. Thomas Nagel, for example, avers, in his review of *Anarchy, State, and Utopia*, that Nozick's strongly inegalitarian conclusions are boringly unsurprising in light of the strongly inegalitarian premisses with which he begins.[33] But I believe that Nozick can be presented more sympathetically than that, and that he needs to be so presented in order that we may understand the otherwise unaccountable allure of his ideas.

Nagel thinks what he does about Nozick because[34] he shares Nozick's view that freedom is antithetical to equality, the difference between these thinkers being that Nagel does not regard the antithesis as a reason for rejecting equality wholesale. Being less disposed to regard freedom and equality as incompatible, I am less inclined to treat Nozick's inegalitarian conclusions as a rewrite of his (would-be) freedom-affirming premisses. Let me, then, say how I think Nozick gets from the latter to the former, and, then, in what ways his progress can be blocked.

Nozick aims to defend the inequality that makes socialists angry and liberals uneasy by exploiting the commitment to freedom which is common to socialists, liberals, and rightists of the Nozick free-market-supporting kind. There exist other kinds of rightists, such as Roger Scruton, who affect scepticism about freedom itself, but, whatever impact they have achieved on contemporary upper middle-brow intellectual culture, they do not, like Nozick, disturb socialists and liberals intellectually, precisely because they do not pretend to build their edifice on shared normative foundations.

But how does Nozick go from freedom to inequality? He departs from

[33] See his 'Libertarianism Without Foundations', especially p. 193.
[34] See Chapter 2, subsection 2e above.

essentially two premisses, the first of which is that no one should be a slave, in whole or in part, to anyone else. No one, that is, may rightfully be owned by anyone else, but each is, rightfully, a self-owner. And, since I am not a slave, but a sovereign self-owner, then you may not co-opt my services when I have not contracted to supply them. If you had the right to command them independent of contract, then I would be, to that extent, your slave. It supposedly follows that a welfare state, in which, for example, quadriplegics are sustained by income extracted from the able-bodied on pain of coercive sanction, involves the partial slavery of some to others. It involves, so Nozick would contend, exactly that subordination of some to others to which socialists object when they plead against the power of capitalists over workers. Yet that is a legitimate power, being the fruit of contract, whereas no contract is involved as background to the service which the welfare state demands.

We may summarize this first part of Nozick's argument as follows:

(1) No one is to any degree the slave of anyone else. Therefore
(2) No one is owned, in whole or in part, by anyone else. Therefore
(3) Each person is owned by himself. Therefore
(4) Each person must be free to do as he pleases, if[35] he does not harm anyone else: he is not required to help anyone else.

Now the conclusion just stated does not by itself legitimate extensive inequality of distribution. For inequality to begin to form, people must have rights not over themselves but over external things, and no such rights can be excogitated from the foregoing argument. In order to establish them, Nozick needs a further premiss, a second premiss, and that is the premiss to which I now turn.

Whereas Nozick's first premiss is about people and their powers, his second premiss ((5), below) is about everything else and its powers, which is to say that it is about nature and about the unmodified resources of nature. These, for Nozick, are, antecedently to anyone's actions or labour on them, not owned by anyone. They pre-dated the appearance of human beings in the world, and while each human being is born with the natural rights over himself implied by the first premiss, none is born with any natural rights over things. Accordingly, any rights which anyone establishes in things must derive from exercises of rights over

---

[35] Not 'if and only if', since some harmings do not violate self-ownership, just as some damages to your property do not violate your rights in it. The issue of which harms are permissible, and which not, is addressed in section 6 of chapter 9 below.

himself.[36] And the way, in particular, that original rights in things are formed is through each person's entitlement to appropriate any amount of raw resources if (see (4), which is a consequence of (1)) he does not thereby harm anyone (including in 'anyone' not only those who exist when he appropriates but also anyone who comes later). Non-harming appropriation is simply a case in point of the 'natural liberty' endorsed in (4).

So the second premiss is:

(5) The external world, in its native state, is not owned, in whole or in part, by anyone.

And (5), together with (4), enables inference of:

(6) Each person may gather to himself unlimited quantities of natural resources if he does not thereby harm anyone.

The next step requires a view about what it means to harm somebody by appropriating an unowned natural resource. Nozick's answer is that it is to make him worse off than he would have been had the resource not been appropriated at all. But unappropriated resources, like common land, tend to be used less productively, for organizational and incentive reasons, than resources that have been taken into secure private control and that are therefore transformable for private gain. It is relatively easy to obtain sufficient benefit from private exploitation of resources that appropriators will have enough to compensate others for the latter's loss of access to them. Non-appropriators will not then be worse off than they would have been had the resources not been appropriated. Along these lines, the comprehensive privatization of almost everything, by those who are quick enough to privatize before others do, is readily justified. Some, who form what we may call a proletariat, will have been too slow or will have been born too late to privatize anything, but they will not be relevantly worse off, so they have no just grievance to press. In sum, (6) enables inference of:

(7) Unequal quantities of natural resources may become, with full legitimacy, privately owned by a section of the population.

Now if each owns himself, in the sense of (4), and the resources of the external world are monopolized by a section of the population, the

---

[36] On the plausible principle that a creature lacking certain rights could acquire them only as a result of exercises of rights by a creature (for example, as in this case, itself) that already has rights of some kind.

resulting economy will, on ordinary assumptions about human motivation (which is to say, on the assumption that people are not extra-ordinarily altruistic), exhibit extensive inequality of condition, on any view of what equality of condition is, be it equality of income, or of utility, or of need satisfaction or whatever. So (4) and (7) yield the desired conclusion, which is that:

(8) Extensive inequality of condition is unavoidable, or avoidable only on pain of violating people's rights to themselves and to things.

Now, there are (at least) three ways of resisting the foregoing line of argumentation, each of which is featured in this book. The first is to challenge the derivation of (4) from (1), and, more generally, to subject the rhetoric of self-ownership to critical scrutiny: that will be the task of Chapter 10 below. But I think that it is interesting and important that we can resist Nozick in two decisive ways which involve no rejection of the self-ownership idea. One is to challenge his notion of harm, by means of which he passes from (6) to (7). One can question the test Nozick uses for determining whether an appropriation of private property harms someone, and argue, against him, that the fact that a person is no worse off than he would have been had the resource not been privately appro-priated at all does not show that he is not harmed, since he may neverthe-less be far worse off than he would have been had the resource not been appropriated by whoever actually appropriated it: that was the burden of section 3 of Chapter 3 above. And the other way of objecting to Nozick without questioning the idea of self-ownership is to challenge his second premiss, (5), the premiss that the external world is originally unowned. It is, of course, legally speaking, originally unowned, but we are here discussing not its original legal condition, but its original moral condition. (If we were discussing legal, as opposed to moral, truth, then the claim that people own themselves would also be evidently false.) One may, then, press against Nozick an alternative view of the original moral relationship between people and things, under which we regard nature as, from the start, collectively owned by everyone. If that different conception of rights over the world is united with the principle of self-ownership, extensive inequality of condition is avoidable: and that was a principal claim of the chapter that ends here.

5. Self-ownership, communism and equality: against the Marxist technological fix

... only then can the narrow horizon of bourgeois right be crossed in its entirety and society inscribe on its banners: From each according to his ability, to each according to his needs! (Karl Marx, *Critique of the Gotha Programme*)

I Self-ownership

1. In this chapter I argue that Marxist reliance on material super-abundance as the solution to social problems is connected with Marxist reluctance to effect an absolute break with certain radical bourgeois values. The 'Marxist technological fix' has served as a means of avoiding questions about justice which those who seek to carry the Marxist tradition forward cannot now conscionably ignore.

I shall call the bourgeois thought structure from which, so I claim, Marxism has failed to distinguish itself (sufficiently thoroughly), 'left-wing libertarianism'. Since the meaning which I assign to that phrase is not the only one it could reasonably be thought to bear, I must explain how I shall use it here.

A libertarian, in the present sense, is one who affirms the principle of self-ownership, which occupies a prominent place in the ideology of capitalism.[1] That principle says, as we have seen, that every person is

---

[1] The first two sections of this chapter revise and expand pp. 114–17 of my 'Self-Ownership, World-Ownership and Equality', which appeared in Frank Lucash (ed.), and which reappears, shorn of the material on those pages, and otherwise revised, as Chapter 3 of this book. In the 1986 paper what is here called 'libertarianism' was called 'liberalism', because of *one* of the senses which the latter term has traditionally borne, but I have been persuaded that it makes for confusion so to use 'liberal' that John Rawls and Ronald Dworkin, who are widely and rightly called liberals, come out emphatically anti-liberal. Hillel Steiner uses 'liberal' in the old and disappearing sense I had in mind in his 'Liberal Theory of Exploitation', and Antony Flew laments the passing of that sense in his entry on 'libertarianism' at p. 188 of his *Dictionary of Philosophy*.

morally entitled to full private property in his own person and powers. This means that each person has an extensive set of moral rights (which the law of his land may or may not recognize) over the use and fruits of his body and capacities, comparable in content to the rights enjoyed by one who has unrestricted private ownership of a piece of physical property.

One right in physical property which is especially important for the explication, by analogy of the content of self-ownership, is the right not to be forced to place what you own at the disposal of anyone else. My land is not *fully* mine if someone else has a right of way over it, or a non-contractual claim to a portion of the income it generates. Analogously, I am not fully mine, I do not own myself fully, if I am required, on pain of coercive penalty, and without my having contracted to do so, to lend my assistance to anyone else, or to transfer (part of) what I produce to anyone else, either directly or through state-imposed redistribution. This prohibition on forcing a person to bestow his service or product on another follows from the freedom to use his powers as he wishes with which each person is endowed under the self-ownership principle. Whatever else self-ownership means, and there is room for reflection about *exactly* what it encompasses,[2] the stated prohibition is one of its entailments, and, moreover, the polemically crucial one, the entailment of chief significance for controversy in political philosophy.

The libertarian principle of self-ownership has been put to both progressive and reactionary use, in different historical periods. It was put to progressive use when it served as a weapon against the non-contractual claims of feudal lords to the labour of their serfs. By contrast, it is, in our own time, put to reactionary use, by those who argue that the welfare state unjustifiably enforces assistance to the needy. In this chapter I shall largely abstract from differences in the import of the principle of self-ownership which reflect differences in the historical context of its application.[3] What interests me here are differences in its import which emerge when libertarianism is conjoined with other principles, as I shall now explain.

Libertarianism, as I have defined it, may be combined with contrasting principles with respect to those productive resources which do not inhere in persons, to wit, the substances and powers of nature. As a result,

[2] See Chapter 9 below for some of that reflection.

[3] One historically oriented remark. If we ask why Marx and/or Marxism have been wary of rejecting self-ownership, the answer might lie in a desire to carry forward the energy of the bourgeois revolution, which is a revolution of self-ownership against the feudal unfreedom that negates it, into the socialist one. If that is so, then this would be among the bourgeois inheritances that disfigure Marxism. (Another one might be what some people call 'productionism'.)

libertarianism comes in both right- and left-wing versions. All libertarians say that each person has a fundamental entitlement to full private property in himself, and consequently, no fundamental entitlement to private property in anyone else. (The qualification 'fundamental' caters for the fact that, just as I may transfer my physical property to another, so I may transfer my ownership of myself, and become another's slave: full self-ownership allows – indeed, it legitimates – derived rights of property in others, and a corresponding derived lack of property in oneself.) Right-wing libertarianism, of which Robert Nozick is an exponent, adds,[4] that self-owning persons can acquire similarly unlimited original rights in virtually unrestricted[5] unequal amounts of external natural resources. Left-wing libertarianism is, by contrast, egalitarian with respect to initial shares in external resources:[6] Herbert Spencer, Leon Walras, Henry George, Hillel Steiner and James Grünebaum have occupied this position.[7]

Two major contemporary thinkers whose doctrines embody a rejection of libertarianism are Ronald Dworkin and John Rawls. They would, to a certain significant extent, restrict self-ownership,[8] for they say that, because it is a matter of brute luck that people have the talents they do, those talents do not, morally speaking, unambiguously belong to them: they are resources over the fruits of whose exercise the community as a whole may legitimately dispose.

---

[4] Some right-wing libertarians, such as Nozick himself, would regard what follows as not so much an addition to as an implication of the principle of self-ownership: see footnote 6 below.

[5] 'Virtually unrestricted', because Nozick imposes a weak proviso on appropriation: see Anarchy, p. 178, and Chapter 3 above, sections 2 and 3.

[6] I am here bracketing off the question of the relationship between the self-ownership tenet and the tenet about resources in each variant of libertarianism. Some might hold that self-ownership requires left-wing libertarianism, others that it requires right-wing libertarianism, and still others that the question of justice with respect to external resources is not settled by the self-ownership thesis. (In Chapter 3 above I criticized what can be described as Nozick's attempt to derive right-wing libertarianism from libertarianism.)

[7] See Herbert Spencer, Social Statics, 1st edn, Chapter IX: this chapter was omitted from the book's second edition, because Spencer had by then become a right-wing libertarian; Léon Walras, Théorie de la propriété, and for good exposition and criticism of Walras, see Ugo Pagano, Work and Welfare, pp. 112ff.; Henry George, Progress and Poverty, esp. Books V–X; Hillel Steiner, 'The Natural Right to the Means of Production', 'Capitalism, Justice, and Equal Starts', and An Essay on Rights, Chapters VII, VIII; and James Grünebaum, Private Ownership, Chapter VII.

[8] Or so I say: I do not claim that Dworkin and Rawls would find that description of their views appealing. Nevertheless, Rawls regards 'the distribution of natural talents as a common asset', in the benefits of which people should share, in amounts decided by his egalitarian difference principle: A Theory of Justice, p. 101; and Dworkin's scheme for taxing talent has a similarly egalitarian rationale: 'Equality of Resources', pp. 290ff.

Now, in my contention, Marxists must oppose what I have called left-wing libertarianism more forthrightly than they have done if they are to be true to some of their most cherished beliefs. I do not here claim that Marxists have accepted the libertarian principle,[9] but that, in their handling of two large issues, they have failed frontally to oppose it. They have dealt with those issues as though it were unnecessary for them to reject the thesis of self-ownership. I believe that those failures to reject it disfigure the standard Marxian treatment of the two issues, and that, for superior treatment of them, in the spirit of Marxism, it is necessary to embrace the anti-self-ownership tenet attributed to Rawls and Dworkin above.

(Note that, in urging Marxists to reject the principle of self-ownership, I do not say that they should affirm no self-ownership rights at all. Rejecting the principle of self-ownership is consistent with affirming many self-ownership rights, and, while I would claim that universal full self-ownership contradicts not only equality but also autonomy,[10] the latter patently requires maintenance of some rights of self-ownership.)

2. The first area in which Marxists have failed to oppose left-wing libertarianism is in their critique of capitalist injustice. In the standard Marxian version of that critique, the exploitation of workers by capitalists, that is, the appropriation without recompense by capitalists of part of what workers produce, derives entirely from the fact that workers have been deprived of access to physical productive resources and must therefore sell their labour power to capitalists, who enjoy a class monopoly in those resources. Hence, for Marxists, capitalist appropriation is rooted in an unfair distribution of rights in external things. The appropriation has its causal origin in an unequal distribution of productive resources, and it suffices for considering it unjust exploitation that it springs from that initial unjust inequality. The Marxist critique of capitalist appropriation thus requires no denial of the thesis of self-ownership.[11]

---

[9] That claim might, nevertheless, also be mounted, on the basis of certain Marxist understandings of the grounds for saying that capitalists exploit workers: see Chapter 6, sections 2 and 3 below.

[10] See Chapter 4, section 6 above, and Chapter 10, section 3 below.

[11] In Chapter XXIV of Vol. I of *Capital*, Marx purports to show that exploitation can also occur without the original unfair distribution of external resources that characterizes what I have just called 'the standard Marxist critique' of capitalist injustice. In the relevant pages, Marx grants, for the sake of argument, that the capitalist's initial capital was accumulated 'from his own labour and that of his forefathers' (*Capital*, Vol. I, p. 728). Once possessed of that

When social democrats (or liberals, in the American sense of the term) call for state intervention on behalf of the less well off, they are demanding that the better off lend them assistance, and they are, accordingly, rejecting the thesis of self-ownership: they forthrightly endorse (what they consider to be) justified constrained helping of the unfortunate by those who are well placed to provide it. The social democratic attitude is visible in those anti-Thatcherite *Guardian* leader columns which complain about the fate of those who are ill-equipped to provide for themselves in market competition, however 'fair' that competition may be.

The political rhetoric of Marxists is quite different. Marxists do not, in their critique of capitalist injustice, demand that the well off *assist* the badly off. In the Marxist focus, the badly off people under capitalism are the proletariat, and they are badly off not because they are (merely) unlucky, but because they are misused, because well off people, or their forebears, have dispossessed them. What afflicts the badly off is that they are forcibly denied control of physical resources, and, under that construal of their plight, the demand for its redress needs nothing stronger than left-wing libertarianism as its ground. In the Marxist claim, the badly off suffer injustice in the left libertarian sense that they do not get their fair share of the external world.

Now, the Marxist posture of non-opposition to left libertarianism in the matter of the critique of capitalist injustice cannot be sustained. What Marxists regard as exploitation, to wit, the appropriation, without recompense, of surplus product, will indeed result when people are forcibly denied the external means of producing their existence. One case of that is what Marx called 'primitive accumulation', the process whereby, in his account of it, a relatively independent British peasantry was transformed into a proletariat through being deprived, by legal and other violence, of its land. But such forced dispossession, while assuredly a sufficient causal condition of what Marxists think is exploitation, is not also a necessary condition of it. For if all means of production were distributed equally across the population, and people retained self-ownership, then differences in talent and time preference and degrees of willingness to take risk would bring about differential prosperity which would, in due course, enable some to hire others on terms that Marxists would regard as

capital, however, the capitalist causes it to grow through the appropriation of unpaid labour, and, hence, through unjust exploitation, until 'the total capital originally advanced becomes a vanishing quantity' (*ibid.*, p. 734). I argue below that this conception of exploitation both presupposes *and* rejects the principle of self-ownership: see the discussion of 'cleanly generated capitalism' in section 8 of Chapter 6 below.

exploitative. (To be more precise, that scenario would unroll at least at levels of development of the productive forces below those at which, according to Marxists, capitalism, and therefore capitalist exploitation, will not obtain. With very advanced productive forces, on the other hand, forces, that is, which enable even relatively unproductive people to produce a lot without assistance, equal distribution of external resources might not lead to exploitation, but you do not, in any case, on a Marxist view, get *very* advanced productive forces while capitalism still prevails.) It might be difficult to imagine each of a total population of n individuals being privately endowed with $1/n$th of the productive forces of a modern society, but essentially the same point applies if we begin with what some would regard as a more feasible hypothesis: if all means of production were socially owned and leased (renewably) to workers' co-operatives for finite periods, then, once again, differences other than ones in initial resource endowments could lead to indefinitely large degrees of inequality of position and, from there, to exploitation, with some co-ops in effect exploiting others.

Marxists have, then, exaggerated the extent to which what they consider exploitation depends on an initial inequality of rights in worldly assets. The story about the dispossession of the peasants from the soil does not impugn capitalism as such. It impugns only capitalisms with one sort of (dirty) pre-history. Libertarians, both left and right, would condemn capitalisms with that sort of pre-history, but Marxists are against capitalism as such, and they must therefore condemn a capitalism in which the exploitation of workers comes from deft use by the exploiters of their self-owned powers on the basis of no special advantage in external resources. Libertarians could not call that exploitative, but Marxists must, and so, to prevent what they consider exploitation, an initial equal distribution of external resources is not enough, and yet they standardly proceed, in their critique of capitalism, as though it would be. ('As though': I do not mean that Marxists think that enforcing initial external resource equality would safely eliminate exploitation. They amply realize that it would not do so. But that is inconsistent with their claim that lack of means of production is the whole cause of exploitation.) To block the generation of the exploitation characteristic of capitalism, people have to have claims on the fruits of the powers of other people, the claims which (even) left-wing libertarianism denies.

I should add that some left-wing libertarians display little awareness of how unstable the initial equality they favour would be. Their attempt to combine the attractions of egalitarianism and self-ownership is bound to fail, and the implications of their view (as opposed to its motivation) are much closer to those of right-wing libertarianism than they readily realize. (The work of Hillel Steiner illustrates this claim.)[12]

II Communism

3. The second important topic, in their reflection on which Marxists fail frontally to oppose left-wing libertarianism, is that of the nature of the good society. I do not mean that all left-wing libertarians have the same vision of the good society as Marxists do, but rather that no left-wing libertarian could base any normative objection to Marx's vision of it on his left-wing libertarianism, considered just as such. For in Marx's good society, productive resources are available, *gratis*, to all, but the individual remains effectively sovereign over himself. He conducts himself 'just as he has a mind',[13] developing himself freely not only without blocking the free development of others, but even as a 'condition'[14] of the free development of others. An overflowing abundance renders it unnecessary to *press* the talent of the naturally better endowed into the service of the poorly endowed for the sake of establishing equality of condition, and it is therefore unnecessary to trench against or modify self-ownership, in order to achieve that equality.

One way of picturing life under communism, as Marx conceived it, is to imagine a jazz band each player in which seeks his own fulfilment as a musician. Though basically interested in his own fulfilment, and not in that of the band as a whole, or of his fellow musicians taken severally, he nevertheless fulfils himself only to the extent that each of the others also does so, and the same holds for each of them. There are, additionally, some less talented people around who obtain high satisfaction not from playing but from listening, and their presence further enhances the fulfilment of the band's members. Against a backdrop of abundance, players and audience alike pursue their own several bents: no one cleans the streets[15] (unless he gets a kick out of that) or spends his life as an appendage to a machine. Everyone is guided by his self-regarding goal, yet there is no inequality in the picture to exercise an egalitarian.

---

[12] For a pertinent discussion of Steiner's work, which offers something similar to the 'bound to fail' verdict ventured above, see Eric Mack, 'Distributive Justice and the Tensions of Lockeanism'.

[13] Karl Marx and Frederick Engels, *The German Ideology*, p. 47.

[14] See the text to footnote 16 below.

[15] See footnote 27 below.

So, as I understand Marx's communism, it is a concert of mutually supporting self-fulfilments, in which no one takes promoting the fulfilment of others as any kind of obligation. I am not, of course, denying that each delights in the fulfilment of the others. Unless they are crabby people, they probably do so. But no such delight is required: it is not something in the dimension of affect which is supposed to make communism possible. Instead, a lofty material endowment ensures that 'the free development of each is the condition for the free development of all'.[16]

In speaking of the Marxist vision of the good society, I have in mind Marx's 'higher phase of communist society',[17] which later Marxists came to call communism, for Marx made a distinction between lower and higher phases of communist society, and subsequent tradition renamed it by distinguishing between socialism and communism. What the subsequent tradition has called socialism, Marx's lower phase, is, for Marx, a society in which means of production are owned by the community as a whole and in which, after certain deductions from it have been made, people receive from the total social product something *'proportional* to the labour they supply',[18] so that those who contribute more get more: I shall call that the 'socialist proportionality principle'. (The deductions effected before the principle is applied cover depreciation and investment, insurance and contingency funds, the costs of government, the supply of schooling, hospitals and other facilities catering to 'the common satisfaction of needs', and, finally, funds for those who are unable to work.)[19]

Marx thought that socialism would be a great advance over capitalism, under which some able-bodied people live without labouring at all, by appropriating the fruits of the labour of others. But he also thought that it would be only a restricted advance. Although no able-bodied person could live without working, because the basis for doing that, private ownership of the means of production, would have disappeared, Marx

---

[16] Karl Marx and Frederick Engels, *The Communist Manifesto*, p. 506. Compare *The German Ideology*, p. 78: 'Only within the community has each individual the means of cultivating his gifts in all directions'. Note that community is here a *means* to the independently specified goal of the development of each person's powers. See, further, p. 618 of *Capital*, Vol. I, where Marx insists that 'the partially developed individual, who is merely the bearer of one specialized social function, must be replaced by the totally developed individual, for whom the different social functions are different modes of activity he takes up in turn'.

[17] Karl Marx, *Critique of the Gotha Programme*, p. 324.

[18] *Ibid.*, p. 324.

[19] *Ibid.*, pp. 322–3.

thought that the socialist proportionality principle had limited moral appeal, and I shall now examine some of his criticism of it.

'The right of the producers', he says, 'is proportional to the labour they supply', and he regards that as an advance on capitalist society. But 'in spite of this advance, this equal right is still constantly stigmatized by a bourgeois limitation':

[For] one person is superior to another physically or mentally[20] and so supplies more labour in the same time, or can labour for a longer time . . . This equal right is [therefore] an unequal right for unequal labour. It recognizes no class differences, because everyone is only a worker like everyone else; *but it tacitly recognizes unequal individual endowment and thus productive capacity as natural privileges.*[21]

In saying that it treats a person's productive capacity as something over which he enjoys a 'natural privilege',[22] Marx is characterizing the socialist proportionality principle as a truncated form of the principle of self-ownership.[23] To be sure, he does not expressly acknowledge that the privilege of self-ownership is truncated here, but it clearly is, since the socialist principle demands what self-ownership would demand in a world of communally owned means of production only *after* deductions prejudicial to self-ownership (see p. 123 above) have already been applied.[24]

Because it preserves the income entitlement of self-ownership, albeit in a restricted form, the socialist proportionality principle 'is therefore a right of inequality': the more talented will, *pro tanto*, do better than the less talented, and those with few dependants will be able to sustain each of

---

[20] For an inexplicable failure to register the import of the foregoing part of Marx's sentence, and a consequent entirely misplaced criticism of Marx's claim that socialism violates the idea of equality, see Richard Norman, *Free and Equal*, p. 115.

[21] *Critique of the Gotha Programme*, p. 324 (my emphases). The further passages from the *Critique* quoted below follow more or less immediately.

[22] It is hard to be sure what Marx means when he says that socialism '*recognizes* unequal individual endowment . . . as [a] . . . natural privilege' (emphasis added). On an entirely literal reading of his statement, he means that the socialist regime affirms the piece of bourgeois ideology which says that people have fundamental moral rights of self-ownership. But it is more likely that Marx means that socialism treats personal endowment *as though* it were a natural privilege: not the ideology as such, but the principle of distribution it mandates, is preserved. There is, in any case, no need to decide between these two interpretations of Marx here.

[23] At *Capital*, Vol. I, p. 271, Marx implies that a person who is the 'proprietor of his own labour-capacity' is thereby proprietor of his own 'person'.

[24] One might question whether all of the deductions contradict self-ownership, but some of them certainly do.

them better than those with many. But these departures from equality of provision, 'these defects',[25]

are inevitable in the first phase of communist society as it is when it has just emerged after prolonged birth pangs from capitalist society. Right can never be higher than the economic structure of society and its cultural development conditioned thereby.

You cannot expect the principle of self-ownership, after centuries of sway, to lose all of its power on the very morrow of the socialist revolution. For practical reasons,[26] socialists must sustain the continued writ of self-ownership, which is not to say that they must espouse it as a fundamental principle.

Well, how do we get beyond the defective – because still partly bourgeois – regime which prevails in this lower phase of communist society, socialism? You might think that we get beyond it by confronting the source of the inequality of condition which is the defect of that society, namely that the society 'tacitly recognizes unequal individual endowment and thus productive capacity as natural privileges'. You might think that we get beyond it by repudiating the persisting legacy of the self-ownership principle. But no. Here is where Marx fails forthrightly to reject left-wing libertarianism. He side-steps the issue, by resorting to a technological fix. Having said that the defects of socialism are inevitable, given its emergence from capitalist society, he immediately goes on to write a paragraph which has inspired many people, including me, but about which I shall presently make some complaints. Here is what Marx says:

---

[25] Note, by the way, that these inequalities of provision are without any ado called 'defects'. If, as some contend, Marx did not believe in equality of condition, why would he consider them to be defects? (For a sophisticated presentation of the stated contention, see Allen Wood's 'Marx and Equality'. For a refutation of Wood's contention, see Norman Geras, *Literature of Revolution*, pp. 48–51.)

[26] The persistence of self-ownership (whether it be as ideology or just as practice: see footnote 22 above) under socialism is, in part, a hang-over from the recent capitalist past: reward is still needed as an incentive to contribution because people are used to it. But Marx presumably also here means (in line with his historical materialism, as that theory is understood in my *Karl Marx's Theory of History*) that the bourgeois principle (or practice) is most suitable for advancing the development of the productive forces towards abundance in virtue of their immediately post-capitalist level, and not (only) because of a form of ideological lag. If he had thought that such a lag was the whole explanation of the defect in socialist justice, he would not have been so certain that the defect would persist until abundance had been achieved: a more perfect justice might have come in advance of abundance, as bourgeois consciousness wore off.

In a higher phase of communist society, after the enslaving subordination of the individual to the division of labour, and therewith also the antithesis between mental and physical labour, has vanished;[27] after labour has become not only a means of life but life's prime want; after the productive forces have also increased with the all-round development of the individual, and all the springs of co-operative wealth flow more abundantly – only then can the narrow horizon of bourgeois right be crossed in its entirety and society inscribe on its banners: From each according to his ability, to each according to his needs!

What communist society inscribes on its banners might seem to be inconsistent with libertarianism. Does it not imply that the individual must lend his ability to the community, for the sake of equality of condition, and therefore exercise it differently from how he might otherwise have chosen to do? But in communist society everyone develops freely, and, so I infer, without any such constraint, and the reason why universal free development is compatible with equality of condition is that labour has become life's prime want: the unconstrained exercise of the ability of each not only allows but also promotes satisfaction of the needs of all. And the reason why labour has become life's prime want is that it has become attractive, because of the high level of productivity posited earlier in the paragraph: 'the material means of ennobling labour itself' is to hand.[28] Hence my claim that Marx side-steps rejection of left-wing libertarianism by resorting to a technological fix. At the high material level of abundance, the incentive of reward for labour contribution is no longer necessary, and so it is not now necessary to maintain the writ of self-ownership. But the same thing that makes it unnecessary to maintain its writ also makes it unnecessary to reject the principle itself. When labour is life's prime want, it is performed both without the remuneration enjoined by the principle of self-ownership and without the coercion which presupposes rejection of that principle.

In both phases of communism people contribute whatever labour they choose: that is why nothing is said about how much they should contribute in the lower phase. Since labour is then their only means of life, there is no danger that they will not contribute. In the higher phase, labour, having become 'ennobled', is now 'life's prime want': so, again, there is no danger of deficient contribution. 'From each according to his ability' is not an imperative, but part of communism's self-description:

[27] With the vanishing of that antithesis, 'labour in which a human being does what a thing could do has ceased': Karl Marx, *The Grundrisse*, p. 325.
[28] Karl Marx, letter in *The People's Paper*, p. 58.

given that labour is life's prime want, that is how things go here. People fulfil themselves in work which they undertake as a matter of unconditional preference rather than in obedience to a binding rule.

III Equality

4. Marx's (higher phase of) communism is characterized by an egalitarian distribution which is not achieved by (the threat of) force: I shall use the phrase 'voluntary equality' to denote that feature. I shall now ask, How might voluntary equality be possible, in a large modern society?, and I shall treat Marx's own reply to that question (it is possible when and because material abundance prevails) as only one of the answers that it might receive. Some will think that a society of voluntary equality is *ipso facto* a communist society, while others will insist that, to be communist, a society must also have further (e.g. distinctive institutional) features. I shall here take a stand neither on that question nor on how Marx himself would have answered it. The immediate topic of this part of the chapter is voluntary equality. Communism continues to be discussed only because voluntary equality is (at least) a necessary condition of it.

I shall not be trying to show that society-wide voluntary equality *is* possible, though I do believe that it is. My question, which is how it *might* be possible, is not the same as the question how it *is* possible. The former question, as I mean it here, asks: What, most plausibly, would make voluntary equality possible, if it is possible? In this part I discuss (and reject) what I have taken to be Marx's answer to that question; a different answer, which I endorse; and a third answer, which is often attributed to Marx, and which I deplore. The two answers attributed (by me, and by others) to Marx are consistent with left-wing libertarianism. The answer I prefer is not.

In what I understand to be Marx's account of how voluntary equality is possible, a plenary abundance ensures extensive compatibility among the material interests of differently endowed people: that abundance eliminates the problem of justice, the need to decide who gets what at whose expense, and *a fortiori*, the need to implement any such decisions by force. But while it might have been excusable, a hundred years ago and more, to ground the possibility of voluntary equality on an expectation of effectively limitless productive power, it is no longer realistic to think about the material situation of humanity in that pre-green fashion. The 'springs of co-operative wealth' will probably never 'flow' so 'abundantly'[29] that no one will be under the necessity of abandoning or revising what he wants, because of the wants of other people. The problem of justice will not go away.

But a lesser abundance might make voluntary equality possible, albeit in a different way. I have in mind a level of productive capacity which is too low to prevent significant conflicts of material interest from arising, but which is high enough to enable their peaceful egalitarian resolution. For not all conflicts of interest generate a need for coercion. A conflict of interest obtains when there are things a person wants which he can get only if, as a result, someone else fails to get something he wants.[30] But a conflict of interest generates a need for coercion only when at least one party to the conflict is unwilling either to modify what he wants or to forbear from pursuing it, unless he is forced to do so. I think that it is not Utopian to speak of a level of material plenty which, while too low to abolish conflicts of interest as such, is high enough to allow their resolution without coercion and in favour of equality.[31] Notice that I do not here have in mind just any old peaceful compromise somewhere or other between opposed demands. I am speaking of an uncoerced *egalitarian* resolution of conflicts of interest, and I conceive such a resolution to be possible when and because people act from a belief in egalitarian justice which, material conditions being favourable, demands only some and not a heroic sacrifice of their self-regarding interests. I project such a society as feasible, not because I think that people might become *entirely* just, and therefore prepared to sacrifice their interests to whatever degree, in whatever circumstances, the virtue of justice would require; but because I think that they are or might become *sufficiently* just willingly to support an egalitarian distribution, in conditions of modest abundance. That is my solution to the problem of how voluntary equality might be possible. (I am here concerned with motivations, and I want to leave institutional details open, but let us suppose, for vividness, that equality is secured through a swingeingly redistributive egalitarian tax law, with non-payment of the required tax generating no penalty except, perforce,

[29] *Critique of the Gotha Programme*, p. 324.
[30] Cf. Lars Bergström 'What is a Conflict of Interest?', p. 208. So defined, a conflict of *interest* may or may not generate conflict between *people*, that is, antagonistic struggle in which each side strives to get what it wants at the expense of the other; and social harmony can obtain either because there *exist* no conflicts of interest, or because whatever conflicts that do exist are resolved without antagonism.
[31] I believe that per capita income in advanced capitalist societies is already beyond the required level, but that belief is not, of course, integral to the above claim.

disapproval.[32] But even that penalty is never applied, since everyone believes in paying, and willingly pays, the required tax).

Someone might ask why I insist on considerable (even though not unlimited) abundance as a presupposition of voluntary equality. He might say that it is just as likely to be displayed under less bounteous, and perhaps even harsh, conditions, where it indeed demands more sacrifice from the talented, but where they might be moved by the greater (than in more benign conditions) liability to deprivation of the less able. Well, I do not need to reject a view about the material conditions of voluntary equality that is more optimistic than the one I have affirmed. But anyone who is drawn to such a view should bear in mind that we are here considering the regular long-term operation of a large-scale, non-primitive society which is not at war. This means that behaviour characteristic of one-off situations of shared distress, such as famine or disastrous accident, is here irrelevant, that familial and tribal forms of solidarity are here ruled out,[33] and that the civic virtues that go with war are not here to be expected. With all of those pertinent stipulations in place, it seems to me unrealistic to hope for voluntary equality in a society which is not rich. But, however that may be, I am here chiefly concerned to address not the optimists described above but Marxists who believe that substantial conflicts of interest make equality impossible, and I ask them to consider whether the material progress on which they rest their hope might not enable an egalitarian resolution of those conflicts at a stage earlier than the one at which that progress causes them to vanish.

5. It should be evident that Marx's account of the possibility of voluntary equality does not contradict left-wing libertarianism. And one might think that left-wing libertarians also need not object to the society my own solution describes, since it, too, displays no coercion invasive of self-ownership. But in my solution the absence of coercion is consistent with social equality only because the citizens disbelieve in self-ownership and willingly follow a law (or practice)[34] which reflects that disbelief. They

---

[32] Some might say that a law with the character of a primary rule (in Herbert Hart's sense: see *The Concept of Law*, Chapter V) must have a penalty attached to it. But I do not think that is true, and, even if it is, its truth is irrelevant here, for I could speak without loss of a recorded and accepted principle of redistribution, and not call it a 'law'. (For a good discussion of whether laws require penalties, see Joseph Raz, *Practical Reason and Norms*, pp. 157–62.)

[33] See, further, *Karl Marx's Theory of History*, pp. 211–12.

[34] One could rephrase everything that follows to satisfy the view of those with whom I expressed disagreement in footnote 32.

believe that those who cannot produce as much as others can are nevertheless entitled to comparable provision, and they consequently also believe that force should be imposed in (at least some) societies unlike their own, where force *is* necessary to promote greater equality. Because everyone has those beliefs, and is true to them, the better endowed fulfil their equality-seeking obligations without being forced to do so. And because the constitution of the society imposes no penalties to sustain equality, it is thus far acceptable to left-wing libertarianism. But the tenets of the society, which are what render coercive laws unnecessary, are not ones that a left-wing libertarian could endorse.

Left-wing libertarians will have stronger reservations still about the society I am describing if, although it functions in an egalitarian fashion because the population believes that justice demands equality, and therefore follow the egalitarian law, that law does have penalties attached to it. One might think that, because such penalties would, *ex hypothesi*, be unnecessary as a means of ensuring that people act in the prescribed egalitarian way,[35] there could be no point in adding them. But a case for adding penalties that are never meted out might nevertheless be made, and I sketch it in the next four paragraphs.

The reason for having such penalties, their proponent urges, is to emphasize that infirm people (to take an extreme case of lesser ability) are not sustained because of the mere generosity of others. The penalties serve to underline the message that the infirm have rights: it is not just a failure of charity when the able do not succour them. Since infirm people have a right to support which is incompatible with granting to the able full rights of self-ownership, there should be a (hypothetically) coercing state, or state surrogate, that sustains their right to support, *even* when people would support them anyway. (A state surrogate is, for example, a general disposition among people to apply coercive sanctions against miscreants, without a special institutional apparatus for applying them.)

What the state here directs the able citizen to do conforms to his independently determined will, but he is still under threat of penalty if he does not do as it directs. It is, to be sure, a mistake to think that, just because the citizen would anyway do what the state directs him to do, he

---

[35] I am here supposing that everyone knows that everyone knows (and so on) that everyone is a committed egalitarian. Since that is 'common knowledge', in the sense of David Lewis' *Convention*, legal penalties are not even necessary for 'assurance game' reasons. (For the concept of an assurance game, see A. K. Sen, 'Isolation, Assurance and the Social Rate of Discount'.)

could have no reason to object to the threat attached to its directive. There are at least two reasons why a person might justifiably feel aggrieved when forcibly obliged to do what he would do anyway. But neither applies in the present case.

The first reason is illustrated when a repressive state forbids people to visit countries to which, as it happens, they do not want to go. They might nevertheless quite reasonably resent the prohibition, since they might think that what countries they visit should be wholly up to them. But the citizens of the egalitarian society we are contemplating do not have this reason for resenting the fact that they would be forced to do what they anyhow want to do, since they recognize the justice of the infirm's claims and they therefore agree that they should be forced to respect those claims of justice if, what is false, it is necessary to force them to do so.

A different reason for objecting to the existence of a penalty against doing what I have no intention of doing is that I might resent the lack of confidence in my moral sense which the existence of the penalty could be thought to betoken. But that ground of grievance is also absent here. For the penalties are not in place because of what able people might otherwise do. Their rationale is to reinforce the status conferred by the law on under-endowed people. That rationale means that there might be a point in having the penalties even though everyone knows that no one would act otherwise than they actually do in their absence. The penalties are not adopted because of adverse beliefs about anyone's motivation.

So much in favour of the claim that unused penalties would lend emphasis to the rights of less talented people. Whatever should be thought about that claim, I am confident that persons of left-wing disposition should reject Marx's Utopian abundance as the basis for projecting a future voluntary social equality, and that they should ground the possibility of that equality in a willingness, in the context of a lesser abundance, to act on beliefs about justice which are inconsistent with any form of libertarianism.

6. I express optimism when I say that we may envisage a level of material plenty which falls short of the limitless conflicts-dissolving abundance projected by Marx, but which is abundant enough so that, although conflicts of interest persist, they can be resolved without the exercise of coercion. I think that Marx himself would have been more pessimistic on that particular score. I think that he thought that anything short of an abundance so fluent that it removes all major conflicts of interest would guarantee continued social strife, a 'struggle for necessities . . . and all

the old filthy business'.[36] I think that it was because he was needlessly pessimistic about the social consequences of anything less than limitless
abundance that Marx needed to be so optimistic about the possibility of
that abundance. A pessimism about social possibility helped to generate
an optimism about material possibility.[37]

Consider this statement, from *The German Ideology*:

so long as the productive forces are still insufficiently developed to make
competition superfluous, and therefore would give rise to competition over
and over again, for so long the classes which are ruled would be wanting the
impossible if they had the 'will' to abolish competition and with it the state and
the law.[38]

What can it mean for competition to be *superfluous*, as opposed to just
non-existent, not actual? It can only mean, I suggest, that there is nothing
for anyone to compete *about*: competition is superfluous when everyone can have everything he wants without prejudice to the wants of
others.

Now, Marx says here that as long as competition is *not* superfluous,
competition is 'therefore' inevitable: competition, he implies, is necessary
as long as it is possible. But what makes competition inevitable, what
'give[s] rise to it over and over again', is an insufficient development of
the productive forces: only when the productive forces are sufficiently
developed is competition superfluous and therefore only then is it
possible to transcend it.

Since competition is necessary as long as it is possible, it follows that, as
long as it is possible *not* to have communism, communism is impossible.
The only thing, moreover, that can make communism possible is a plenary
development of the productive forces. Having burdened himself with that
gloomy confidence, Marx had to believe either that capitalism would last
forever or that such a development of the productive forces would one
day come. And, since he hated capitalism, he needed his technological fix.

Now, what *is* a society of competition, in the sense of the *German Ideology*
passage? It is a society in which people use their powers to get as much as
they can for *themselves*, without regard to the needs of others. But they can
do that only if they are free to use their powers as they wish, only, therefore, if the principle of self-ownership prevails. Then, since Marx thought
– so our text proves – that it is impossible to extinguish competition in

---

[36] *The German Ideology*, p. 49.
[37] I do not say that Marx's social pessimism was the only source of his materialist optimism:
see the Introduction to this book, footnote 13.
[38] *The German Ideology*, pp. 329–30.

advance of the achievement of absolute abundance, he almost certainly thought that it would be impossible to abolish the juridical presupposition of competition, to wit, self-ownership, as long as any kind of scarcity obtained. Had he thought it possible to transcend self-ownership in scarcity, why, for what further and unconnected reason, would he have nevertheless thought it impossible to abolish competition?

When there is no abundance, it is, so Marx thought, impossible to abolish self-ownership. But once abundance is achieved, and that possibility is established, the abolition of self-ownership is not necessary. The beauty of abundance is not that it makes it possible to abolish self-ownership, though it does, but that it makes it unnecessary to do so (see p. 126 above).

7. Some students of Marx would say that I have exaggerated the extent to which he relied for the success of communism on an abundance which extinguishes conflicts of interest, and I admit that I get the idea not just from poring over texts but from remembering how bourgeois objections to communism were handled in my childhood and youth. For I was brought up in the Canadian communist movement, and my first ingestion of Marxism, which no doubt had a lasting effect, was in that movement, and it might be claimed that the emphasis on limitless abundance in my own understanding of Marxism comes not from Marx but from that movement. (The movement's gospel was Stalin's *Dialectical and Historical Materialism*: for Joseph Vissarianovitch, the development of the productive forces was the key to history and to human liberation.)[39] The students of Marx whom

---

[39] To provide the reader with a taste of what Stalinist faith in the development of the productive forces was like, I quote from the Soviet textbook *Fundamentals of Marxism-Leninism*, which appeared in the early 1960s. Its account of what occurs in 'the advance to the shining heights of communist civilization' begins with a long quotation from the work of academician V. A. Obruchev, 'the well-known Soviet scientist', who, we proceed to learn, did not go far enough:

> It is necessary:
> to prolong man's life to 150–200 years on the average, to wipe out infectious diseases, to reduce non-infectious diseases to a minimum, to conquer old age and fatigue, to learn to restore life in case of untimely, accidental death;
> to place at the service of man all the forces of nature, the energy of the sun, the wind and subterranean heat, to apply atomic energy in industry, transport and construction, to learn how to store energy and transmit it, without wires, to any point;
> to predict and render completely harmless natural calamities: floods, hurricanes, volcanic eruptions, earthquakes;
> to produce in factories all the substances known on earth, up to most complex – protein – and also substances unknown in nature: harder than diamonds, more heat-resistant than fire-brick, more refractory than tungsten and osmium, more flexible than silk and more elastic than rubber;

I have in mind would agree that, according to Marx, there will be few conflicts of interest under communism, but they would say that he based that expectation *not* on belief in a future towering abundance but on confidence that, after the abolition of capitalism, individualist *motivation* will gradually wither away. People will no longer think in terms of mine and thine. Each person will become a 'social individual' who *identifies* himself with the interests of other people.

Now, I have reservations about this interpretation of Marx, and I shall develop them in section 9. Here I want to criticize reliance on the transcendence of individualist motivation, whether or not there is a basis for it in Marx. One can, of course, question whether such a transcendence is possible. But, putting that aside, I want to urge that it is extremely undesirable. For unless the phrase 'transcendence of individualist motivation' is used as a misleading description of something different, to wit, my own idea that conflicts of interest persist but people are willing to resolve them in an egalitarian way, it denotes a pretty hair-raising prospect, in which self-ownership is protected at the expense of over-socialization of the self-owning individuals. The Soviet jurist E. B. Pashukanis looked forward to the 'social person of the future, who submerges his ego in the collective and finds the greatest satisfaction and the meaning of life in this act',[40] but I do not find the ideal portrayed in that formulation attractive.

In the Pashukanis scenario, the constitution lets people behave as they please, 'just as they have a mind', and what they are minded to do is to please each other. My own solution to the problem projects no such extreme change in people's motivation. *I believe that it is far better to reject the bourgeois normative principle of self-ownership and not look to a big*[41]

---

to evolve new breeds of animals and varieties of plants that grow more swiftly and yield more meat, milk, wool, grain, fruit, fibres, and wood for man's needs;
to reduce, adapt for the needs of life and conquer unpromising areas, marshes, mountains, deserts, taiga, tundra, and perhaps even the sea bottom;
to learn to control the weather, regulate the wind and heat, just as rivers are regulated now, to shift clouds at will, to arrange for rain or clear weather, snow or hot weather.

It goes without saying that even after coping with these magnificent and sweeping tasks, science will not have reached the limits of its potentialities. There is no limit, nor can there be any, to the inquiring human mind, to the striving of man to put the forces of nature at his service, to divine all nature's secrets (pp. 876–7).

[40] *Law and Marxism*, p. 160.
[41] I need not claim that the scenario that I myself project (see pp. 128–9 above) involves *no* change in human psychology.

*transformation in human psychology than it is to defer to the bourgeois principle
and then rely on an extravagant degree of socialization.*

The insistence on overcoming all conflicts of interests, in both its
abundance and its 'social individual' versions, reflects, I think, an infantile
unwillingness to countenance a measure of self-denial as a way of dealing
with the inevitable difficulties of social existence. We should accept that
there will always be substantial conflicts of interest, but that people may
be able to handle them with mutual forbearance and a sense of justice
when they are blessed with material circumstances which are clement, yet
not Elysian. For this to be feasible, people do not have to be zealously just
and altruistic, since I am premissing an abundance which, while smaller
than what I think Marx prophesied, is great enough to ensure that very
considerable self-sacrifice for the sake of equality of condition will not be
necessary.

Figure 1 summarizes much of the foregoing discussion. It depicts three
bases for believing that radical equality without coercion is possible.[42]

8. Figure 1 displays two traditional Marxist answers to the question as to
how voluntary equality might be possible, and my own different answer.
It omits a fourth candidate-answer, which is neither Marxist nor my own,
and which I shall call the Sumner solution, because Wayne Sumner
suggested it to me.

The Sumner solution is unlike any Marxist one in that it tolerates
conflicts of interest, but it is also unlike mine, in that its mechanism is
not a sense of egalitarian justice, and it therefore does not contradict
libertarianism. The Sumner solution depends on a material level like the
one I invoke, at which large sacrifices are not needed for equality to be
achieved. It bases its achievement on a form of limited altruism. Under
Sumner, people have sufficient (not unlimited) sympathy for one another,
so that, whenever anyone falls below the common level of well-being,
others notice his plight and take remedial action. The assistance they give
is not offered with a redolence of pitying kindness, which could offend the
dignity of under-endowed people, but in a spirit of comradeship. Sumner
citizens are not Pashukanis people, since they do sacrifice goals that
they would wish to pursue, in the way that one might for the sake of a
friend.

---

[42] For a challenging critique of an earlier version of the preceding sections of this chapter, see
Keith Graham's 'Self-Ownership, Communism and Equality', my reply to which is
available on request.

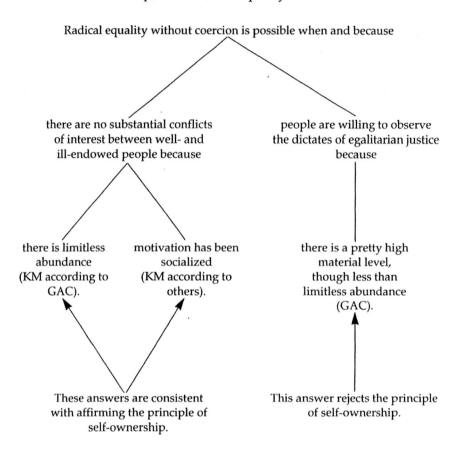

Figure 1

In the Sumner scenario, no one aims at equality as such, as he would if he were actuated by justice, but an egalitarian upshot is nevertheless achieved. I find that conjunction of conditions unrealistic, at any rate for societies which exceed villages in size. It might be unrealistic to suppose that, even in a large society, people moved neither by justice nor by charity could be firmly disposed to help anonymous others who are in special difficulty, but the most which that would provide is an anarchical analogue of the welfare state: relief from serious trouble and acute deprivation. I do not see how the Sumner motivation could be expected to secure the more demanding goal of equality.

9. I expressed doubt (p. 134) about the attribution to Marx of a Pashukanis-like view of what would make communist equality possible. Perhaps

Marx relied on radical sociality at the time of his earlier writings, but socialized individuals, in the required sense, do not seem to me to be what makes communist equality possible in his later works, from *The German Ideology* on. When *The Communist Manifesto* predicts that 'the free development of each [will be] the condition for the free development of all', it does not, so I have suggested (see section 3 above), forecast an eruption of altruism, or any other similarly large change of affect. Let me revert to the music-making example. If a saxophonist, a bass player, a drummer and one or two others form a jazz band, because it is the heart's desire of each to develop his own talent by playing in one, they are not actuated by altruism, and no one joins the band in order to promote another's self-realization. Each joins it to fulfil himself, and not because he wants it to flourish for any independent reason (which is not to say that he does not also have such independent reasons).

In his *Marxism and Morality* Steven Lukes overlooks the jazz band interpretation of the relevant texts, and consequently embraces a strongly oversocialized and textually unsustainable characterization of the Marxist communist individual. I know no evidence, in Marx's mature writings, for Lukes' view that he 'inclined towards the maximum' erasure of distinction between individual interests.[43] Communism is not, Marx said, the 'love-imbued opposite of selfishness'.[44]

In my view, when the mature Marx spoke of an overcoming of the antagonism between the individual and the social interest, he did not mean that the individual would make the social interest his own. What he had in mind was a happy harmony of individual interests, and, consequently, a cessation of the expression of social unity in alienated forms.[45] Lukes misconstrues the absence of conflict between the individual and a *separate* social interest as an identity of the interests of individuals.[46] Marx did not, moreover, posit an absurdly complete harmony of individual interests. The antagonisms deriving from 'the social process of production' have gone, and so, therefore, has the need to project an illusory harmony in the state and religion, but not all 'individual antagonism' disappears.[47]

---

[43] Lukes, *Marxism and Morality*, p. 98.
[44] Marx and Engels, 'Circular Letter Against Kriege', p. 41. Cf. *The German Ideology*, p. 439: 'The individuals' consciousness of their mutual relations . . . will no more be the "principle of love" or *dévouement* than it will be egoism.'
[45] See my *Karl Marx's Theory of History: A Defence*, pp. 125–9, on how, according to Marx, antagonism between individuals leads to sociality in alienated forms.
[46] See Lukes, *Marxism and Morality*, pp. 97–8. The passage from *The German Ideology* which Lukes quotes at p. 98 has nothing to do with socializing the individuals.
[47] Preface to *The Critique of Political Economy*, p. 183.

To be sure, Marx did use the phrase 'social individual', and it suggests, out of context, the product of a radically socializing transformation in the structure of individual motivation. But a look at the passage in which the phrase occurs dispels that initial impression. When Marx affirms that, with communism, 'the development of the social individual . . . appears as the great foundation-stone of production and of wealth',[48] he is not talking about altruistic motivation or any other sort of affective bond. He is talking about sociality no longer being confined to an alienated expression in repressive state and social structures:[49] with the supersession of alienation, society now exists *only* in its constituent individuals.

In that way the 'social individual' of the *Grundrisse* recalls the individual of the *Jewish Question*, who will recognize and organize his own forces 'as *social* forces, and consequently no longer separate social power from himself in the shape of *political* power'.[50] But in that early work the idea that sociality as oppressive superstructure will subside *is* linked to a motivational doctrine. For when the self-emancipating individual of the *Jewish Question* transcends the state, he transcends, in the same movement, the egotism in civil society that made the state necessary. That is one reason why I restrict my rejection of the socialized individual (in the Pashukanis sense) as an interpretation of Marx's basis for believing in the possibility of communism to his *German Ideology*-and-after writings. Another is the apparent textual support for the socialization notion in the extraordinarily ambitious description of what it is to '[carry] out production as human beings' to be found in Marx's 'Comments on James Mill' of 1844.[51]

10. Does communism, as Marx depicts it, and given the nature of his reason for thinking it possible, realize justice, or is it, as some people think, 'beyond justice'?[52] That question is different from each of two other ones, namely: Does communism, as Marx depicts it, realize justice, *on Marx's understanding of justice?* and: *Did Marx himself think* that communism

---

[48] *The Grundrisse*, p. 705. For similar phrasing, see *ibid.*, p. 832.

[49] For this different interpretation of 'social individuality', see, further, David Archard, 'The Marxist Ethic of Self-Realisation', pp. 28ff.; and Will Kymlicka, *Liberalism, Community, and Culture*, pp. 114–19. The socialization of the individual, as interpreted by those authors, is related to the notion of communism as 'the liberation of the content', which I explore in section (7) of Chapter V of *Karl Marx's Theory of History*.

[50] 'On the Jewish Questions', p. 168.

[51] See those 'Comments', p. 227.

[52] 'Beyond justice' is multiply ambiguous. 'Beyond' could mean 'beyond the need for' or 'beyond the possibility of', and 'justice' can be a feature of persons, or of institutions, or of distributions. I do not treat all of the resulting possible disambiguations in what follows.

would realize justice? I am asking only the first question, which is the least exegetical of the three. The three questions are plainly distinct, and, in my view, they have different answers, partly because, as I have argued elsewhere,[53] while Marx believed that capitalism was unjust, and that communism was just, he did not always realize that he had those beliefs. This discrepancy within his attitude to justice has generated extensive exegetical controversy, on which I shall not comment here, partly because I should have so little to add to Norman Geras' excellent treatment of the issue.[54]

Part of the controversy with respect to whether or not Marx's communism is beyond justice reflects failure to distinguish categorially different subjects of the predicate 'is just'. One thing that can be just or unjust is the distribution of goods and services. I think that it is just when it has a certain egalitarian shape, whose exact character need not here be specified, but which I shall suppose characterizes distribution under Marxian communism. It would follow that communism, as Marx depicts it, indeed realizes justice. But it does so either (as in my interpretation of Marx) by virtue of abundance or (as in the interpretation of him offered by others) by virtue of a certain socialization of motivation. In neither case, then, is the justice it realizes due to justice as a moral virtue in its citizenry. And since one can think of justice not as a rightful state of affairs but as a way of achieving one, then, given how the rightful distribution is achieved in communism, as Marx depicts it, one may conclude that it is beyond justice. But there is no reason for someone who thinks that communism is just because its distribution is just to resist the conclusion that it is (also) beyond justice, in the sense in which I used 'beyond justice' in the foregoing sentence. (Note that, under my own non-Marxist proposal about what might make communism possible, the society is in no sense beyond justice in either of the two senses – justice as a distribution and justice as a moral virtue – distinguished above.)

The importance of being clear about what justice, in different discussions, is a property of, is borne out by an interesting relationship between three views of what might make communism possible which I have discussed in this essay and certain distinctions in David Hume's account of the personal virtue of justice.

For Hume, one subjective condition and one objective condition are individually necessary and jointly sufficient for the virtue of justice to be

---

[53] In my review of Allen Wood's *Karl Marx*.
[54] See 'The Controversy about Marx and Justice', in his *Literature of Revolution*.

140   Self-ownership, freedom, and equality

both necessary and possible in human society. The conditions are limited generosity and moderate scarcity.[55] When limitations on generosity are removed, so that each man 'feels no more concern for his own interest than for that of his fellows',[56] justice is unnecessary, and, when people lack generosity entirely, justice is impossible. Under complete absence of scarcity, which is the same thing as unlimited abundance, justice is, once again, unnecessary, and under dire scarcity, where there is less than enough to sustain everyone, it is impossible: you cannot expect human beings to be just in such circumstances. Justice is a normal feature of human affairs, since its subjective condition is fulfilled as a matter of human nature, and its objective condition is almost always fulfilled, since dire scarcity cannot last (it wipes people out), and few people live on naturally bountiful South Sea Islands.[57]

[55] ' . . . 'tis only from the selfishness and confin'd generosity of men, along with the scanty provision nature had made for his wants, that justice derives its origin', *A Treatise of Human Nature*, p. 495. For a well-argued claim that Hume's list is incomplete, see Lukes, *Marxism and Morality*, pp. 32–3, and also his 'Taking Morality Seriously', pp. 104–5. Lukes follows, and develops, Allen Buchanan, *Marx and Justice*, p. 167. For further sapient criticism of Hume, see James Griffin, *Well-Being*, pp. 285–6, 382.

[56] *An Enquiry Concerning the Principles of Morals*, p. 185. Note that this is not the paradoxical altruism in which people care only about the interests of other people, which is paradoxical, because there are then no interests for anyone to care about. It is, rather, an immediate attitude of conformity to the policy of either maximizing or equalizing welfare (depending on how the equality of concern is to be understood: see p. 142 below).

[57] Here is a more systematic presentation of Hume's account of the conditions of justice. Each of generosity and scarcity may be entirely absent, moderate, or unconfined. That creates nine possible conjunctions of objective and subjective conditions. I tabulate them here, together with some consequences I think Hume would draw, in each case, for whether the virtue of justice is possible and necessary:

		GENEROSITY		
S		Absent	Moderate	Unconfined
C				
A	Unconfined	1 Impossible	4 Impossible	7 Unnecessary
R	(= dire scarcity)			
C	Moderate	2 Impossible	5 Possible and	8 Unnecessary
I	(= moderate		necessary)	
	abundance)			
T	Absent	3 Unnecessary	6 Unnecessary	9 Unnecessary
	(= unlimited			
	abundance)			
Y				

Entries 3, 6, 7, 8 and 9 are justified by this *Treatise* sentence: 'Encrease to a sufficient degree the benevolence of men, or the bounty of nature, and you render justice useless, by supplying its place with much nobler virtues, and more valuable blessings' (p. 495). And Hume's brilliant discussion in Part I of section III of the *Enquiry* appears to me to justify the remaining entries in the table.

When scarcity is moderate, generosity makes justice possible, and its confined character makes justice necessary. When generosity exists but is confined, the absence of dire scarcity makes justice possible, and the presence of (moderate) scarcity makes it necessary.

That is Hume's answer to the question: when is justice, as a virtue of persons, both necessary and possible? I asked the different question: what might make communism possible, where communism is conceived as egalitarian distribution without coercion? The questions are different, but the answers map on to one another. The first answer to my question is the one I think Marx gave, to wit, the circumstance of massive abundance, which is the same as one of Hume's two answers to the question: what would make justice unnecessary? The second answer to my question, which others think Marx gave, I called socialized motivation, and that is like unlimited benevolence, which is Hume's alternative answer to the question of what makes justice unnecessary. The answer I favour to my question is: voluntarily just behaviour. That is what Hume says occurs[58] when people are neither wholly uncaring about others nor thoroughly mutually identified and nature neither imposes dire scarcity nor offers a cornucopia; and in my account of communism, by contrast with the two accounts of it attributed to Marx, it too displays those subjective and objective features.

One might say, in Humean vein, that, in the two Marxian views of it (as opposed to in my own), communism is beyond justice, because it is beyond one or other of its two conditions. Or one might, on the other hand, say that what, for Hume, makes justice unnecessary is precisely what, for Marx, makes justice possible. But the air of paradox disappears once we recall what justice, in the two cases, is a feature of.

If we predicate justice of communism, as Marx depicts it, then we do so because of its egalitarian distribution, and not because of a virtue in its citizens. For Hume, by contrast, justice is always a virtue of persons. It is, among other things, and most relevantly here, the artificial virtue that restrains our natural tendency to appropriate what a generally welfare-promoting property institution assigns to others.

Is justice possible in the cases where it is unnecessary? It seems to me impossible in cases 7 through 9, for the reasons given at pp. 142–3 below, where the inconsistency of increased benevolence and justice is discussed. But is justice possible in cases 3 and 6, where what makes it unnecessary is not special generosity but abundance alone? One might say: no, it is not possible, because abundance renders creation of the institutions cleaving to which counts as justice unnecessary, so they will not be there to be cloven to. But one might also say: yes, it is possible, since it is possible for people pointlessly to erect and honour those institutions; you could have property rights where, for abundance reasons, they are not necessary, so you could have pointless justice, 'an idle ceremonial' (*Enquiry*, p. 184), in cases 3 and 6. Or should one still say: no, since honouring those institutions would not go against the grain, so it would not be an artificial virtue, so it would not be justice?

[58] Except that Hume and I regard very different things as the content of just behaviour: the parallel is more formal at this point than it is at the other two.

Both 'generally' and 'welfare-promoting' need explaining. The institution obedience to which is justice is only *generally* welfare-promoting because, in particular instances, sticking to the property rules can do more harm than good, and it is a mark of the artificiality of justice (by contrast with a natural virtue like benevolence) that this should be so. There are no feasible property rules that are better, all things considered, than ones which in some instances enjoin something harmful.

The expression *welfare-promoting* is, by design, ambiguous across two alternatives. Some commentators think that Hume was a utilitarian, so that the institution obedience to which is justice promotes aggregate happiness, if necessary at the expense of the happiness of some. Others, like Gauthier, think that Hume supposes that the relevant institutions promote the welfare of each person.[59] I use the vague term 'welfare-promoting' because the difference between its aggregative and individualized interpretations is not important here.

Institutions like private property are not in themselves, for Hume, just or unjust, but welfare-promoting or -frustrating; and people are just or unjust according as they do or do not observe the rules of welfare-promoting institutions. Justice is 'a regard to the property of others'[60] but that regard counts as justice only because the institution of property is generally welfare-promoting.

Since Humean justice is adherence to the rules of property, there can be no justice, for Hume, where property rules do not exist. Accordingly, when full abundance makes those rules unnecessary, it also dissolves justice. Justice is the artificial virtue that combats our natural tendency to take what belongs to others. But there is no scope for the expression of that tendency when abundance obtains, because human beings can then get all they want without taking from others (and they are not so malicious as to want to take from others for non-instrumental reasons). Abundance means that there is nothing for the artifice of justice to oppose.

It might seem less clear that increased benevolence will 'render justice useless'.[61] Why should a disposition to respect rules of property not coexist with an expansion of generosity? As long as there is scarcity, there seems to be a point in distinguishing mine from thine, and if, being benevolent, people observe the distinction willingly, then are they not being willingly just, rather than benevolent-and-therefore-not-just?

[59] See his excellent 'David Hume, Contractarian'.
[60] 'Of the Original Contract', p. 367. Sometimes sticking to promises is *also* part of justice – see e.g., *Treatise*, p. 526.
[61] *Treatise*, p. 495.

That line of questioning mistakes what is involved when the limitations on human generosity are lifted. When each 'feels no more concern for his own interest than for that of his fellows', the use of any material object, on any occasion, falls, with everyone's consent, to whomever would appear likely to get the most satisfaction from it.[62] There would, accordingly, be no 'land-marks between my neighbour's field and mine',[63] and not merely no walls or fences. Its definitional association with property makes justice by nature a 'cautious, jealous virtue',[64] a regard for mine and thine ungoverned by immediate welfare consequences, and therefore strictly incompatible with the degree of generosity which Hume says banishes justice.

If justice is a disposition to honour certain institutions and injustice is a disposition to violate them, then neither exists, we are truly beyond both, when the institutions in question do not exist. But if justice is regarded as a feature of distributions, then a variety of motives is consistent with justice, and also a variety of circumstances, including abundance. If justice is, for example, distribution proportional to need, then abundance might be thought to make justice easy to achieve, rather than unnecessary. And, where abundance is lacking, then special generosity, even Humean unlimited generosity, might be what makes justice possible. In the widest sense of distribution[65] there always is a distribution of goods and bads in society, and it always has a certain shape. Then where justice is a distribution of a certain shape, it is impossible to go 'beyond' justice and injustice. They are contradictories, and not merely contraries.

---

[62] Or to whomever has some differently grounded welfare claim on it, depending on how equality of concern is understood: see p. 142 above.
[63] *Enquiry*, p. 185.
[64] *Ibid.*, p. 184.
[65] Wider, for example, than one that restricts itself to distributions of property *per se*.

6. Marxism and contemporary political philosophy, or: why Nozick exercises some Marxists more than he does any egalitarian liberals

It is we who ploughed the prairies, built the cities where they trade,
Dug the mines and built the workshops, endless miles of railroad laid;
Now, we stand outcast and starving, mid the wonders we have made . . .
(Ralph Chaplin, 'Solidarity Forever')

1. Although I belong to a school of thought which has been called *analytical Marxism*, I am, like other partisans of this position, and as is manifest in the preceding chapters of this book, engaged by questions in moral and political philosophy which have not, in the past, attracted the attention of Marxists. Analytical Marxists are concerned with exactly what a commitment to equality requires, and with exactly what sort of obligations productive and talented people have to people who are relatively unproductive, or handicapped, or in special need. We seek a precise definition of what exploitation is, and we want to know exactly why it is wrong.

What explains this rather novel involvement, novel, that is, for Marxists, or even – for it is no doubt, by now, more accurate to call us this – for semi-Marxists? I do not think that it is explained by the fact that, unlike the Marxists of yore, we are academics with relatively well paid jobs who get money and recognition through pursuing those questions and propounding our answers to them. For we can also get money and recognition through pursuing questions which always *have* concerned Marxists, such as the questions about base and superstructure and forces and relations of production which occupied me for some fifteen years, before my interests shifted decisively in the direction of moral and political philosophy.

I think, instead, that our shift of attention is explained by profound changes in the class structure of Western capitalist societies, changes which raise normative problems which did not exist before, or, rather, which previously had little political significance. Those normative problems have great political significance now.

One purpose of this chapter is to identify some of those normative problems and to explain why they were less interesting in the past and why they now arise in a poignant way.

2. People like me, who were nurtured on a politically committed Marxism long before they encountered academic political philosophy, come to academic political philosophy with a certain paradigm of injustice governing their reflections. That paradigm is the relationship between the propertied capitalist and the propertyless wage worker, which Marxists take to be a relationship of unjust exploitation. It is a moral datum for politically committed Marxists, or, at any rate, for politically committed Marxists of the not eccentric kind that surrounded me when I was growing up,[1] that there is injustice whenever an owner of capital, by virtue of his ownership of it, extracts product from a worker who lacks capital of his own and who is therefore forced to yield part of his product to a capitalist in exchange for access to means of production.

Why do such Marxists think that the extraction in question is unjust? I believe that they think so largely because they think that the transfer of product from the worker to the capitalist involves what Marx called 'the theft of another person's labour time':[2] the wage the worker receives matches only part of the time he spends at work, so that hours which should, as a matter of justice, belong to the worker are stolen by his capitalist superior. I do not say that this is the only criticism Marxists make of the capitalist relationship, nor even that it is, for them, the most important one. The criticism that a society based on the capitalist relationship represses the development of human potential is at least as important, but that criticism does not entail that the capitalist relationship is *unjust*.[3] My claim is that, for Marxists, the central justice objection to capitalism is the labour theft objection, and that, to the extent that Marxists

---

[1] I was born in 1941 in a part of Montreal which returned a communist to Parliament in 1945, and my parents, and eventually I too, were active in the communist movement in Montreal, which was vigorous until 1956: see Chapter 11, section 1, below.

[2] *The Grundrisse*, p. 705.

[3] To see that non-entailment, notice that a social system might repress the potential of all of its members equally, to no one's benefit, and not at the behest of any particular section of society: there would then be no ingredient of injustice in the repression. By contrast, there could not be a system under which each person suffers, through expropriation, a net loss of labour time.

have other justice-inspired objections to capitalism, they do not clearly distinguish them from this one. (The unequal distribution of means of production, for example, which could be regarded as unjust on independent grounds, is thought unjust by Marxists chiefly because it forces some to do unpaid labour for others.)

To support his condemnation of capitalism, Marx argued that the relationship between buyers and sellers of labour power was in several central respects substantially the same as the relationship between feudal lords and serfs. Feudal law and usage require that the serf give up part of his life to the lord. The theft of the serf's labour time begins when he leaves his own plot and proceeds to fulfil his duties on the lord's demesne. It is manifestly true, a matter not of theory but of observation, that the serf spends part of his time working for himself and another part in unrecompensed[4] work for the lord. According to Marx, it is no less true of the wage worker that he is forced to give up part of his life to a powerful superior. But the truth is, in his case, much less manifest. For two surface features of capitalism conceal its underlying reality. First, under capitalism exploitation is mediated by a contract which the worker is formally (albeit only formally) free not to enter: the serf, by contrast, enjoys no formal freedom not to work for the lord. And second, the division of the worker's labour time into time that he works for himself and time that he works for the capitalist requires economic analysis and is not, as it is in the feudal case, a matter of observation.

Marxists say that capitalists steal labour time from working people. But you can steal from someone only that which properly belongs to him. The Marxist critique of capitalist injustice therefore implies that the worker is the proper owner of his own labour time: he, no one else, has the right to decide what will be done with it. But he could hardly have that right without having the right to decide what to do with his own *capacity* to work, his labour power. The claim that capitalists steal labour time from working people therefore implies that the worker is the proper owner of his own power. But Marxists could not think that the worker is the proper owner of his own power unless they thought that the same is true of people in general. Hence the Marxist contention that the capitalist exploits the worker depends on the proposition that people are the rightful owners of their own powers. That proposition is the thesis of self-

---

[4] Some people think that the protection he receives from the lord compensates the serf for his surplus labour. Suffice it to say, here, that Marx is not one of them.

ownership, and I claim that (something like)[5] it undergirds the Marxist case for the proposition that the capitalist relationship is inherently exploitative. The underlying idea is that a person should be sovereign with respect to what he will do with his energies. He should not deploy them under another person's orders in the manner of a slave *and* have part or all of his product taken from him for nothing in return.

I emphasize 'and' to indicate that one may distinguish two (not usually distinguished but nevertheless distinct) elements in the charge that the worker suffers injustice. The serf is, in part, the slave of his lord, because for part of his life he is subject, independently of his own agreement, to the lord's will, and that is wrong because a person should always ultimately be subject only to his own will. He should be in command of what he does, in the way that he is in command of what is done with a piece of private property that he owns. (That command is not, of course, unqualified, and the same applies to the analogous command called for by the idea of self-ownership.) But that rendering of what is wrong with slavery and serfdom (and claimed by Marxists also to be wrong with capitalism) does not refer to a person's being deprived of something he produces. To be sure, the wrong done to a slave is compounded if he indeed produces and does not receive (all of) his product, but his time is stolen whether or not he is also forced to yield up product. So, similarly, the serf is wronged, and, if Marx is right, the proletarian is too, whether or not they produce anything in the time during which they are captive to their superiors, since captivity itself is wrong. A proletarian is wronged even if he is not, in Marx's sense, exploited, because his inefficient employer never gets round to assigning a task to him while he waits, idly, in the factory.

A connoisseur of *Capital*[6] might object that, even if Marx did affirm some principle of self-ownership, he could hardly have thought that the wage relationship involved a theft of labour power that violated it, since he so strongly insisted that the worker receives the full value of the labour power which he sells to the capitalist (that being the value of what is

---

[5] The parenthesis is a gesture in the direction of a weaker claim: it is no doubt unnecessary to affirm an *unrestricted* version of the self-ownership principle in order to claim that the capitalist relationship is inherently exploitative. But Marxists have certainly not reflected on the possible restrictions, and they consequently have not distanced themselves from the unqualified self-ownership thesis. It is therefore a permissible simplification to attribute it to them in that form. (One possible restriction would be a prohibition on *transfer* of self-ownership, which means selling oneself into slavery. That restriction is consistent with describing capitalists as stealing from workers. The same does not hold for all restrictions on the exercise of income rights that go with self-ownership.)

[6] Readers who find labour theory of value Talmudics boring may wish to skip these final paragraphs of section 2 and proceed to section 3.

required to produce the worker's labour power, to wit, the subsistence goods which he buys with his wage).

Now, the premiss of this objection (that the worker, according to Marx, receives the market value of his labour power) is correct, but the suggested conclusion (that Marx did not think that the worker's rights in his labour power were violated) is hastily drawn.[7] For Marx frequently spoke of the theft of labour time[8] and, as I argued at p. 146 above, theft of labour time implies theft of labour power. Accordingly, if the *Capital* connoisseur is right that the claim that the worker's labour power is *stolen* by the capitalist is inconsistent with the proposition that the capitalist pays the worker the full market value of his labour power, then Marx himself was inconsistent: the fault lies not with me but with him.

But we can, I think, acquit Marx of the present charge of inconsistency. To do so, we need to be clear about the status of Marx's claim that the capitalist steals from the worker. Such a claim is, of course, false, when 'stealing' is restricted to its legal sense: no law of bourgeois property is violated in the wage relationship. But that is not to the point here, since it is equally true that no law of feudal property is violated in the relationship between the lord and the serf, to whom Marx assimilates the proletarian in order to show that the latter is defrauded. In each case, there is, according to Marx, a theft in fact but not in legal form: if he is right, the ruling legal forms serve to facilitate the very (non-legally speaking) thefts that Marx describes. In legal form the worker is 'the free proprietor of his own labour-capacity, hence of his person',[9] but he is no more that in fact than a serf is.

There is, finally, a further and subtler way in which Marx's consistency might be vindicated. For although the capitalist pays the full market value

---

[7] Those who draw this conclusion like to quote Marx's *Capital* comment on the circumstance that the capitalist obtains more value from the worker's labour than the value represented by the latter's wages: 'this circumstance is a piece of good luck for the buyer, but by no means an injustice towards the seller' (Vol. I, p. 301). But I think it singularly wooden (pun intended: see Allen Wood, *Karl Marx*, p. 134) to treat 'injustice', in this excerpt, as denoting (straightforward) injustice. 'Injustice', here, means what Engels shows he thought it means, in this parallel passage: '[This] circumstance . . . is a piece of especially good luck for the buyer, but *according to the laws of exchange of commodities* by no means an injustice to the seller' (*Anti-Dühring*, p. 284, emphases added).

[8] See the *Grundrisse* passage quoted at p. 145 above. There are many other relevantly similar passages, including the following one, which is especially interesting and pertinent, since it shows that Marx himself regarded the charge that the capitalist steals (at any rate something) as consistent with his paying the worker what his labour power is worth: 'Although equivalent is exchanged for equivalent, the whole thing still remains the age-old activity of the conqueror, who buys commodities from the conquered with the money he has stolen from them' (*Capital*, Vol. I, p. 728).

[9] *Ibid.*, p. 271.

of the worker's labour power, and therefore cannot readily be said to steal any of its market value, he might be said to steal part of its use-value, since part of its use-value is its power of producing more than is necessary to keep itself in being, and the capitalist might be said to appropriate that without supplying anything in return: perhaps, then, he achieves the feat of stealing use-value without stealing market value.[10]

3. I do not say that anyone who thinks that certain workers are exploited, or even that anyone who thinks that workers are, on the whole, exploited, must affirm a principle of self-ownership. Instead, I say two things. First, and as I argued in section 2, Marxists *in fact* base the exploitation charge on some notion of self-ownership. Second, and as I now want to argue, if, as Marxists do, you take appropriation of labour time as such, that is, in its fully general form, as a paradigm of injustice, then you cannot eschew affirmation of something like the self-ownership principle.

To see that this is so, it is necessary to bear in mind that the traditional Marxist thesis, that forcible appropriation of another's labour time and product by virtue of ownership of means of production is unjust, is expressed as a fully general claim. It does not matter, for that claim, what *sort* of capitalist, or what *sort* of worker, we are talking about. Accordingly, if the traditional Marxist thesis is correct, then the particular case which I am about to describe has to be regarded as one of unjust exploitation.[11]

Think of a worker who very much enjoys both his work and the wages it brings him and who works for a wholly infirm neighbour who leads a miserable life but who, unlike the worker, has managed to possess himself of a stock of capital. This infirm capitalist lops off just enough of the worker's product so that he, the capitalist, can stay alive. We can suppose that, if something like the stated capital imbalance did not obtain, then the worker would produce for himself alone and callously let his infirm neighbour die. And we can also suppose that it was because he knew that

---

[10] I am here indebted to Douglas Ehring's ingenious argument that you can steal the use-value of a thing without stealing its market value. I should add that I do not accept Ehring's less important complementary and converse claim that you can steal market value without stealing use-value, and I also do not accept his criticism of some claims that I have made about labour, desire and exploitation. See Ehring's 'Cohen, Exploitation, and Theft', pp. 30ff. For the claims Ehring criticizes, see 'The Labour Theory of Value and the Concept of Exploitation', in my *History, Labour, and Freedom*, pp. 229–30.

[11] Everyone will agree that the case to be described is one of exploitation in a morally neutral sense of that term, *if there is one*, but the question of whether it should be regarded as one of *unjust* exploitation is, it will be seen, rather more delicate.

he would die without the power over the worker that capital would give him that the infirm man decided to acquire and exercise that power.

Now Marxists are committed by their unqualified claim that appropriation of another's labour time is, as such, unjust, to calling the relationship between the joyful worker and the infirm capitalist unjustly exploitative. And this reinforces my contention that the thesis that appropriation is *always* unjust requires affirmation of a principle of self-ownership. For how could you consider *that* relationship to be one of unjust exploitation without affirming the worker's self-ownership? There is, *ex hypothesi*, no unfairness in the distribution of benefits and burdens which would show that the exchange is unjust.

I see no way of regarding it as unjust without regarding the sadly infirm capitalist as violating the joyful worker's rights in his own powers. So strong is the case for saying that this uncharacteristically unfortunate capitalist should have some rights over this worker's labour power, if necessary through the mechanism of capital imbalance, that you cannot call him an unjust exploiter unless you say that no one should ever have rights in another's labour power.

Someone might say: what Marxists would think wrong here is not that a right of self-ownership is violated but that the worker is *forced* to work for the capitalist. But it is not always wrong to force people to do things. It is, for example, not always wrong to force people to honour other people's rights. If Marxists think (as they undoubtedly do) that it is wrong to force a surplus out of the worker, then that would be explained by a belief that doing so violates the worker's rights over his own powers. I contend that there is no plausible alternative way of explaining why they believe the forcing is wrong.

Someone might now protest that few Marxists would think that the transfer from the joyful worker to the infirm capitalist is unjust. But I am not predicting what Marxists would think. I do not claim that Marxists would *want* to say that there is an injustice here: some might want to and some might not. It is hard to know what Marxists would want to say about the case, since they do not usually discuss such out-of-the-way examples. Being a philosopher, I study out-of-the-way examples to probe the commitments of doctrines, and I claim that, whatever Marxists would *want* to say about the case, they are committed to identifying an injustice in it because of their uncritical belief that extraction of product from a worker through the instrumentality of capital ownership is, as such, unjust. (By calling that belief uncritical I mean, *inter alia*, that it has not been tested through consideration of possible counter-examples to it.) The example shows that their unreflective doctrine of exploitation commits Marxists to an affirmation of the principle of self-ownership. That principle contradicts the idea that there should be an equality of benefits and burdens among people. Marxists are, of course, very friendly to the latter idea: it occupies a larger place in their hearts than does the principle of self-ownership, which they should reject. The egalitarian idea suggests that the infirm person's possession and use of his capital is blameless, which implies that there is no injustice in it, and that implies that the Marxist doctrine of exploitation is an overgeneralization. The egalitarian thing to say about the case is that no person should be left to die and that it is a piece of luck for the worker that he has sufficient labour capacity to sustain both himself and someone who, if unsupported, would die. It is also a piece of luck for the infirm capitalist that he has the power, through his ownership of capital, to exact support from the worker, and, in the given idiosyncratic circumstances, there is nothing wrong with his having and using that power.[12] Exploiting a person is taking unfair advantage of him. The infirm capitalist takes advantage of the joyful worker, but not an unfair one.

4. Through their uncompromising line on the capital/labour relationship, Marxists come implicitly to accept the notion of self-ownership. But that notion is, as we have seen,[13] the foundation of libertarianism, which is a reactionary position in contemporary political philosophy. According to libertarianism, the welfare state does to tax-paying workers exactly what, in the Marxist complaint, capitalists do to workers: it forcibly extracts product from them, and, libertarians would add, without benefit of the contract that workers sign with capitalists. Since Marxists regard that contract as a sham, they need not agree that welfare state extraction is *worse* than capitalist extraction. But their theory of exploitation makes it hard for them to regard it as *just*. For they cannot deny that the welfare state makes the productive worker do by force of law what he does for the capitalist by force of circumstance.[14]

---

[12] Needless to say, the above statement implies no retreat from the proposition that a *society* founded on minority private ownership of the means of production is unjust; and the peculiar example which I used to make a key conceptual point has no policy consequences for socialists, who favour a society in which infirm people would obtain support as a matter of basic right.

[13] See Chapter 3, section 1, above.

[14] Some socialists think that it suffices in rebuttal of Nozick's claim that taxation is forced labour to point out that, unlike a slave, the taxpayer is not forced to *labour*, but only to yield

Thus libertarians lay siege to, and embarrass, Marxists in political philosophy. For it is hard to see how welfare state extraction from a worker could be justified if the infirm capitalist's extraction is not. And it is, I conjecture, the difficulty Marxists have with that sort of analogy which explains why so much energy has been, and is now, devoted to political philosophy by me and some of my colleagues. We have to rethink the theory of exploitation in a fundamental way, in order to condemn neither the redistribution enforced by the welfare state, nor, *a fortiori*, the still more egalitarian redistributive dispensations which, as Marxists, or semi-Marxists, we endorse.

I have rejected (see p. 150) the suggestion that the Marxist complaint about the exploited worker is not that his self-ownership rights are violated but just that he is wrongfully *forced* to yield his labour to the capitalist. Suppose now that I am mistaken, and that what Marxists deplore in the capitalist relationship is *just* that it forces the worker to put in time for the capitalist. (This means supposing that I am wrong to think that Marxian rhetoric about theft and robbery implies commitment to a principle of self-ownership and also wrong in the argument I build on the joyful worker/infirm capitalist case.) Then a libertarian challenge to Marxists would still apply, namely, why is it not similarly wrong to force the taxpayer to put in time for the state?

I am, accordingly, offering a general hypothesis and also a more specific one which entails it but on which it does not depend. The general hypothesis is that the reason why Marxists are vulnerable to libertarians is that it looks as though the latter can say about worker taxpayers in the welfare state what Marxists say about workers exploited by capitalists. The specific hypothesis adds that the relevant statement about exploited workers is that their self-ownership rights are violated. The general hypothesis survives replacement of that specific hypothesis by the alternative that the relevant statement about workers is that they are forced to engage in unrequited labour.

5. I now want to deal with two objections to what I have said. The first objection is based on the political activity of Marxists, and the second is based on their description of the communist future.

The first objection is that the communist movement was, in many

product *if* she labours. I doubt that they would also say, as consistency requires, that the proletarian is, similarly, not forced to *labour* for the capitalist, but only to yield product to him, *if* she labours.

countries, including my native Canada, in the forefront of the struggle for the welfare state. And communists never experienced any intellectual difficulty in sustaining their commitment to that struggle. But how could that have been so, if I am right that there is a serious tension between the justification of the welfare state and the Marxist doctrine of exploitation? How does their struggle for the welfare state square with my attribution to Marxists of a self-ownership principle which the welfare state violates?

And the second and somewhat related objection is that the rule which governs distribution in the Marxist ideal society, communism, seems to contradict the principle of self-ownership. The communist rule says 'From each according to his ability, to each according to his needs',[15] and its first part seems to impose a duty to labour for society which is inconsistent with the self-ownership principle.

The fact that the communist movement promoted the welfare state does not, in my view, present any problem for my claims. For communists saw the struggle for the welfare state as a struggle for basic minima for *working* people in particular: public provision was regarded as a modest rectification of the wrongs done to labour with respect to the product of its activity, its products being (in the words of the song an excerpt from which forms the epigraph of this chapter) 'the wonders [it had] made'.[16] In 'Solidarity Forever', the outcast and starving people who need the welfare state are the very people who created the wealth of society. Compare the famous American lamentation of the 1930s, 'Buddy, Can you Spare a Dime'. The man says 'Once I built a railroad, made it run . . . once I built a tower, up to the sun', and those creations are supposed to show that he should have at least a dime.

In the lines of those songs, people do not demand relief from starvation on the ground that they cannot produce but on the ground that they have produced and should therefore not be left to starve. Two claims to recompense, *need* and *entitlement through labour*, are fused, in a fashion typical of the communist rhetoric of the time in the 'Solidarity' verse which forms the epigraph to this chapter. It was possible to fuse them at the time when the song was written because revolutionaries and progressives saw the set of exploited producers as roughly coterminous

---

15 'The Critique of the Gotha Programme', p. 325.
16 A Marxist with a strong commitment to *The Communist Manifesto* might find it difficult to justify welfare state provision for the chronically unemployed and unproducing lumpen-proletariat. Here is how the *Manifesto* describes them: 'the "dangerous class", the social scum, that passively rotting mass thrown off by the lowest layers of old society may, here and there, be swept into the movement by a proletarian revolution; its conditions of life, however, prepare it far more for the part of a bribed tool of reactionary intrigue' (p. 494).

with the set of those who needed the welfare state's benefits. Accordingly they did not sense any conflict between the producer entitlement doctrine implied by the second part of the third line ('Mid the wonders we have made') and the egalitarian doctrine suggested in its first part ('Now, we stand outcast and starving'), when it is read on its own. For it does not require much argument to show that there is indeed a difference of principle between the appeals in the two parts of the line. Starving people are not necessarily people who have produced what starving people need, and, if what people produce belongs as of right to them, the people who have produced it, then starving people who have not produced it have no claim on it. The old image of the working class, as a set of people who *both* make the wealth *and* do not have it, conceals, in its fusion of those characteristics, the poignant and problematic truth that the two claims to sustenance, namely, 'I made this and I should therefore have it' and 'I need this, I will die or wither if I do not get it' are not only different but potentially contradictory pleas.[17] The libertarian trick is to turn the first plea against the second.

That they created the wonders and that they were outcast and starving were two of four characteristics which communists perceived in the working class in the heyday of the communist movement. The four features never belonged to any single set of people anywhere, but there used to be enough convergence among them for an impression of their coincidence to be sustainable, given a dose of enthusiasm and a bit of self-deception. The communist impression of the working class was that its members

1 constituted the majority of society
2 produced the wealth of society
3 were the exploited people in society, and
4 were the needy people in society.

There were, moreover, in the same impression, two further characteristics consequent on those four. The workers were *so* needy that they

5 would have nothing to lose from revolution, whatever its upshot might be

[17] Cf. Anton Menger, *The Right to the Whole Produce of Labour*, p. 5: 'Any attempt to carry to a logical conclusion the idea of the labourer's right to the whole produce of his labour is immediately confronted with the numerous persons who are incapable of work (children, the aged and invalids, etc.), and who must depend for the satisfaction of their wants on unearned income'. Cf. *ibid.*, pp. 28, 109.

and, because of 1, 2 and 5, it was within the capacity (1, 2) and in the interest (5) of the working class to change society, so that it

6 could and would transform society.

I shall use these names to denote the six features: *majority, production, exploitation, need, nothing-to-lose* and *revolution*.

Many of the present problems of Marxism, and, indeed, of the British Labour Party,[18] reflect the increasing lack of coincidence of the first four characteristics. Of special relevance to this chapter is the coming apart of the exploitation and need features. It forces a choice between a principle of self-ownership embedded in the doctrine of exploitation and a principle of equality of benefits and burdens which negates the self-ownership principle and which is required to defend support for very needy people who are not producers and who are, *a fortiori*, not exploited.[19]

If you can get yourself to believe that the features cohere, you then have a very powerful political posture.[20] You can say to democrats that they

---

[18] Every Labour Party membership card still reproduces the fabled phrase from 'Clause IV' of Labour's constitution, which promises 'to secure for workers by hand or by brain the full fruits of their labour'. If that promise were fulfilled, then full-time single parents, infirm people and other unemployables would get nothing.

[19] Which here means just that they do not work more hours than are necessary to produce what they consume. It is here irrelevant that they may nevertheless be exploited in some broader sense.

[20] That posture is struck in 'Solidarity Forever', which brings all of the features together, and whose verses run as follows:

> When the union's inspiration through the workers' blood shall run,
> There can be no power greater anywhere beneath the sun;
> Yet what force on earth is weaker than the feeble strength of one,
> For the union makes us strong.

> It is we who ploughed the prairies, built the cities where they trade,
> Dug the mines and built the workshops, endless miles of railroad laid;
> Now we stand outcast and starving, 'mid the wonders we have made,
> But the union makes us strong.

> They have taken untold millions that they never toiled to earn,
> But without our brain and muscle not a single wheel can turn;
> We can break their haughty power, gain our freedom when we learn
> That the union makes us strong.

> In our hands is placed a power greater than their hoarded gold,
> Greater than the might of atoms magnified a thousandfold;
> We can bring to birth a new world from the ashes of the old,
> For the union makes us strong.

Feature 1, that the workers constitute the majority of society, is not explicitly affirmed, but it is surely implied as part of the explanation of the immense potential power of the working class asserted in the first, third and fourth stanzas. The other part of the should embrace socialism, because workers form the immense majority of the population. You can say the same to humanitarians, because workers suffer tremendous need. And, very importantly, you are under less pressure than you otherwise would be to worry about the exact ideals and principles of socialism, and that is so for two reasons. The first is that, when the features are seen to cohere, several kinds of normative principle will justify a struggle for socialism, and there is then no practical urgency about identifying which principle or principles are essential: from a practical point of view, such discussion will appear unnecessary, and a waste of political energy. And the second reason for not worrying too much about principles, when the features (seem to) cohere, is that you do not then need to recruit people to the socialist cause by articulating principles which will draw them to it: success of the cause is guaranteed, by the majority, production and nothing-to-lose features.

It is partly because there is now patently no group that has those features and, therefore, the revolution feature that Marxists, or what were Marxists, are increasingly impelled to enter normative political philosophy. The disintegration of the characteristics induces an intellectual need to philosophize which is related to a political need to be clear as never before about values and principles, for the sake of socialist advocacy. Normative socialist advocacy is less necessary when the features coincide. You do not have to justify a socialist transformation as a matter of principle when people are driven to make it by the urgencies of their situation, and in a good position to succeed.

Each of characteristics 1–4 is now the leading motif in a certain kind of left-wing or post-left-wing politics in Britain. First, there is (what is sometimes called *rainbow*) majority politics, adopted by socialists who recognize the disintegration and look to generate a majority for social change out of heterogeneous elements: badly paid workers, the unemployed, oppressed races, people oppressed because of their gender or their sexual preference, neglected old people, single-parent families and so forth. (Many of those people suffer special need, but they are not selected because they are the neediest people, as such.) Ernesto Laclau and

---

explanation of that power is that the workers are the producers, as the second stanza, and the all-important second line of the third, assure us. The feature of exploitation is apparent in the first line of the third stanza, and the third line of the second indicates how utterly deprived the workers are, no doubt on such a scale that the fifth feature (nothing-to-lose) obtains. As for the revolution feature, the third lines of each of the last two verses, and the second of the first, imply that the workers *can* change society, and it is clearly part of the message of the whole song that they will.

Chantal Mouffe seek to theorize this perspective.[21] A producer politics with reduced emphasis on exploitation characterized the Wilsonian rhetoric of 1964, which promised a melting away of reactionary British structures in the 'white heat' of a technological transformation of the country in which an alliance of proletarian and highly educated producers would overcome the power of City and landed and other drones.[22] Producer politics projects a Saint-Simonian alliance of workers and high-tech producers with greater emphasis on the parasitism of those who do not produce than on the exploitation of those who do (since some of the high fliers who fall within the Saint-Simonian inclusion could hardly be regarded as exploited).[23] An exploitation politics, with a degree of pretence that the other features are still there, characterizes various forms of obsolescent Scargillian labourism.[24] And, finally, there is the need-centred politics of welfare rights action, a politics of those who think that suffering has the first claim on radical energy and who devote it to new organizations such as Shelter, the Child Poverty Action Group, Age Concern, and the panoply of groups which confront world-wide hunger, deprivation, and injustice. Such organizations did not exist when the disintegration was less advanced and the labour movement and the welfare movement were pretty well identical. (Philanthropic activity on

[21] See their *Hegemony and Socialist Strategy*. A meticulous critique of their over-reactive retreat from traditional Marxist claims is provided by Norman Geras in 'Post-Marxism?'. For a less meticulous critique, see Chapter 4 of *The Retreat from Class*, by the enraged Ellen Meiksins Wood. Wood is right that those who say *Farewell to the Working Class* (the title of a book by André Gorz) fail to identify an agency of change comparable to the working class, as it was traditionally conceived, in power. But she exaggerates the extent to which the traditional agency is intact: see the features she attributes to the working class at pp. 14–15 of her book. It may be crazy to forgo the traditional agency and then say 'business (more or less) as usual', but Wood says 'business as usual' without forgoing the traditional agency, and that could be regarded as crazier.

[22] The phrase 'white heat of technology' was actually used without irony in the 1964 parliamentary election campaign.

[23] The Wilson wheeze was revived by Michael Meacher, in an article in *The Guardian* which appeared less than a fortnight after Labour's 1987 election defeat. According to Meacher, 'Labour cannot regain power simply by relying on its traditional manual worker vote . . . It is the technocratic class – the semi-conductor "chip" designers, the computer operators, the industrial research scientists, the high-tech engineers – who hold the key to Britain's future. That is the class that Labour must champion and bring to power.' Meacher contrasts his faith in that group's possibilities with two alternative bases of Labour power: a 'Rainbow Coalition of minorities', and 'the growing underclass of have-nots'. It is depressing that a figure who is usually regarded as on the *left* of the Labour Party should depart so expressly from an egalitarian perspective.

[24] The present account sheds some light on how and why that form of politics is disastrous when it is obsolete. Old-style revolutionary labourism plays the bourgeois *force majeure* bargaining game: 'Give us the means of production or we'll go on permanent general strike.' When the capitalists can reply, 'Fine, we don't need you any more, go on strike', then it is time to forsake might and think about right.

behalf of deprived children, the homeless and the indigent old long predates the founding of the organizations named above, but they pursue their aims in a spirit not of providing charity but of rectifying injustice; injustice, moreover, which cannot be brought under the concept of exploitation.)

6. I now turn to the second objection to my attribution to Marxists of the self-ownership thesis, which is that the principle governing distribution under communism ('From each according to his ability, to each according to his needs') contradicts it. I shall call it the 'communist objection'. There are two answers to it.[25]

First, one may concede that the communist principle indeed contradicts the thesis of self-ownership, while denying that this undermines the attribution of that thesis to Marxists. One may, in short, take the view that a thesis to which Marxists are committed by their critique of capitalism contradicts the principle Marxists themselves legislate for communism. For the communism objection does not address the *argument* for attributing the self-ownership thesis to Marxists (see sections 2 and 3 above), and it therefore does not exclude this first response.

But there is a reply to this first answer to the communism objection. It is that, in drawing implicitly on the self-ownership thesis, the Marxist critique of capitalism is *ad hominem*: it is a critique which aims to hoist capitalism on its own petard, without, as it were, affirming that petard, and, therefore, without generating self-contradiction in the total Marxist doctrine.

I now offer three rejoinders to this reply to my first answer to the communism objection. The first rejoinder begins by noting that the afore-stated reply does not deny that Marxists *employ* the self-ownership thesis:

---

[25] The argumentation of this section is complicated, and readers may find this summary of its course helpful:

The communism objection: The communist principle contradicts the thesis of self-ownership, which therefore cannot be attributed to Marxists.

My first answer: If the communist principle contradicts the self-ownership thesis, then perhaps Marxists contradict themselves.

Objector's reply: They do not contradict themselves, since they invoke self-ownership only in an *ad hominem* way.

My first rejoinder: They nevertheless ceaselessly employ it, and that might be enough to explain their vulnerability to libertarianism.

My second rejoinder: The *ad hominem* gambit does not work.

My third rejoinder: Merely *ad hominem* use of the self-ownership thesis would not explain the passion which accompanies the Marxist claim that the worker is robbed.

My second answer to the communism objection: The communist principle does not, in fact, contradict the self-ownership thesis.

it grants that they employ it while denying that they believe it. But habitual, systematic employment of the self-ownership thesis, even if it does not express or issue in full-hearted belief, could generate a serious confusion of purpose which suffices to explain Marxist vulnerability to libertarianism. My second rejoinder is that the hoisting of capitalism on its own petard will not, in fact, work: I shall show in section 8 that you cannot condemn capitalism on the bourgeois grounds that condemn serfdom. Finally -- and this is my third and decisive rejoinder -- it is implausible that the passion which accompanies the Marxist assertion that the worker is robbed of his substance is confected for *ad hominem* purposes. That would mean that Marxists do not really think that the serf is being robbed, since, unless their use of the *ad hominem* gambit is dishonest, they must believe that the situations of the serf and the proletarian are truly parallel.

My second answer to the communism objection withdraws the concession I made in the first one. This is the answer I prefer, because, as I have explained in section 3 of Chapter 5, I think it is a misinterpretation of the communist principle to see in it a denial of self-ownership. The communist citizen who conducts himself 'just as he has a mind'[26] *is* effectively sovereign over himself.

It is, in fact, harder (though not impossible), from the perspective of the claims of this chapter, to accommodate what Marx says in *The Critique of the Gotha Programme* about the lower stage of communism, or what later came to be called socialism. For, in that society, there unquestionably *is* some abridgement of the principle of self-ownership. But for a fuller discussion of both stages of communism, in relation to Marxian failure to repudiate the idea of self-ownership, I must, once again, refer the reader back to section 3 of Chapter 5.

7. So much in rebuttal of two objections to my attribution of the self-ownership thesis to Marxists. I now resume my main theme.

When those who suffer dire need can be conceived as coinciding with, or as a subset of, the exploited working class, then the Marxist doctrine of exploitation does not cause much difficulty for the Marxist principle of distribution according to need. But, once the really needy and the exploited producers cease to coincide, then the Marxist doctrine of exploitation is flagrantly incongruent with even the minimal principle

---

[26] Marx and Engels, *The German Ideology*, p. 47.

of the welfare state. Marxist anxiety about libertarianism is a reflection in thought of the separation of features 3 and 4 (see p. 154 above) going on in fact. And one may say, without exaggeration, that libertarians have forced Marxists to be more consistent egalitarians. (Much of the recent work of John Roemer, and, in particular, his claim that exploitation lacks fundamental normative significance, can be understood in this perspective.)[27]

An attempt to pursue a consistent egalitarianism in political philosophy will be found within the literature of contemporary liberalism, which Marxists must, accordingly, address. Unlike Marxists, liberals enjoy a degree of immunity to the Nozick challenge. Suppose that one enters political philosophy not as a Marxist but as a liberal of the Brian Barry or Ronald Dworkin or John Rawls or Thomas Scanlon sort. Then one does not conceive oneself as the intellectual representative of a particular class or movement. One can consequently think about the big issues in political philosophy without that sort of constraint on one's reflections, and, in particular, one consequently does not begin with the exploitation paradigm. The liberals that I have named begin with more widely focused concerns both with respect to the possible sites of injustice and with respect to the possible modes of injustice. In thinking about those sites and modes they go immediately for a principle of equality, and much of their work is an attempt to explicate its content. They will apply that principle of equality to, among other things, the relationship between capital and labour, and that will lead to criticisms, of many kinds, of various instances of the relationship. Some of the criticism will reflect a sensitivity to the egalitarian value of democracy, and so we get liberal critiques of the capital/labour relationship from authors like Michael Walzer[28] and Robert Dahl[29] which focus not on exploitation but on the undemocratic character of relations in the capitalist workplace. Also possible is a Rawlsian critique of capitalism (suggested to me by Tim Scanlon) under which its use of unemployment to keep the economy in smooth motion is condemned as a serious violation of the Difference Principle. Since the unemployed are not, while unemployed, producing anything, Marxists can bring them under their paradigm of injustice only by representing them as temporary outcasts from the exploited working class: Marxists

[27] See John Roemer, 'Should Marxists be Interested in Exploitation?'. For criticism of the Roemer article, see section 6 of Chapter 8 below.
[28] See his *Spheres of Justice*, pp. 117–19, 161–3, 301–3.
[29] See his *Preface to Economic Democracy*.

tend to represent the unemployed as disemployed.[30] But, for liberals like Scanlon, the fact that they are denied the opportunity to produce suffices to establish the injustice of their situation: there is no pressure to represent them as erstwhile producers who are idling.

Those are examples of possible severe liberal criticisms of capitalism, about the details of which there is plenty of room for dispute. What is, however, indisputable is that, since liberals do not take the injustice of the capitalist relationship in its general form as a datum, they have no consequent propensity to accept the principle of self-ownership.

8. The contrast between the vulnerability of Marxists and the security of liberals on the topic of production and justice is nicely brought out by the case of what I shall call 'cleanly generated capitalist relationships'. In a cleanly generated capitalist relationship there is, as there always is in a capitalist relationship, a capital-lacking worker on one side and a capital-endowed capitalist on the other, but the relationship is cleanly generated in that here the differential endowment is the upshot of a history which begins with equal capital endowment in a context of self-ownership and which reaches its capitalist stage as a result of no force or fraud but of the greater frugality and/or talent of those who come to have all the capital.

Such relationships trouble Marxists deeply. For they will want to say that even in such a relationship the worker is unjustly exploited. They need to say that, on pain of giving up the claim that the capitalist relationship is inherently unjust. Yet, given their commitment to self-ownership, on what basis can Marxists complain about clean capitalist relationships? Those relationships derive from equality of external resources in the context of self-ownership. The Marxist cannot object to the self-ownership component of the derivation, since he implicitly affirms the rights of self-ownership himself. But it would be absurd for the Marxist to reject the

---

[30] As in the left-wing song, 'The Banks of Marble', by Les Rice:

> I saw the seaman standing, idly by the shore,
> I heard the bosses saying, 'Got no work for you no more'.

The song concerns disemployed farmers, miners and seamen, but it says nothing about those who never had a chance to farm, mine or work at sea in the first place. Those who never had such opportunities fall outside the set of 'my brothers working' who will 'together make a stand' so that they will come to own what they have 'sweated for'.

For a brilliant attempt to treat the unemployed not as disemployed but as a class more or less permanently deprived of 'job assets', see Philippe Van Parijs, 'A Revolution in Class Theory'. Van Parijs points out that 'the unemployed would gain much more from a redistribution of jobs than from a redistribution of wealth' (*ibid.*, p. 469).

initial external resource equality, given Marxism's strong opposition to inequality of access to means of production.[31] Accordingly, the Marxist is hoist with *his* own petard. The principle he implicitly relies on to establish the claim that the worker is exploited here operates to subvert that very claim. Let e = in any capitalist relationship the worker is unjustly exploited, and let s be the self-ownership thesis. The Marxist's account of e (his condemnation of the capitalist as a thief) shows that he is committed to s, and, if I am right in my reflection on the case of the infirm capitalist, there is no way of asserting e without affirming s. But the case of the cleanly generated capitalist relationship shows that s disproves e. So, if e is true, s is true; but, if s is true, e is false. And that is a *reductio ad absurdum* of the Marxist claim that propertyless workers are, as such, exploited.

Liberals, by contrast, experience no difficulty with the case of cleanly generated capitalist relationships. They do not need to say that they are exploitative, but they are also not disabled from saying that they are. If, for certain reasons, liberals want to condemn (some) clean capitalist relationships, no commitment to self-ownership obstructs them. According to Ronald Dworkin, or so I would interpret him, clean capitalist relationships are not unjust when they come about wholly because people of comparable material endowment and personal capacity have different preferences; but they are probably unjust when and because they reflect differences of talent. The latter statement contradicts the self-ownership thesis.

The way Marxists get hoist with their own petard in the matter of cleanly generated capitalist relationships is a consequence of a failed attempt on their part to hoist the bourgeois defence of capitalism with *its* own petard. Marxists have always relished the idea of exposing capitalism in the light of bourgeois ideology itself. They would like to show that only a false account of capitalism can make it pass muster under its own justifying ideology. They try to condemn capitalism on the ground that it violates self-ownership, or bourgeois liberty: the labour contract, they say, is *fictio juris*, for it conceals a relationship substantially similar to the one

---

[31] An egalitarian might reject initial external resource equality on the ground that resources need to be differentially distributed to compensate for talent differences. But that ground of rejection of resource equality requires denial of the tenet, derived from the thesis of self-ownership, that people are entitled to the differential rewards which (uncompensated for) talent differences produce, and is therefore unavailable to Marxists. (There is more to be said about how, precisely, the Marxian condemnation of unequal access to means of production is related to the Marxian condemnation of extraction of surplus product: see Chapter 8 below.)

between lord and serf. But, however true that may be for the case of a worker dispossessed of resources from the start, it has no purchase against cleanly generated capitalist relationships, and there is enough cleanliness in actually existing capitalism to discommode a critique of it which rests on the bourgeois self-ownership principle. (Banks will advance capital to people who are manifestly endowed with entrepreneurial talent even when they can put up only modest collateral.)

Because they lack the disabling commitment to self-ownership which burdens Marxists, contemporary liberal philosophers do not find libertarians like Nozick challenging. Their attitude to him was expressed in the title of Thomas Nagel's review of *Anarchy, State, and Utopia*: 'Libertarianism Without Foundations'. Liberals are unimpressed by what they regard as Nozick's unargued affirmation of self-ownership rights. Marxists find it difficult to dismiss Nozick as readily as liberals do, since they tend themselves to use self-ownership in a foundational way.

Since the liberals I have named find Nozick undisturbing, they show surprise at how seriously people like myself and Jon Elster and John Roemer and Philippe Van Parijs take him. They think that, being to their left, we should find Nozick even less disturbing. But I think that we find him more disturbing because of the particular way in which we are to the left of the liberals. We are to their left because of our attitude to the capitalist relationship, but that attitude turns out to be sustainable in its pristine form only if self-ownership is affirmed. (Not *if* and only if, since if it is affirmed, then the Marxist attitude to capitalism is not sustainable, for the reasons given in my discussion of clean capitalist relationships.)

One thing that might follow from all this is that the liberals, through being less vulnerable to the libertarian challenge, are therefore also less well placed to appreciate its force. Because they have no belief of their own in self-ownership to exorcize, the decisive encounter with libertarianism must be joined by us rather than by them. And, in my view, Dworkin, Nagel and Rawls do not take Nozick seriously enough to do what is necessary to defeat his position.[32] Through serious confrontation with Nozick, Marxists may hope not only to refute him[33] but also, thereby, to

[32] Relevant failures by liberals to take self-ownership seriously are discussed in section 9 of Chapter 4 above and in sections 3 and 5 of Chapter 9 below.
[33] One way of undermining Nozick's case for self-ownership is to distinguish carefully between the idea of self-ownership and the idea of freedom: see Chapter 4, section 6 above, and Chapter 10, section 3 below. Being more prone than egalitarian liberals are to confuse these two ideas, Marxists are also more strongly motivated than they are to expose the roots of that confusion.

reach a deeper characterization of their own conception of justice than the one associated with undiscriminating use of the traditional idea of exploitation.[34]

---

[34] In 'Self-Ownership, Reciprocity, and Exploitation, or: Why Marxists Shouldn't be Afraid of Robert Nozick', Paul Warren mounts a comprehensive critique of the article-predecessor of this chapter. He argues against my claim that (1) the Marxist conception of exploitation leans in the direction of the principle of self-ownership, and, independently, against my distinct claim that (2) the principle of self-ownership is inconsistent with Marxist distributive egalitarianism. I am unconvinced by each of Warren's criticisms, and I note with satisfaction that, at his fn. 20, he comes close to acknowledging that they are inconsistent with one another. I am more impressed by the positive part of Warren's article, which defends a *marxisant* notion of capitalist exploitation on the basis of a certain norm of reciprocity.

7. Marx and Locke on land and labour

... labour makes the far greatest part of the value of things we enjoy in this world. And the ground which produces the materials is scarce to be reckoned in as any, or at most but a very small, part of it ... (John Locke, *Second Treatise of Government*)

1. We have seen[1] that the axial distinction between self-ownership and world-ownership generates three views about the powers of nature and the powers of people. The views differ according as they do or do not encourage an egalitarian approach to the substances and capacities of nature on the one hand, and to the powers of people to modify nature on the other.

There are, first, those who defend an egalitarian approach to both natural resources and human labour. They argue that talented people are merely lucky to be so, and that, to counter the unjustly unequalizing influence of that luck, not only what nature produces but also the product of the powers of people should be distributed according to principles of equality (of, perhaps, in the two cases, appropriately different kinds). John Rawls and Ronald Dworkin are leading exponents of this position.

Others, however, such as Robert Nozick, oppose egalitarianism with respect to both human and non-human productive capacity. Nozick claims that, to avoid endorsement of the slavery which he thinks implicit in an egalitarian attitude to people's powers, each person must control his own powers and their products. He holds, moreover, that people exercise their powers legitimately when they gather to themselves virtually unrestricted amounts of unowned natural resources. That legitimate gathering justifies a skewed distribution of resources, the inequality of which is increased by the fact that Nozick's individuals are entitled not

---

[1] See, especially, section 1 of Chapter 5 above.

only to what they have themselves taken, but also to the takings of others which come to them by way of trade or gift.

It is possible, finally, to attempt an intermediate course, in which a Nozickian principle of self-ownership is conjoined with an egalitarian regime over the resources of nature only. In Chapters 3–6, I have commented on that third approach, which might be called *partial egalitarianism*, to contrast it with the comprehensive egalitarianism of Rawls and Dworkin on the one hand, and the comprehensive anti-egalitarianism of Nozick on the other. I have asked how far one can go, in the direction of some sort of final equality of condition, on the basis of an egalitarianism of external resources which concedes each person's sovereignty over herself.

My interest in partial egalitarianism reflects a left-wing political sympathy. It is good strategy for a socialist to postpone engagement against the beguiling idea that each individual should decide what is to be done with his own person and powers. Leftists should proceed, initially, as partial egalitarianism does, by rejecting only that part of right-wing thinking which is relatively easy to reject, namely, its cavalier treatment of external resources, which so readily become, in right-wing thinking, unequal private property. In the end, so we have seen, socialists will have to place some limits on people's claims to self-ownership, since they will not otherwise be able to secure as much equality of condition[2] as they believe to be justified. But I believe that they can move far further in the direction of equality of condition from a merely partial egalitarian starting point than many seem to think. For many suppose that the first thing socialists must do is deny self-ownership, and that the debate between left and right is primarily about the rights individuals have over themselves, against the claims of other people. That way of posing the key political question is too kind to the right: it leaves the right's weak side out of consideration.

2. In this chapter I expound and criticize a pair of arguments, which derive from John Locke's *Second Treatise of Government*, and which threaten to undermine the hope that some support for equality of condition might come from an egalitarianism of worldly resources alone. But, before I turn to Locke, I want to describe an anomaly in Marxist views about distributive justice, which must be removed if Marxists are to avert the threat of Locke's arguments.

---

[2] Or, indeed, as much freedom and autonomy: see Chapter 10, section 3 below.

As everybody knows, Marxists believe in the labour theory of value, or, at any rate, fully orthodox Marxists believe in it, and they are the Marxists about whom I shall speak here. Such Marxists believe that the value of commodities is entirely due to the labour required for their production. And, because of their allegiance to the labour theory, Marxists must assert, and they do in fact assert, that the raw worldly resources to which labour is applied neither possess value, since labour did not create them, nor themselves create value, since they are not themselves labour. Marxists maintain, moreover, that profit on capital comes from exploitation of labour. Capitalists exploit workers when they appropriate part of the value which only the labour of workers can produce.

Yet when Marxists indicate how workers come to be exploited by capitalists, as opposed to what that exploitation consists in, they suddenly assign extreme importance to natural resources, as I now proceed to explain.

Slaves are exploited because they do not own their labour power, and serfs are exploited because they do not own all of it,[3] but wage-workers, who do own their labour power,[4] are exploited only because they own no means of production. They must therefore sell their labour power to capitalists, on adverse terms. Now most means of production are not raw natural resources, but products of labour, such as tools, machines, and already worked, or at least extracted, materials. But, since means of production which are not themselves natural resources are the product, in the end, of natural resources and labour power, 'the two primary creators of wealth',[5] and, since workers under capitalism do not lack ownership of their own labour power, it must, ultimately, in the Marxist view, be their lack of ownership of natural resources which accounts for their vulnerability to exploitation by capitalists.

In conformity with that line of thought, Marx is emphatic that the answer to the question, how workers come to be exploited, lies in facts about natural resources alone. His commitment to that answer shows up in his discussion of what he calls 'the secret of primitive accumulation', which reveals how exploiting capital came into being. Marx disparages

---

[3] See my *Karl Marx's Theory of History*, p. 65.

[4] It suffices here that they enjoy that ownership as a matter of formal legal fact, even if, because they own no means of production, they are *in effect* as lacking in self-ownership as serfs are: see Chapter 6, section 2 above.

[5] Marx, *Capital*, Vol. I, p. 752. Marx identifies those 'creators' as 'labour-power and land' (or, *ibid.*, as 'man and nature'), and he explains at *ibid.*, p. 758 that 'land' 'means, economically speaking, all the objects of labour furnished by nature without human intervention'.

the apologetic story in which it was a result of the industry and saving of a 'diligent, intelligent, and, above all, frugal elite'.[6] If that account were true, then a provident use of self-owned labour power, in the context of an initial equality of external resources, would have created capital. But, according to Marx, the truth is that capital came into being when and because exploitable labour did, as a consequence of the resource dispossession of pre-capitalist peasants. 'The expropriation of the . . . peasant from the soil was the basis of the whole process'.[7] Soil, however, is a natural resource, and it follows that, according to Marx, it was a critical loss of natural resources that generated the proletariat. (To be sure, only virgin soil is a natural resource in the strict sense required in this chapter, but it was not because his soil was cultivated that the peasant was exposed to exploitation when it was taken from him.)

It might be objected that, even if lack of land brought the proletariat into being, what they now signally lack are not raw resources but the means of production characteristic of established capitalism. And it is indeed true that, were they provided with those means, then exploitation would cease. But it does not follow that they need those advanced means to escape the necessity of contracting with capitalists. In Marx's account, they sell their labour power to capitalists because otherwise they die, and, if they need existing means of production to live well, a ruder resource provision might nevertheless suffice for them to avoid starvation. It is no doubt for this reason that Marx wrote, in a sentence whose topic was 'present-day' capitalism, and not its origin, that 'the monopoly of land is even the basis of the monopoly of capital'.[8]

But the objector could argue that the growth of population which capitalist productivity made possible means that there is no longer enough land per person for each to survive on the basis, initially, or raw resources alone. Yet, even if that is true, it is of questionable relevance in a discussion of the implications of *Marx*'s account of the basis of exploi-tation. It is, moreover, a controversial claim, when, as might be thought appropriate, the land endowment of the whole planet is taken into account. But suppose that it is indeed both true and relevant that contemporary workers would, because of their numbers, need relatively sophisticated means of production to escape exploitation. Then why did their forebears not furnish them with them, or with the wherewithal to make them? Not, of course, because they lacked the necessary labour

---

[6] *Capital*, Vol. I, pp. 873–4.   [7] *Ibid.*, p. 876.
[8] *The Critique of the Gotha Programme*, p. 321.

power, but because they, in turn, lacked means of production, having been furnished with none by their forbears, who were themselves similarly deprived: and so on, backwards in time. By reiterating that impeccably Marxist explanation of each proletarian generation's lack of means of production we arrive at an original loss of natural resources as the ultimate cause of the exploitability of today's proletariat.

Now there is an (at least) apparent tension here, between the extreme importance imputed to the distribution of worldly resources in the Marxist diagnosis of the root cause of exploitation, and the total unimportance of worldly resources in the Marxist account of the source of value. If raw worldly resources do not create or possess value, why should it matter that workers were deprived of them?

3. The Marxist diagnosis of the origin of exploitation is congenial to a policy of egalitarian redistribution. But the claim with which it is uneasily conjoined, to wit, that labour is the sole source of value, can be made to serve inegalitarian ends, and such are the ends which, we shall find, something *like* a labour theory of value is made to serve by John Locke.

To see how the falsehood of the proposition that labour creates value is encouraging from an egalitarian point of view, let us imagine that nature offers all its resources to us in the form of final consumption goods which there is no need to alter by labour. Suppose, that is, that anything physical which anybody wants comes from nature as a very ripe apple does when it falls from the tree on to a hungry person's lap. Under those benign conditions, labour would not be creating any value, and an equal distribution of worldly resources would tend to foster the final equality of condition which Marxists favour.[9] But in the real world the things we desire depend, in part, for their desirable qualities on labour. Hence, given that people are differentially good at labouring, we have here the makings of a justification of inequality of reward and circumstance, under which more redounds to the more productive and their chosen beneficiaries. Inequality of condition is harder to defend on the hypothesis that, or to the extent that, labour is *not* responsible for the value of commodities. In virtue of the comparative appeal of the self-ownership thesis, which

---

[9] Not everyone thinks, as I do, that Marxists are egalitarians. A good case for the proposition that Marx himself was not an egalitarian is made by Allen Wood in his 'Marx and Equality'. For pretty conclusive argument to the contrary, however, see Norman Geras, 'The Controversy About Marx and Justice', in his *Literature of Revolution*.

endorses the naturally unequal distribution of personal powers, and the comparative lack of appeal of a similarly unequal distribution of natural resources and energy, the claim people make to the fruits of their labour is the strongest possible basis for inequality of distribution.[10]

There is, then, a danger of discrepancy between Marxism's egalitarianism and Marxism's depreciation of the role of non-labour inputs in the formation of value. To sustain their egalitarianism, orthodox Marxists must distinguish their position from a Locke-like one which asserts both the pre-eminent place of labour in value creation and the labourer's right to his labour and hence to its products.

There are, in principle, two ways out of this dilemma. The first is to reduce the significance of labour in the account of value creation. But that means giving up the labour theory of value, and, therefore, extinguishing orthodox Marxism. The other, and seemingly more eligible, way out is to deny the labourer's claim to his product. This path seems more open, but two obstacles lie upon it. The first is that, if Marxists deny that the worker has a right to his product, they must then explain why they nevertheless think he counts as exploited, yet they do not usually offer any such alternative explanation.[11] And the second obstacle is that Marxists are, for political reasons, reluctant forthrightly to deny the principle of self-ownership, since they would lose allies if they did so. One expression of that reluctance is the Marxist attachment to the diagnosis of the cause of exploitation which I described in the last section. When Marxists trace exploitation to the producers' dispossession of worldly resources, they account for it without denying self-ownership, and they thereby attract left-libertarian (that is, partial egalitarian) support to the anti-capitalist

[10] Consider a fantasy world in which nature contributes nothing to human satisfaction, and which is therefore relevantly opposite in character to the labourless one figured in the above paragraph. In this second imaginary world, people float in space, and all necessary and luxury services take the form of other people touching them in various ways. For simplicity, suppose that all get the same satisfactions, in the same degree, from the same touchings: this is not a world of different strokes for different folks. But it is a world of different strokes *from* different folks. For although utility functions are identical, talent endowments (capacities to touch well) are not. Under self-ownership of talent, gifted touchers will get more stroking by others than they have to dish out, since the stroking they provide is of such rare quality, and there will consequently be enormous inequality in the distribution of what people care about, which is, on the positive side, the strokes they get, and, on the negative, the effort of stroking others. This inequality cannot be traced to unequal division of non-human resources, since no such resources are in play here. It is far more difficult to object to inequality in this world than it is to object to it in the labourless world described above.

[11] For a modest attempt at one see my 'Labour Theory of Value and the Concept of Exploitation', in *History, Labour, and Freedom*, p. 230 fn. 37.

cause.[12] But if I am right, Marxists can retain their distinctive account of value creation, and yet be egalitarians, only if they assert more difference between themselves and left-wing libertarians than they have found it convenient to do.

4. But now I must deal with an objection which informed partisans of Marxist economics would be eager to press. They would complain that, in the foregoing discussion, I rode roughshod over a crucial distinction, the distinction, namely, between (what Marxists call) *exchange-value* and *use-value*. The first, exchange-value, is the power of a thing to exchange against other things on the market, the measure of its power to do so being given by the number of things of any other kind for which it will exchange.[13] And exchange-value is different from use-value, which is the power of a thing to satisfy human desire, whether directly or indirectly. A thing satisfies desire indirectly when, for example, it is used to produce another thing which satisfies desire directly, in the sense that, to satisfy desire, that other thing need only be consumed. The term 'use-value' denotes, moreover, not only such a power, but also anything that has such a power, for it is a Marxian verbal convention that whatever *has* a use-value *is* a use-value. Hence anything which contributes to the satisfaction of desire is a use-value, and so, for example, a tract of fertile land both has and is a use-value, since it may be used to produce a use-valuable crop.

Now the Marxist critic would remind me that the labour theory of value is a theory of exchange-value only. The theory does not pretend to explain why a commodity has the amount of use-value it does, but only why it exchanges against a certain number of other use-values on the market. The labour theory's answer to that question is that market exchange ratios are, in the final analysis, a function of the amounts of labour required to produce commodities. And while Marx did say that labour alone creates

[12] For characterizations of partial egalitarianism and left libertarianism, see, respectively, p. 166 above and pp. 118–19 of Chapter 5. Another expression of Marxist reluctance to reject the principle of self-ownership is the Marxist account of communism: see Chapter 5, section 3.

[13] I here give Marx's initial definition of exchange-value, as we find it in the opening pages of Vol. I of *Capital*. Later, he implicitly and cheatingly redefines it, in terms of labour time, and thereby turns what was supposed to be the *explanans* of exchange-value into a combined *explanans/explanandum*, a manœuvre that renders the labour theory of value tautologous. Under the original definition of exchange-value, virgin land would possess some, but it loses it under the tautologizing redefinition. (Marx's illicit definitional transition is discussed at pp. 221–6 of my 'Labour Theory of Value and the Concept of Exploitation', in *History, Labour, and Freedom*. See also pp. 325–8 of my 'More on Exploitation and the Labour Theory of Value'.)

exchange-value, he amply acknowledged that land, or nature, contributes to use-value, and he was contemptuous of socialists who denied that truth. He criticized the German socialists for opening their Gotha Programme of 1874 with the declaration that 'labour is the source of all wealth and all culture', and admonished them that 'nature is just as much the source of use-values as labour' is.[14] Labour alone produces exchange-value, but nothing has exchange-value unless it has use-value, and, since natural resources are needed to produce use-value, they are a presupposition of the creation of exchange-value, even though they do not themselves have or create any. Thereby, so my Marxist critic would conclude, the seeming tension of which I spoke at the end of section 2 is dissipated. The worker's lack of worldly resources sets the scene for his exploitation, even though exploitation is expropriation of exchange-value, and worldly resources neither possess nor create exchange-value. One can affirm both that labour is the source of all (exchange-) value and that, because of their immense use-value, inequality of natural resources is fateful and unjustified. Consequently, one can affirm the labour theory of value but also protest against the resource dispossession from which workers suffer. That answers the question at the end of section 2. And the dilemma constructed at the end of section 3 may also, now, be avoided. One can affirm the labour theory of value and yet call for egalitarian redistribution, without denying the principle of self-ownership, by emphasizing the importance of natural resources in the generation of use-value.

5. But this solution to the problems for orthodox Marxism which I raised in sections 2 and 3 will not work: the reminder that the labour theory is a theory of exchange-value is of no avail in the present context. For, as I have argued elsewhere,[15] the notion that labour creates exchange-value carries ideological weight only because it is confused with the distinct claim that Marxists officially deny, namely, that labour is the sole creator of the use-valuable product itself. It is only because Marxists (and also their opponents) conflate those two ideas that they are able to suppose that the labour theory of value is a suitable basis for raising a charge of exploitation against capitalists.

---

[14] *The Critique of the Gotha Programme*, p. 319. Marx interestingly here fails to mention non-natural means of production as a third source of use-value. This confirms the approach of section 2 above, in which such means are treated as deriving from the ultimate factors of production, which are land and labour.

[15] See 'The Labour Theory of Value and the Concept of Exploitation', in *History, Labour, and Freedom*, pp. 214–32.

To see how the conflation arises, notice, to begin with, that sentences like 'labour creates exchange-value' provide a merely metaphorical rendering of the labour theory of value. What the labour theory literally says is that the exchange-value of a commodity varies directly and uniformly with the amount of labour time required to produce commodities of its kind under currently standard conditions of production, and inversely and uniformly with the amount of labour time currently required to produce commodities of other kinds. That statement does not imply that labour creates anything. It is the amounts of labour time that *would* now be required to produce things, a certain set of counterfactual magnitudes, and not any actual sweating toil, which accounts for how much exchange-value things have, if the labour theory of value is true. The past history of a commodity, and, hence, how much labour was spent on it, or even whether any labour was spent on it, have strictly nothing to do with how much exchange-value it has. A commodity has a lot of exchange-value if a lot of labour would be required to replicate it, even if the commodity fell from the sky and therefore has no labour 'embodied' in it at all.

What was required in the past, and still more what happened in the past – these facts are irrelevant to how much exchange-value a commodity has, if the labour theory of value is true. But they are not epistemically irrelevant. For, since technical conditions change relatively slowly, the labour time required to produce something in the recent past is usually a good guide to the labour time required to produce it now. Typical past actual labour time is, moreover, the best guide to how much labour time was necessary in the past. Thereby what did occur, the labour actually spent, becomes a good index of what is now required, and, therefore, a good index of the exchange-value of the commodity. But it does not follow that, in any sense of 'creates', it creates the exchange-value of the commodity.

The creation metaphor widely used[16] to convey the labour theory of value makes people think that the theory says that workers produce something, and, since the most obvious candidate for something produced by workers is the physical product, the labour theory of value is, in the end, confused with the idea that the workers create the product itself. *It is, more-over, only because of that confusion that the labour theory attracts ideological*

---

[16] For example, by Marx. For a list of his uses of the metaphor, see 'The Labour Theory of Value and the Concept of Exploitation', in *History, Labour, and Freedom*, p. 216 fn. 14.

interest. It has none when it is clearly and distinctly conceived. For real ideological interest lies in claims about the creation of the use-valuable thing in which exchange-value inheres.

To see that this is so, suppose, by way of thought-experiment, that something other than counter-factual labour 'creates' exchange-value, in the very sense in which, in the labour theory, counter-factual labour 'creates' it. (I place scare-quotes around 'creates' in contexts where its use is, at best, metaphorical.) Imagine, in particular, that the magnitude of every commodity's exchange value is wholly determined by the extent and intensity of desire for it, and that we can therefore say that desire, not labour, 'creates' exchange-value.[17] But imagine, too, that labour creates the product itself, out of in all senses worthless raw materials, or – the product being a pure service – out of none. Do we now lose our inclination (supposing, of course, that a belief in the labour theory of value induced one in us) to sympathize with the labourer's claim to the product, and, hence, to its exchange-value, even though we are no longer supposing that labour 'creates' that exchange-value? I do not think that we do. The worker continues to look exploited if he creates the exchange-valuable thing and does not get all the exchange-value of the thing he creates. What matters, ideologically, is what creates that thing, or so transforms it that it has (more) exchange-value,[18] not what makes things of its sort have the amount of exchange-value they do, which is what the labour theory of value is really supposed to explain.

If I am right, the labour theory fulfils its ideological function only when it is mistaken for a theory that labour alone creates the product itself. But the latter theory is both false and hard to reconcile with the extreme importance (see section 2 above) assigned to non-labour resources in the Marxian diagnosis of what enables capitalists to exploit workers. It is because worldly resources *do* contribute to the creation of the product that they enjoy the importance they have in that diagnosis. The distinction between 'creating' exchange-value and creating the use-valuable product

---

[17] That desire 'creates' exchange-value may be untrue, but it is not an absurd supposition when, as here, it is the supposition that facts about desire, and not facts about socially necessary labour time, determine exchange-value ratios. The reader who finds absurd the idea that desire 'creates' exchange-value is probably himself confusing exchange-value 'creation' with product creation, and therefore confusing the idea that desire 'creates' exchange-value with the magical idea that it (really) creates the desired product.

[18] Whatever creates a valuable thing or enhances the value of a thing in *that* sense creates (some of) its value, but that is not the sense of 'creates value' in which labour is supposed to create value in the labour theory of value: see my 'Labour Theory of Value and the Concept of Exploitation', in *History, Labour, and Freedom*, pp. 232–3.

therefore provides no escape from the dilemma in which I sought to place orthodox Marxists at the end of section 3.

6. Recall that the third approach to distributive justice, partial egalitarianism (see section 1 above), does not restrict people's rights in their own powers, nor, therefore, in the fruits of the exercise of those powers. It follows that the third approach will not enable much movement in the direction of equality of condition if one can say that the things people want are largely the product of human labour, as opposed to of non-human resources. And that, to turn now to Locke, is precisely what he says. He claims that labour is responsible for virtually all of the use-value[19] of what human beings want or need, while natural resources are responsible for virtually none of it.

Some typical embodiments of Locke's claim:

. . . labour makes the far greatest part of the value of things we enjoy in this world. And the ground which produces the materials is scarce to be reckoned in as any, or at most but a very small part of it . . .

'Tis labour, then, which puts the greatest part of value upon land, without which it would scarcely be worth anything . . . Nature and the earth furnished only the most worthless materials, as in themselves.[20]

Uncultivated land creates virtually no value, and, Locke infers, it therefore possesses virtually no value. It is 'scarcely . . . worth anything', since it 'furnishe[s] the most worthless materials' only.

Locke repeatedly emphasizes the claims that labour creates almost all of the value of things and that natural resources have almost no value. Clearly, then, he thought something pretty important followed from them. But it is not so clear what he thought the important conclusion was. I shall presently describe two conclusions which might be thought to follow from Locke's contrast between the contributions of land and labour. Each conclusion has been attributed to him by commentators. I shall not try to say which of them he really drew himself, partly because my

[19] Locke uses the word 'value' when he makes this claim, but, as I argue in section 7 below, the claim concerns use-value, since, for Locke, 'the intrinsic value of things . . . depends only on their usefulness to the life of man' (*Second Treatise on Government*, para. 37). Elsewhere, Locke contrasts 'intrinsic' and 'marketable value', that being his way of anticipating the Marxian 'use-value'/'exchange-value' distinction: see *Some Considerations*. In the rest of this chapter, I use 'value' to mean 'use-value', in conformity with Locke's *Second Treatise* practice.

[20] *Second Treatise of Government*, Chapter V, paras. 42 and 43, and see, too, paras. 36, 37, 40, and 41. Further references to Locke's two *Treatises of Government* will be by *Treatise* and para. number.

philosophical interest in Locke is not so historical as that, but also because, when I come to criticize Locke, I shall focus, for the most part, on his premiss that labour creates virtually all value, and what plainly was his argument *for* it, rather than on what, not equally plainly, his inference *from* it was.

One conclusion which Locke has been thought to draw from the premiss that labour creates virtually all of the value of things is that no one should object very strongly to currently existing inequality, since it largely descends from people's exercise of their self-owned powers and subsequent disposal of what they created by using them. And the other conclusion is that the original formation of private property in unowned external things was justified by the fact that those things were nearly valueless before their labouring appropriators envalued them: appropriators gathered nothing worth mentioning when they established exclusive control over tracts of natural resources.

So we find in Locke, or attributed to Locke, a pair of arguments, with a common premiss. The common premiss is that labour is responsible for virtually all the value of what we use and consume. The conclusion of one argument, which I shall call the value/appropriation argument, is that a person who labours on unowned natural resources becomes, thereby, their legitimate owner. And the conclusion of the other argument, here called the value/inequality argument, is that inequality in distribution is justified, since, or to the extent that, it reflects unequal value-creating applications of labour. I am sure that Locke wanted to draw one or other of these conclusions, or both of them, or conclusions similar to them, from his premiss that labour creates nearly all value, since it is otherwise impossible to explain the importance which he attached to that premiss.

The common premiss of the value/appropriation and value/inequality arguments should not be identified with another, and more famous, Lockean claim. That different claim is that, when one labours on something, one mixes one's labour with it, thereby placing within it something one owns. Locke uses the labour mixture claim as a premiss to justify the original formation of private property out of what nobody privately owns. By mixing what he owns, to wit, his labour, with something unowned, the labouring appropriator becomes the legitimate owner of the resulting mixture, since he alone has any right to any of it.[21]

Let us call that the 'labour mixture argument'. Note now that the labour

---

[21] I apologize for reproducing, in the next two paragraphs, material that also appears at pp. 108–9 of Chapter 4 above: unfortunately, these points are needed in both places.

mixture argument is different from the value/appropriation argument, whose *conclusion* it shares. The value argument for legitimate appropriation has a different rationale from the argument for labour mixture, although many (and sometimes, perhaps, Locke)[22] are prone to confuse the two. It is easy to confuse them, since it is (at least standardly) by labouring on something that you enhance its value, and perhaps your action on it should count as labour only if it does enhance its value. Nevertheless, in the logic of the labour mixture argument, it is labour itself, and not value-creation, which justifies the claim to private property. If you own what you laboured on because your own labour is in it, then you do not own it because you have enhanced its value, even if nothing deserves to be called 'labour' unless it creates value. And, for the value/appropriation argument, it is the conferring of value as such, not the labour by which it is conferred, that is essential. If you magically enhanced something's value without labouring, but say, by wishing that it were more valuable,[23] then you would be entitled to whatever the value argument justifies you in having, even though you had not performed any labour.

Locke's principal labour mixture paragraphs in Chapter V of his *Second Treatise of Government* do not, in my view, invoke the consideration that labour enhances the value of that to which it is applied.[24] And Karl Olivecrona may be right that when, in later paragraphs of the chapter, Locke does bring value enhancement to the fore, he is not there trying to defend the initial appropriation of private property, but, instead,

---

[22] Locke's most explicitly 'labour mixture' paragraph is II: 27:

> Whatsoever then he removes out of the State that Nature hath provided, and left it in, he hath mixed his Labour with, and joyned to it something that is his own, and thereby makes it his Property. It being by him removed from the common state Nature placed it in, hath by this labour something annexed to it, that excludes the common right of other Men.

I think what gets 'annexed' (or, in II: 28, 'added') to nature is labour, not value, but, if it is value, then Locke is confusing the two arguments. Better evidence that he confuses them is II: 44, which, after several value-creation paragraphs (i.e., II: 40–3), reverts to the labour mixture theme, as though continuing the same discussion; and also the first sentence of II: 40, which, given what precedes and follows it, seems to represent labour's prodigious power to create value as the explanation why its mixture with things confers title on them in the labourer.

[23] Note that the magical supposition that wishing creates use-value is different from the unmagical one (see p. 174 above) that desire 'creates' exchange-value, and that the wisher would not desire what he wishes were use-valuable unless and until his wish had worked.

[24] The principal labour mixture paragraphs are II: 27–34. Paras. 27 and 28 *perhaps* invoke value enhancement, but as I said in footnote 22, I do not think that they do.

advancing the differently concluding value/inequality argument.[25] He is purporting to justify the extensive inequality of goods that obtains now, when original appropriation has long since ceased. The justification Locke offers is that almost all of present inequality is due not to any unequal initial appropriating but to the labour which followed after initial appropriation. Locke is prepared to concede that untouched natural things have some little value, but he urges that at least 90 per cent (and probably 99 per cent) of the value of things which have been transformed by labour is due to that transforming labour,[26] so that, unless you would rob people of what they produced, or of what they rightfully received, directly, or at the end of a chain of transfers, from labouring producers, you cannot object to the greater part of the inequality that now prevails.

I shall show, in section 8, that Locke provides inadequate support for the premiss of the value arguments; then, in section 9, that that premiss is indefensible; and finally, in section 10, that, even if it were true, it would not sustain the conclusions that are drawn from it. But, before offering those criticisms, I must first clarify what the value-creation premiss says, and why Locke was so confident that it was true.

7. Locke's premiss is often described as a rough statement of what, since Marx, has been known as the labour theory of value. That is misleading,[27] since the value which Locke says is (nearly all) due to labour is not the value Marx says labour created. Locke's topic is use-value, not exchange-value. Suppose you own a quantity of wheat. Then the use-value you own is measured by the number of bushels of wheat you have, or, more

---

[25] See Olivecrona, 'Locke's Theory of Appropriation', pp. 231–4. The relevant later Locke paragraphs are II: 40–3.

[26] 'I think it will be but a very modest computation to say that of the products of the earth useful to the life of man nine-tenths are the effects of labour; nay, if we will rightly estimate things as they come to our use, and cast up the several expenses about them – what in them is purely owing to nature, and what to labour – we shall find that in most of them ninety-nine hundredths are wholly to be put on the account of labour' (I: 40). II: 37 gives the same figures, and II: 43 multiplies the larger of them by ten.

[27] The frequency of the misleading description is no doubt due to 'the emotional appeal' of the labour theory of value, which 'has induced some historians to interpret as many authors as possible' as proponents of it: Joseph Schumpeter, *A History of Economic Analysis*, p. 98. See, for example, Richard Aaron, *Locke*, p. 280; John Gough, *John Locke's Political Philosophy*, p. 81; George Sabine, *A History of Political Theory*, p. 528. John Dunn (*Locke*, p. 44) says that 'the tangled history of the labour theory of value ever since, in the justification and rejection of capitalist production, was already foreshadowed in the ambiguities of the theory which he [Locke] fashioned'. That is strictly wrong, since Locke did not fashion *that* theory. But Dunn is nevertheless substantially right, to the extent that the theory of value typically enters the debates to which he refers in the misread, ideologically motivated, form described in section 5 above.

abstractly, by the amount of life and enjoyment, or 'utility', those bushels will afford, whereas their exchange-value is measured by the quantity of other commodities they would fetch on a market in equilibrium. And use-value and exchange-value can vary independently of each other: the self-same quantity of wheat, with the self-same use-value, will undergo a change in exchange-value as (equilibrium) market conditions change, and different quantities of wheat, and hence of use-value, will, under appropriately different market conditions, possess the same exchange-value.

If you read Locke with this distinction in mind, I think you will agree that his labour-praising premiss praises labour as the source of use-, not exchange-, value. Consider, for example, these excerpts from II: 37:

the provisions serving to the support of human life produced by one acre of enclosed and cultivated land are (to speak much within compass) ten times more than those which are yielded by an acre of land of an equal richness lying waste in common . . . I have here rated the improved land very low, in making its product but as ten to one, when it is much nearer a hundred to one.

Hence land without labour is, as we saw, 'scarcely . . . worth anything'. But the increase in its value which is here assigned to the action of labour is an increase in its use-value. For Locke's figures have to do with the comparative physical yields, or use-values, which virgin and cultivated land produce, not with what virgin and cultivated land would respectively fetch on the market.

Notice, now, how Locke determines the contribution of labour to use-value.[28] He does so by comparing the yield of the land with and without labour, his tool of comparison being what I shall call 'the subtraction criterion'. It operates as follows: you subtract what the land yields without labour from what it yields with it, and then you form the fraction got by putting the result of that subtraction over what the land yields with labour. The resulting fraction, to wit,

$$\frac{\text{Amount land yields with labour minus amount it yields without it}}{\text{Amount land yields with labour}}$$

is supposed to indicate the proportion of use-value which is due to labour, with the rest, consequently, being due to land. I shall later criticize this procedure for gauging comparative contributions to use-value creation, but, for the moment, just note what it is, and that it has nothing to do with

---

[28] See, in particular, II: 40, 42, 43.

exchange-value. Land which produces one-tenth without labour of what it would produce with it is not consequently going to fetch, on the market, one-tenth in its virgin state of what it would fetch if it were cultivated.

Since Locke's *explanandum* is use-value, his is not the *explanandum* of the Marxian labour theory, exchange-value. But the *explanans* in Locke's theory is also not the same as the labour-theoretical *explanans*, since, in the labour theory, exchange-value is a positive linear function of labour time,[29] and labour *time* plays no comparable role in Locke's theory. And that is because the amount of a thing's use-value could not conceivably be imagined to co-vary in a simple way with the labour time required to produce it, even by someone who thought that its use-value was entirely due to labour. As Karl Marx saw, Locke's *explanans* is 'concrete labour', which is to say labour considered in its concrete form of ploughing, sowing and so forth, not, as Marx put it, labour 'as a quantum'.[30]

To see how labour times play no essential role in Locke's theory, suppose that every piece of land within a given economy is of the same fertility, and that an economy-wide deterioration in fertility, affecting every piece equally, now supervenes. Both before and after the deterioration one acre of the land would yield one bushel of corn per day without labour and a maximum of ten with it, but three hours a day was required to make it yield its maximum ten bushels when the land was good and six hours after it has deteriorated. Then the yield of the cultivated land would not have more value for Locke in stage two than it had in stage one, and that is because the use-value of its yield would have remained the same, even though, on labour-theoretical premisses, its exchange-value would, *ceteris paribus*, have risen.

A simple proof that Locke's is not a labour theory of value in the Marxian sense is that he says only that *almost* all of the value of the product is due to labour. But that point aside, he was not a Marxian labour theorist, for the two reasons rehearsed above.

The second of those reasons was that Locke's *explanans* of value is not the amount of labour time required to produce the product. Yet he does emphasize how prodigious is the amount of labour that goes into elementary consumption goods, reminding us that

---

[29] The qualifications which need to be put on that statement to cope with the complexities addressed in Volume III of *Capital* are not relevant here.

[30] *Theories of Surplus Value*, Vol. I, p. 366. On the difference between concrete and abstract labour see my *Karl Marx's Theory of History*, p. 101.

'tis not barely the ploughman's pains, the reaper's and thresher's toil and the baker's sweat, is to be counted into the bread we eat; the labour of those who broke the oxen, who dug and wrought the iron and stones, who felled and framed the timber employed about the plough, mill, oven, or any other utensils, which are a vast number, requisite to the corn, from its being seed to be sown to its being made bread, must all be charged on the account of labour, and received as an effect of that. Nature and the earth furnished only the almost worthless materials as in themselves. (II: 43)

Still, the extensive labour catalogued here is not here measured in the relevant Marxian way, as a quantity of undifferentiated labour time with which exchange-value might be thought to vary. Locke's point is rather that a great deal of variously concrete labour is needed to get consumable bread from an almost worthless natural starting point. It is, moreover, not entirely clear how Locke's catalogue is supposed to serve his own purpose, which is to affirm that labour is the source of (almost all) use-value. For his reason for saying that unworked materials are worthless would apply even if only very little labour were needed to transform them into something worthwhile. The application of the subtraction procedure for determining labour's contribution requires no information about the amount of labour, in any sense, that has been spent. (A speculation about Locke's motive for nevertheless emphasizing labour's amount is offered in the following section: see footnote 33 below.)

Finally, a remark about Marx. As I observed earlier (p. 180), he knew that Locke was not propounding a labour theory of exchange-value. But the passage in which Marx expresses that insight is also interesting for another reason. Having observed that, for Locke, 'labour gives things almost all their value', Marx then adds this partly curious gloss:

value here is equivalent to use-value, and labour is taken as concrete labour, not as a quantum; but the measuring of exchange-value by labour is in reality based on the fact that the labourer creates use-value.[31]

The curious part follows the semicolon. Almost certainly, Marx is there stating something he believes to be true, rather than merely something he believes Locke thought true. But then Marx's statement is curious, for how could he think that labour's creation of use-value was the basis for 'the measuring of exchange-value by labour' (alone) when, as he knew (see p. 172 above), land too creates use-value? A Marxist might reply that creating use-value is but a necessary condition of a factor's being a measure of exchange-value. But then what further relevant condition does

---

[31] *Theories of Surplus Value*, Vol. I, p. 366.

labour, and not also land, satisfy?[32] To answer that question, one must say more than merely: that it is labour.

8. My main criticism of Locke's value arguments is an objection to the basis on which he asserts their premiss, which is the premiss that labour is responsible for almost all of what the land yields. He establishes that premiss on the basis of his subtraction criterion (see p. 179 above).

Consider a piece of cultivated land which yields ten times as much crop as it did before it was cultivated. Is it true, for the reason Locke gave, and with the sense that he attached to the following statement, that labour is responsible for 90 per cent of the crop of the cultivated land? In its intended sense, the statement contrasts the contribution of labour with that of the land itself, which here would be 10 per cent of the crop: the point of the statement is to depreciate the contribution of land itself to use-value.

In my view, the desired statement is not true in the required contrastive sense for the reason Locke gave, since that reason, to wit, Locke's subtraction criterion, is unacceptable. One ground for saying that it is unacceptable is that it has intuitively unacceptable consequences. Another ground is that it generates a logical contradiction.

To see that the subtraction criterion has intuitively unacceptable consequences, suppose that only one hour a year of labour is required to draw a hundred bushels of wheat per year from a field which produces only a single bushel per year spontaneously. Or, to take a more realistic example, suppose that just one hour of digging creates a well which yields a thousand gallons of water a year, where before there was only a measly annual ten-gallon trickle. It would surely be wrong to infer, from the fact that the digging *raised* the water yield from ten to a thousand gallons, that the digging is responsible for 99 per cent of the water yielded by, and, hence, of the use-value produced by, the dug land, while the land itself is responsible for only 1 per cent of it.[33]

As Locke recognized, land frequently produces consumables without

---

[32] For several attempts to distinguish in a Marx-supporting way between labour and land see Nancy Holmstrom, 'Marx and Cohen on the Labour Theory of Value', pp. 300–2. But see, too, my 'More on Exploitation and the Labour Theory of Value', p. 327, on why, in my view, all of her attempts fail.

[33] *Perhaps* Locke emphasizes how extensive labour's contribution is in II: 32 (see p. 181 above) to still the sort of doubt I have here raised about the consequences of his criterion, and of which he may have been obscurely aware. But his catalogue will not silence that doubt, if only because, as the well example shows, a lot of labour is not always required to draw extensive consumables from spontaneously unfruitful land.

any labour having been applied to it. Contrast the hide of a cow, which produces no shoes, and not merely very few, when no tanning and cutting and shaping of it goes on. Must we therefore say that land which is, spontaneously, modestly productive, makes some small contribution to the use-value of the bread baked from its wheat, whereas cowhide makes none to the use-value of shoes? The contrast is absurd, but it is forced upon us by Locke's subtraction criterion.

Locke's criterion fails because the *difference* application of a factor makes to output, its marginal contribution, cannot be treated as its contribution to that output *by contrast* with the contribution of other factors. But it is just such a contrast that Locke needs, so that he can upvalue the contribution of labour and devalue the contribution of land. He needs, in other words, to pass from the unexceptionable premiss of the following argument to its invalidly derived conclusion. It will often be true that:

(1) The application of labour makes virgin land produce ten times what it did before.

But it does not follow that, in such a case:

(2) Labour produces 90 per cent of the product of applying it to virgin land.

No one can think such an argument valid once he gets its premiss and conclusion distinguished from each other in his mind, but that sometimes takes effort, since many sentences can be used to express either its premiss or its conclusion, and thereby the argument can acquire an appearance of validity. One might think that (2) follows from (1) because one inattentively uses such a sentence as 'the additional output of 90 per cent is due to labour' to express now (1) and now (2).

Some claim that the fallacy exposed above is too simple to attribute to a thinker of Locke's stature. They say that I have not captured the intuitive power of his reply to the egalitarian, which is that the goods the latter would redistribute are so largely due to labour that redistribution of them would violate rightful claims in them. But I think that the intuitive power of that reply depends entirely on its ambiguity. It is true in sense (1), but polemically interesting only in sense (2). Unless we represent Locke as confusing (1) and (2), or as unjustifiably inferring (2) from (1), we cannot explain why he lays so much emphasis on (1); (1) serves no labour-praising and land-diminishing polemical purpose when (2) is neither derived from it nor confused with it.

I said that Locke's criterion for determining relative contributions to use-value not only has unintuitive consequences, but also leads to a contradiction. On that criterion, if a piece of land is cropless without labour, but yields a crop with it, then labour is responsible for all of that crop, and land is responsible for none of it. But, although the land is entirely cropless without labour, it is equally true that the labour, the ploughing and harrowing and so on, would yield no crop on infertile land. The value of the following fraction, is consequently, 100 per cent:

$$\frac{\text{Amount labour yields with land minus amount it yields without it}}{\text{Amount labour yields with land}}$$

Then, on a natural generalization of Locke's procedure, we should have to add conclusions (5) and (6) to the ones he draws, which are (3) and (4):

(3) Labour is responsible for all of the crop.
(4) Land is responsible for none of the crop.
(5) Land is responsible for all of the crop.
(6) Labour is responsible for none of the crop.

This set of sentences fails to award the palm to labour. But, beyond that, it also entails a manifest contradiction. For, even if (3) and (5) are somehow consistent with each other, (3) and (6) (and (4) and (5)) are certainly not. *If* there exists a defensible criterion for assigning relative contributions to output of labour on the one hand and the original properties of the soil on the other, then it is not Locke's.

For my part, I doubt that there exists such a criterion, and I must therefore distinguish what some economists might think would supply such a criterion from the sort of criterion that I do not think exists. Economists call the problem of rewarding co-operating factors of production *the value allocation problem*. An early solution to that problem was provided by Lloyd Shapley. He laid down seemingly plausible axiomatic constraints on any solution, and he proved that the only procedure consistent with them was to allocate to each factor the average of its marginal contributions in all possible orders in which the factors might be combined with one another.[34]

Now the reason why I nevertheless say that there is no criterion which should replace Locke's unacceptable one is that, while Locke seeks, in the

[34] The 'Shapley value' is explained in Lloyd Shapley, 'A Value for N-person Games', pp. 307–17. A brief exposition of Shapley's solution and of subsequent work developing out of it will be found in Martin Shubik, *Game Theory in the Social Sciences*, pp. 180ff.

end, to answer something like[35] the Shapley allocation question, his criterion is, immediately, not of how to allocate portions of what is produced to factors, in the sense of rewarding them, but of how to diagnose what different factors contribute to the product (in order, on that basis, to do some appropriate rewarding). In short, Locke goes from (i) facts about marginal contributions, to (ii) claims about comparative physical contributions, to (iii) conclusions about rewards. His argument says, roughly, that, since land without labour produces hardly anything, and land with labour produces an enormous amount, labour contributes vastly more to output than land does, and labour should, accordingly, be appropriately rewarded. There is nothing in Shapley which corresponds to the second stage of this argument. He proceeds directly, by dint of his axioms, from (i) to (iii), and thereby, unlike Locke, refrains from addressing what may be a pseudo-question. I am confident that Locke affirms (ii), since he starts with (i) and ends with (iii), and I do not see how he could otherwise think that he has traversed the distance between them. He certainly did not anticipate Shapley's axioms, which have, by the way, distinctly non-Lockean distributional consequences.[36]

To conclude, if J. R. Ewing, or Donna Krebs, produces a well yielding one thousand barrels of oil per day after five minutes' excavation, then we cannot infer, on the Lockean ground that no oil comes without digging, that his or her labour, *as opposed to the land*, is responsible for all of that oil. That conclusion is unavailable, not only because it is absurd so to praise so mere a whiff of labour, but also because, by the same Lockean token, labour is responsible for *none* of the oil, since a digger on oil-less land produces no oil: the digger cannot be both responsible for all of the oil and responsible for none of it.[37]

---

[35] Something *like* it, because Locke's question is explicitly normative, whereas the Shapley value is presented as an answer to the question of what rewards owners of factors should *expect*, as a matter of fact, to get from co-operation. Shapley's answer to that question might nevertheless be treated as an answer to the corresponding normative question of what it would be appropriate for them to get, as sovereign owners of the factors they supply.

[36] Suppose that some land yields one gallon of water without labour and ten gallons with it. Since it is also true that labour yields no water without land, the Shapley value assigns 5.5 gallons to the land and 4.5 gallons to labour.

[37] (i) According to Israel Kirzner, there is no vexing problem about the original appropriation of valuable resources, since resources are valueless, and even, 'in the relevant sense', non-existent, until appropriators perceive the uses to which they can be put, and thereby endow them with value. An argument similar to the foregoing one against Locke might also apply against Kirzner's bizarrerie, since perception that a resource could be used thus and so would yield nothing if the resource lacked the properties that made the perception correct. See Kirzner's 'Entrepreneurship, Entitlement, and Economic Justice', especially pp. 400–7.

9. So Locke's defence of his premiss, that labour is responsible for nearly all of the use-value of things, is unacceptable. And the premiss is, moreover, indefensible, even if my suspicion that it answers a pseudo-question is unfounded.

I say that it is indefensible for two reasons. The first is that I do not see how one might try to defend it other than on Locke's unacceptable basis: what else could lead one to think that it is true? But my second reason for saying that it is indefensible is more positive. If Locke is right, then land in general has nearly no use-value. Well, consider some land which Locke would regard as particularly friendly to his case, because it yields nothing without labour, though very much with it. One could not say of such land that it has virtually no use-value, let alone, as Locke's criterion would have it, none at all. One could not say that, precisely because the land yields so much *with* labour. Its use-value cannot be considered trivial, since it has a prodigious power to satisfy human desire, in virtue of how it reacts when labour is applied to it.

10. But even if we were to accept Locke's indefensible – and, perhaps, meaningless – premiss, we should still be able to resist the conclusions he is supposed to have derived from it, which are that original appropriation and/or currently existing inequality are justified. For even if land never produced anything without labour, so that, Locke here being assumed to be right, labour was responsible for all the use-value drawn from the land, the landowner would not thereby be justified in taking all of the land's fruit, on the supposition that he or relevantly connected predecessors had performed all the labour on it. For that inference ignores the consideration that not everyone might have had an equivalent opportunity to labour on land, because there was no land left to labour on, or because the land left to labour on was less good than what the more fortunate laboured on.[38]

(ii) In the examples used above, a single labourer applies himself to the land, so there is no problem of disaggregating the contributions of a plurality of interdependent labours. For that problem, see Amartya Sen's critique of Locke-like defences of inequality by reference to differential productive contribution, in Sen's 'Just Desert' and 'The Moral Standing of the Market', pp. 14–17. Note, by the way, that a critique of an argument for rewarding productive contribution which turns on the collective nature of labour does not defeat the claims of productively discrete collectives to all of what they produce, however it should be divided among the individuals within them.

(iii) For ingenious, but, in my view, unsuccessful, criticism of sections 6 through 8 of this chapter, see Andrew Williams, 'Cohen on Locke, Land and Labour'. To see why I say it is ingenious, read it. To see why I say it is unsuccessful, read an unpublished reply by me that I will supply on request, together with Andrew Williams' response to that reply.

[38] This rejection of the Lockean inference might be thought inconsistent with my criticism of orthodox Marxism in section 2, for I there imply that, since land is needed for production,

It is generally thought[39] that, when Locke advanced his labour mixture argument (see p. 176 above), he made it a condition of the power of labour to create title in land that the labourer leave 'enough and as good' land for others to labour on. To cope with the consideration just mentioned, something similar would have to be added to the value creation premiss, in both of its uses. But then both of the arguments based on it would fail, since enough and as good has not in fact been left for others.

To that complaint of opportunity denied, Robert Nozick has responded that no grievance results, since the landless are no worse off than they would have been had the appropriated land remained unowned. But in focusing only on how the landless in a fully appropriated world would have fared in a wholly unappropriated one, Nozick suppresses other pertinent questions, such as how they would have fared had they, or their forbears, had the opportunity to do some appropriating, and his response therefore fails to allay the grievance here envisaged.[40]

This is the right place to comment on a brilliant Lockean argument for private property, which exploits labour's creative powers in a quite different way from the arguments discussed above. I mean Locke's contention that the improving cultivator

who appropriates land to himself by his labour does not lessen but increase the common stock of mankind . . . he that encloses land, and has a greater plenty of the conveniences of life from ten acres than he could have had from a hundred left to nature, may truly be said to give ninety acres to mankind: for his labour now supplies him with provisions out of ten acres, which were but the product of a hundred lying in common.[41]

This argument has the virtue that it requires no claim that the cultivator is responsible for 90 per cent of what he draws from nature. The cultivator's gift to 'the common stock' is not, I think, the surplus provision he produces on his own ten acres,[42] all of which he might himself consume,

---

it must have use-value. But there is, in fact, no inconsistency. I am saying that the necessity of land for production defeats the Lockean inference even if (what I am sure is false) the fact that land is needed does not prove that it has use-value.

[39] But see, for impressive, and, in my view, nearly convincing, dissent, Jeremy Waldron, 'Enough and As Good Left for Others', which is criticized by Thomas Baldwin at p. 21 of his 'Tully, Locke, and Land'.

[40] For Nozick's position on the grievances of non-appropriators see *Anarchy, State, and Utopia*, pp. 175–82. For criticism of Nozick's position, see Chapter 3 above, especially sections 3–6.

[41] II: 37. This passage did not appear in the original composition of the *Treatise*: Locke added it years later. See the remarks by Laslett at p. 336 of his edition of the text.

[42] Though see the Spain example near the end of II: 36, which suggests that Locke may mean, rather oddly, what I think he does not mean.

but the bounty of nature on the ninety acres he is able to vacate for the use of the rest of mankind, because of his productivity on the ten he privatizes. And the argument does justify private property, at any rate if people own their own powers and therefore owe no fruit of them to others, since, on that assumption, this privatizer only benefits the rest of mankind when he retires to his own plot: they now have an additional ninety acres to reap the fruit of. But the argument justifies private property only as long as appropriation generates an expanding common for the privately unendowed to forage on, and it therefore fails to justify actual private property in the real and fully appropriated world. To justify private property in a fully appropriated world in which some do not own any, something like Nozick's move would be needed, but that move, as I have said, fails.

11. I expressed uncertainty (see section 6 above) about what conclusion(s) Locke hoped to draw from his premiss that labour created (nearly all) value, but I also expressed confidence that he thought that something important followed from it in favour of private property and/or inequality. I believe, moreover, that he thought that what followed favoured private property and/or inequality both in the pre-governmental state of nature and in society under government. James Tully's interpretation of Chapter V of the *Second Treatise* would, if correct, create difficulty for that understanding of Locke, and I must therefore explain why I reject Tully's interpretation of Locke.

According to Tully, Locke does not seek to justify property which is truly private, either in the state of nature or under government. What God gives to men in common undergoes what Tully calls 'individuation', but not full privatization. And one reason why Tully's Locke refuses to endorse fully private property is that such property entitlements would militate against the welfare of the community. But both (a) Tully's attribution to Locke of welfarist intentions, and (b) his denial that individuated property is private seem to me to depend on misuse of Locke's texts.

(a) Some of the material offered by Tully in defence of the first thesis gives it no support whatever. He refers to II: 39 to sustain his statement that 'it is the duty of governments to organize the community's possessions and strength for the public good', but nothing in II: 39 bears on that issue.[43]

---

[43] *A Discourse on Property*, p. 170. Here is the whole of II: 39: 'And thus, without supposing any private dominion, and property in Adam, over all the world, exclusive of all other

He cites II: 50 to show that the community's laws must 'confine the possession of land' so that everyone can enjoy it,[44] whereas all II: 50 says to the point is that 'in governments the laws regulate the right of property, and the possession of land is determined by positive constitutions'. And he invokes II: 135 in justification of the amazing claim, about which II: 135 says nothing,[45] that, for Locke, 'government is required to constitute a new order of social relations which will bring the actions of men once again in line with God's intentions'.

Tully thinks that the actions of men fell out of line with God's intentions in the state of nature, when the introduction of money disrupted naturally ordered relations by facilitating a development of inequality which would have been impossible or unlikely before money appeared.[46] Yet it is not, as Tully groundlessly says, the wealthy themselves who -- for Tully's Locke, unjustifiably -- 'claim to be entitled to their enlarged possessions'[47] in the texts he cites, but John Locke who presents that claim for them. According to Locke, the accumulator of monetary wealth 'invade[s] not the right of others', since 'the exceeding of the bounds of his just property' lies not 'in the largeness of his possession', but in 'the perishing of anything uselessly in it' (II: 46), and money does not perish.

In the *First Treatise* (I: 42) Locke imposes on those who have more than they need a duty to give to those who are in want, and we might reasonably suppose that a Lockean government would enforce that duty.[48] But there is little reference to a duty of charity in the *Second Treatise*, notwithstanding Tully's straining efforts to show the contrary, some of which I now expose.

Citing II: 37, Tully says:

if a case of need arises then, *ipso facto*, one man's individual right is overridden by another's claim, and the goods become his property. By failing to hand over the goods, the proprietor invades the share now belonging to the needy and is liable to punishment.[49]

men, which no way can be proved, nor any ones property be made out from it; but supposing the world given as it was to the children of men in common, we see how labour could make men distinct titles to several parcels of it, for their private uses; wherein there could be no doubt of right, no room for quarrel.'
[44] Tully, *Discourse*, p. 152.
[45] *Ibid.*, p. 154. II: 135 is too long to reproduce here, so the reader is invited to verify my allegation for herself.
[46] Tully, p. 154.
[47] *Ibid.*, p. 152.
[48] For an argument that it would, see Waldron, *The Right to Private Property*, p. 241.
[49] *Ibid.*, p. 132.

This twists what II: 37 says. It says nothing about needy people. It does say that if a man takes more than he can use, so that some of it spoils, then he invades 'his neighbour's share', but he invades it *whether or not his neighbour is needy*. It is not as though a person is allowed to keep fruit which he cannot use unless and until 'a case of need arises'.[50] Rather, he is not supposed to have it at all. He has no presumptive right to it which someone else's need might, as in I: 42, override.

The duty of charity laid down in I: 42 might be called a duty of the abundantly endowed to *preserve* others, but I have not found a duty to preserve others, in the I: 42 sense, imposed on the well endowed, or on anyone else, in the *Second Treatise*. Hence I do not agree with Tully when he cites II: 6 in support of 'a natural duty of each man to preserve himself, and, *ceteris paribus*, others'.[51] In fact, II: 6 forbids people to harm others, or to deprive them of what they have produced for themselves, but it does not, as Tully's gloss on it suggests, lay down that, having succeeded in preserving himself, a person is obliged to set about working for the preservation of others, should such activity now be necessary and possible.[52] Note that not even I: 42 obliges a person to labour for the sake of anyone else's preservation.

Tully quotes from II: 149[53] in further supposed support of a 'natural duty to engage in the end-directed activity of preserving man', but no duty of the individual to preserve anyone but himself is mentioned in II: 149.[54] And when Tully points to II: 11, in which Locke speaks of 'the right he [man] has of preserving all mankind',[55] he refrains from mentioning that the said right is here exercised solely in preventing or deterring others from killing people. Locke is here grounding a right to

---

[50] *Ibid.*

[51] *Ibid.*, p. 62.

[52] The most Tully-supporting clause of II: 6 reads as follows, 'he' being 'every one': 'when his own Preservation comes not in competition, ought he, as much as he can, *to preserve the rest of Mankind*', but the sentence concludes as follows: 'and may not unless it be to do Justice on an Offender, take away, or impair the life, or what tends to the Preservation of the Life, Liberty, Health, Limb or Goods of another'. I do not think the 'and' at the beginning of that concluding segment is an ordinary conjunction, but one that introduces a clause in apposition to what went before, in order to specify what is here *meant* by preserving the rest of mankind. I think it is because 'and' is here used to introduce an apposition that, unlike what precedes it, what follows it is not italicized.

[53] Tully, *Discourse*, p. 62.

[54] To be sure, there is a reference to 'the preservation of the Community' in the first sentence of II: 149, but the duty to achieve it lies on the legislative, in execution of the trust reposed in it. It does not follow that anyone ever has a duty, independently of contract or fiduciary relationship, to preserve anyone.

[55] Tully, *Discourse*, p. 62.

punish aggressors against oneself and others, not addressing himself
to need and to the preservation of needy people.

Although the *First Treatise* might be taken to imply that the duty of
charity is to be enforced by government, I do not agree with Tully that it
'attributes to Filmer the theory that property in land is independent of
social functions and admonishes that it is the "most specious thing" '.[56] For
the thing Locke here calls 'most specious' is the idea that if one man (e.g.
Adam) were the legitimate proprietor of the whole world, he would have
a consequent right to starve everyone else into submission to him. It
hardly follows that Locke would think it similarly specious to deny social
functions to property where it was distributed with less extravagant
inequity.

Tully also cites the *Essays on the Law of Nature* to support his claim that
Locke 'finds a theory of property which is not conditional upon the
performance of social functions as an "absurdity" '.[57] But what Locke there
declares to be an 'absurdity' is not some theory of property, but a theory
of morally correct motivation according to which

it would be unlawful for a man to renounce his own rights or to impart benefits to
another without a definite hope of reward . . . to grant or give anything to a friend,
incur expenses on his behalf, or in any other manner do him a favour out of pure
kindness.

Locke is denying that 'the rightness of a course of action be derived from
expediency', not affirming that property rights are conditional on social
service. He urges that, if it were wrong for a man to act against his own
selfish interest, then, absurdly, it would be wrong for him to 'renounce his
own rights' for the sake of a friend. The words I just quoted imply that, for
Locke, property rights include, as one might expect, the right not to give
away what one owns (on which a kind man will not always insist). Hence,
far from sustaining Tully's eccentric interpretation, the *Essays* passage
actually contradicts it.

(b) So much against Tully's attribution to Lockean texts of welfarist
intentions which are not to be found in them. I turn to the connected issue
distinguished at p. 188 above, to wit, Tully's denial that the legitimate
'individuation' of what God gives to men in common amounts to the
formation of private property.

According to Tully, what most commentators have thought was
private property in Locke is, in fact, 'exclusive property within positive

[56] Tully, *Discourse*, p. 99, quoting I: 41.
[57] *Ibid.*, p. 103, citing Locke, *Essays on the Law of Nature*, pp. 213–15.

community'. The individuation of the world 'does not dissolve, but merely realises property in common'. This is supposed to be demonstrated by II: 26, in which, comments Tully, an 'agent with an exclusive right still remains "a tenant in common" '.[58]

But that comment is a misuse of II: 26. The agent in II: 26 is an Indian who has established an exclusive right in some fruit or venison. The fruit did belong to mankind in common, but, once the Indian has appropriated it, it no longer does: the common property in the fruit is entirely 'dissolved'. What he remains 'a tenant in common of' is the land itself, over no part of which, however, does he have any exclusive right, and Locke's point in II: 26 is that private property is so unavoidable that even a tenant in common must privatize the fruit of the common to get any benefit from it. The individuation of land itself arises only later, at II: 32, where Locke says 'it is plain, that property in that too is acquired' as property is acquired in venison and fruit, with full private right. The idea that individuation 'does not dissolve, but merely realises property in common' is entirely without foundation.

Continuing his advocacy of 'exclusive property within positive community', Tully makes curious and unjustified use of paragraphs 28 and 35 of the *Second Treatise*:

Locke is quite explicit in saying that his model is the English Common. 'We see in Commons, which remain so by compact, that 'tis the taking any part of what is common, and removing it out of the state nature leaves it in, which begins the property; without which the common is of no use' (2. 28. cf. 2. 35).[59]

Now, as II: 35 makes clear, a common by compact is, by contrast with a common in the state of nature, one whose parts may not be privatized: the compact is an agreement that the land will remain held in common. All that one can privatize here is the fruit of the common, not the land itself, and Locke's point in II: 28 is that *even* when the land is held in common by compact, something must be privatized for it to be of any use. So II: 28 supports the idea that individuation 'realises property in common' just as little as the Indian example in II: 26 does.

Tully's 'cf. 2. 35' is, moreover, hard to construe. II: 35 adverts to the impossibility of privatizing the land of a 'common by compact', but points out that 'it is quite otherwise' for commons lacking in legislated status.[60] Where the common is natural you can take land, but you thereby cancel common ownership of the part you take. Where the common is by

---

[58] Tully, *Discourse*, p. 105.
[59] *Ibid.*, pp. 124–5.   [60] Cf. II: 32–4.

compact, you can take only fruit, thereby dissolving the common ownership of that fruit. The formula favoured by Tully, of 'exclusive property
within positive community', is in no case satisfied, and I do not understand why he refers us to II: 35.

12. In my conventional perception of Locke, he holds that men enter
political community in order to secure their lives and their possessions,
both of which are at risk in the state of nature.[61] Now it is obviously,
because necessarily, the very lives which they had in the state of nature,
and not, *per impossibile*, some freshly distributed ones, which come under
communal protection once men enter political society. And I believe, with
most commentators, and against Tully, that, although it is not equally
necessary, it is equally true that, for Locke, the possessions men enjoy in
society are, initially, the very possessions which belonged to them in the
state of nature, and which they had aimed to make more safe: they do not
enter community in order to have some or other secure possessions, but in
order to secure the possessions they already precariously enjoyed. In the
paragraphs bearing on this issue Locke's language does not distinguish
between preservation of life and preservation of property in the way it
would if there were not between the two preservations the similarity on
which I am here insisting.

In Tully's different view of Locke, once government is established, 'all
the possessions a man has in the state of nature . . . become possessions of
the community',[62] which determines the members' use of them. But
Tully's interpretation confuses possession, or ownership, with political
rule. When people join the community, they submit *themselves* to its rule,
and, as Locke makes plain (II: 120), they must, on pain of contradiction,
submit their property to its rule too. But it no more follows from the
community's rule over a person's possessions that they now 'belong to
the community'[63] than it does from its rule over him that *he* belongs to it,
in the relevant parallel sense of being its slave. The community does not
own his goods any more than it owns his person. To be sure, it enacts and
enforces rules of criminal and civil law, to which his property and person
are now subject, and both are consequently more secure than they are in
the pre-political condition, since the pre-political law of nature is both
indeterminate in detail and hard to enforce (II: 136). One may therefore
say, as Locke does, that government 'regulates' (II: 50, 139) property, but

[61] See, e.g., II: 123ff., 138.
[62] Tully, *Discourse*, p. 164.   [63] *Ibid.*

it hardly follows that 'the *distribution* of property' is 'in the hands of government'.[64] Its distribution is, temporally speaking, pre-politically grounded, and, speaking in terms of justifying principle, sub-politically grounded. That is why II: 138 emphasizes – on Tully's account, unintelligibly – that the legislature 'cannot take from any man any part of his property without his own consent': if the legislature distributed property in the first place, it could surely redistribute it, when circumstances have changed, on whatever basis underlay the original distribution.[65]

When Locke writes that men, 'by compact and agreement, settled the property which labour and industry began' (II: 45), the natural reading of his words is that it was the very property which each compactor had gathered as a result of his own labour (or that of relevantly connected others) which was now to be 'settled': it was rendered secure, by being placed within a political framework. On Tully's alternative reading, the pre-politically well endowed would, improbably, have agreed to a dispossession which reduced them to equal standing with the pre-politically indigent. Commenting on II: 45, he tells us that, for Locke, 'property in political society is a creation of that society',[66] but there is no warrant there, or elsewhere, for this assertion, or for Tully's extravagant conclusion that 'community ownership of all possessions is the logical consequence of the premises of Locke's theory in the *Two Treatises*'. It is no more entailed by Locke's premises than community ownership of individuals is.

---

[64] *Ibid.*, p. 171, emphasis added. In another place ('A Reply to Waldron and Baldwin', p. 37), Tully invokes the authority of John Dunn, who writes that, once government is formed, 'property *now* is what the legal rules specify' ('Consent in the Political Theory of John Locke', p. 140). But Dunn's statement does not entail that legal rules decide property's distribution. For pretty conclusive evidence that Locke distinguishes between the power to regulate property and the power to decide who owns it, see the first sentence of II: 139.

[65] Cf., on this and related matters, Jeremy Waldron's decisive 'Locke, Tully and the Regulation of Property', pp. 98–106, or the revised version of that text at pp. 232–41 of *The Right to Private Property*.

[66] Tully, *Discourse*, p. 98. Compare the comments at p. 165 on II: 136, 138, which seem to me to be similarly incorrect, albeit less demonstrably so.

8. Exploitation in Marx: what makes it unjust?

... the money owner now strides in front as capitalist; the possessor of labour-power follows as his labourer. The one with an air of importance, smirking, intent on business; the other, timid and holding back, like one who is bringing his own hide to market and has nothing to expect but – a hiding. (Karl Marx, *Capital*)

1. In the standard Marxist account of capitalist exploitation, workers are constrained by their propertylessness to sell their labour power to capitalists, who own all the means of production. Workers are thereby forced both to submit to capitalists' directives and to yield some of what they produce to them: the workers keep part of what they produce, and the capitalists take the rest (the surplus product), for no return.

Now, there exists a debate about whether or not Marx regarded capitalist exploitation as *unjust*. Some think it obvious that he did believe it to be unjust, and others think that he patently did not. I shall not pursue that debate here. Here I take for granted, what I have argued for elsewhere, that Marx did think that capitalist exploitation was unjust.[1]

That being given, let us return to the standard account of exploitation,[2] sketched a moment ago, in order to ask: where, precisely, did Marx think that the injustice of exploitation lay? For notice that three logically distinct things occur in the Marxist account of exploitation, each of which carries a redolence of injustice. One is that (1) workers are at the short end of an unequal distribution of means of production. A second is that (2) they are forced to work as others direct them to. And a third is that (3) they are

---

[1] See my review of Allen Wood, *Karl Marx*; and, for an (in my view) sound and comprehensive treatment of the issue, see Norman Geras, 'The Controversy About Marx and Justice', in his *Literature of Revolution*.

[2] I shall often, as I do here, use 'exploitation' to mean 'capitalist exploitation'. Exploitations characterizing other modes of production play no role in this chapter.

forced to yield surplus product to others. (In the standard story, (1) causes each of (2) and (3).)

As I said, these are logically independent features of the workers' condition. Logically, there could be any one of them without the other two, and any two without the third. If workers lacking means of production choose to die, then only (1) is true. Or, if workers have less or worse means of production than capitalists, rather than none, and they choose to work autarchically,[3] because that makes sense in material terms, or in a spirit of defiance, because they hate exploitation more than they do poverty, then, again, only (1) is true. If, by contrast, workers are equitably endowed with means of production but forced to work at gunpoint by oppressors who reap nothing from their labour (maybe the workers are forced to break up rocks), then only (2) is true. And if workers are equitably endowed with means of production, and work for themselves, but others then take, by force, part of what they produce, then only (3) is true. (One can also compose cases where only (1) and (2), (2) and (3), and (1) and (3) are, respectively, true.)

Let us now ask: *which* of these features makes or make (for it might be more than one of them) exploitation unjust, not so much according to Marx, but, more broadly, within a Marxist outlook? The question is not (directly) about Marx's mind. Canonically put, it is this: *if* the story of capitalist exploitation is the one Marx tells (and which I summarized in the first paragraph of this chapter), then where, precisely, does the injustice lie (on independently reasonable views about justice)?

Now, in each of two recent chapters of this book, I discussed the Marxist account of exploitation, and I protested, in each, against a relationship that I discerned between that account and the thesis of self-ownership. I said, in Chapter 5 (see, in particular, its first two sections), that Marxists seek to represent exploitation as unjust without rejecting the thesis of self-ownership (and I argued that you cannot represent it as unjust without rejecting that thesis). In Chapter 6 I went further. I accused Marxists of implicitly *affirming* the thesis of self-ownership in their account of exploitation (with grave consequences for the coherence of that account: see sections 2, 3 and 8 of that chapter).

That Marxists fail to reject self-ownership and that they actually affirm it: those are, of course, mutually consistent claims. But the premises of my arguments for the two claims appear to be inconsistent with one another. For, in Chapter 5, I treated the injustice of exploitation as lying,

---

[3] For further comment on this case, see section 4 below.

fundamentally, according to Marx, in the unequal distribution of means of production (distinguished as feature (1) above) that generates the surplus extraction, whereas, in Chapter 6, I treated the injustice of exploitation as (again, for Marx) fundamentally a matter of the extraction of the surplus itself (feature (3)): I did not present it as a secondary injustice deriving from a maldistribution of resources which is the primary injustice. In this chapter, I shall briefly recall the apparently contrasting treatments, show why they seem inconsistent, attempt to arbitrate between them, and then criticize some formulations of John Roemer which relate to my theme.[4]

2. In Chapter 5 I said that, in the Marxist critique of capitalist injustice, the exploitation of workers by capitalists derives entirely from the fact that workers lack access to physical productive resources. Here the Marxist charge is that the badly off suffer injustice in the left libertarian sense that they do not get their fair share of the external world (a charge, I noted, that requires no rejection or modification of the thesis of self-ownership). But in Chapter 6 the prime site of injustice appears to shift from the pre-production asset distribution to the forced extraction of product itself, from feature (1) (see p. 195 above) to feature (3). I do not say in Chapter 6 that Marxists think that the extraction is unjust because of what enables or induces it (the pre-production distribution), but because it involves what Marx called 'the theft of another person's labour time' (and this charge, I argued, requires affirmation of the thesis of self-ownership).

So I seem to say, in Chapter 5, that, for Marx, the initial unequal asset distribution is unjust, and that the consequent flow of product from worker to capitalist is unjust *for that reason*. Yet, in Chapter 6, the emphasis shifts to the forced product flow itself, that being treated as the essential injustice for Marx, so that the asset distribution counts as unjust precisely *because* it gives rise to such a flow. And these accounts of the matter look inconsistent with one another. *Can it be true both that the extraction is unjust because it reflects an unjust distribution and that the asset distribution is unjust because it generates that unjust extraction?* The answer, I believe, is 'yes', when the two 'because's in that question are appropriately and differently interpreted: that is what I hope to show.

It is often helpful, when faced, as we are here, with a conundrum, to model it in another area of thought where we can expect fewer prejudices

---

[4] The attentive reader may have noted that feature (2) (see p. 195 above) thereby falls out of view here. That is appropriate, since it is not germane to exploitation as such: see Chapter 6, p. 147 above.

to interfere with perception. So here is a relevant partial analogy to our problem. Suppose that whoever is in a position to do so distributes guns unequally, that is, to some people but not to everybody, and that guns enable those who have them to engage in highway robbery. Suppose that equal distribution of guns would have meant no highway robbery, because of mutual deterrence, and suppose also that the only relevant use of guns is to commit or deter highway robbery. Nobody cares about how elegant guns are, for example. They are valuable only as a means of destruction and threat.

Before we reflect further on the gun example, let me say why I have modelled it as I have. Distribution of guns is meant to parallel distribution of means of production, robbing parallels forcible extraction of a surplus, and the important requirement that people care about guns only as means of effecting or preventing highway robbery matches a stipulation we should make about means of production, to wit, that no one cares about them except *as* means of production. This means, for example, that no landowner wants to use (part of) his land as a private park, and no seed-corn can be eaten instead of being sown. That is, of course, false, but I am sure that its falsehood is irrelevant to the question of where the basic injustice lies in exploitation: no such fungibility in means of production, such possibility of their use as means not of production but of consumption, is required in Marx's story.

We can say this about the guns. We can say that highway robbery is unjust[5] and that an unequal distribution of guns is unjust. And we can say that the unequal distribution of guns is unjust because it enables highway robbery, meaning thereby that the gun inequality owes its injustice to what it enables: it counts as unjust because of the injustice (highway robbery) that it facilitates.

By contrast, it would be wrong to say that highway robbery owes its injustice to the unjust distribution of guns which makes it possible. What makes highway robbery unjust is simply that it is a forced unreciprocated transfer of money to the robber (by contrast with an unreciprocated transfer which is not unjust because it is a gift, and a forced reciprocal transfer the puzzling question of the justice of which need not be confronted here). Highway robbery is unjust because it is a transfer of money *for the wrong reason* (to wit, in this case, the victim's fear that the highwayman will kill him).

---

[5] Except, perhaps, in Robin-Hood-type cases where robbery rectifies injustice and might therefore be thought not unjust: we can set aside such cases here.

The maldistribution of guns is not *normatively* fundamental, even though transfer of money is unjust when and because it is effected by such means as gun threat. That fact does not make the maldistribution of guns normatively fundamental, for it is wrong only because of the unjust transfer that it enables, despite the fact that, where such maldistribution occurs, it is *causally* fundamental in the explanation of the possibility and the occurrence of unjust transfers. Even if gun maldistribution were the only possible cause of wrongful money extraction, that maldistribution would remain a normatively secondary (though causally primary) wrong.

Return now to the Marxist context. As long as we distinguish between causal and normative fundamentals, we can indeed say, to revert to the formulation under challenge (see p. 197 above), *both* that the extraction is unjust because it reflects an unjust distribution *and* that the asset distribution is unjust because it generates that unjust extraction. In parallel with the robbery example, the correct things to say about exploitation in Marxism are as follows. First, forced extraction of a surplus is wrong because of what it is, and not because it inherits the wrong of something else. Second, on our reasonable assumption that the sole purpose of means of production is to make product, a distribution of means of production is unjust only if and because it enables an unjust transfer of product. Finally, and in proper analogy with the gun example, the fact that the transfer of product is unjust when and because it is enabled by maldistribution of (this time) means of production does not make that maldistribution normatively fundamental. To think so is to confuse causal and normative fundamentality.

A transfer of product is unjust if and only if it occurs for the *wrong reason*. If an unreciprocated product transfer reflects nothing but different (unmanipulated) preferences in a straightforward way,[6] the transfer is not unjust. But it is unjust when and because it is caused by an unequal asset endowment, an unequal asset endowment which is unjust because it induces a wrongful, because forced, and not, for example, preference-based, flow. So we can say both that the extraction is unjust because it comes from an unequal (and therefore unjust) asset distribution, and that the latter is unjust because it generates an unjust extraction. *The flow is unjust because it reflects an unjust division of resources which is unjust because it tends to produce precisely such a flow.*

Articulation of the basis of the two conjuncts of the foregoing sentence shows that their joint affirmation generates no inconsistency or circle:

[6] As in the example from Roemer described at p. 205 below.

(i) The worker (*W*) is exploited by the capitalist (*C*), since *C* gets some of what *W* produces (for no return) by virtue of differential ownership of means of production, and where that causes *C* to get some of what *W* produces, *C*'s getting it is unjust.

(ii) Unequal distribution of means of production is unjust because it causes the unjustly unreciprocal transfer described in (i)

Many would accept the distinction I shall now draw between descriptive and normative features, and this and the next paragraph are not addressed to those who reject it, since there can be no attempt here to defend that distinction in general terms. A feature is descriptive if and only if affirming that a thing has it entails no judgement of value, whereas value judgements are entailed when normative features are predicated. Descriptive features of exploitation are that it is a forced and unreciprocated flow, and a descriptive feature of the pre-production asset distribution is that it is unequal. It is a normative feature of each (according to Marxists) that it is unjust.

The normative/descriptive distinction enables a reasonably precise statement of what is due to what in the present domain: the descriptive features of the flow are due to the descriptive features of the pre-production distribution; the normative feature of the flow is due to its descriptive features (and therefore, by transitivity, to the descriptive features of the pre-production distribution); and the normative feature of the pre-production distribution is due to the normative feature of the flow it enables. In a word (or two), the transfer in exploitation is unjust because of the nature (the descriptive features) of its cause, and that cause counts as unjust, has that normative feature, because what it causes is unjust.

For further clarification, let us distinguish three topics of assessment: an unequal asset distribution, its tendency to induce a forced product flow, and a forced product flow. My view is that the normatively fundamental injustice is such a flow, even though it counts as unjustly exploitative because it is caused by an unequal asset distribution. That distribution is unjust because of its tendency to induce a forced product flow, and that tendency makes the distribution unjust because the realization of the tendency is unjust.[7]

---

[7] Further clarification of that tripartite statement is available in section 3, which some non-philosophers will find tedious. (Some philosophers may find it even more tedious.)

3. I claim that an unjust distribution of means of production owes its injustice to the injustice of the surplus extraction that such a distribution facilitates. Some will be moved to resist that claim on the ground that an unjust distribution of means of production is *intrinsically* unjust, unjust, that is, no matter what its actual effects are. I agree with the latter statement, but I do not think that it refutes my claim that injustice in a distribution of means of production is secondary.

Different senses of 'intrinsic', 'intrinsically' (etc.) need to be distinguished here. The relevant pre-production distributive injustice is indeed intrinsic to that distribution in the first sense of 'intrinsic' that I shall introduce. But I shall also introduce a second sense of 'intrinsic' in which injustice is not intrinsic to the pre-production distribution: the derivative status of its injustice is related to the latter's not being intrinsic to it in that second sense.

I have said that, if y is unjust because it enables or tends to produce x and x is unjust,[8] then y's injustice derives from x's (even when x counts as unjust only when y produces it). Now, in one sense of 'intrinsically', a good or evil is intrinsically so if it is so apart from its effects. And, in that sense, an unequal distribution of means of production is indeed intrinsically unjust, even though its injustice is not primary but secondary, normatively speaking. Such a distribution is intrinsically unjust because its injustice resides in its *disposition* to produce a certain effect, a disposition which might not be activated. Its injustice does not depend on any effect that it *actually* produces, and it is, therefore, independent of whatever its actual effects may be.

Consider an instructive partial analogy. The intention to do something wrong is bad apart from its effects, and, in particular, even if no wrong act ensues from it (because the agent changes his mind, because his plan is thwarted, etc.). And doing something wrong, too, is bad apart from any (further) effects it may have. Both, thus, are, in the stated sense, intrinsically wrong, yet one may nevertheless think[9] that doing wrong is the primary bad here, that intending to do wrong is bad because of what it is an intention to do (whereas doing wrong is not bad *because* it issues from a bad intention (even if it does not count as *doing* wrong unless it so issues)).

---

[8] Note that 'and x is unjust' comes within the scope of 'because' here: x's injustice must be part of the explanation of y's injustice for the forthcoming consequent to follow.

[9] Some may think otherwise: the issue is a contested one, on which I need not take a stand here. What matters here is the logical co-tenability of 'intentions can be wrong apart from their effects' and 'wrong intentions are wrong because of what they are intentions to do'.

Analogously, an initially unequal distribution of means of production is unjust, apart from what its actual effects are, and, therefore, it is (in the stated sense) intrinsically unjust: it is unjust because of its tendency to cause injustice, which tendency is intrinsic to it, in the sense that it has that tendency whatever the actual effects of the tendency may be. But the injustice of the distribution nevertheless remains normatively derivative: the core generative injustice is forced unreciprocated transfer itself.

I allow, then, that a maldistribution of means of production is intrinsically unjust (unjust, that is, apart from its consequences), but I also say that *such a distribution is unjust because of what it causes* (and that it is therefore derivatively unjust). That sounds contradictory, so I must clarify the meaning which I attach to the phrase 'what it causes' in the italicized claim. 'What it causes' means, here, not what it has caused, is causing, or will cause, but, instead, what it *tends* to cause. A maldistribution of means of production is indeed unjust because of what it causes, because, that is, of a tendency inherent in it. Accordingly, it is intrinsically (though derivatively) unjust, because it is unjust no matter what its actual consequences are.

Up to now, a normative property of x has qualified as 'intrinsic' just in case x has it independently of the actual effects of x. A tougher condition for 'intrinsic' adds that the relevant normative property must be had non-relationally, that is, no matter how *other* things are.

To illustrate. A given batch of TNT is explosive whether or not it actually explodes. On our initial definition of 'intrinsic', its explosiveness is therefore an intrinsic property of the TNT. Yet one might say that the batch of TNT would not be explosive if it were placed on a planet that lacked oxygen, and, for that reason, one might deny that it is intrinsically explosive. In short, one might add to the conditions of 'x is intrinsically f' that x be f regardless not only of its effects but, more generally, of its *relations* to other things in the world.

A bad intention (which, we continue to suppose, is bad because of the badness of the action it is an intention to perform) remains bad no matter what happens in the world. Such an intention is intrinsically bad even in our second and stronger sense of 'intrinsic'. For its object, being an intentional (or 'intensional') object in the technical sense, does not vary with variations in the world. Nor, therefore, is the answer to whether or not an intention is bad exposed to such variation.

By contrast, and analogously with the TNT case, something can be bad because of its tendency *as things are*, a tendency it would lose if things were different. So, for example, an unequal distribution of means of production might be thought unjust if it is to people of identical preference orderings and talents, but just if to people who differ in those respects and where the inequality of the means of production distribution is appropriately compensating. Injustice of a distribution of means of production is, then, intrinsic in the first of the two senses of 'intrinsic' that I defined, but not in the second and stronger one. Its injustice depends on how other things stand, and, in particular, on whether other things so stand that the means of production distribution enables an unjust appropriation of surplus product.

4. I have thus far supposed that the characteristic effect of unequal distribution of means of production is to force some to produce for others. I have operated under this supposition because that is how Marx conceived economic injustice, and my question (see p. 196 above) has been: if this is the story of economic injustice, then where, precisely, does the injustice lie?

The injustice generated by maldistribution of means of production may, however, be described in more general terms, in terms, that is, of the leisure-and-income sets available to differently endowed (with means of production) agents, whether or not some extract product from others. Under some conditions, for example, an inequitable distribution of means of production will mean not that A is exploited by B but that A works harder than B for the same product, or gets less product for the same labour input.

Such a case was noted at p. 196 above, but I have not explored it, for two reasons. First, the case falls outside the Marxist frame within which my discussion is placed. Second, the interesting question that poses itself with respect to the non-exploitation case is structurally analogous to the one that has occupied us: it therefore does not require independent investigation. That question is: is the central injustice the means of production distribution or the skewed result it tends to produce? And the answer to it is: the normatively generative injustice is the final distribution, its propensity to produce which derivatively makes the causally generative injustice unjust.

5. An example in Volume I of *Capital* that I cited in footnote 11 of Chapter 5 shows that Marx was himself firmly against rooting the injustice of exploitation in the injustice of an *initial* unequal distribution of means of production. For, in Marx's example, there is an unjust flow without an initial unjust external asset distribution. Everyone starts out equal in

external assets, but, by dint of (so Marx is willing to suppose) 'his own labour and that of his forefathers', A's assets are so improved that he is now in a position to exploit B, who, we can further suppose, allowed his external assets to decay. (Marx seems to have meant that a generation or two passes by before exploitation begins. Let us, however, delete the 'forefathers' and treat the example as intra-generational, to forestall unhelpful objections.)

Because, in this example, there is an unjust flow without an unjust initial asset distribution, the injustice of the flow is not a function of any such initial distribution, and this confirms that the injustice of such initial distributions is a function, for Marx, of the injustice of the exploitative flow which they enable. But even if exploitative flow were, as the Marxian example shows that it is not, causally impossible without an initial skewed distribution of means of production, then, so we have seen, the latter would remain a (causally primary but) normatively derivative injustice.

6. John Roemer has argued, using ingenious examples of a sort that would not have occurred to Marx, that *not all unequal product flow on the market*[10] *is unjust, and, indeed, that such a flow is unjust only if it reflects an unjust initial asset distribution.* Roemer infers that the issue of flow is uninteresting, and that Marxists are therefore wrong to focus on it.[11] But I think that, although Roemer's premiss (the italicized statement) is substantially true,[12] it follows neither that unreciprocated flow is normatively uninteresting nor that (as Roemer also thinks) the normatively fundamental injustice is the asset maldistribution: so Roemer is wrong on two counts. I shall expound Roemer's position and then spell out why I believe it to be incorrect.

Now, I said that[13] we can agree with Roemer that all unjust exploitative flow requires an initial unjust distribution. And that seems to conflict with what Marx says about the special example discussed in section 5 above. But, if we readily agree with Marx about that example, then, so I suggest, that is because we suppose that there are certain assets unmentioned

---

10 'On the market', here, establishes a contrast with directly forced extraction (e.g. at gunpoint), fraud, etc.

11 He replies negatively to the title question of his essay 'Should Marxists be Interested in Exploitation?', which is my target here. (I do not ask whether Roemer's positions in that essay are consistent with what he says elsewhere.)

12 It is false only because ignorance and accident can affect the upshot of market transactions (see subsection 2c of Chapter 2 above). But it is convenient to forget about ignorance and accident here.

13 Setting aside special cases: see footnote 12.

by Marx which are initially, and perhaps also continuingly, unequally distributed, to wit the intangible assets of talent and foresight that can undermine an initial equality in external assets. Roemer would say that, in the *Capital* example, thus elaborated, the initial situation is unjust, and I would agree. It is unjust because the external asset distribution should compensate for, not facilitate the natural consequences of, the unequal intangible asset distribution. If, through some degree of commitment to self-ownership, we flinch from saying that, then it is hard to see how we can regard the *Capital* case, at any rate in the intra-generational form that I imposed on it, as one of unjust exploitation.

Now, Roemer says that an unequal flow, which is what he means by 'exploitation' in the article I am discussing, is not unjust when it does not reflect an unjust asset distribution. And, being free of commitment to self-ownership, Roemer treats an initial asset distribution as just only if it can be judged equal when both external *and* intangible assets (talent) are taken into account. Consider now this Roemeresque example: X and Y are equal in talent and in external assets *but* they have different preferences, and, in particular, different income/leisure trade-offs. X is a basker and Y is a workaholic. So X lets Y work on X's means of production after Y has finished working on his own. Y works ten hours, five on his own and five on X's means of production, and some of Y's product, say, 2½ hours worth, goes to X.[14] We can agree with Roemer that there is nothing unjust here. There is nothing unjust because (although there is extraction) there is no unjust extraction.[15]

Such examples establish Roemer's premiss, which is that unequal flow is not, as such, unjust. But his conclusion from that premiss, which is that unequal asset distribution, not exploitative flow, is the (normatively) fundamental injustice, does not, in my view, follow. If that conclusion followed, then the reasoning in section 2 of this chapter would have been mistaken.

The reason why Roemer's conclusion does not follow is that it remains possible, and plausible, for all that his premiss (unequal flow is not, as such, unjust) is true, that *it is the unequal flow that is unjust, when it reflects an unjustly unequal asset distribution, which distribution is unjust precisely*

---

[14] These means of production conk out if they are used for more than five hours a day.

[15] The extraction reflects nothing but different preferences. But, contrary to what Roemer says at p. 272 of 'Should Marxists . . . ?', it is false that unjust exploitation can never occur on the basis of different preferences. For a splendid counter-example to that generalization, see the Appendix in 'The Relation between Self-Interest and Justice in Contractarian Ethics', by Christopher Morris.

because it enables an unjustly equal flow so that, pace *Roemer, the latter injustice is normatively fundamental.* After all, what *else* is unfair about the distribution, on the legitimate assumption[16] that all people care about in means of production is that they *are* means of production? It is absurd to advise us to be interested in asset distribution *as opposed to* flow of product when it is flow of product that makes asset distribution interesting!

The Marxian position is that, since labour and labour alone creates the product, and since (differential) ownership of means of production enables non-labourers to obtain some of what labour creates, just *because* they own means of production, their ownership of means of production is morally illegitimate. Here, indeed, is a great crux dividing Marxist from bourgeois thought. For Marxists say, in effect, that *since* labour produces the product and private owners of capital appropriate part of it, private capital is morally illegitimate and workers are exploited; and bourgeois thinkers say, in effect, that *since* private capital is morally legitimate, workers are not exploited, despite the fact that they produce the product and part of it redounds to capital.

I nail my colours to the formulation italicized two paragraphs back. I therefore part company with Roemer when he declares that

exploitation theory . . . does not provide a proper model or account of Marxian moral sentiments: the proper Marxian claim, I think, is for equality in the distribution of productive assets, not for the elimination of exploitation.[17]

(where, as always in Roemer's paper, exploitation just means unequal flow). Roemer neglects to consider what the point of equality of distribution of productive assets is, if that point is not to make an unjust flow impossible. If, as Roemer insists, 'the proper Marxian claim . . . is for equality in the distribution of productive assets', then that is because such a distribution makes (unjust) exploitation impossible, and, that being so, it is entirely inappropriate to *contrast* the quoted 'claim' with the one that Roemer seeks to degrade. The bottom line must include preventing unjust treatment of some by others: it cannot be (only) preventing what enables such treatment to occur.

Entering another's house is not wrong when you have its owner's permission and he has given you a key, but it is wrong when you have no such permission and you use a gun to enter it. Yet it does not follow that what is wrong when you use a gun to enter is not that you enter but that you use a gun, in this case, merely as it happens, to enter. *The entering is*

---

[16] See p. 198 above.   [17] 'Should Marxists . . . ?', pp. 274–5.

wrong because it is by means of a gun and the possession of guns is wrong precisely because they enable wrongful entry: wrongful entry is the normatively generative (though causally secondary) wrong here.

Analogously: Roemer is right that (defining 'exploitation', here, as unequal flow, not as unjust flow) exploitation is not by nature unjust. But exploitation, and not unequal means of production, is, in its unjust form, the central and normatively generative injustice, even though it is not always an injustice.

Consider, again, the highwayman. It is not in general an injustice that a cheque is signed. It is an injustice when it is signed because a highwayman threatens the signer with death if she does not sign. An injustice then occurs over and above that of the highwayman's having and threatening with his gun, since the victim might have chosen to die instead of signing. That this *counts* as an injustice because of the gun (cheque-signing is not in general unjust) manifestly does not prevent it from *being* unjust, and, so I have argued, it also does not prevent gun inequality from being merely secondarily unjust: gun inequality is unjust *because* it enables unjust transfers, such as highway robbery, to occur. And, similarly, although 'the injustice of an exploitative allocation depends upon the injustice of the initial distribution',[18] what makes the latter unjust is its propensity to generate the primary injustice, an exploitative allocation.

In my solution to the conundrum introduced at p. 197, I say that the asset distribution is unjust because it enables or makes possible an unjust flow. I do not say that it necessitates such a flow, since I am aware that, for various reasons (for example, a concern for her own dignity), a poorly endowed worker might prefer extreme poverty to working for a capitalist; and a philanthropic capitalist could distribute the whole product to his workers (and remain a capitalist only because he loves making decisions about investment and so on). Simplifying matters[19] like the economist he is, such cases are ruled out by Roemer's assumptions, under which people maximize utility and find utility in income and leisure alone. On those axioms, the asset distribution necessitates a certain flow, so that process or flow disappears from view as irrelevant precisely because it is, as it were, squeezed into the asset distribution itself, by virtue of the stated ruling assumptions. That is why Roemer can say 'that the existence of exploitation [in the standard circumstances on which Marxists focus –

---

[18] Roemer, *Free to Lose*, p. 57.
[19] Which is permissible in relation to many economic problems and disastrous in relation to many ethical problems, such as the one to which this chapter is devoted.

GAC] is *equivalent* to inequality in distribution of initial assets'.[20] The two are indeed equivalent, within Roemer's constraining frame, but they are otherwise quite different, and their specially constructed equivalence is a poor reason for concluding that exploitation is not the primary injustice.[21]

---

[20] 'Should Marxists . . . ?', p. 274, emphasis added.

[21] Contrast the last-mentioned Roemerian argument with the one I confronted in section 3 above. The latter ran as follows:

> (Unjust) inequality need not cause exploitation.
> ∴ (Unjust) asset inequality is intrinsically unjust.
> ∴ (Unjust) asset equality is not merely derivatively unjust.

Roemer's goes thus:

> (Unjust) asset inequality *must* cause exploitation.
> ∴ (Unjust) asset inequality is not merely derivatively unjust.

The premiss and the first inference of the section 3 argument are correct, but its second inference is not. The premiss of Roemer's argument is only artificially true. I believe, moreover, that its inference is incorrect, but that somewhat refined claim has not been argued for above.

9. Self-ownership: delineating the concept

To every Individuall in nature is given an individual property by nature, not to be invaded or usurped by any: for everyone as he is himselfe, so he has a self propriety, else could he not be himselfe . . . Every man by nature being a King, Priest and Prophet in his owne naturall circuit and compasse. (Richard Overton, *An Arrow Against all Tyrants*)

. . . every man has a property in his own person; this nobody has any right to but himself. The labour of his body and the work of his hands we may say are properly his. (John Locke, *Second Treatise of Government*)

Man can neither be inherited, sold, nor be made the object of a gift; he can be no one else's property because he is his own property. (Johann Gottlieb Fichte, *A Discourse on the Reclamation of the Freedom of Thought from the Princes of Europe, who have hitherto Suppressed it*)

1. In Chapters 3–7 I studied the implications of the thesis of self-ownership for the question of the justice of the distribution of goods of all kinds. With respect to that general question of distributive justice, principles about the ownership of the physical world have a bearing no smaller than that of principles about who owns whose powers. But, over the course of this chapter and the next, I abstract so far as possible from the world-ownership side of the problem of distribution, in order to focus on the concept, and the thesis, of self-ownership itself.

The concept of self-ownership is not identical with the thesis of self-ownership: the latter might be false, while the former, being a concept, cannot be false, save where 'false' is used, floridly, to mean incoherent, or inconsistent, or irredeemably vague, or irremediably indeterminate. It should not be necessary to lay emphasis on the distinction between the concept and the thesis, but my polemical experience shows that it is wise to do so. For, in the resistance and criticism that greeted the publication of the articles on self-ownership which form the basis of Chapters 3–7 of this book, not all commentators distinguished their confidence that the thesis of self-ownership is false from a conviction that the very concept of self-ownership is confused. In conformity with that propensity to conflate the two issues, some mistook my insistence on the coherence of the concept of self-ownership, as such, as a concept, as a form of approval of the thesis of self-ownership.[1]

The present chapter unrolls as follows. In section 2 I confront the claim that the concept of self-ownership is incoherent, or, as an argument from Kant has it, self-contradictory. In section 3 I argue against the view, expressed by Ronald Dworkin, that the concept is too indeterminate to serve any purpose in political philosophy. Section 4 takes up and, I think, defeats the claim of David Gauthier that self-ownership is consistent with redistributive taxation (of, in particular, market rent), and section 5 argues against a related Rawlsian claim, that such taxation does not force some to help others. Section 6 comments on the complex relationship between the concept of self-ownership and the harming/not helping distinction.

2. Some philosophers think that the phrase 'self-ownership' purports to conjoin semantic elements that cannot be united in the required way. If they are right, self-ownership is just a would-be concept, like the would-be concept of a green number, or (Wittgenstein's example) the would-be concept of its being 5 o'clock on the sun. There is nothing wrong with the phrases '5 o'clock' and 'on the sun', but the phrase that results when they are concatenated relates to no coherent concept. And some say that while one may, similarly, speak of persons, and of ownership, it does not follow, and is false, that one may speak of self-ownership, of a person owning the person that she is.

But what is there in the content of the concepts of ownership and personhood that might disqualify the concept of self-ownership? Persons and their powers can be controlled, among others by themselves, and there is surely always an answer to the question, with respect to anything that can be controlled, who has the right to control it? – even if that answer is: no one.[2] The thesis of self-ownership says that the answer to all such questions about persons and their powers is: the person herself. Why should that answer be judged incoherent?

---

[1] There is, for example, no textual basis for Alan Ryan's attribution to me of the claim 'that anyone who minds very much about liberty is committed to the idea that we are self-owning creatures' (Review of Jonathan Wolff, *Robert Nozick*, p. 155.) Cf. footnote 23 below.

[2] Which is the answer suggested by Joseph Raz for certain questions bearing on the issue of self-ownership: see Chapter 10, section 2, below.

The claim that the concept of self-ownership is incoherent comes in a number of versions, but they are variations on a theme of Kant that I shall look at in a moment. First, though, I remind the reader of a point already made (see Chapter 3, p. 68 above), that 'self-ownership' does not denote the ownership of a self. I do not myself believe, as some appear to do, that there exist selves, as opposed to persons, who shave themselves, criticize themselves, and (so some think) own themselves. But whether or not there exist selves,[3] when a person shaves or criticizes himself, he no more performs those operations on some deeply inner thing called a 'self' than a self-starting engine does something to an especially intimate part of itself when it gets itself to go.

We do not say that a person owns some deeply inner thing when we say that he owns himself. To say that A enjoys self-ownership is just to say that A owns A: 'self', here, signifies a reflexive relation. I see nothing in the concept of ownership which (like fatherhood) excludes a reflexive instance of it. Anyone who purports to see in the concept something that excludes its reflexive use must say what that is.

Immanuel Kant rose to that challenge, when he argued that the would-be concept of self-ownership was an impossible concept, because self-contradictory. It is ironical that Kant made such an argument, in the light of Robert Nozick's view that Kant's prohibition against using a person merely as a means *supports* the principle of self-ownership. I show (at Chapter 10, section 4 below) that, contrary to what Nozick thinks, Kant's doctrine about means and ends does not support the principle of self-ownership, but I am with Nozick and against Kant on the issue of whether the very concept of self-ownership is coherent.

Kant said:

Man cannot dispose over himself because he is not a thing; he is not his own property; to say that he is would be self-contradictory; for insofar as he is a person he is a Subject in whom the ownership of things can be vested, and if he were his own property, he would be a thing over which he could have ownership. But a person cannot be a property and so cannot be a thing which can be owned, for it is impossible to be a person and a thing, the proprietor and the property.[4]

There might be more than one argument embedded in this jumble of statements (which derive from students' lecture notes), but, however that

---

[3] As opposed to minds, some of whose recesses are remote.
[4] *Lectures on Ethics*, p. 165. (Note the contrast between what Kant says and the doctrine in the excerpt from Fichte at the head of this chapter.)

may be, I doubt that an argument better than the following can be extracted from them:

Man is a person.
Nothing can be both a person and a thing.
∴Man is not a thing.

But

Only things can be owned.
∴Man cannot be owned.
∴Man cannot own himself.[5]

That is a valid argument, with three premisses. I need not challenge either of the first two premisses. But the third premiss ('Only things can be owned') is entirely question-begging in the present context: nothing argued here shows that only things (where, by the second premiss, persons are not a subset of things) can be owned, to one who does not already accept that persons cannot own themselves. Kant's argument therefore fails to establish that self-ownership is self-contradictory.

In propounding the foregoing argument, Kant is trying to pull a normative rabbit out of a conceptual hat. For the ulterior purpose of his argument is to show that it is morally unacceptable for human beings to sell parts of themselves, engage in prostitution, etc. Kant's idea is that, since self-ownership is incoherent, acting as though one owned one's parts and powers is immoral.

Kant no doubt has another argument for the latter conclusion, which does not depend on conceptual *legerdemain*. It is this: human beings are ends-in-themselves, and parts of ends-in-themselves ought not to be sold for gain. Therefore (whether or not the very concept of self-ownership is self-contradictory) acting as though one owned one's parts and powers is immoral. Whatever one thinks of that different argument, it does not

---

[5] You might think that, contrary to my representation of him, Kant is relying on the idea that what owns and what is owned could not be identical, which is different from the idea that man is of the wrong metaphysical type to be an item that is owned. But, unlike the premisses that I have featured, this different argument, from the supposed irreflexivity of the ownership relation, allows that *others* might own a man, and Kant clearly means his argument to exclude that too.

Again, you might think that Kant is objecting only to the *phrase* 'self-ownership', and its cognates, that he has no objection to persons' having the *rights* associated with self-ownership by those who are not allergic to the phrase. But that is a misinterpretation, since the whole point of Kant's demonstration is to show that 'Man cannot dispose over himself' as those rights would license: he argues, in the surrounding context, against prostitution, sale of parts of one's body, etc.

impugn the conceptual coherence of self-ownership, which is what has been at issue in this section.

3. Some think that the concept of self-ownership is vitiated not by incoherence but by indeterminacy. Ronald Dworkin objected,[6] in just such terms, to my use of the concept of self-ownership to identify libertarianism. He said that the principle of self-ownership is too indeterminate to pick out a distinct position in political philosophy. He reasoned as follows: to own something is to enjoy some or other set of rights with respect to that thing. But one might envisage a number of importantly different sets of rights over themselves and their own powers in virtue of which we could say of people that they are self-owners. The principle of self-ownership therefore lacks determinate content.

The premises of this sceptical argument do not appear to me to sustain its conclusion. They do not show that the principle of self-ownership legislates indeterminately. For one thing, they do not refute the hypothesis, which I hereby propose, that the principle achieves determinacy through its requirement that *everyone* enjoys *full* self-ownership rights. It might indeed make no determinate sense to say, in the abstract, that Jones owns himself. But when one stipulates that *each* person has *full* private property in himself, then the constraints of universality and fullness combine to disqualify some sets of rights as possible denotations of 'self-ownership', and, on the hypothesis proposed here, only one set of rights survives, with which self-ownership can then be (uniquely) identified.

In the present proposal, the stipulation that self-ownership confers the fullest right a person (logically) can have over herself provided that each other person also has just such a right[7] generates a procedure for determining the content of self-ownership. Determinacy might be achieved through the identification of a set of rights S which is such that every person can have them over herself and where S confers fuller rights over

---

[6] He put the objection I go on to describe at a seminar in Oxford in the summer of 1986. Compare Richard Arneson, 'Lockean Self-Ownership', p. 54: 'The idea of self-ownership is not nearly so determinate as competing conceptions of justice, such as act-utilitarianism or Rawls's principles of justice . . .'

[7] It should go without saying, even though many have said this in past misplaced criticism of me, that one could construct a concept of self-ownership less ample in the rights it confers than the maximal concept which I seek to construct here: Judith Thomson's well-considered concept of self-ownership as 'first property' (see Chapter 8 of *The Realm of Rights*) is a case in point. But I seek a maximal concept because, as the informed reader will, I am sure, agree, that is the concept to which libertarians are attached. That one might use the term 'self-ownership' to denote something less extravagant is here beside the point.

herself than any other set of universally enjoyable rights does. Dworkin's premises do not show that there is no such set.

Self-ownership, one might say, is the principle which, in a phrase of Dworkin's, allows 'differences in ability' to 'produce income differences in a laissez-faire economy among people with the same ambitions'.[8] Laissez-faire economies vary in their rules of operation, but that is not a reason for condemning the unexplicated idea of a laissez-faire economy (which Dworkin uses) as hopelessly indeterminate. And, while the idea of a person's ownership of himself might indeed be capable of different interpretations (perhaps the hypothesis discussed in the foregoing two paragraphs is misconceived), it is no less determinate than the unexplicated idea of his ownership of other resources, to which Dworkin has qualmlessly helped himself in his own writing.[9] I do not think that it is harder to say what rights I have if I own myself than it is to say what rights I have if I own a knife, or a tract of land, or a horse, or a slave. Those ownerships are different, in all kinds of ways, but that is because knives, tracts, horses and human beings differ in ways that induce different ownership structures when they enter the relation of ownership, not because a different concept of ownership applies in each case. And the case of slave ownership is particularly instructive, since it affords a way of introducing the concept of self-ownership that I used at p. 68 of Chapter 3 above: to own oneself is to enjoy with respect to oneself all those rights which a slaveowner has over a complete chattel slave.

Return to the procedure for constructing a list of self-ownership rights laid out two paragraphs back. Perhaps no set of rights meets the condition the procedure defines. Consider a possibly parallel case. If we stipulate that every piece of land is maximally owned by some person, we can infer that no one has rights of way on others' land, but there is no similarly obvious inference available with respect to what sort of structures (of, say, a light-obstructing kind) each of the full owners can erect on her land. The requirement of universal maximal land-ownership may not settle that. And universal maximal person-ownership might be similarly indeterminate. But, in all cases of ownership, the requirements of universality and maximality will generate core rights that are indisputable. The residual

---

[8] 'Equality of Resources', p. 311.
[9] See *ibid.*, p. 283. Dworkin later defended a maximal freedom of use of personally owned resources. Whether or not he was right in his normative claim that that is how equally distributed resources should be owned, applying the concept of maximal freedom of use to the case of self-ownership raises no difficulty not also raised by Dworkin's normative claim. (See 'The Place of Liberty', section IV.)

indeterminacies will no doubt frustrate some intellectual projects, but not, I am confident, the one in which I am engaged. For, while there might indeed be a plurality of maximal rights-sets that compete for the title of 'full self-ownership', they will not differ in ways that matter to the questions about distributive justice which dominate this book and which motivate interest in self-ownership. Universal maximal self-ownership delivers everything that we need, even if it does not deliver everything.

Thus, for example, universal maximal self-ownership ensures that my right to use my fist as I please stops at the tip of your nose, because of your rights, under universal maximal self-ownership, over your nose. True enough, if each of us had less right over his nose and more over his fist, so that each was entitled to punch the other's nose, then in no clear sense would our respective budgets of rights be smaller. But we are not looking for universal maximal rights, *tout court*, but universal maximal rights of *ownership*, over a particular body, by the person whose body (in the natural sense) it is, and all that, together, fixes rights over fists and noses in the stated way. This is but an elementary application to self-ownership of what we would say about private property in things. The individual's budget of rights may not shrink when he gets a right of way across the land of another who at the same time gets such a right of way across his, but private property rights in land are thereby, nevertheless, incontestably pared down.

The polemically crucial right of self-ownership is the right not to (be forced to) supply product or service to anyone. The claim that we have no such a right speaks to central questions in political philosophy, and the principle of self-ownership unambiguously confers that right. Failing to help another person cannot be construed as interfering with his right to use himself as he wishes, and not being required to help others leaves everyone with more rights over their own powers than they would otherwise have. Accordingly, the right not to supply service or product forms part of any plausible reading of the self-ownership principle.

If you think those asseverations dogmatic, consider, again, the ownership of material things, which is the proper model for the concept of self-ownership. If I am the (full) legal owner of a knife, then the state may prevent me from putting it in your back, but it may not, in the ordinary course of events, direct me to place it at your disposal, because, for example, you need it at the moment, or because you deserve it more than I do. The state can ensure that I do not use my knife aggressively, but it may not force me to use it to help you. Nor, importantly (from the point of view of the analogy with self-ownership), may it direct me to use it to some extent on your behalf as a condition of my using it on my own behalf. The state cannot both recognize my full property in the knife and regulate my use of it on such property-ignoring bases.

Now, those principles about the ownership of knives come from the concept of ownership, not from anything special in the concept of a knife. Accordingly, if I own myself, then analogous points apply with respect to my rights in my arm, or my brain. I do not fully own them, nor, hence, myself, if someone else has a right, not based on prior agreement with me, to tell me how to use them. Nor is my full ownership of them consistent with a directive that, whenever I use them for my own benefit, I must, to a stated extent, use them to benefit others too: that is the essence of redistributive income taxation. I do not (fully) own myself if I am required to give others (part of) what I earn by applying my powers.

True enough, if a person uses an asset (for example, her talent) to generate income to pay a tax which she owes to the government, it does not follow that her ownership of that asset is prejudiced. But if a portion of her earnings from the asset is collected by the state just *because* she earns money through its use, then her ownership of the asset is indeed prejudiced: her right to the income it generates, which is a key incident in private ownership of an asset,[10] is breached. There are reasons consistent with self-ownership for imposing taxes: to pay for police protection of property,[11] to correct for externalities, to redistribute land rent (on Georgian grounds) and so on. But a tax on earned market income as such is inconsistent with self-ownership.

I am here showing agreement with the view of Robert Nozick that differentially high taxation of the market income of unusually productive people contradicts the principle (which he affirms and I reject) that each person is the legitimate owner of his own powers, and may therefore not be forced to use them to help others, as redistributive taxation requires. Because I agree with Nozick about that, I disagree both with David Gauthier, who believes that self-ownership (which he, like Nozick, endorses) is consistent with (a certain form of) redistributive taxation, and

---

[10] See Tony Honoré, *Making Law Bind*, pp. 169–70. For more on rights to income, see section 4 below, especially pp. 220–1.

[11] Notice that, for all the complexities with respect to what is voluntary and what is coerced which characterize Nozick's *hypothetical* 'invisible-hand' construction of the legitimate state (see *Anarchy, State, and Utopia*, Part I), he does not regard voluntary individual subscription by a person to an *actual* state as a necessary condition of its right to tax that person.

with a Rawlsian view which denies that redistributive taxation (of the usual form) makes the better off *help* the worse off. I shall first pursue my dispute with Gauthier, and then turn to Rawls.

4. Gauthier notes that many will suppose that a person's

right to his basic endowment – his natural capacities – gives him the right to factor rent deriving from the endowment. Wayne Gretzky has the right to his unique hockey skills; he may use them as he pleases; does he not therefore have the right to the rent which they command? But his right to use his hockey skills as he pleases is not affected by the distribution of rent . . . a confiscatory tax on rent would not, and could not, affect his willingness to play hockey. Each person's right to his basic endowment is a right to the exclusive use of that endowment in market and co-operative interaction. But market interaction is not affected by the distribution of the surplus represented by rent; each person's exclusive use of his capacities is left untouched if rent is confiscated . . . The benefit represented by factor rent is part of the surplus afforded by [society considered as a single co-operative enterprise], for it arises only in social interaction.[12]

Accordingly, Gauthier favours a redistribution of rent under his principle of minimax relative concession, whose nature need not occupy us here, since what matters here is *that*, not how, rent is to be redistributed. Gauthier does allow that confiscating rent restricts

a particular liberty – specifically the freedom to collect factor rent. But this is no part of the freedom of a solitary being; the surplus represent by rent arises only through interaction. And so it is not a necessary part of market freedom conceived as an extension of the natural freedom enjoyed by a Robinson Crusoe.[13]

Gauthier's argument for his claim that a person's 'right to his basic endowment'[14] does not give him 'the right to factor rent deriving from the endowment' conflates three distinct magnitudes. There is, first, a conflation of *factor rent* and *producer surplus*. This conflation, which I shall presently expose, is made, routinely, by economists, and, under assumptions suited to economists' purposes,[15] the two magnitudes indeed become extensionally equivalent. But economists' purposes are not philosophers', and confusion between the two ideas in the context of Gauthier's argument is damaging. Each of the aforementioned magni-

[12] *Morals by Agreement*, pp. 273–4.
[13] *Ibid.*, p. 276.
[14] Which either *is* his right of self-ownership or (if 'endowment' covers not the whole person but just his productive capacity) is the particular self-ownership right of prime concern to questions of distributive justice: see p. 215 above.
[15] Such as, for example, that persons have identical utility functions.

218 Self-ownership, freedom, and equality

tudes is, moreover, different from a third one with which Gauthier identifies them: the difference between a person's market earnings and what he could get for his efforts in the absence of social interaction.

Factor rent is the difference between the price of a factor and the lower price at which it would sell if, contrary to fact, it were possible to expand its supply. Factor rent thus reflects insuperable scarcity: high-grade land commands a factor rent when there is less of it than is demanded and less good land cannot be brought up to the same high grade. Analogously, Gretzky's talent earns a factor rent, since no one, or too few, can produce new Gretzkys, or make themselves Gretzky-like, with a view to underselling him.

Factor rent is not the same thing as *producer surplus*, which is the difference between the price of a factor in a use to which it is allocated and the minimum price its supplier would accept for it in that use (which is sometimes called his 'reservation price'). It is true by definition that a supplier continues to supply what he otherwise does even when his producer surplus is taxed away.

Now Gauthier seems to regard it as crucial to his claim that a tax on rent is legitimate[16] that imposing it would not diminish the supply of the rent-attracting service. But that is true of rent only when it happens to coincide with, or to be less than, the producer surplus afforded to the service-supplier at the rent-inclusive rate. It is true not, as Gauthier implies, of rent as such, but of producer surplus as such. Thus, if Gretzky hates playing hockey, his rent-including salary might be identical with his reservation price: it is logically possible, for all that his salary is indeed swollen with rent, that Gretzky would hang up his skates and sell insurance if he got one dollar less a year for playing hockey. Contrariwise, if Gretzky loves hockey, then it is possible that taxing much more than just the rent element in his salary would not turn him away from his current occupation.[17]

In any reconstruction of his argument, Gauthier would have to decide whether what is taxable, consistently with self-ownership, is rent proper or producer surplus. But, whichever of those magnitudes he might be inclined to choose, he would also have to clear up a further and more

---

[16] That is: does not prejudice the taxed person's 'right to his basic endowment'.
[17] For further severe criticism of Gauthier's doctrine on rent, see John Harsanyi's review of *Morals by Agreement*, pp. 346–8. Among other things, Harsanyi refutes Gauthier's claim that 'market interaction is not affected by the distribution of the surplus represented by rent' (see above, p. 217). Harsanyi's excellent points are unconnected with the critique of Gauthier prosecuted in this section.

serious conflation that appears in his text: between factor rent/producer surplus, and the fruit of social interaction.

For it is a crucial claim about rent/producer surplus in Gauthier's argument that it 'arises only in social interaction': it is because it arises thus that it is subject to redistribution, within the terms of Gauthier's hypothetical contractarianism. Now, I shall presently show that producer surplus (as opposed to economic rent) does not, in fact, require social interaction,[18] but the important immediate point is that if its origin in social interaction is what makes rent taxable, then the floodgates have been opened very widely indeed. For it is no more true of rent than of producer surplus, and, indeed, of most consumer demand, that it is due to social interaction. It is only in virtue of social interaction that there is any demand for my service, even at its reservation price. It is only in virtue of social interaction that not only Gretzky but also the most mediocre and marginal hockey player acquires his skills.[19] Gauthier rejects pure *laissez-faire* in favour of *laissez-faire* constrained by, *inter alia*,[20] the redistribution of rent. But the present ground of that restriction on *laissez-faire*, that the stated *redistribuendum* is a result of social interaction, would justify taxing virtually all income. And even if what is to be taxed is not just *anything* that arises through social interaction, but only that part of what arises through it which exceeds what would redound to a given person in the state of nature, the taxman's take would certainly be more than it is in contemporary states that effect more redistribution than (so I suppose) Gauthier would wish to encourage or permit.

To clarify the conceptual position further, it is worth noting that, on empirically implausible but entirely coherent assumptions, the surplus-over-state-of-nature criterion for taxability might justify no taxing of Gretzky. Suppose that Gretzky' source of both sustenance and pleasure in the state of nature would have been coconuts, which he would have got by shaking certain trees until the coconuts dropped. And suppose that he would have got just so many coconuts that he is indifferent between what his life would have been in the state of nature and his life as a trained hockey player on a vast salary in contemporary society.[21] Then

---

18 See p. 220 below for a possible case of producer surplus in an autarkic state of nature.
19 Daniel Hausman makes a similar point and draws devastating conclusions from it: 'Are Markets Morally Free Zones?', pp. 324–6.
20 Taxation is also required, he says, to cater for externalities, and to sustain the state activities (e.g. protection of private property) required by market interaction.
21 This kind of comparison might seem mind-boggling, but it is essential to Gauthier's theory that it be possible. (For my own part, I find the comparison difficult epistemically, but not conceptually.)

(1) Gretzky's income in society would still contain a huge component of rent, but (2) he would be no better off in society than in the jungle, and should therefore not be taxed, on Gauthier's surplus-over-state-of-nature criterion. And all that is so whatever assumptions we make about Gretzky's producer surplus either in society or in the state of nature. (Gretzky's producer surplus in the state of nature is the difference between the number of coconuts that fall as a result of his tree-shaking and the lesser number that he would regard as rendering *just* worthwhile the amount of effort he devotes to that shaking.)

But those are unlikely assumptions about anyone's condition in the state of nature, and, on plausible ones, Gauthier's argument would, as we have seen, when properly generalized, license much more redistribution than he would wish to allow. Yet I do not think that the premises of Gauthier's argument, under any interpretation of them,[22] justify any redistribution at all, if, as Gauthier does, one affirms a person's 'right to his basic endowment'.

I do not say the absurd thing that redistributive taxation completely removes that right. I say the banal thing that such taxation reduces it, and I say this, banal though it is, because many (not only Gauthier) implicitly deny it. Look at it this way. Suppose that I own three frying pans and you own three feather dusters, and we trade them with one another. The state then claims the right to confiscate one of my post-trade dusters and one of your post-trade pans, on the Gauthier grounds that (1) I would have accepted two dusters, and you two pans and (2) there are no dusters or pans in the state of nature. Then, although (1) and (2) are true, the state's claim trenches against our rights in what we originally owned: we have not been allowed to get what others are willing to give us for them. And the same goes, *mutatis mutandis*, when what I offer is not my frying pans but a day's *use* of them, which is, of course, relevantly analogous to my offering you a day's use of my talent, which is what you get when you hire me for a day. If my wage for that day, whether it be paid in dusters or in dollars, has tax docked off it for Gauthier's reasons, however good, independently considered, those reasons for taxing may be, then my rights over my talent are restricted.[23] (Suppose that whenever I scratch

---

22 There are six (at least abstractly) possible versions of the premises of Gauthier's argument: they feature rent or producer surplus or surplus-over-state-of-nature or any two or all three of those.

23 I disagree with the view of Jeremy Waldron that 'there is no sense to the idea that there is a natural phenomenon called "reaping the benefits of one's talents" which is understood apart from the social arrangements and institutions that define one's relationships to other

my back I am required by the state to scratch someone else's. It surely follows that I lack full ownership of my hand. And the implication of non-(full) ownership survives when we suppose that if I scratch your back in return for your scratching mine, then some further scratching of the backs of third parties can be exacted by the state from each of us, after the fashion of redistributive income taxation.)

Accordingly, even if (what is not necessarily true)[24] 'a confiscatory tax on rent would not . . . affect [Gretzky's] willingness to play hockey', it does not follow that such a tax does not affect 'his right to use his hockey skills as he pleases'. It is also true that, as Gauthier contends, 'the surplus represented by rent arises only through interaction', and maybe it follows that 'it is not a necessary part of market freedom conceived as an extension of the natural freedom enjoyed by a Robinson Crusoe', but why should it follow that taxing the surplus is not a violation of a person's right to dispose of his capacities as he chooses? Persons are exclusive owners of what they own only if they are entitled to set the terms on which they will exchange what they own with one another.[25] Self-ownership goes with market freedom, not with 'market freedom conceived as an extension of the natural freedom enjoyed by a Robinson Crusoe', whether or not that phrase articulates a coherent idea.

I have argued that Gauthier goes astray when he denies a person's 'right to his basic endowment – his natural capacities – gives him the right to factor rent deriving from the endowment' (see p. 217 above). A right to

---

people' (*The Right to Private Property*, p. 404), where such arrangements are, as Waldron means them to be here, socially *legislated*. We do not have to contemplate specific social legislation to find sense in the idea that, if *A* fully owns *X* and *B* fully owns *Y*, then *A* and *B* are entitled to agree on the terms on which they will exchange those ownables. It is not true that a self-owned 'talent has to be understood as a sort of a function that takes social structures as its argument' (*ibid.*, p. 406). The concept of a social structure (roughly, *laissez-faire*) which maximally respects the self-ownership talent is easy to understand.

Section 3 of Chapter XI of Waldron's book, from which the foregoing passages have been drawn, illustrates my complaint (see section 1 above) that some authors fail to distinguish between the concept of self-ownership and the thesis of self-ownership. Waldron presents (good) arguments against the thesis in the guise of (false) claims about the content of the concept.

[24] See p. 218 above: it is true only if his rent is equal to or less than his producer surplus.

[25] I agree here with Jan Narveson, who complains that Gauthier's view of rent constitutes a 'denial of our entitlement to make the best use we can of our natural endowment. It seems scarcely compatible with that entitlement to deprive people of whatever percentage of their incomes would leave them with an amount they would still be willing to do the same thing for' (*The Libertarian Idea*, p. 206). That is, I agree with Narveson about what the content of the stated entitlement is, but not that we have it.

factor rent is an ineliminable part of a right to one's basic endowment, and, therefore, of (full) self-ownership. Now, for completeness, I want to note a further respect in which the schedule of rights assigned to people by Gauthier differs from the rights implied by full self-ownership. But this further difference between Gauthier people's rights and full self-ownership involves no distortion of the notion of a 'right to one's basic endowment', of the sort that, so I claimed, Gauthier accomplishes in his doctrine of economic rent.

The Gauthier formulation which requires attention here is the proviso which his contractors satisfy before they sit down together to agree on morals. That proviso 'prohibits worsening the situation of others except where this is necessary to avoid worsening one's own position'.[26] (More colloquially, an agent may harm someone only when the agent would otherwise herself suffer harm.) Gauthier remarks that 'the crucial distinction . . . is between worsening someone's situation and failing to better it, since the proviso prohibits only the former, not the latter'.[27] In further explication of the proviso, it is stipulated that worsening someone's situation means, here, making it worse than it would have been had one not interacted with her.[28] Although Gauthier uses the indicative mood to formulate his proviso, its canonical statement should be in the subjunctive mood, since it specifies a counterfactual requirement.

Now, Gauthier's proviso does not bind all individuals in all circumstances. It binds only those individuals for whom co-operative interaction is in prospect: the proviso determines what prospective co-operators may bring to the bargaining table at which principles of co-operation will be decided. They may bring all and only those assets that are acquired without violation of the proviso. Where co-operation is not in prospect, the principle stated in the proviso does not apply.

It follows from the content of the proviso and the stated restriction on its application that Gauthier agents are in some respects more and in some respects less endowed with rights and liberties[29] than agents are under an unrestricted principle of full self-ownership. Gauthier people have more liberty than self-owners do because they are allowed to kill, coerce,

[26] Morals by Agreement, p. 203.
[27] Ibid., p. 204.
[28] Ibid., p. 203.
[29] I here invoke W. N. Hohfeld's distinction (see his Fundamental Legal Conceptions), which runs as follows: X has the liberty to do A if he has no duty not to do A and even if others have no duty to let him do A; and X has the right to do A if he both has no duty not to do A and others have a duty to let him do A.

enslave, etc., anyone with whom they cannot profitably co-operate.[30] And, correlatively, they lack some rights in the state of nature that self-owners have, for the proviso vests them with rights against aggression only in those states of nature that are prelude to market and co-operative inter-action. To the extent that, for whatever reason, the state of nature is going to persist, they lack those rights: Gauthier's state of nature, when it is not the threshold of society, is Hobbesian rather than Lockean, with an appropriately diminished conception of self-ownership in place, one in which each person has, in Hohfeld's senses of the terms, the liberty to do anything and the right to do nothing. (Hobbesian self-ownership is diminished, since *full* self-ownership requires the right and not merely the liberty to use one's parts and capacities as one pleases: that is a Hohfeldian way of expressing the conclusion of the argument about fists and noses given at p. 215 above.)

Finally, and to remind the reader of the main burden of the section that ends here, Gauthier agents lack (full) self-ownership in the social order established by the bargaining to which the proviso is prelude, for the surplus of social interaction is divided according to the principle of mini-max relative concession, and dividing it, in that or any other redistributive way, runs against self-ownership.

5. I have argued that the principle of self-ownership forbids forcing one person to assist another. I regard redistributive taxation as other-assisting, and, therefore, as inconsistent with self-ownership. We have just reviewed – and rejected – David Gauthier's claim that, whether or not common forms of redistribution count as constrained assistance (that issue was not on the table in section 4), not all redistributive taxation violates self-ownership. What I now examine is the claim that, whether or not the redistribution mandated by John Rawls' difference principle contradicts self-ownership, that principle does not direct some to *assist* others. I take up this claim because some Ralwsians[31] have resisted my view that the difference principle commands assistance.

When I speak of Able *helping* Infirm, I suppose that Able would be better off, in self-interested terms, if he left Infirm to his own meagre devices. According to my Rawlsian critics, that supposition is relevantly unsatisfied within the Rawlsian framework. They argue as follows: the

---

[30] Something which he emphasizes – see, e.g., *Morals by Agreement*, p. 268. He should also have emphasized that the enslavable unfortunates have as much liberty to kill or to steal from productive co-operators as the latter have to enslave the former.

[31] Mainly John Rawls and Joshua Cohen, in private exchanges.

theory constructed in *A Theory of Justice* is proposed for a context of mutual provision in which, although people's productive powers are different in kind and in extent, the activity of each enhances the reward available to all. Everyone is a net contributor to and a net beneficiary of social co-operation, and the question answered by principles of justice is not: who should (unilaterally) help whom, and to what extent? but: how should the fruits of co-operation, a process in which everyone benefits everyone, be divided? The difference principle answers that question and does not thereby direct anyone to help anyone, in a unilateral sense. The principle gives each person more than he could secure autarkically, and what the worst off get cannot, therefore, be unambiguously described as part of the product of the powers of other people. Under the assumptions framing the Rawlsian theory, the difference principle, though contradicting *laissez-faire*, cannot be described as enjoining a distribution in which the more able *help* the less able:

> The least advantaged are not if all goes well, the unfortunate and unlucky – objects of our charity and compassion, much less our pity – but those to whom reciprocity is owed as a matter of *political justice* among those who are free and equal citizens along with us, and who, though they control less resources, are doing their full share on terms seen by each as *mutually* advantageous and consistent with everyone's self-respect.[32]

I have two replies to this attempt to show that Rawlsian justice does not direct some to assist others. '

First, it has the consequence, supposing that it is sound, that *A Theory of Justice* is importantly incomplete: on the present description of the scope of that work, those who cannot benefit others, those who would gain from association with others without being able to confer advantage in return, those who indeed *are* 'unfortunate and unlucky', are simply not part of the Rawlsian game: the book says nothing about radically unproductive people who make no contribution to the social product. The principles of justice, being principles for dividing the benefits of co-operation, do not apply to them. Because they cannot relevantly operate, they cannot *co*-operate. It is obvious that John Rawls the person would favour their sustenance as a matter of right, but no such favour is justified in *A Theory of Justice*. (Rawls indeed says, in various places, that we should address the problem of radically handicapped people at a later stage. 'If we can work out a viable theory for the normal range [of human capacity], we can

---

[32] John Rawls, 'Justice as Fairness: a Briefer Restatement', p. 127. For a lucid and friendly elaboration of the quoted Rawlsian claim, see Thomas Pogge, *Realizing Rawls*, section 5.

attempt to handle these other cases later.'[33] But I claim that they resist 'handling' as long as we stay with the contractarian standpoint of *mutual* advantage. David Hume knew that, and being, in the relevant sense, a contractarian,[34] he would have had to deny that justice is owed to the wholly infirm.)

One can show, secondly, that either Rawls' criterion for reciprocal benefit is too weak or his principles apply only to societies very different in composition from our own. Which of these unwelcome consequences we confront depends on whether, in comparing what an individual can obtain through social interaction to what he can get without it, in order to determine whether he is a net beneficiary of social interaction, we are to consider only what he would get in the autarkic alternative in which he withdraws completely from society; or, alternatively, and more appropriately, we are to consider the rewards he would get in all the possible withdrawing coalitions (all members of which would benefit from withdrawal) in which he would be a member.[35] The former criterion of reciprocal benefit is arbitrarily weak. The most talented individual in society might benefit even from a flatly equal distribution of the social product, relative to what he can produce entirely on his own, but he is nevertheless likely to get much more than what the difference principle gives him if he withdraws with a suitable set of other talented individuals. If, however, the criterion of reciprocal benefit is strengthened to allow for such coalition withdrawal, then reciprocal benefit will be consistent with the difference principle only in societies strikingly unlike the sort Rawls would want his theory to cover, societies, that is, which are comparable in size and variety to our own.[36]

---

[33] 'The Basic Structure as Subject', p. 70(9). Cf. *Political Justice*, p. 20, and 'Social Unity and Primary Goods', p. 168: 'It is best to make an initial concession in the case of special health and medical needs. I put this difficult problem aside in this paper and assume that all citizens have physical and psychological capacities within a certain normal range. I do this because the first problem of justice concerns the relations between citizens who are normally active and fully cooperating members of society over a complete life.' Against this view, I believe that an appropriate starting point for reflection on justice is the problem of justifying provision to the non-contributing infirm, and that the problem of distribution among differentially contributing non-infirm people is best seen as a generalization of that first problem.

[34] As Gauthier shows: see his 'David Hume, Contractarian'.

[35] Cf. Nozick, *Anarchy, State, and Utopia*, p. 193, Barry, *Theories of Justice*, p. 243. At pp. 61–2 of 'The Basic Structure as Subject' Rawls protests against the coherence of comparisons of this kind, but I do not see how they can be avoided if one wishes to speak of 'beneficiaries of social co-operation'.

[36] This statement remains true even when we acknowledge indirect benefits got by the talented from the presence of less talented people, such as the enhancement of their social status.

On the plausible assumption that Rawls legislates for large societies which are indefinitely heterogeneous with respect to talent distribution, we can say that the better off get less under the difference principle than they would in some feasible society which raises each of them above his autarkic alternative. This produces the difficulty for Rawls that I have tried to expose, a difficulty identified by Gauthier when he says that if we

agree with Rawls that society is a co-operative venture for mutual advantage, we must disagree with his view that natural talents are to be considered a common asset. The two views offer antithetical conceptions of both the individual human being and society.[37]

The root of the difficulty is that Rawls' contractualist characterization of the *problem* of justice is inconsistent with the Rawlsian *principles* of justice[38] (even when we set aside the problem of wholly infirm people). Rawls avoids the profoundly inegalitarian conclusions a consistent contractualist would reach only by being untrue to his own contractual starting point.[39]

6. I argued in section 3 that Dworkin fails to show that self-ownership cannot be explicated satisfactorily under the constraints of universality and maximality: it might be true, consistently with Dworkin's premises, that we can derive a (sufficiently) determinate schedule of self-ownership rights from the requirement that *each* person has *as much* right over herself as possible. In this section, I examine an alternative strategy for explicating self-ownership, which does not rely on the universality / maximality idea, and which is also not excluded by Dworkin's premises.

The strategy is suggested by the proposition, defended above (see pp. 215ff.), that self-owners may not be forced to *help* others. The suggestion is that one can go further with the notion of helping, and its contrast, harming; that, in particular, and to a first approximation, the meaning of the principle of self-ownership is that no one may harm anyone else *and* no one may be required to *help* anyone else.

This proposal fits the structure of typical disputes between critics and supporters of self-ownership. The critic emphasizes the parlous lot of

---

[37] *Morals by Agreement*, p. 221.
[38] I do not mean that the original position will not generate the principles Rawls says it generates. That is another matter. I mean that, *if* it generates those principles, then *either* it violates the contractual setting of the problem of justice which precedes recourse to the original position, *or* the principles (supposedly) generated in that position apply only to less inclusive forms of society than those to which they are meant to apply.
[39] For further elaboration of this claim, see my 'Limits of Contractual Equality'.

the poorly endowed when the principle of self-ownership prevails. The supporter of the principle responds that the lot of the ill-endowed is not the fault of the well-endowed: the latter have not placed the former in their unfortunate position. The well-endowed have not harmed those who are unlucky, and it would unfairly harm the well-endowed to force them to help the less fortunate.

One may sketch two extreme views with respect to the proposed connection between self-ownership and the harming/not helping distinction. There is, first, the just suggested view that the concept of self-ownership can be explicated without remainder by reference to the harming/not helping distinction, treated as independently understood. And then there is an opposite view, according to which the notions of harming and helping are so labile that we cannot fix their senses, in the appropriate way, until we are possessed of an independently secured concept of self-ownership. I believe that both extreme views are incorrect: the harming/not helping distinction contributes to the explication of self-ownership, but it does not take us all the way.

An analysis of self-ownership in the suggested terms says: people should be free to do anything with themselves that does not harm others. Accordingly, I am never required to help others, except in cases where failing to help itself counts as harming. There may indeed be such cases, and, if there are, then they pose no problem for the suggested analysis, as it is phrased in the first sentence of this paragraph.

That analysis is, however, too simple, for a different reason, which is that universal self-ownership, intuitively understood, is plainly consistent with *some* harmings. For market competition harms losers, and market competition is the social soul of self-ownership.[40] What may be worse, it is unclear with respect to some disadvantages from which market traders sometimes suffer whether they should count as effects of harming. Does the seller harm the buyer, or just not help him, when he withholds disturbing information about the product from him?

If the initial analysis is too simple, an intermediate course might nevertheless be viable, under which self-ownership is explicated in terms of a list of forbidden harms, but formation of the list is guided by the notion of ownership in general. Since, in the attempt to complete the analysis, the

---

[40] Also consistent with universal self-ownership are harmings associated with legitimate punishment and self-defence. But they are legitimate in virtue of aggressors' and criminals' forfeiture of self-ownership rights: nothing similar holds for market competition harm, which therefore poses a more serious counter-example to the analysis on exhibit.

idea of *self*-ownership in particular would not be invoked, there is no circularity in the proposed procedure.

It is useful to remind ourselves, here, why self-ownership excludes a duty to help (save where not helping also counts as harming). If I own myself, I own my parts and powers, which are the wherewithal for helping others. Since it is in general true of ownership that I need not devote what I own to another's benefit, it is true of self-ownership that I need not devote myself to anyone else's benefit, and I therefore have no duty to help others. And the harming induced by market competition qualifies as acceptable in the light of the concept of ownership. For I harm you in market competition by selling what you might not want me to sell or by buying what you might not want me to buy, and freedom to buy and sell, and, therefore, the harmings it may occasion, are integral to the concept of ownership.

If I own something, then no one else may damage that thing without my consent. So you may not chip a piece off my clock. But you do not damage my clock if you make a better one, and thereby bring it about that no one any longer wants to buy my clock at a price that appeals to me. Analogously, although you harm me by out-competing me on the labour market, you do that without relevantly damaging my self-owned property. There are, to be sure, lots of hard questions here. Do you violate my self-ownership by telling lies that harm my reputation? What if you tell damaging truths about me? Is it appropriate to be guided, here, by the answer to the question whether you violate my ownership of my clock by telling lies or truths which diminish its attractiveness to others? And if that is indeed an appropriate guide, then what guidance does it give?

Lots of questions would require attention, but the general course of the suggested account is reasonably clear. We begin with the simple idea that each is free to do what harms no one. We then notice that some harms are permitted, and we draw on the concept of ownership in general to determine what they are. And if there are obscurities regarding what sorts of harmings of owned things count as damages which violate their owners' rights in them, then the notion of self-ownership is not to be disparaged for inheriting those obscurities. A serious problem would, however, arise if for some reason (I cannot think of one) permissible harming uses of fully owned objects turned out to be a poor guide to permissible harming uses of fully self-owned personal powers.

10. Self-ownership: assessing the thesis

Seizing the results of someone's labour is equivalent to seizing hours from him and directing him to carry on various activities. If people force you to do certain work, or unrewarded work, for a certain period of time, they decide what you are to do and what purposes your work is to serve apart from your decisions. This process whereby they take this decision from you makes them a *part-owner* of you; it gives them a property right in you. (Robert Nozick, *Anarchy, State, and Utopia*)

1. As I said in section 1 of Chapter 3, it is an initially attractive strategy, for egalitarians, to grant libertarians the premiss of self-ownership and then, by insisting on equality of raw worldly resources, to deny the libertarian conclusion that equality of condition contradicts justice. But, as I also said in Chapter 3, and as I demonstrated in Chapters 4 and 5, that strategy will not succeed, and egalitarians are therefore obliged to criticize the thesis of self-ownership itself. It is, however, difficult to criticize it in a non-question-begging way. Thus, for example, it is, in my opinion, a considerable objection to the thesis of self-ownership that no one should fare worse than others do because of bad brute luck,[1] for no luck is bruter than that of how one is born, raised and circumstanced, the good and bad results of which adhere firmly to individuals under the self-ownership principle. But the fact that it sanctions the results of luck will not move a moderately sophisticated believer in self-ownership. The conflict between the relevant principles is too basic, and too evident, for her not already to have countenanced it and (*ex hypothesi*) stood her ground.

Yet there is a way of arguing against the self-ownership principle without invoking the luck principle or any other tenets which conflict so fundamentally with self-ownership that the relevant argument might be

---

[1] I explore the consequences of this tenet in 'On the Currency of Egalitarian Justice'.

thought question-begging. And that is by showing that self-ownership is different from other conditions its confusion with which explains (at least) *some* of the favour it attracts. Such arguments do not *refute* the thesis of self-ownership: I do not think that it can be refuted. But, if the arguments are sound, they diminish the appeal of the principle, sufficiently, I am sure, to detach many people from their allegiance to it. That, at any rate, is the strategy pursued in this chapter, in which the thesis of self-ownership is at issue.

Libertarians think that, if you reject the thesis of self-ownership, then you license slavery, you restrict human autonomy, and you endorse the treatment of people as mere means. In sections 2–4 of this chapter I dispute these charges, by distinguishing self-ownership from three conditions with which the foregoing three charges confuse it: not being a slave, possessing autonomy, and not being used merely as a means. Finally, in section 5, I return to the eye transplant example which I used to motivate the thesis of self-ownership in section 1 of Chapter 3, and I argue that the example does not support the thesis.

2. The central form of rejection of the thesis of self-ownership is in the affirmation of non-contractual obligations to serve other people. According to Robert Nozick, principles that impose non-contractual obligations 'institute (partial) ownership by others of people and their actions and labour. These principles involve a shift from the classical liberals' notion of self-ownership to a notion of (partial) property rights in other people.'[2] I take the quoted passage to be an *argument* against the obligation-imposing principles, rather than a characterization of them which even their proponents can be expected to accept. The argument I discern exploits an aversion to property rights in other people, which is to say, an aversion to slavery, an aversion that need not reflect an antecedent commitment to the principle of self-ownership itself. The purpose of the argument is to convert non-believers in self-ownership by showing them that rejection of self-ownership is tantamount to endorsement of slavery.

The polemically operative sequence in the argument runs, I think as follows:

(1) If X is non-contractually obliged to do A for Y, then Y has a right of disposal over X's labour of the sort that a slave-owner has.

---

[2] *Anarchy, State, and Utopia*, p. 172, and see, further, the associated passage which forms the epigraph of this chapter.

(2) If Y has a right of disposal over X's labour of the sort that a slave-owner has, then X is, *pro tanto*, Y's slave.

(3) It is morally intolerable for anyone to be, in any degree, another's slave. Therefore

(4) It is morally intolerable for X to be non-contractually obliged to do A for Y.

The argument, as reconstructed above, is valid. Accordingly, opposition to it must fix on one or more of its three premisses. A clever person might find subtle reasons for rejecting premiss (2), but I do not think that it would be profitable to speculate about that. The interesting premisses are (1) and (3), and I shall begin with (3), since what I have to say about (1) is rather complicated, and what I have to say about (3) is not.

An objection to (3) might be developed as follows. Consider, for a moment, a condition different from (though also partly similar to) slavery, to wit, the condition of imprisonment. Suppose that you are an innocent person and that I forcibly detain you in a room for five minutes. Then, indeed, I forcibly detain you, albeit for only five minutes. Now, whether or not such brief detention should qualify as short-term *imprisonment*, whether or not to call it 'imprisonment' would be a preposterous exaggeration, there is a massive *normative* difference between this brief detention and life-long imprisonment. Brief detention of an innocent person might be justified by, for example, temporary needs of social order, even if life-long imprisonment of an innocent person could never be justified. And, similarly, even if premiss (1) in the argument under examination is true, so that redistributive taxation does mean, as Nozick insists, slavery-like forced labour, a limited dose of forced labour is massively different, normatively, from the life-long forced labour that characterizes a slave.[3]

I turn, now, to premiss (1), and to a way of resisting Nozick's argument that was put to me by Joseph Raz. Raz argued that, when X is non-contractually obliged to Y, it does not follow that anyone has a slave-owner-like right to dispose over X's labour.[4] Raz resisted (1) by pressing

---

[3] Thomas Scanlon makes what is in effect this objection to Nozick at 'Liberty, Contract and Contribution', p. 66 fn. 8.

[4] My exposition of Raz's argument together with responses to it and associated rejoinders generates sufficient complexity to warrant the following overview of what lies ahead. I begin with Raz's argument that, as my obligation to help my mother shows, an obligation of A does not entail a slave-holder-like right over A on the part of some B. Objection: the example is of the wrong sort, since my obligation to my mother is not enforceable. Reply: even if the state enforces the stated obligation, it remains true that no one has a slave-holder-like right over me. Broader objection to Raz: I am sufficiently like a slave in having

the following example: although I might be obliged to assist my mother if she falls ill, she might have no right to absolve me from that obligation, and, therefore, no more right than I have to decide whether my capacity to assist, in this respect, is or is not exercised. Even if, moreover, my mother does have the right to absolve me from that particular obligation, it remains untrue that she has unrestricted disposal, of the kind a slave-owner has, over the personal power that I must use to discharge the obligation. She cannot tell me to do with my power whatever she happens to want me to do with it.

Three progressively weaker claims might be made about the rights-entailments of my obligation with respect to my mother, and the third and weakest claim, and, therefore, the hardest one to deny, suffices to show that my obligation to her need not reflect a right of the sort that a slave-holder has – which is the sort of right Nozick needs for his argument.

First, it might be said that my having an obligation to her need not mean that my mother has any right against me at all. But the notion of a right against someone is not so clear that one can expect everyone to agree with that first claim. Some will find it very difficult to separate in their minds the idea that I have an obligation to my mother from the idea that she has a corresponding right against me. (I would defend the separation by saying that, if I fail in my obligation, then it might be that she has no stronger basis for complaining about my failure than others have.)

The second, weaker, claim is that, although my mother may indeed have a right against me, although it may be she and no one else who has a grievance if I do not fulfil my obligation, she may yet lack the right to absolve me of my obligation, and therefore lack the sort of right that a slave-holder has.

Finally, even if my mother does have the right to absolve me of the obligation, or even to forbid me to carry it out, it does not follow that she has the slave-holder-like right to tell me to do whatever she chooses with whatever resource I would use to carry out the stated obligation.

The general point is that the question of how, in certain conditions, I am entitled to use my power to assist might be settled not by anyone's exercise of a right, but by the existence of a relevant obligation, or, in the weakest claim, by truths about rights which are consistent with gaps in the

non-contractual obligations to others even if they do not imply that *someone else* has slave-holder rights over me. Reply: in that case Nozick himself (by implication) countenances slavery, since (a) citizens of his minimal state are obliged to pay tax to support its police force, and (b) Nozick believes that contractually based full slavery is possible, and should therefore also regard less comprehensive types of contract as instituting partial slavery.

space of rights, gaps which mean that 'nobody' is the answer to some questions of the form: who has the right to decide whether or not I do *A*? And this defeats Nozick's claim that, to the extent that I do not own myself, I am a slave. Slavery is characterized by non-contractual obligation, and, when I lack a right with respect to some aspect of my power or activity, then that may indeed be because I have such an obligation. But it does not follow that I am then a slave, for it does not follow that another then has the right that I lack. Accordingly, absences of self-ownership need not be presences *pro tanto* of slavery.[5]

Some will object that this excursus about my obligation to my mother is beside the point. They will say that the thesis of self-ownership does not exclude moral obligations, but only legally enforceable obligations. Only those obligations betoken slavery, and my obligation to my mother would not normally be regarded as legally enforceable. Call that the 'enforcement objection'.

One way of resisting the enforcement objection is to question the consistency of self-ownership and (even) non-enforceable obligations to others. And that style of resistance certainly appears in the anti-libertarian polemical literature. But, even if such resistance is correct, the consequent conceptual gain – that self-ownership is inconsistent with intuitively evident moral obligations of a non-enslaving sort – is not matched by victory at the level of political philosophy. For the libertarian bottom line in political philosophy is not, indeed, that we are self-owners but that the state has no right to impose or enforce non-contractual obligations on us, and the line of resistance canvassed here leaves that claim intact. It is, moreover, unclear that even a conceptual victory is available on this front. For it is not clearly inconsistent to say both that I am the unambiguous full owner of this tract of land and that I have a moral obligation to let my neighbour peacefully traverse it when he desperately needs to get water from the brook to which he has no other means of access. It is not obviously false that all that relevantly follows from my unambiguous full ownership of the land is that I have a right to exclude him (which I might be morally obliged not to exercise) and that he has no right to traverse it.

So the nettle must be grasped, we need a different way of meeting the

---

[5] Raz adds that, to oppose self-ownership, defined as the absence of non-contractual enforcible obligation to (even partial) slavery, as though the two were exhaustive, is to commit the ancient fallacy of the international lawyers who thought that, if the state is sovereign, then it lacks obligations. In fact, its sovereignty consists in the absence of a body superior to it, and not being a slave to anyone, means, similarly, that no one rules over you, not that you have a right to self-rule of the unrestricted self-ownership kind.

enforcement objection, which says that Raz invokes the wrong sort of obligation against premiss (1) in the Nozick argument. Let us, then, suppose that, whether or not I would otherwise have any kind of obligation to her, the state imposes on me a legal obligation to serve my mother, or the needy in general. Does this not, indeed, show that it arrogates to itself the sort of right over my labour that a slave-holder has?

It does not, for points similar to those made above about my mother's not relating to me as a slave-owner in the original example can now be made about the state. Thus one might believe that the state has no right to absolve me from this obligation, that it has a duty to tax me, and, consequently, no right to decide whether or not I should transfer income to the needy. The state therefore lacks the relevant right to dispose over my labour even if it has the right to direct this particular other-assisting use of it. Nor do my mother, or the needy, now have slave-holder-like rights over me, by virtue of the enforcement by the state of whatever rights they do have against me. The reasons offered previously against saying that they are my partial owners remain intact.

A defender of the enforcement objection might now say that the state simply cannot have the particular right here attributed to it unless it has the comprehensive right over me that betokens slavery. But that is just not true. The socialist constitution requires the state to tax redistributively; the Nozick constitution forbids it to do so. It is equally false in each case that the state is thereby vested with a right to decide whether or not some will serve others. Of course, and this could confuse the issue in the minds of some, the redistributive state may have the *de facto* power to do something forbidden by its constitution. But that is also true of Nozick's state, and it is therefore irrelevant.

In sum, we could all have enforceable obligations to one another which imply no slave-owner-like rights of disposal in anyone over anyone's labour. Indeed, such obligations form the normative substance of a redistributive state. In that state, there are no self-ownership rights with respect to certain dimensions of the capacity to assist, but there are also no slave-owner/slave relations.

The objection to Raz, that his case against Nozick's argument collapses when we turn to obligations of the relevant enforceable kind, does not succeed. But, even if Raz has refuted premiss (1) of Nozick's argument, there is a broader objection to his response to Nozick which seems to me correct, although the objection also shows, ironically, that Nozick somewhat mis-states his own case in the passage quoted at the beginning of this section.

Here is the broad objection. Suppose that I am obliged to spend a stretch of time carrying out a task for you that no one has the right to absolve me from performing and that it is so precisely specified that there are only trivially different ways in which it might be performed. Then, for the Razian reasons articulated at pp. 231–3 above, my being weighted with this task does not mean that anyone is my short-term slave-holder or partial owner. But, for all that, my own condition, so far as I am concerned, is not in every important way different from that of a short-term or partial slave. For *I* have no more right to decide what to do with my faculties within the given frame of task and time than I would have if my obligation had been whimfully imposed by an arbitrary master. What matters to an agent is not only whether he is subject to the comprehensive concentrated control of a single alien will but whether what he does is subject to his own will. Accordingly, and here I turn this strategic objection to Raz against Nozick's own formulations, he, Nozick, should not have brought forth the motif of partial ownership rights in other people, but emphasized, instead, the predicament of lack of full ownership rights in oneself. Mere absence of self-ownership turns out, ironically, to be a more robust objection to enforced obligation than the ownership by another that was supposed to point up the awfulness of absence of self-ownership.

Does the indicated re-orientation of Nozick's argument make it safe? No, because there are two decisive objections to it, each of which turns on Nozick's own theoretical commitments. In two ways, those commitments disentitle him to say that welfare state redistribution is to be rejected because it makes the citizen's condition like that of a slave.

The first point is that citizens in the minimal state whose coercion Nozick regards as legitimate are obliged to pay taxes which support that state's coercive apparatus whether or not they want the protection they get in exchange. It is impossible to argue that an hour's labour that ends up as part of somebody's welfare payment is like slavery, while an hour's labour that ends up as part of a policeman's salary is not, when focus is on the condition of the putative slave himself. To be sure, and this is not here denied, if Nozick is right, then taxation for policemen is justified and taxation for the poor is not, because the principle of self-ownership, through a complicated argument to do with self-defence, licenses the first taxation and forbids the second. But the principle of self-ownership cannot here be invoked to distinguish the cases, nor, in particular, to show that one case is like slavery and the other is not, since the slavery consideration is here supposed to be an argument *for* the principle of self-ownership.

And a second internally based criticism of the suggested re-orientated form of the slavery argument (away from other-ownership and pivoting, now, on non-self-ownership) is also powerful. Nozick needs to distinguish between contractual obligations, which do not, in general, constitute slavery, and non-contractual obligations, which, so he says, do. Now, Nozick allows that a person might, in certain circumstances, voluntarily contract into full and, because contractually based, legitimate slavery: he would not say that what the contemplated person enters is not slavery because he enters it voluntarily. To be sure, this is not logically inconsistent with his further view that it distinguishes non-contractual obligations that they always betoken (at least partial) slavery, since that view is that they are sufficient, not necessary, for slavery. But Nozick must nevertheless explain why there is more slavery in every non-contractual obligation than there is in any contractual obligation (short of full slavery) regardless of why it was entered, and however close that contractual obligation comes to completely binding over all of a person's labour power. Pending further argument, it seems entirely arbitrary to rule that there cannot be a contractually based partial slavery, when there can be contractually based complete slavery.

3. Many libertarians say that people control their own lives, or enjoy *autonomy*, if and only if they possess the rights constitutive of self-ownership.[6] In what follows I question the liaison between self-ownership and autonomy. ('Autonomy', here, denotes the range of a person's choice, as opposed to a feature of a person's character, related to his powers of deliberation and self-control. Autonomy of the latter kind is not under discussion here, which is not to say that universal self-ownership poses no threat to it, e.g., by disinsuring the availability of resources required to nourish children's capacity to choose.)

Now, the first thing to note, in an investigation of the relationship between self-ownership and autonomy, is that autonomy is a matter of degree, a matter of the quantity and the quality of the options that a

---

[6] Thus, for example, Nozick associates self-ownership rights with the *ability to lead one's own life* (see *Anarchy, State, and Utopia*, p. 34, and see, too, *ibid.*, pp. 48–51). Note that the relevant text is subject to two interpretations. In one, the underlined is a rhetorical or (would-be) persuasive redescription of what self-ownership rights come to. In another, it links the latter to an idea which has independent standing. Under the first interpretation of Nozick's text, it provides no argument for self-ownership. There is a case to answer only under the second interpretation of the self-ownership/autonomy association, and I mount an answer to that case in the present section.

person has. Accordingly, the claim that self-ownership favours autonomy needs to be made more precise. It can hardly be the preposterous claim that a person has no autonomy if his self-ownership is to any extent incomplete, and/or that full self-ownership guarantees so much autonomy that more would be inconceivable. The relevant claim must be that there is more autonomy under universal complete self-ownership than under any alternative dispensation.

But, against that claim, there is good reason to suppose that, at least in a world of people with different measures of talent, self-ownership is hostile to autonomy, for, in such a world (see section 6 of Chapter 4 above), the self-seeking authorized by self-ownership generates propertyless proletarians whose life prospects are too confined for them to enjoy the control of a substantial kind over their own lives that answers to the idea of autonomy. Accordingly, if everyone is to enjoy a reasonable degree of autonomy, it is necessary, at least in some circumstances, to impose restrictions on self-ownership.

Self-ownership might fail to maximize autonomy (and, *pari passu*, to maximinize it, to ensure, that is, that those with the least autonomy have as much of it as possible) even in a world of equally talented individuals. For autonomy, the range of choice you have in leading your life, is a function of two things: the scope of your rights over yourself, with which it varies positively; and the rights of others over themselves and over things, with which it varies variously. There are many scenarios where some, or even all, have less autonomy than some, or all, would have with certain restrictions on self-ownership. We can all benefit in terms of autonomy if none of us has the right to do certain things.

It might be objected that, where that is so, rational self-owning individuals who care about autonomy would contract to reduce or suspend their own self-ownership rights. But the assumption of equality of talent does not itself ensure universal rationality, and, even if universal rationality prevails, and transaction problems do not prevent institution of the rationally preferred restrictions, the very fact that they are rationally preferable shows that it is not self-ownership as such, but a certain self-cancelling use of it, that allows autonomy to flourish. If we had to choose between self-ownership, when it might be exercised in a manner detrimental to autonomy, and the exogenous imposition of the required restrictions, then a commitment to autonomy would counsel the latter course.

Joseph Raz argues that 'some collective goods are intrinsically desirable if personal autonomy is intrinsically desirable. If this is so then right-based theories cannot account for the desirability of autonomy',[7] and so, we can add, the principle of self-ownership, a paradigm case of a rights-based theory (or 'theoryette'), also cannot cater adequately to autonomy. 'A person is autonomous only if he has a variety of acceptable options available to him to choose from, and his life became as it is through his choice of some of these options.'[8] Since 'the existence of many options consists in part in the existence of certain social conditions',[9] including the availability of collective goods such as educational and welfare institutions, the provision of such goods must be assured for autonomy to prevail. Accordingly, that provision, being 'constitutive of the very possibility of autonomy . . . cannot be relegated to a subordinate role, compared with some alleged right against coercion, in the name of autonomy'.[10]

Using the persuasive example of a creative artist, Simon Green argues that opportunities to pursue his art must be afforded to him if he has a 'right . . . to an autonomous deployment of his talents in artistic creation'. That right would, Green remarks, impose obligations on others, 'but it will not entail what would be the additional, and quite distinct, requirement that [he] also have a right to private ownership of the fruits of [his] talent exchanged as commodities in an open market'.[11] Since that latter right is, as I have argued, integral to self-ownership, it follows that autonomy no more implies self-ownership than it is implied by it. Putting together the two points made by Green, we can say that, to promote the autonomy of artists, we do not have to confer self-ownership on them, and we do have to restrict the self-ownership of others.

4. Nozick says that the rights he affirms 'reflect the underlying Kantian principle that *individuals are ends and not merely means*: they may not be sacrificed or used for the achieving of other ends without their consent'.[12] Nozick thereby seeks to attach to self-ownership the prestige associated with the name of Kant.

Call the underlined *Kant's principle,* and what follows it (after the colon) *Nozick's consent principle.* For the sake of clarity, and ready reference back to them, I exhibit the two principles distinctly here:

---

[7] *The Morality of Freedom,* p. 203.   [8] *Ibid.,* p. 204.
[9] *Ibid.,* p. 205.   [10] *Ibid.,* p. 207.
[11] 'Competitive Equality of Opportunity', p. 18.
[12] *Anarchy, State, and Utopia,* p. 31, my emphases.

| Kant's principle: | Individuals are ends and not merely means. |
| Nozick's consent principle: | Individuals may not be sacrificed or used for the achieving of other ends without their consent. |

In this section I deal with three issues: first, I discuss the relationship between Kant's principle and self-ownership; next, I ask whether Nozick's consent principle is the same as Kant's principle; finally, I discuss the relationship between self-ownership and Nozick's consent principle: do rights of self-ownership really 'reflect' Nozick's consent principle?

a. I begin by arguing that Kant's principle does not entail the thesis of self-ownership, and that the thesis does not entail Kant's principle.

Kant's principle says, in its full statement,[13] that you must treat humanity both in yourself and in others never as a means only but always also as an end in itself. The principle does not forbid me to use another as a means. It allows me to do so, *provided that* I at the same time honour his status as an independent centre of value, as an originator of projects that demand my respect. *Of course* I treat the ticket-seller as a means when I hand him the money and thereby get him to hand me my ticket. For I interact with him only *because* he is my means of getting a ticket. After all, I undoubtedly treat the ticket *machine* as a means when I put my money in it, and there is plainly something in common between how I treat or regard the machine's action, what its place within my purposes is, and what the ticket-seller's place within my purposes is. The action that I induce in each case serves as a means to my purposes, and that is why I induce it. But, if I obey Kant's principle, then the difference in my stance is not, indeed, that I do not treat the ticket-seller as a means, but that I also treat him as an end. Thus, for example, if the machine breaks down, I just get cross: now I cannot get my ticket. But, if the man breaks down, if he is suddenly seized with a fit, I do something about it, I try to help, and I thereby show that I never regarded him as a means *only*.[14] My response might not suffice to show that I treat him as an end in the full Kantian sense: by contrast with the comparatively clear idea of not treating someone as a means, the idea of treating a person as an end is neither

---

[13] Nozick quotes that full statement at *ibid.*, p. 32.
[14] Note that I might also not regard a machine as a means only, because it might have aesthetic or sentimental or other non-instrumental value for me.

particularly clear nor well explained by Kant.[15] But while it may be unclear what Kant's demand, in full, amounts to, it is clear that whatever it requires is consistent with the customary instrumental uses that people (perforce) make of others.

Now, suppose I think[16] that able-bodied people have a duty, which the state should enforce through taxation, to produce a surplus over what they need to support themselves, to sustain disabled people who would otherwise die. Then I am committed against the principle of self-ownership. For self-ownership implies that you have no non-contractual enforceable obligations to anyone else with respect to the use of your powers, just as (full) thing-ownership implies that you have no such obligations with respect to the use of a thing that you own. But, committed against self-ownership as I am, I may nevertheless be true to Kant's principle. For, although I believe that the labour of the able-bodied should be used as a means and, if necessary, against their will, in order that the unfortunate may be supported, it does not follow that I am unconcerned about the able-bodied themselves: among other things, I may believe that they should provide the indicated service only because I also believe that giving it will not blight their lives. Accordingly, rejection of self-ownership does not imply rejection of Kant's principle: you can affirm the second while rejecting the first.

Now, the opposite point, that you can affirm self-ownership but reject the Kantian principle, also holds good. For observing rights of self-ownership implies nothing about my attitude to others, how I regard them, and I am sure that *treating* others as ends implies, in Kant's discourse, a particular form of regard for or attitude to them. To see this, return to the example of the malfunctioning human ticket-seller. I can observe his rights of self-ownership but regard him completely as a means and therefore do nothing for him when he collapses. Of course, I may not threaten to punch him in the nose in order to get him to give me my ticket more quickly. But that does not mean that I must treat him as an end. For, just as I observe his right of ownership of his nose, I can also observe British Rail's right of ownership of its machine, and I therefore do not

---

[15] Kant recognized that not treating someone merely as a means does not suffice for treating him as an end. (See *The Metaphysics of Morals*, p. 198.) He thereby in effect acknowledged that obscurity with respect to the notion of treating someone as an end is possible, although he did not, of course, acknowledge that such obscurity pervades his own discussion of the matter.

[16] As, incidentally, Kant did: see *The Metaphysics of Morals*, p. 136.

punch the machine in the face when *it* malfunctions. But that hardly means that I treat British Rail as an end.

b. So much for Kant's principle and self-ownership. I shall shortly inquire into the relationship between self-ownership and the principle that Nozick says it reflects, to wit, that people 'may not be sacrificed or used for the achieving of other ends without their consent'. But first I want to indicate how Nozick's consent principle differs from Kant's means–ends principle. The difference between them is in the condition satisfaction of which does allow you to use another person as a means: for Kant, using someone is all right provided that you treat the person you use as (also) an end, while, for Nozick, it is all right provided that you have his consent. To see the difference between those provisos notice that a capitalist employer may scrupulously observe Nozick's consent requirement while not caring two hoots about the welfare (or anything else that relates to their status as ends) of his employees, and that the state which taxes the able-bodied violates Nozick's consent requirement but may nevertheless respect their humanity.

A passage in the *Grundlegung* might be thought to cast doubt on the contrast I have drawn between Nozick's consent principle and Kant's principle. And, although I do not think it shows that I am wrong to contrast their teachings as I did, it does suggest that my explication of the Kantian principle needs further refinement:

he who intends a deceitful promise to others sees immediately that he intends to use another man merely as a means, without the latter at the same time containing the end in himself. For he whom I want to use for my own purposes by means of such a promise cannot possibly assent to my mode of acting against him and thus share in the purpose of this action.[17]

As I understand this passage, what defeats the liar is not that his victim *does* not, but that he *could* not, consent to the way the former proposes to treat him. Unlike Nozick, Kant does not require the actual, but the possible, consent of the person I deal with. And 'possible', here, means '*normatively* possible', so that the criteria for the consent whose possibility Kant requires differ from the criteria for the consent whose actuality Nozick requires. Thus I might actually consent, in a sense that satisfies Nozick, to acts that treat me merely as a means, for example, to my enslavement by the person who wins a 'slavery

---

[17] *Foundations of the Metaphysics of Morals*, pp. 46–7.

gamble'[18] against me, yet that would evidently not prove that it was possible, in Kant's sense, for me to consent to my enslaver's act, since, for Kant, it is impossible, in the relevant sense, to consent to that.[19] Contrariwise, if I refuse consent to a particular treatment of me, it would not follow that I *could* not have consented to it, in Kant's sense. If I actually consent to your use of me, my self-ownership is intact. If I actually refuse consent, but you go forward, my self-ownership is violated. Since Kant's motif is not self-ownership – as we saw in section 2 of Chapter 9 above, he even thinks that self-ownership is a self-contradictory notion – actual consent and its absence are not the crucial things for him.

But if the *Grundlegung* text on exhibit fails to vindicate Nozick's Kantian posture, it also expresses a requirement which must be added to what was said in subsection 4a above about the conditions for treating someone as a Kantian end. Kant's text suggests that the test of not using a person as a means must be satisfied in each of my actions, and not merely in the attitude and dispositions collateral to them. True enough, I should remember, even as I use him as a means, that the ticket-seller is a person with interests to which I must be sensitive, but the Kantian constraint on my use of him goes beyond that. If British Rail employed slaves as ticket-sellers, I might help them if they fell ill, and respect their projects, but in the act of buying a ticket from them I would be disrespecting their status as ends in so far as, in that act, I was collaborating with British Rail's degradation of them to slave status.

c. Having (I hope) clarified the difference between Nozick's consent principle and Kant's means-end principle, I turn, finally, to the question of the relationship between Nozick's (as we now see) non-Kantian consent principle and the principle of self-ownership itself. Nozick says that self-ownership *reflects* the consent principle, that the principle 'underlies' self-ownership. Well, to begin with, does Nozick's consent principle imply the principle of self-ownership? I believe that it does not, although I also concede that it is not particularly interesting that it does not. I say that it does not because it appears that you can observe Nozick's consent principle while rejecting self-ownership. For, if you punch someone in the nose without his consent, you violate his self-ownership, but you do not necessarily thereby use him to achieve some end, not even in the way a punching bag is standardly so used.

[18] For the idea of a slavery gamble, see Chapter 2 above, subsection 1d.
[19] See *The Metaphysics of Morals*, pp. 101, 139–40, 248.

By contrast, if people are self-owners, then they indeed may not be used without their consent: the entailment does stand in the reverse direction. That is, they may not be caused to do on behalf of their users, and without their consent, what they otherwise would not do. You have to put in 'what they otherwise would not do' because it is all right (self-ownership-wise), at least in certain cases, to use you, without your consent, by taking advantage of what you are doing *anyway*. It is all right for me to use you without your consent to prevent the light from shining in my eyes, by positioning myself in an appropriate way.

But Nozick says that the rights of self-ownership *'reflect'* the principle that people may not be used without their consent, which means that he offers the consent principle as a ground or reason for self-ownership. Yet I do not see how the consent principle can fulfil that role, since it is just an immediate entailment of self-ownership: it formulates a right which covers almost all of the ground, and nothing more, covered by the principle of self-ownership itself. You may agree both with the idea of self-ownership and (therefore) with this major entailment of it, but you cannot think that its entailment is an *argument* for self-ownership.[20] Nozick's principle is, moreover, nothing like as attractive as it sounds, once it has been distinguished from the properly Kantian principle with which it is readily confused. Various of the examples reviewed above expose the limitations of the consent principle. To drive those limitations home, I remind you of the case of the abject proletarian, Nozick's Z,[21] who has nothing to sell but his labour power, and who therefore might be used as a means without scruple, *with* his consent, by someone who hires him. One way to make that severely un-Kantian treatment impossible is by increasing Z's bargaining power through state provision of a welfare minimum. But that means exacting services from other people regardless of whether or not they consent, and thereby violating Nozick's non-Kantian principle.

5. I return, in closing, to the example of the eye lottery which was used to motivate sympathy with the thesis of self-ownership in section 1 of Chapter 3 above.

Suppose that people are born with empty eye sockets (because a radiation-originating disease destroyed the genes for eyes) and there is

---

[20] I do not mean that the entailment of a principle is never an argument for it, but I do not see how this entailment of it can be regarded as an argument for the self-ownership principle.
[21] See Chapter 4 above, section 6.

a well-established practice of perinatal implantation of perfect artificial eyes by the state. Sometimes a mishap occurs in which a grown-up loses her eyes, and the only way to endow her with an eye is to take one from a 'sighted' person, because unused artificial eyes are no good for adults: they turn into eyes good for adults only through being used from birth to adulthood. If an eye lottery is proposed by way of remedy, should we not feel as unhappy about it as we would about such a lottery for natural eyes? If so, the suggestion arises that our resistance to a lottery for natural eyes shows not belief in self-ownership but hostility to severe interference in someone's life. For the state need never vest ownership of the eyes in persons: they could be regarded as on loan, with one of them being retrievable if your number comes up in a lottery.

Notice that, even if coerced eye transfer is horrendous, it scarcely follows that there is nothing untoward about marketing one's own eye, whether by selling it or by hiring it out. This too suggests that self-ownership need not be what motivates resistance to the eye lottery. (You can condemn rape (the violent borrowing of sexual organs) while also condemning prostitution (the peaceful hiring out of same), and thereby questioning some rights of self-ownership. If the only basis for condemning rape were the principle of self-ownership, prostitution would have to be regarded as just a particular use (by the prostitute) of her rights over her body.)

Now, stalwart believers in self-ownership will think that, contrary to what was suggested above, the difference between congenital and state-implanted eyes makes a big difference to the acceptability of the proposed lottery, precisely because the former are owned by the sighted person and the latter are not. But I wonder how they would react to the following alternative fantasy. Here, all are born with empty eye sockets, but most, a bare majority, have eyes that fall into their sockets as they pass under the ocular trees, while others, a minority, do not. The accidentality of the acquisition might suggest that redistribution to the sightless of one eye by lottery would not be so bad. Can believers in self-ownership convince themselves that there is an important difference between the luck of the eye-tree and the luck of the genetic draw?

Unfortunately, they can. As I said in section 1, the thesis of self-ownership cannot be refuted. But, as I also said, many lose confidence in it when certain contrasts and analogies are presented. And I hope that some people will be impressed by the sub-demonstrative considerations adduced in this closing section.

11. The future of a disillusion

The real purpose of socialism is precisely to overcome and advance beyond the predatory phase of human development (Albert Einstein, 'Why Socialism?')

1. It looks as though the Soviet Union, or the pieces that it may soon become, will embrace capitalism, or fall into a severe authoritarianism, or undergo both of those fates.[1] That is not an original thought. While a certain amount of humane socialist rhetoric survives even now in the Soviet Union, few observers believe that from its present crisis there will emerge a state, or states, characterized by an attractive form of socialism. But it costs me a lot to endorse that unoriginal thought, and I want to explain why.

In 1912 my mother was born, in Kharkov, to secular Jewish parents of ample means, her father being a successful timber merchant. When she was just five years old, the Bolshevik revolution occurred. My grandfather's business continued to provide well for the family during the period of the New Economic Policy,[2] and my mother was consequently quite well-heeled, with plenty to lose, but she nevertheless developed, across the course of the nineteen-twenties, in schools and in youth organizations, a full-hearted commitment to the Bolshevik cause. This she took with her in 1930 when, the NEP having given way to a regime less amenable to bourgeois existence, her parents decided to immigrate to Canada, and she left the Soviet Union, not because she wanted to,

---

[1] The present chapter was written, substantially, in 1989, and the above remarks, and some further conjectures below, may now read somewhat strangely. But they belong to the mood in which the chapter was written, and I cannot revise them without spoiling its integrity.

[2] I do not know what the family's condition was in the turbulent post-revolutionary period which preceded the adoption of the NEP in 1921.

but because she did not want to part with her emigrating parents and sister.

In Montreal, my mother, who could not speak English, and without, at eighteen, an advanced education, tumbled down the class ladder to a proletarian position. She took employment as a sewing machine operator in a garment factory. Before long, she met my father, a dress cutter, who, unlike her, had an impeccably proletarian pedigree (his father was a poor tailor from Lithuania), and no secondary education. Their courtship unrolled in the context of long hours of factory work, struggles to build unionism in the garment trade, and summer week-ends at the country camp some forty miles from town that was set up by and for left-wing Jewish workers. My parents married in 1936 and I appeared, their first-born, in 1941.

My mother was proud to be – to have become – working class, and through the thirties and forties, and until 1958, she was an active member of the Canadian Communist Party. My father belonged to the United Jewish People's Order, most of whose members were anti-religious, anti-Zionist, and strongly pro-Soviet. He was not in the Party itself, not because he had ideological reservations, but because his personality was not conducive to Party membership. Members of the Communist Party were expected to express themselves frequently, and with confidence, at branch meetings, and my father was an unusually reticent man with a restricted capacity for self-expression.

Because of my parents' convictions, my upbringing was intensely political. My first school, which I entered in 1946, was named after Morris Winchevsky, a Jewish proletarian poet. At Morris Winchevsky we learned standard primary school things in the mornings, from non-communist gentile women teachers;[3] but, in the afternoons, we were taught Jewish (and other) history and Yiddish language and literature, by left-wing Jews and Jewesses whose first (and in some cases, so it seemed, only) language was Yiddish. The instruction we got from them, even when they narrated Old Testament stories, was suffused with vernacular Marxist seasoning: nothing heavy or pedantic, just good Yiddish revolutionary common sense. Our report cards were folded down the middle,

---

[3] They were gentile because discrimination against hiring Jewish teachers in the Quebec school system meant that there were few Jewish aspirants to the profession. And they were non-communist not only because most people were, but also because the communist minority consisted mainly of French Canadians (the majority linguistic group), Jews and Ukrainians. Most English-speaking Montreal schoolteachers at primary level were genteel Protestant women of British Isles extraction: not a category abounding in subversives.

with English subjects on the left-hand side and Yiddish on the right, because of the directions in which the two languages are written. One of the Yiddish subjects was *Geshichte fun Klassen Kamf* (History of Class Struggle), at which, I am pleased to note, I scored a straight *aleph* in 1949.

One Friday in 1952, the Anti-Subversive (or, as it was commonly known, the Red) Squad of the Province of Quebec Provincial Police raided Morris Winchewsky and turned it inside out, in a search for incriminating left-wing literature. We were at our desks when they came, but, whatever happened in other classes, the raid was not frightening for those of us who were then in Lehrerin ('teacheress') Asher's charge, because, having left the room for a moment in response to the knock on the door, she soon returned, clapped her hands with simulated exuberance, and announced, in English: 'Children, the Board of Health is inspecting the school and you can all go home for the rest of the day!' So we scurried down the stairs, and lurking at the entrance were four men, each of them tall and very fat, all of them eyes down, and looking sheepish.

In the event, no compromising materials were found, since the school had been careful to keep itself clean, but a parallel raid on the premises of the United Jewish People's Order, which ran the school, did expose pamphlets and the like. Those premises were consequently padlocked by the police and their owners were denied access to them, within the terms of a Quebec law later struck down by the Supreme Court of Canada. And, although Morris Winchewsky was not forbidden to continue, the raids caused enough parents to withdraw their children from the school to make its further full-time operation impractical.

Accordingly, we were cast forth, as far as our formal schooling was concerned, into the big wide non-communist world. But some of us, and I, now eleven, was one of them, departed with a rock-firm attachment to the principles it had been a major purpose of Morris Winchewsky to instil in us, and with full and joyous confidence that the Soviet Union was implementing those principles.

The first blow to that confidence fell in June of 1956, when the American State Department published the text of the speech discrediting Stalin that Nikita Khruschev had delivered, four months earlier, at a closed session of the Twentieth Congress of the Communist Party of the Soviet Union. The Party in Quebec was stunned by the 'Khruschev revelations'. Its top six leaders resigned their memberships in September of 1956. They were, like most Party people, dismayed by what Khruschev had said, because it implied that they had conducted their political lives (and, therefore, their lives) under a massive illusion. But they also felt dismayed for the further reason that national (that is, Toronto) Party leaders who were fraternal delegates at the Twentieth Congress had concealed the de-Stalinization speech when reporting back to the Canadian Party. The six Montreal-based Quebec leaders felt betrayed by the national leadership, and, once they had left, the membership of the Party in Montreal felt not only, like its erstwhile local leadership, betrayed by Toronto, but also abandoned, by six admired and much-loved comrades whose departure was accompanied by no explanatory statement, who called no meeting to share their burden with the membership, who just went without saying good-bye.

In an atmosphere of confusion and distress, high-tension meetings of an unstructured kind and open to all Party members were held in the remaining months of 1956, at the premises of the Beaver Outing Club,[4] which was a recreational society sponsored by the Party. As leader of the younger teenage portion of the Quebec Division of the National Federation of Labour Youth,[5] I sat agog at those meetings, a silent witness of a little piece of history in the making. I watched the Party split into two groups: hardliners and softliners. While willing (just) to repudiate Stalin, the hardliners were for minimal change in the Party's mode of work, while the softliners had an appetite for reconstruction and renovation.[6] The hardliners called themselves 'Marxists' and their opponents 'revisionists', and the latter called themselves 'the New' and the others 'the Old' (or, sometimes, the 'dogmatists'). My mother was enthusiastically New, as were the other members of the Party branch she chaired: the line of fracture in the Party was running between rather than within branches.

After eighteen further months of factional dispute, a convention was called to elect a new executive for the still leaderless Quebec Party. Two high functionaries came from Toronto, where the Party was far less wracked, to supervise accreditation of delegates to an electoral con-

---

4 Those familiar with Montreal might like to know that this place was on the north side of Mount Royal Avenue, opposite Fletcher's Field, just west of what was then the Young Men's Hebrew Association and what is now a Université de Montréal sports centre, and above a delicatessen called, at different times, Shap's, Dunn's, Nu-Park and Nu-Way.

5 The NFLY (pronounced 'enflï') was, in all but name, the Young Communist League. The Communist Party had been outlawed when, because of the Molotov–Ribbentrop Pact, it refused to support the war against Germany. So it changed its name to the Labour Progressive Party, and the YCL became the NFLY. (The Party reassumed its original name in 1959. In announcing the nomenclatural reclamation, the *Canadian Tribune* (the Party paper) explained that 'Communist Party' was being readopted because it was 'scientifically more correct'.)

6 The line of the softliners was not all that soft. Thus, for example, the Soviet action in Hungary in the autumn of October 1956 was regarded, at the time, by virtually everyone in the Party as an entirely justified suppression of a Fascist rebellion.

vention. The sympathy of the men from Toronto was with the hardliners, and they ensured that duly selected representatives of 'New' Party branches were denied their right to vote, on spurious technical grounds. I believe – but here my recollection is somewhat hazy – that this was the trick the Toronto supervisors pulled: they delayed dispatch to New branches of the forms on which delegates' names were to be inscribed, so that, when those forms were filled in and returned, they could be declared invalid for having arrived too late. Through that or some comparable form of manipulation, the convention was made to produce a uniformly Old executive, and, in the aftermath, those of the New persuasion, my mother included, gradually fell away from the Party: they had, in effect, been disfranchised. Six or seven years later, when my mother taxed one of the Toronto emissaries, a personal friend, with the role he had played in the misconstruction of the 1958 convention, I heard him say something like: 'Bella, in politics you sometimes have to do things that are not pleasant.'

A year or so before the 1958 Convention, the leader of the Quebec division of the National Federation of Labour Youth resigned in disillusionment (to become an academic anthropologist), and the Quebec NFLY just collapsed, so fast that I would not have been able to leave it had I wanted to. Nor would I have wanted to leave it then: my mother, after all, was at the time still a committed Party member. I felt, morosely, that the NFLY was leaving me.

In September of 1957, with the NFLY gone and me too young for a Party that was anyway growing too Old for me, I entered McGill University, a convinced Marxist with no suitable organization to belong to, and I joined the thoroughly tame Socialist Society which was all that McGill then had to offer.

2. Through the rest of the fifties, and into the early sixties, I was what some would have called a 'fellow-traveller'. The Party rapidly became too rigid for me to consider submitting myself anew to its authority, but I remained basically pro-Soviet. Seeds of doubt had been sown, and I knew that there was much over there that deserved to be criticized, yet I still believed that the Soviet Union was a socialist country, struggling towards community and equality, and amply meriting every leftist's allegiance.

But in the thirty years and more that separate the disappearance of the National Federation of Labour Youth and the disappearance, now occurring, of both the Sovietness and the Unionhood of the Soviet Union, my views have undergone further evolution, and for a long time – perhaps two decades – they have included a pretty adverse assessment of the Soviet Union's claim to be a socialist society. Some people have therefore found it surprising that I should be saddened by what I perceive to be the impending final abandonment of the Bolshevik experiment. They can understand that I must regret the impact of the experiment's termination on how socialism is assessed, an impact which results from the widespread tendency to identify the Bolshevik and socialist causes. But they notice that my dejection goes beyond such matters of political calculation, and they wonder why.

The answer is that, although I have long since sustained little hope that things in the Soviet Union might get substantially better, in a socialist sense, there is, in certain domains, and people are prone to overlook this, a vast difference between nourishing little hope and giving up all hope. The small hope that I kept was, as it were, an immense thing, since so much was at stake. And now that residual hope has to be forsworn. So a feeling of loss is not surprising.

And there is also another and perhaps less rational motif here, which I would do well to avow. It is true that I was heavily critical of the Soviet Union, but the angry little boy who pummels his father's chest will not be glad if the old man collapses.[7] As long as the Soviet Union seemed safe, it felt safe for me to be anti-Soviet. Now that it begins, disobligingly, to crumble, I feel impotently protective towards it.

3. Since this piece is for a volume dedicated to Richard Wollheim, he is present to my mind as I write, and his presence causes me to remember how impressed I was by something that Sigmund Freud said about the Soviet Union in his 1927 essay on *The Future of an Illusion*, when I first read it, more than twenty-five years ago.

In Chapter 1 of that book, Freud propounds a theory about the structure of society which any leftist would judge reactionary. He begins by remarking – and with this many leftists, I among them, would readily agree – 'that there are present in all men destructive, and therefore anti-social and anti-cultural trends'.[8] It is Freud's next step which is reactionary, for he proceeds to bisect humanity into radically distinct groups. On one side of the divide are the 'lazy and unintelligent masses'

---

[7] Those of us on the left who were stern critics of the Soviet Union long before it collapsed needed it to be there to receive our blows. The Soviet Union needed to be there as a defective model so that, with one eye on it, we could construct a better one. It created a non-capitalist mental space in which to think about socialism.

[8] *The Future of an Illusion*, p. 7. 'Trends' translates '*Tendenzen*': 'tendencies' would be better.

in whom the destructive tendency is so strong that it 'determine[s] their behaviour in human society'. What is more dangerous, these people are not isolated from each other in their submission to unruly instinct, for they 'support one another in giving free rein to their indiscipline'. It is, accordingly, 'impossible to do without control of the mass by a minority',[9] and, fortunately, such a minority exists. For there is also another group of people, who possess the capacity for self-control that the masses lack, who have 'master[ed] their own instinctual wishes', and who therefore have the ability to exercise mastery over others. That ability endows them with the right – and the duty – to rule, for

it is only through the influence of these individuals who can set an example and whom masses recognize as their leaders that they can be induced to perform the work and undergo the renunciations on which the existence of civilization depends.[10]

Having read thus far, I was disappointed to see Freud, who was in so many ways above conventional notions, endorsing the old aristocratic fiction that because of their deficient inherent nature, 'for the mass of mankind . . . self-control chiefly means obeying their governors'.[11]

But now, having laid out his own view, Freud acknowledges the counter-argument that 'cultural regulations' superior to those which have prevailed to date might reduce the negative consequences of biology, and, in deference to that argument, he enters a moderately hopeful qualification. The destructive instinctual drives are, he insists, basic biological fact, but the fact that, as things stand, only a minority are able to discipline them without assistance might not be a biological one:

One may question whether, and in what degree, it would be possible for a different cultural environment to do away with the two characteristics of human masses which make the guidance of human affairs so difficult.[12] The experiment

---

[9] *Ibid.*, pp. 7–8.   [10] *Ibid.*, p. 8.

[11] Plato, *The Republic*, p. 78. For an argument against the Plato-Freud view, see my *Karl Marx's Theory of History*, pp. 212–13.

[12] These are that 'they are not spontaneously fond of work and that arguments are of no avail against their passions' (*ibid.*, p. 8). But, given the rest of the chapter, and Freud's ideas about gratification-deferral, the first of these characteristics, the 'spontaneous' aversion to work, is best interpreted as a biological universal, so that it is, for Freud, only the second characteristic, the insensitivity to argument, that distinguishes the masses from their leaders: in other words, the latter, too, have 'no love for instinctual renunciation', but *they* are 'convinced by argument of its inevitability' (*ibid.*, p. 7). I grant that so interpreting Freud goes awkwardly with his entertaining the possibility that 'a different *cultural* environment' might 'do away with' the masses' lack of 'spontaneous fondness' for work, but, as far as I can see, the line between nature and culture cuts at different points in different formulations in Freud's chapter.

has not yet been made. Probably a certain percentage of mankind (owing to a pathological disposition or an excess of instinctual strength) will always remain asocial; but if it were feasible merely to reduce the majority that is hostile towards civilization today into a minority, a great deal would have been accomplished – perhaps all that *can* be accomplished.[13]

That was somewhat better than what went before, but the whole message was still hard for a committed Marxist to take, so it was with relief, and pleasure, that I read, in the final paragraph of the chapter, that Freud had

not the least intention of making judgments on the great experiment in civilization that is now in progress in the vast country that stretches between Europe and Asia … What is in preparation there is unfinished and therefore eludes an investigation for which our own long-consolidated civilization affords us material.[14]

That Freud did not propound the negative prognosis on the Soviet experiment suggested by the general tenor of his chapter was doubly satisfying, for a still pro-Soviet reader with a strong affection for Freud and his writings. First, it showed that Freud was not, so early as 1927, as anti-Soviet as the main course of his chapter had caused me to fear, and I therefore did not have to classify him, with a heavy heart, as a paid-up member of the enemy camp. But second, my pro-Soviet (as opposed to my socialist) convictions being, at the time, already embattled, it was a relief not to have to cope, on top of everything else, with an acid Freudian scepticism, which I would have respected, despite my confidence in the falsehood of the premisses on which it would have been based: people are not always consistent, especially in things that matter a lot to them.

4. That solace means little now, for we can no longer say about the Soviet Union that 'what is in preparation there is unfinished'. It is finished, all washed up, and the question that arises for those of us who think that and who were attached to the Soviet Union is: having sustained this loss, what do we do now?

The loss affects both those who (like me) had once believed, and had not abandoned all hope, that the Soviet Union would realize the socialist ideal, and, *a fortiori*, those who still believed, only yesterday, that it was in fact realizing it. And although the ideal in question presented itself differently to different believers, it included, for all of us, the following elements,

---

[13] *Ibid.*, p. 9.   [14] *Ibid.*, p. 9.

and it was, consequently, prodigiously demanding: instead of the class exploitation of capitalism, economic equality; instead of the illusory democracy of class-based bourgeois politics, a real and complete democracy; instead of the alienation from one another of economic agents driven by greed and fear, an economy characterized by willing mutual service.

People have reacted in different ways when they have concluded that no progress towards the ideal which they once thought the Soviet Union was realizing will occur there in the foreseeable future. Their reactions depend on how they are disposed to explain the Soviet failure, on how they conceive the relationship, in general, between political ideals and political practice, and on aspects of their emotional make-up, such as how robust they are. These variations generate a ramified taxonomy, and, without trying to depict all of it, I want to describe some of its salient branches.

First, there are those who both preserve their belief in the ideal and sustain their commitment to pursuing it, with a fresh view about how and/or where and/or when it is to be achieved.

Others repudiate the unachieved ideal, sometimes after careful reconsideration of its claims, and sometimes through a form of self-deception in which they let those claims fade from their minds. In either case, a new ideal is adopted and a new politics elected, but those who pass on to them without reflection and in recoil from their loss are practising what has been called Adaptive Preference Formation. Adaptive Preference Formation is an irrational process in which a person comes to prefer A to B just because A is available and B is not. That A is more accessible than B is not a reason for thinking that A is better than B, but A's greater availability can nevertheless cause a person to think that A is better. The fox who tries and fails to reach the grapes has no *reason* to conclude that they are sour, but his failure *causes* him to fall into that conviction.[15]

Still others among the politically bereaved form a mixed collection of types who have it in common that they turn away altogether from politics. Some of them still acknowledge the authority of the original ideal, but they are convinced that it is impossible to realize, or virtually impossible, or anyway something they can no longer summon the energy to fight for: perhaps, when they let the baton fall, they hope that somebody else will pick it up. Others reject the ideal and are unable to embrace a different one. To all of these nothing now achievable seems worth achieving, or worth

---

[15] For further discussion of this phenomenon, in general terms, see footnote 17 below.

the effort of their own depleted power. When they look at the political world, 'Vanity of Vanities' is what they are inclined to say.

In what follows, I shall endorse sustained pursuit of something like the original ideal, but first I want to say a word about the Vanity of Vanities response, because I have been tempted by it myself in moments when the old ideal has appeared to me to be hopelessly over-ambitious; and also about the response of Adaptive Preference Formation, because, so it seems to me, it is a temptation to which many on the left are currently succumbing.

5. Vanity of Vanities, or rather, the form of it that has tempted me, says: genuine socialism is impossible, or virtually impossible, to achieve. It is overwhelmingly likely that the best we shall ever get is some kind of capitalism, and it is for others to find the strength to fight for a better capitalism. Here the old ideal remains bright, but the will collapses, and, integral to its collapse, both helping to induce it and feeding on it, is a pessimistic judgement of possibility that spreads its gloom across perception of the whole feasible set, so that the person says: what is *really* good is not to be had, and there is nothing else that is good enough for me to devote myself to.

A period of withdrawal following disappearance of what one hoped would fulfil one's dream is, of course, entirely natural. Time is needed to work things through. What is more, depression about the failure of the Soviet Union, as it supervenes in those of us who reluctantly rejected its claims decades ago, perforce has a complex structure, one element in which is self-reproach, since what is lost is a long-since denied (yet also fiercely clung to) love.[16] Against such a psychological background, it may be unwise to expect to reach full clarity of purpose quickly. It is neverthe-less right to resist the movement from a perhaps necessary depression to a settled Vanity of Vanities attitude.

If Vanity of Vanities sees nothing good when the best appears lost, Adaptive Preference Formation[17] treats the best it can find as the best that

---

[16] See Freud's telling remarks at 'Mourning and Melancholia', p. 240.

[17] That is the name applied by Jon Elster to the phenomenon in question: see his brilliant (albeit, as we shall see, verbally flawed) discussion of (what he also calls) 'Sour Grapes' (*Sour Grapes*, Ch. III), to which I am greatly indebted. 'Sour Grapes' is undoubtedly a snappier name than 'Adaptive Preference Formation', but, despite Elster's official or at least initial identification of them with one another (see *ibid.*, p. 110), 'Sour Grapes' is not a good name for Adaptive Preference, because the latter is a general phenomenon and the fox's attitude in the Sour Grapes story is in two ways but a specific form of it, as I shall now explain.

could be conceived. In Adaptive Preference the grass looks greener on *this* side of the fence: the agent's assessment ordering bends round to favour what (he thinks) is in the feasible set. In my opinion, this pathology is visible in a movement of thought which is widespread in contemporary Western socialism.

6. Let me explain. Nineteenth-century socialists were for the most part opposed to market organization of economic life. The pioneers favoured something which they thought would be far superior, to wit, comprehensive central planning, and their later followers were encouraged by what they interpreted as victories of planning, such as Stalin's industrialization drive and the early institution of educational and medical provision in the People's Republic of China. More recently, however, many socialists have concluded that central planning is a poor recipe for economic success. And now there is among socialist intellectuals an intelligent movement, but also alongside it, an unthinking and fashion-driven rush, in the direction of a non-planning or minimally planning *market* socialist society. Market socialism is socialist because it overcomes the division between capital and labour: there is, in market socialism, no class of capitalists facing workers who own no capital, since workers themselves own the firms. But market socialism is unlike traditionally conceived socialism in that its worker-owned firms confront one another, and consumers, in competitive market-contractual fashion; and market

---

In all adaptive preference formation, *A* is preferred to *B* because *A* is (readily) available and *B* is not, but the comparative preference can be the upshot *either* of judging *A* better than it would otherwise (that is, but for the unavailability of *B*) be judged *or* of judging *B* worse than it would otherwise be judged (or, of course of both). The fox is in the second position. He downgrades the grapes he does not have: he does not upgrade the condition of grapelessness. But much Adaptive Preference Formation, including some of the preference for market socialism discussed in the next section, goes the other way: the available thing gets upgraded. (At p. 119 Elster appears to restrict 'Sour Grapes' to downgrading the unavailable, despite his use of it as an alternative name for Adaptive Preference Formation as such at p. 110.)

One may, moreover, come to prefer available *A* to unavailable *B* *either* because of a change of criteria caused by knowledge of the feasible set *or* because of a (similarly caused) change of factual judgement about how *A* and *B* stack up against unrevised criteria. Sour Grapes proper, in the story of the fox, illustrates the second thing, an irrational change of factual judgement (and, despite what Elster says at p. 123, in the English version of the story as well as in the French). As for the recent turn towards market socialism, it surely reflects reassessment, to different degrees in different cases, *both* of facts *and* of criteria, so 'Sour Grapes' would, once again, be misleading here. (To make matters more tangled, as far as Elster's exposition goes, at p. 123 he (not unreasonably) *contrasts* 'adaptive preferences' and 'adaptive [factual] perception' and in effect treats the Sour Grapes story as a case of the latter, so that Sour Grapes is in the end not even an *instance* of what he originally *identified* it with!)

socialism is also, and relatedly, unlike traditionally conceived socialism in that it reduces, even though it does not entirely eliminate, the traditional socialist emphasis on economic equality. Equality is prejudiced because market competition means winners and losers, who end up less well off than the winners do.

I believe that it is good for the political prospects of socialism that market socialism is being brought to the fore as an object of advocacy and policy: these socialist intellectuals, even some of the fashion-driven ones, are performing a useful political service. But I also think that market socialism is at best second best, even if it is the best (or more than the best) at which it is now reasonable to aim, and that many socialist intellectuals who think otherwise are indulging in Adaptive Preference.

Now, the Adaptive Preference response sometimes has some good effects. Like the rational policy of Not Crying Over Spilt Milk, it may prevent fruitless lamentation and wasted effort. But Adaptive Preference also has great destructive potential, since it means losing standards that may be needed to guide criticism of the *status quo*, and it dissolves the faith to which a future with ampler possibilities may yet be hospitable. If you cannot bear to remember the goodness of the goal that you sought and which is not now attainable,[18] you may fail to pursue it should it come within reach, and you will not try to bring it within reach. When the fox succeeds in convincing himself that the grapes are sour, he does not build the ladder that might enable him to get at them.

In 1983 there appeared an important book by Alec Nove, called *The Economics of Feasible Socialism*. One point of including the word 'feasible' in its title was or should have been to abjure the claim that the arrangements recommended in the book are the best conceivable. I do not think that Nove would say, for example, that the market socialism he recommends fully satisfies socialist standards of distributive justice, though he would rightly say that it scores better by those standards than market capitalism does. Notwithstanding that relative superiority, market socialism remains deficient from a socialist point of view, if only because, in socialist perception, there is injustice in a system which confers high rewards on people who happen to be unusually talented and who form highly productive co-operatives.

---

[18] If you cannot do that, you will be relevantly like those who 'fail to experience mourning. Feeling incapable of saving and securely reinstating their loved objects inside themselves, they must turn away from them more than hitherto and therefore deny their love for them.' (Melanie Klein, 'Mourning', p. 336.)

In 1989 there appeared another important book, by David Miller, called *Market, State and Community*, which, like Nove's, advocates market socialism. But in Chapter 6 of his book, Miller seems to me to promote Adaptive Preference Formation. It is, in my view, a serious mistake to suppose that any market system (except, perhaps, the very special one – of which I shall say more later – designed by Joseph Carens) could conform to the requirements of distributive justice. Yet in Chapter 6 Miller argues that market socialism tends to reward personal desert and therefore is, substantially, distributively just. I disagree both with the premiss (that market socialism tends to reward desert)[19] and with the inference (that it follows that it is just)[20] of that argument, and I also reject its conclusion (that market socialism is just).[21]

I do not say that we should aim to achieve, in this era of ideologically rejuvenated capitalism, a form of socialism very different from what Nove and Miller describe. As far as immediate political programmes are concerned, market socialism is probably a good idea. But Miller's (and others') claims for it are grander, and they should not be accepted. One reason why they should not be accepted is found in the thought of Karl Marx, to an aspect of which I now turn.

7. Marx was no friend of the market, even in its socialist form. The communist society which he envisaged proclaimed the slogan 'From each according to his ability, to each according to his needs'. One might ask what it means for each to give according to his ability, and to get according to his needs. But, for our purposes, the unambiguous message of the communist slogan is that what you get is *not* a function of what you give, that contribution and reward are entirely separate matters. You do not get more because you produce more, and you do not get less because you are not good at producing. Accordingly, the ideal flourished in

---

[19] For desert, supposing that there is such a thing, divides into what Joel Feinberg would call comparative and non-comparative forms, and I am convinced that the two need to be confused with one another for the stated premiss to seem true. There is, moreover, the further difficulty that the market rewards results, which are imperfectly correlated with effort, which is also (if anything is) a source of desert, and to which the market is blind. (For these and other points, see my 'David Miller on Market Socialism and Distributive Justice', typescript available on request; and see Joel Feinberg's 'Noncomparative Justice' for the distinction between comparative and non-comparative desert.)

[20] For desert is not the only relevant dimension of justice. There is also, for example, need, and Miller's attempt to finesse the latter in the present connection is unsatisfactory. See *Market, State and Community*, pp. 295–6, and my 'David Miller . . .', section 3.

[21] Since I think it is unjust, for reasons that may already be apparent, and which are amplified in the next section.

the communist slogan represents a complete rejection of the logic of the market.

Marx also described a second best to full communism, which he called 'the first phase of communist society',[22] a phase transitional to the final one in which the just-discussed principle of distribution is sovereign. Because of later Marxist verbal usage, the two phases are more familiarly known under the titles 'socialism' and 'communism'. And although Marxist socialism is not a market socialism, Marx's criticism of that transitional form of society also bears against market socialism.

Marxist socialism, the lower phase of communism, is a non-market society in which remuneration is supposed to reward labour contribution. That is the import of its ruling slogan, which says: To each according to his contribution. If, as David Miller thinks, contribution establishes desert and rewarding desert suffices for justice, then Marxist socialism would possess the virtue that it rewards desert and is, therefore, just: perhaps, indeed, more just than any market socialism could be.

That last speculation is, however, a pretty idle one, since measuring contribution in a non-market society requires questionable assignments of product to heterogenous labours, and to labours of different skill levels;[23] and while a market society assigns salaries to labour in an automatic process free of the application of contestable criteria, it is impossible to treat those salaries as measures of *contribution*, influenced as they are by vagaries of bargaining power and other accidental market circumstance. It is, accordingly, difficult to compare the relative merits of the two forms of socialism as devices for rewarding producers according to their contribution.

But let us here set aside the question of whether Marx was right to prefer a non-market socialism to a market one, and also the problem of how labour contributions are to be measured. Of greater present relevance is that Marx's strictures against the principle of reward to contribution expose the anti-socialist (because bourgeois) character of market socialism's reward structure. While pointing out that first-stage communism abolishes capitalist exploitation, since differential access to means of production is gone, and no one now consumes more labour value than he produces, Marx criticized the principle of reward for contribution

---

[22] In *The Critique of the Gotha Programme*, p. 324.
[23] Because of the difficulty of finding criteria for assigning product to individuals, Soviet bureaucrats often got away with defending their bloated salaries on the principle of reward to contribution. They sometimes implied that they would be failing in their obligation to help realize the lower stage of communism if they gave up their large dachas.

The future of a disillusion

because of the (unjust)[24] inequality that it generates. For Marx, it is indeed a recommendation of low-stage communism that the bourgeois principle of reward for contribution is in this society not just invoked as ideological rationalization but actually instituted, so that 'principle and practice are no longer at loggerheads'. But he did not doubt that reward for contribution *is* a bourgeois principle, one which treats a person's talent 'as a natural privilege'.[25] Reward for contribution honours the principle of self-ownership.[26] Nothing is more bourgeois than that principle – it is, indeed, *the* principle of the bourgeois revolution – and the Gotha Critique lesson for market socialism is that, while market socialism may remove the income injustice caused by differential ownership of capital, it preserves the income injustice caused by differential ownership of endowments of personal capacity.

8. Before we settle for market socialism, let us recall why socialists in the past rejected the market. Some of their reasons were better than others, and here I shall review what I take to be the four principal criticisms of the market in the socialist tradition, starting with two that I consider misplaced, and ending with two that I consider sound. The market was judged (1) inefficient, (2) anarchic, (3) unjust in its results, and (4) mean in its motivational presuppositions.

(1) To say that the market is inefficient is to criticize it in its allocative as opposed to in its distributive function, where allocation concerns the assignment of resources to different productive uses (so much steel to housing and so much to automobiles and so many engineers to each and so on) and distribution concerns the assignment of income to persons. Manifestly, allocation and distribution are in intimate causal relationship, but the bottom line of this first criticism relates to allocation alone: it is that the market is wasteful, variously over- and under-productive, and here the question of who in particular suffers from that waste is set to one side. And the reason for the wastefulness, so the criticism goes, is that a market economy is unplanned.

We now know that the traditional socialist view about the market's lack of planning was misconceived. It failed to acknowledge how remarkably

---

[24] The adjective has to go in parentheses because Marx disparaged the notion of justice, and, so I have claimed, did not realize that he believed passionately in it: see my review of Allen Wood's *Karl Marx*.

[25] *The Critique of the Gotha Programme*, p. 324.

[26] It honours that principle even if it does not imply acceptance of it: see Chapter 5 above, pp. 123–5.

well the unplanned market organizes information, and, indeed, how difficult it is for a planning centre to possess itself of the information about preferences and production possibilities dispersed through the market in a non-planning system. Even if the planner's computer could do wonders with that information, there would remain the problem that there are systematic obstacles to gathering it: to that extent, Von Mises and Hayek were right. And the traditional socialist critique also failed to appreciate the degree to which it would prove possible to correct for market inefficiencies through an external regulation which falls far short of comprehensive planning.

(2) There was, however, in the traditional socialist objection to the market, a separate emphasis that the market's generation of massive unplanned outcomes are deplorable as such (that is, apart from the particular disbenefits and injustices of those outcomes). They are deplorable *just* because they are unplanned, since the fact that they are not planned means that society is not in control of its own destiny. Marx and Engels did not favour planning solely because of the particular advantageous economic consequences that they thought it would have, but also because of the significance of planning as a realization of the idea, derived no doubt from the Hegelian legacy under which they laboured, of humanity rising to consciousness of and control over itself. The advent of the planned society was seen as 'the ascent of man from the kingdom of necessity to the kingdom of freedom ... Man, at last the master of his own form of social organization, becomes at the same time the lord over Nature, his own master – free.'[27]

In my view, that idea is entirely misplaced. Individual self-direction, a person's determining the course of his own life, may have value *per se*, but collective self-direction does not.[28] David Miller perceptively claims that five values (conceived not instrumentally but as valuable in themselves) have inspired socialists, and I think (as he does) that we should dump the first one – conscious social purpose – on his list.[29] It is not the same thing as democracy, for a democracy can decide that some things should not be subject to collective purpose. A decision is democratic if it is made (in some appropriate sense) by the people as a whole. But there is conscious

---

[27] Friedrich Engels, *Socialism: Utopian and Scientific*, pp. 82, 86.

[28] Except in the here totally irrelevant sense of non-subjection to another collective. Not wanting your society's course to be determined from without does not imply wanting it to be deliberately determined from within.

[29] The other four are democracy, freedom, equality and community. See Miller, 'A Vision of Market Socialism', pp. 406–8.

social purpose in a social development if that development was planned, decided by society as such, whatever the political character of the society may be, democratic, dictatorial, or something else. A dictator can plan, and a democracy can decide not to.

Now, unlike collective self-direction, democracy *is* good in itself. The case for it, if one is a principled democrat, is not exhausted by the claim that it produces better results. One can believe that, even if *A* was a bad decision, and *B* would have been a better one, it says something for *A* that it was taken democratically. By contrast, I would not say about bad things caused by planning: well, at least they were planned. To the extent that something is democratic, it is good, but it is false that, to the extent that something is planned or controlled, it is good.[30]

We should decide what to put within, and what to leave outside, collective purpose, on a purely instrumental basis, that is, according to the tendency of collective action to promote or frustrate intrinsic values, and, notably, the other four on David Miller's list, which are freedom, equality, community[31] and democracy itself. There is harm to no one in the *mere* fact that social purpose is lacking, although society-wide decision-making is of

---

[30] The contrast between democracy and control (the first being valuable, as such, and the second not) survives in a more nuanced statement of the value of democracy. Reflecting on a monstrous democratic decision, such as the democratic choice of a racist government, one might say that, sometimes, the content of a democratic decision is so awful that it is small (but still some) consolation that it is democratic; or one might say, more subtly, but quite consistently: the intrinsic value of democracy is conditional on the democratic decision not being too awful.

Suppose that you have to decide whether or not to go against the democratic will, and you hold the just-explained subtle view of democracy's intrinsic value. Then there would be three kinds of case in which you regretted that the democratic will went the way it did. First, ones where you would nevertheless co-operate with it. Then, ones where you would not co-operate, but you would still think that it tells in favour of the decision (but not sufficiently for you to support it, given the countervailing value of its bad content) that it was democratic. And, finally, ones where there is no intrinsic value in the decision's being democratic, because its content is so bad.

But whatever may be the precisely correct way of affirming that democracy is not only instrumentally but intrinsically valuable, I am tempted to no similar affirmation with respect to a development occurring in a planned as opposed to in a spontaneous way. I see nothing inherently valuable in the social process being *controlled*, by human will. And I am confident that Marx and Engels did see something valuable in that.

[31] Endorsement of community as an ultimate value might be thought inconsistent with the scepticism that I have just expressed about the ultimate value of collective purpose. For if community is valuable, then identification with community is valuable: and such identification might require subscribing to a group goal which community members could not regard as instrumentally justified (by the propensity of pursuit of that goal to sustain community). That represents a complex challenge to what I have said, and I do not want to deal with it here, save by remarking that even if community members could not regard the communal goal as instrumentally justified, how they could regard it and what its true value would be are different matters.

course required for instrumental reasons, such as, sometimes, to promote individual freedom, and in order to suppress or control the evil aspects of the market, two of which relate to two traditional criticisms of the market which seem to me to be unanswerable.

Those criticisms are (3) that the market distributes in unjustly unequal amounts, about which enough has been said above, and (4) that it motivates productive contribution not on the basis of commitment to one's fellow human beings, but on the basis of impersonal cash reward. The immediate motive to productive activity in a market society is typically[32] some mixture of greed and fear, in proportions that vary with the details of a person's market position and personal character. In greed, other people are seen as possible sources of enrichment, and in fear they are seen as threats. These are horrible ways of seeing other people, however much we have become habituated and inured to them, as a result of centuries of capitalist development.

In (at least one kind of) non-market motivation I produce because I desire to serve my fellow human beings while being served by them. Such motivation embodies an expectation of reciprocation, but it nevertheless differs critically from market motivation. The marketeer is willing to serve, but only in order to be served. He does not desire the conjunction (serve-and-be-served) as such, for he would not serve if doing so were not a means to get service. The difference is expressed in the lack of fine tuning that attends non-market motivation. Contrast taking turns in a loose way with respect to who buys the drinks with keeping a record of who has paid what for them. In the former procedure, we distance ourselves from the rules of the market.

Now, the history of the twentieth century encourages the thought that the easiest way to generate productivity in a modern society is by nourishing the motives of greed and fear, in a hierarchy of unequal income. But that does not make them attractive motives. Who would propose running a society on such motives, and thereby promoting the psychology to which they belong, if they were not known to be effective, did they not have the instrumental value which is the only value that they have? In the famous statement in which Adam Smith justified market relations, he pointed out that we place our faith not in the butcher's generosity but on his self-interest when we rely on him to provision us.

---

[32] People can operate under a sense of service even in a market society, but in so far as they do so, what makes the market work is not what makes them work. Their discipline is not market discipline.

Smith thereby propounded a wholly extrinsic justification of market motivation, in face of what he acknowledged to be its unattractive intrinsic character. Traditional socialists have often ignored Smith's point, in a moralistic condemnation of market motivation which fails to address its extrinsic justification. Certain contemporary over-enthusiastic market socialists tend, contrariwise, to forget that the market is intrinsically repugnant, because they are blinded by their belated discovery of the market's extrinsic value. The genius of the market is that it recruits shabby motives to desirable ends, and, in a balanced view, both sides of that proposition must be kept in focus.

Both self-interest and generosity exist in everyone. We know how to make an economic system work on the basis of self-interest. We do not know how to make it work on the basis of generosity. But that does not mean that we should forget generosity: we should still confine the sway of self-interest as much as we can. We do that, for example, when we tax, redistributively, the unequalizing results of market activity. The extent to which we can do that without defeating our aim (of making the badly off better off) varies inversely with the extent to which self-interest has been allowed to triumph in private and public consciousness.[33] (To the extent that it has triumphed, heavily progressive taxation drives high earners abroad, or causes them to decide to reduce their labour input, or induces in them a morose attitude which makes their previous input hard or impossible to sustain.)

The fact that the first great experiment in running a modern economy without relying on avarice and anxiety has failed, disastrously, is not a good reason for giving up the attempt, forever. Philosophers least of all should join the contemporary choruses of dirge and hosanna whose common refrain is that the socialist project is over. I am sure that it has a long way to go yet, and it is part of the mission of philosophy to explore unanticipated possibilities.

What is true and, as the interest in market socialism shows, widely appreciated, is that different ways forward must now be tried. And in the light of the misallocating propensity of comprehensive planning on the one hand and of the injustice of market results and the moral

---

[33] My views on this matter run alongside those of John Stuart Mill, who averred that '[e]very-body has selfish and unselfish interests, and a selfish man has cultivated the habit of caring for the former, and not caring for the latter.' (*Considerations on Representative Government*, p. 444. For sapient commentary on this and other relevant passages in Mill, see Richard Ashcraft, 'Class Conflict and Constitutionalism in J. S. Mill's Thought', pp. 117–18.)

shabbiness of market motivation on the other, it is natural to ask whether it might be possible to preserve the allocative function of the market, to continue to get the benefits it provides of information generation and processing, while extinguishing its normal motivational presuppositions and distributive consequences.

Such a project of differentiation is the aspiration of a ground-breaking book by Joseph Carens. The book is called *Equality, Moral Incentives, and the Market*, and its significant subtitle is *An Essay in Utopian Politico-Economic Theory*. Carens describes a society in which what looks like a standard capitalist market organizes economic activity, but the tax system cancels the disequalizing results of that market by redistributing income to complete equality. There are (pre-tax) profit-maximizing capitalists, and workers who own no capital, *but* people acknowledge an obligation to serve others, and the extent to which they discharge it is measured by how close their pre-tax income is to what it would be in the most remunerative activity available to them, while taxation effects a fully egalitarian post-tax distribution of income. Here, then, producers aim, in an immediate sense, at cash results, but they do not keep the money that accrues, and they seek it out of a desire to contribute to society.

As Carens has recognized, there are problems with the scheme,[34] but it seems to me one that is amply worth refining. Because the Carens model is an entirely market, even capitalist, society, which yet sustains both a strict equality and an ethic of mutual service, it qualifies, in a certain sense, as the Platonic ideal of market socialism. For the inspiration of market socialism, one to which it necessarily cannot be completely true, is to seize the advantages of market competition while preserving the socialist egalitarian principle. The Carens perfection of that ideal is a star for socialist economists to steer by as they navigate the worldly problems of socialist design.

9. It can be hard to maintain dedication to socialism in a climate where it is regarded as irrelevant. When you are out of joint with the times, you look for sources of confidence, to strengthen your resolve. In closing, I shall mention two of mine.

When I did graduate work at Oxford, it was the prevailing notion that there were in philosophy plainly right and plainly wrong answers, that a hard-headed clear-mindedness would without too much ado generate the right ones, and that the latter were likely to be not surprising but already

---

[34] See his 'Rights and Duties', Parts III and IV.

familiar. In 1963 I left Oxford to lecture in the Department where Richard Wollheim had just become Professor. On Wednesday afternoons he presided over a staff discussion group in which the prevailing notion was different from at Oxford, and one that I experienced as liberating. It was that on any large philosophical question there were bound to be different *views* (that was the operative word), that it could be hard to tell which one was right, and that there was no reason to suppose that the right one was comfortable or long since known. I remember how Richard would restore a sense of perspective, when one of us had rehearsed some accepted wisdom, by uttering a corrective sentence which began 'well, there *is*, of course, the *other* view, that . . . ' And I also remember the thrill I felt, listening to his beautiful inaugural lecture, when he said of his predecessors A. J. Ayer and Stuart Hampshire that they did not encourage 'the desire to agree'.[35] In times like these, Richard's generous liberalism is a good thing to have experienced, and to remember.

The other source of strength that I want to mention relates more to politics than to philosophy, but it too implies an admonition against surrender to the pull of conventional thinking. It is the end of the letter which Friedrich Engels wrote to his comrade Friedrich Sorge, the day after Karl Marx died:

Local lights and lesser minds, if not the humbugs, will now have a free hand. The final victory is certain, but circuitous paths, temporary and local errors – things which even now are so unavoidable – will become more common than ever. Well, we must see it through. What else are we here for?
    And we are not near losing courage yet.[36]

---

[35] *On Drawing an Object*, p. 6.
[36] Marx and Engels, *Selected Correspondence*, p. 340.

Bibliography

Aaron, Richard, *Locke*, Oxford, 1937

Aikin, H. D. (ed.), *Hume's Moral and Political Philosophy*, New York, 1959

Ake, Christopher, 'Justice as Equality', *Philosophy and Public Affairs*, 5, 1975–6

Archard, David, 'The Marxist Ethic of Self-Realisation', in Evans (ed.)

Arneson, Richard, 'Lockean Self-Ownership: Towards a Demolition', *Political Studies*, 39, 1991

Ashcraft, Richard, 'Class Conflict and Constitutionalism in J. S. Mill's Thought', in Rosenblum (ed.)

Baldwin, Thomas, 'Tully, Locke, and Land', *The Locke Newsletter*, 13, 1982

Barry, Brian, *Theories of Justice*, Hemel Hempstead, 1989

　Democracy, Power and Justice, Oxford, 1989

　'Humanity and Justice', in Barry, *Democracy, Power and Justice*

Bergström, Lars, 'What is a Conflict of Interest?', *Journal of Peace Research*, 3, 1970

Brody, Baruch, 'Redistribution without Egalitarianism', *Social Philosophy and Policy*, 1, 1983

Brown, Grant, review of Narveson, *Canadian Journal of Philosophy*, 20, 1990

Buchanan, Allen, *Marx and Justice*, Totowa, NJ, 1982

Carens, Joseph, *Equality, Moral Incentives, and the Market*, Chicago, 1981

　'Rights and Duties in an Egalitarian Society', *Political Theory*, 14, 1986

Cather, Willa, *Death Comes for the Archbishop*, New York, 1927

Chaplin, Ralph, 'Solidarity Forever', in Hille (ed.)

Child, James W., 'Can Libertarianism Sustain a Fraud Standard?', *Ethics*, 104, 1993–4

Cohen, G. A., *Karl Marx's Theory of History: A Defence*, Oxford and Princeton, 1978

　'Illusions about Private Property and Freedom', in Mepham and Ruben (eds.)

　'More on Exploitation and the Labour Theory of Value', *Inquiry*, 26, 1983

　Review of Allen Wood, *Karl Marx*, *Mind*, 92, 1983

　History, Labour, and Freedom, Oxford, 1988

　'On the Currency of Egalitarian Justice', *Ethics*, 99, 1988–9

　'David Miller on Market Socialism and Distributive Justice', All Souls College, typescript, 1989

　'Capitalism, Freedom and the Proletariat', in D. Miller (ed.)

'The Limits of Contractual Equality', *Ratio Juris*, 8, 1995
'Equality as Fact and as Norm: Reflections on the (Partial) Demise of Marxism', *Theoria*, forthcoming
Cohen, Joshua, 'Democratic Equality', *Ethics*, 99, 1988–9
The Commission on Social Justice, *The Justice Gap*, London, 1993
Dahl, Robert, *A Preface to Economic Democracy*, Oxford, 1985
Dunn, John, 'Consent in the Political Theory of John Locke', in Schochet (ed.) *Locke*, Oxford, 1984
Dworkin, G., Bermant, G. and Brown, P. G. (eds.), *Markets and Morals*, Washington, 1977
Dworkin, Ronald, 'What is Equality? Part 1: Equality of Welfare', *Philosophy and Public Affairs*, 10, 1981
'What is Equality? Part 2: Equality of Resources', *Philosophy and Public Affairs*, 10, 1981
'What is Equality? Part 3: The Place of Liberty', *Iowa Law Review*, 73, 1987
Ehring, Douglas, 'Cohen, Exploitation, and Theft', *Dialogue*, 26, 1987
Einstein, Albert, 'Why Socialism?', *Monthly Review*, 1, 1949
Elster, Jon, *Sour Grapes*, Cambridge, 1983
Elster, Jon and Moene, Karl Ove (eds.), *Alternatives to Capitalism*, Cambridge, 1989
Engels, Friedrich, *Socialism: Utopian and Scientific*, London, 1892
Anti-Dühring, Moscow, 1954
Evans, J. G. D. (ed.), *Moral Philosophy and Contemporary Problems*, Cambridge, 1987
Exdell, John, 'Distributive Justice: Nozick and Property Rights', *Ethics*, 87, 1977
Feinberg, Joel, 'Noncomparative Justice', *Philosophical Review*, 83, 1974
Fichte, Johann Gottlieb, *Zurückforderung der Denkfreiheit von den Fürsten Europens, die sie bisher unterdrückten: Eine Rede*, in I. H. Fichte (ed.), *Fichte's Werke*, Berlin, 1845–6
Flew, Anthony, *A Dictionary of Philosophy*, London, 1979
Frankfurt, Harry, 'Coercion and Moral Responsibility', in Honderich (ed.), 1973
Freud, Sigmund, *Complete Psychological Works*, London, 1966–74
'Mourning and Melancholia', in Freud, *Complete Psychological Works*, Vol. XIV
The Future of an Illusion, in Freud, *Complete Psychological Works*, Vol. XXI
Galston, William, *Justice and the Human Good*, Chicago, 1980
Gauthier, David, 'David Hume, Contractarian', *Philosophical Review*, 88, 1979
Morals by Agreement, Oxford, 1986
George, Henry, *Progress and Poverty*, London, 1884
Geras, Norman, *Literature of Revolution*, London, 1986
'Post-Marxism?', *New Left Review*, 163, 1987
Goldman, A. I. and Kim, J. (eds.), *Values and Morals*, Dordrecht, 1978
Gorz, André, *Farewell to the Working Class*, Boston, 1982
Gough, John, *John Locke's Political Philosophy*, Oxford, 1950
Graham, Keith, 'Self-Ownership, Communism and Equality', *Proceedings of the Aristotelian Society*, supp. vol. 64, 1990
Gray, John, 'Marxian Freedom, Individual Liberty, and the End of Alienation', in Ellen Frankel Paul *et al.* (eds.), 1986
'Against Cohen on Proletarian Unfreedom', in Ellen Frankel Paul *et al.* (eds.), 1989

Green, S. J. D., 'Competitive Equality of Opportunity: A Defense', *Ethics*, 100, 1989

Griffin, James, *Well-Being*, Oxford, 1986

Grünebaum, James O., *Private Ownership*, London, 1987

Hale, Robert L., 'Coercion and Distribution in a Supposedly Non-Coercive State', *Political Science Quarterly*, 100, 1923

Harsanyi, John, review of Gauthier, *Morals by Agreement*, *Economics and Philosophy*, 3, 1987

Hart, H. L. A., *The Concept of Law*, Oxford, 1961

Hausman, Daniel, 'Are Markets Morally Free Zones?', *Philosophy and Public Affairs*, 18, 1989

Hille, Waldemar (ed.), *The People's Song Book*, New York, 1948

Hobhouse, Leonard, *The Elements of Social Justice*, London, 1922

Hohfeld, W. N., *Fundamental Legal Conceptions*, New Haven, 1946

Holmstrom, Nancy, 'Marx and Cohen on the Labour Theory of Value', *Inquiry*, 26, 1983

Honderich, Ted (ed.), *Essays on Freedom of Action*, London, 1973
    Morality and Objectivity, London, 1985

Honoré, Tony, *Making Law Bind*, Oxford, 1987

Hume, David, *A Treatise of Human Nature*, Oxford, 1888
    'Of the Original Contract', in Aikin (ed.)
    An Enquiry Concerning the Principles of Morals, Oxford, 1975

Ingram, Attracta, *A Political Theory of Rights*, Oxford, 1994

Kant, Immanuel, *Lectures on Ethics*, Indianapolis, 1963
    Foundations of the Metaphysics of Morals, New York, 1990
    The Metaphysics of Morals, Cambridge, 1991

Kirzner, Israel, 'Entrepreneurship, Entitlement, and Economic Justice', in J. Paul (ed.)

Klein, Melanie, 'Mourning: Its Relation to Manic-Depressive States', in Klein, *Contributions to Psychoanalysis*, London, 1973

Knight, Frank H., 'Some Fallacies in the Interpretation of Social Cost', *The Quarterly Journal of Economics*, Vol. 38, 1924

Kuhn, H. and Tucker, A. W. (eds.), *Contributions to the Theory of Games*, Vol. II, Princeton, 1953

Kuusinen, O. W. (ed.), *Fundamentals of Marxism-Leninism*, Moscow, no date

Kymlicka, Will, *Liberalism, Community, and Culture*, Oxford, 1989

Laclau, Ernesto and Mouffe, Chantal, *Hegemony and Socialist Strategy*, London, 1985

Lewis, David, *Convention*, Cambridge, MA, 1969

Locke, John, *Two Treatises of Government*, Peter Laslett (ed.), Cambridge, 1963
    'Some Considerations of the Consequences of the Lowering of Interest and Raising the Value of Money', in John Locke, *Several Papers Relating to Money, Interest and Trade* (1696), New York, 1968
    Essays on the Law of Nature, Oxford, 1970

Lucash, Frank (ed.), *Justice and Equality Here and Now*, Ithaca, NY, 1986

Lukes, Steven, *Marxism and Morality*, Oxford, 1985
    'Taking Morality Seriously', in Honderich (ed.), 1985

Mack, Eric, 'Nozick on Unproductivity: The Unintended Consequences', in J. Paul (ed.)

'Distributive Justice and the Tensions of Lockeanism', *Social Philosophy and Policy*, 1, 1983

Mackie, John, *Ethics: Inventing Right and Wrong*, Harmondsworth, Middlesex, 1977

Maclean, Douglas and Brown, Peter G. (eds.), *Energy and the Future*, Totowa, NJ, 1983

Macleod, Alistair, 'Distributive Justice, Contract, and Equality', *Journal of Philosophy*, 81, 1984

Macpherson, C. B., *The Political Theory of Possessive Individualism*, Oxford, 1962

Marx, Karl, Preface to *A Contribution to the Critique of Political Economy*, in *Marx/Engels: Selected Works in One Volume*

Critique of the Gotha Programme, in *Marx/Engels: Selected Works in One Volume*

'On the Jewish Question', in *Marx/Engels: Collected Works*, Vol. III

'Comments on James Mill, *Elémens d'économie politique*', in *Marx/Engels: Collected Works*, Vol. III

Letter of 9 March 1854 in *The People's Paper*, in *Marx/Engels: Collected Works*, Vol. XIII

Theories of Surplus Value, Vol. I, Moscow, 1963

Theories of Surplus Value, Vol. II, Moscow, 1968

The Grundrisse, Harmondsworth, Middlesex, 1973

Capital, Vol. I, Harmondsworth, Middlesex, 1976

Capital, Vol. III, Harmondsworth, Middlesex, 1978

Marx, Karl and Engels, Frederick, *Selected Works in One Volume*, London, 1968

Collected Works, London, 1975–

Selected Correspondence, Moscow, 1975

The German Ideology, in *Marx/Engels: Collected Works*, Vol. V

'Circular Letter Against Kriege', in *Marx/Engels: Collected Works*, Vol. VI

Manifesto of the Communist Party, in *Marx/Engels: Collected Works*, Vol. VI

Meacher, Michael, 'Picking Up the Pieces', *The Guardian*, 25 June 1987

Menger, Anton, *The Right to the Whole Produce of Labour*, London, 1899

Mepham, John and Ruben, David-Hillel (eds.), *Issues in Marxist Philosophy*, Vol. IV, Hassocks, Sussex, 1981

Mill, John Stuart, *Considerations on Representative Government*, in *The Collected Works of John Stuart Mill*, Toronto, 1965–86, Vol. XIX

Miller, David, *Social Justice*, Oxford, 1976

Market, State and Community, Oxford, 1989

'A Vision of Market Socialism', *Dissent*, 38, 1991

Miller, David (ed.), *Liberty*, Oxford, 1991

Morgenbesser, S., Suppes, P. and White, M. (eds.), *Philosophy, Science, and Method: Essays in Honor of Ernest Nagel*, New York, 1969

Morris, Christopher, 'The Relation between Self-Interest and Justice in Contractarian Ethics', *Social Philosophy and Policy*, 5, 1987

Münzer, Stephen R., *A Theory of Property*, Cambridge, 1990

Nagel, Thomas, 'Libertarianism Without Foundations', in J. Paul (ed.)

Narveson, Jan, *The Libertarian Idea*, Philadelphia, 1988

Norman, Richard, *Free and Equal*, Oxford, 1987

Nove, Alec, *The Economics of Feasible Socialism*, London, 1983
Nozick, Robert, 'Coercion', in S. Morgenbesser *et al.* (eds.)
  Anarchy, State, and Utopia, New York, 1974
  Philosophical Explanations, Oxford, 1981
Olivecrona, Karl, 'Locke's Theory of Appropriation', *Philosophical Quarterly*, 24, 1974
Overton, Richard, *An Arrow Against All Tyrants*, as quoted in Macpherson, pp. 140–1
Pagano, Ugo, *Work and Welfare in Economic Theory*, Siena, 1983
Pashukanis, E. B., *Law and Marxism*, London, 1978
Paul, Ellen Frankel, Miller Jr, Fred D., Paul, Jeffrey and Ahrens, John (eds.), *Marxism and Liberalism*, Oxford, 1986
  Capitalism, Oxford, 1989
Paul, Jeffrey (ed.), *Reading Nozick*, Totowa, NJ, 1981
Plato, *The Republic*, Oxford, 1945
Plekhanov, George, *The Development of the Monist View of History*, Moscow, 1956
Pogge, Thomas, *Reading Rawls*, Ithaca, NY, 1989
Rawls, John, *A Theory of Justice*, Cambridge, MA, 1971
  'The Basic Structure as Subject', in Goldman and Kim (eds.)
  'Social Unity and Primary Goods', in Sen and Williams (eds.)
  'Justice as Fairness: A Briefer Restatement', Harvard University, typescript, 1989
  Political Liberalism, New York, 1993
Raz, Joseph, *Practical Reason and Norms*, Oxford, 1975
  The Morality of Freedom, Oxford, 1986
Roemer, John, 'Should Marxists be Interested in Exploitation?', in Roemer (ed.)
  Free to Lose, Cambridge, MA, 1988
  'Public Ownership and Private Property Externalities', in Elster and Moene (eds.)
Roemer John (ed.), *Analytical Marxism*, Cambridge, 1986
Rosenblum, Nancy (ed.), *Liberalism and the Moral Life*, Cambridge, MA, 1989
Ryan, Alan, review of Wolff, *Ethics*, 103, 1992
Sabine, George, *A History of Political Theory*, New York, 1958
Scanlon, Thomas, 'Liberty, Contract and Contribution', in Dworkin *et al.* (eds.)
Scheffler, Samuel, *The Rejection of Consequentialism*, Oxford, 1982
Schelling, Thomas, *Strategy of Conflict*, New York, 1960
Schochet, G. (ed.), *Life, Liberty and Property: Essays on Locke's Political Ideas*, Belmont, CA, 1971
Schumpeter, Joseph, *A History of Economic Analysis*, New York, 1954
Sen, A. K., 'Isolation, Assurance and the Social Rate of Discount', *Quarterly Journal of Economics*, 80, 1967
  'Just Desert', *New York Review of Books*, 29, 1982
  'The Moral Standing of the Market', *Social Philosophy and Policy*, 2, 1985
Sen, A. K. and Williams, Bernard, *Utilitarianism and Beyond*, Cambridge, 1982
Shapley, Lloyd, 'A Value for N-person Games', in Kuhn and Tucker (eds.)
Shubik, Martin, *Game Theory in the Social Sciences*, Cambridge, MA, 1982
Simmons, A. John, *The Lockean Theory of Rights*, Princeton, 1992
Spencer, Herbert, *Social Statics*, 1st edition, London, 1851

Stalin, J. V., *Dialectical and Historical Materialism*, in J. V. Stalin, *Leninism*, New York, 1942

Steiner, Hillel, 'Individual Liberty', Proceedings of the Aristotelian Society, 75, 1974–5

'The Natural Right to the Means of Production', *Philosophical Quarterly*, 27, 1977

'Liberty and Equality', *Political Studies*, 34, 1980

'Justice and Entitlement', in J. Paul (ed.)

'The Rights of Future Generations', in MacLean and Brown (eds.)

'A Liberal Theory of Exploitation', *Ethics*, 94, 1983–4

'Capitalism, Justice, and Equal Starts', *Social Philosophy and Policy*, 5, 1987

An Essay on Rights, Oxford, 1994

Thomson, Judith, *The Realm of Rights*, Cambridge, MA, 1990

Tully, James, *A Discourse on Property*, Cambridge, 1980

'A Reply to Waldron and Baldwin', *The Locke Newsletter*, 13, 1982

Review of Grünebaum, *Ethics*. Vol. 98, 1987–8

van der Veen, Robert J. and Van Parijs, Philippe, 'Entitlement Theories of Justice', *Economics and Philosophy*, 1, 1985

Van Parijs, Philippe, 'A Revolution in Class Theory', *Politics and Society*, 15, 1986–7

Varian, Hal, 'Distributive Justice, Welfare Economics, and the Theory of Fairness', *Philosophy and Public Affairs*, 4, 1975

Waldron, Jeremy, 'Enough and As Good Left for Others', *Philosophical Quarterly*, 29, 1979

'Locke, Tully and the Regulation of Property', *Political Studies*, 32, 1984

The Right to Private Property, Oxford, 1988

Walras, Léon, *Théorie de la propriété*, in Walras, *Etudes d'Economie Sociale*, Lausanne, 1896

Walzer, Michael, *Spheres of Justice*, New York, 1983

Warren, Paul, 'Self-Ownership, Reciprocity, and Exploitation, or: Why Marxists Shouldn't be Afraid of Robert Nozick', *Canadian Journal of Philosophy*, 24, 1994

Williams, Andrew, 'Cohen on Locke, Land and Labour', *Political Studies*, 40, 1992

Wolff, Jonathan, *Robert Nozick*, Cambridge, 1991

Wollheim, Richard, *On Drawing an Object*, London, 1965

Wood, Allen, *Karl Marx*, London, 1981

'Marx and Equality', in Roemer (ed.)

Wood, Ellen Meiksins, *The Retreat from Class*, London, 1986

Index of names

Aaron, Richard, 178
Ake, Christopher, 25
Archard, David, 138
Arneson, Richard, 18, 75, 78, 83, 213
Ashcraft, Richard, 263

Baldwin, Thomas, 187
Barry, Brian, 84, 160, 225
Bergström, Lars, 128
Brody, Baruch, 86
Brown, Grant, 101
Buchanan, Allen, 140

Carens, Joseph, 257, 264
Cather, Willa, 104
Chaplin, Ralph, 144, 155
Child, James, 39
Cohen, Joshua, 88, 223

Dahl, Robert, 160
Dunn, John, 178, 194
Dworkin, Gerald, 4
Dworking, Ronald, 18, 93, 102–4, 106–11,
    116, 118–19, 160, 162, 163, 165–6, 210,
    213–14, 226

Ehring, Douglas, 149
Einstein, Albert, 245
Elster, John, 163, 254–5
Engels, Frederick, 2, 5, 123, 137, 148, 260–1,
    265
Exdell, John, 84

Feinberg, Joel, 257
Fichte, Johann Gottlieb, 209
Filmer, Robert, 191
Flew, Anthony, 116
Fourier, Charles, 5
Frankfurt, Harry, 36
Freud, Sigmund, 250–2, 254

Galston, William, 104
Gauthier, David, 18, 66, 142, 210, 216–23,
    225, 226
George, Henry, 118, 216
Geras, Norman, 125, 139, 157, 169, 195
Gorz, André, 157
Gough, John, 178
Graham, Keith, 135
Gray, John, 55, 62–5
Green, S. J. D., 238
Griffin, James, 140
Grünebaum, James, 118

Hale, Robert L., 38
Harsanyi, John, 218
Hart, H. L. A., 129
Hausman, Daniel, 219
Hegel, G. W. F., 260
Hobbes, Thomas, 223
Hobhouse, Leonard, 104
Hohfeld, W. N., 222-3
Holmstrom, Nancy, 182
Honoré, Tony, 216
Hume, David, 139–43, 225

Ingram, Attracta, 21, 83

Kant, Immanuel, 18, 32, 210, 211–13, 238–43
Khruschev, Nikita, 247
Kirzner, Israel, 52, 185–6
Klein, Melanie, 256
Knight, Frank H., 67
Kymlicka, Will, 138

Laclau, Ernesto, 156–7
Laslett, Peter, 187
Lewis, David, 130
Locke, John, 16–17, 74–9, 87, 103, 108–10,
    165–6, 170, 175–94, 209, 223
Lukes, Steven, 137, 140

Mack, Eric, 82, 122
Mackie, John, 47–8
MacLeod, Alistair, 47–8
Marx, Karl, 1–2, 7, 9–11, 17, 30, 56, 72,
    116–17, 119–29, 131–9, 141, 145–8,
    152–3, 158–9, 167–75, 178, 180–2,
    193–200, 203–5, 257–61, 265
Meacher, Michael, 157
Menger, Anton, 154
Mill, John Stuart, 263
Miller, David, 104, 257, 258, 260
Morris, Christopher, 205
Mouffe, Chantal, 156–7
Münzer, Thomas, 81

Nagel, Thomas, 4, 28, 31, 33, 56–7, 112,
    163
Narveson, Jan, 101, 221
Norman, Richard, 124
Nove, Alec, 256–7
Nozick, Robert, 4–5, 7, 12–14, 19–55, 59–94,
    99–102, 104, 108, 110, 112–15, 118, 151,
    160, 163, 165–6, 187, 211, 216, 225,
    229–36, 238–9, 241–3

Obrucher, V. A., 133–4
Olivecrona, Karl, 109, 177–8
Overton, Richard, 71, 209
Owen, Robert, 5

Pagano, Ugo, 118
Pashukanis, E. B., 134–6
Plato, 251
Plekhanov, George, 19
Pogge, Thomas, 55, 224

Rawls, John, 17, 18, 46, 63, 65, 87–8, 93, 116,
    118–19, 160, 163, 165–6, 210, 213, 217,
    223–6
Raz, Joseph, 129, 210, 231–5, 237–8
Rice, Les, 161

Roemer, John, 6, 17, 104, 107, 160, 163, 197,
    199, 204–8
Rousseau, Jean-Jacques, 71, 92
Ryan, Alan, 210

Sabine, George, 178
Scanlon, Thomas, 4, 160, 161, 231
Scheffler, Samuel, 32
Schelling, Thomas, 97
Schumpeter, Joseph, 178
Scruton, Roger, 112
Sen, A. K., 130, 186
Shapley, Lloyd, 184–5
Shubik, Martin, 184
Simmons, A. John, 77
Smith, Adam, 262–3
Spencer, Herbert, 72, 118
Stalin, J. V., 133–4, 247, 248, 255
Steiner, Hillel, 15, 21, 73, 77, 82, 84, 98,
    102–11, 116, 118, 122
Sumner, L. W., 135–6

Thomson, Judith, 213
Tully, James, 17, 69, 103, 188–94

van der Veen, Robert, 24
Van Parijs, Philippe, 6, 24, 161, 163
Varian, Hal, 86
Von Hayek, Friedrich, 260
Von Mises, Ludwig, 260

Waldron, Jeremy, 187, 189, 194, 220–1
Walras, Leon, 118
Walzer, Michael, 160
Warren, Paul, 164
William, Andrew, 186
Winchewsky, Morris, 246
Wittgenstein, Ludwig, 210
Wollheim, Richard, 250, 265
Wood, Allen, 125, 148, 169
Wood, Ellen Meiksins, 157

Subject index

Able and Infirm, story of, 94–101, 103, 223
abundance, 6–7, 10–11, 16, 116, 122–3, 126–9, 131–5, 139–43
accumulation, primitive, 120, 167–8
adaptive preference formation, 253–7
alienation, 137–8, 253
altruism, 115, 134–9, 141, *see also* human nature
appropriation, *see* justice in acquisition, provisos, world-ownership
autonomy, *see* self-ownership, freedom

bargaining, 95–7, 103, 258

Canada, 245–8
capital, *see* capitalism
capitalism
    and equal division, 103
    and exploitation, 1–2, 16–17, 145–52, 158, 160–3, 167–8, 172, 174, 195–7, 199–200, 206–7
    and freedom, 30, 34, 36–7, 68, 94, 101–2
    and justice, 15–17, 28, 34, 119–21, 123, 125, 139, 160–2
    and the market, 253–9
    and Nozick's proviso, 84–7
    and persons as ends, 241
    and scarcity, 132
    see also laissez-faire
capitalists, *see* capitalism
charity (in Locke), 189–90
China, 255
class division, 26, 244–5, 251, *see also* capitalism, exploitation, proletarians, serfdom, slavery
coercion, 35–7, 39, 68, 127–31, 146, 149–52, 195–200, 203, *see also* freedom
common ownership (of land), 78–87, 103, 188, 191–4

communism
    and abundance, 132–4
    and equality, 122, 124–5, 127–30, 135–7
    and freedom, 16, 137
    and human nature, 134–8
    and justice, 138–9, 141, 143
    and labour, 126–7
    and the market, 257–8
    and self-ownership, 16, 122–6, 129–30, 132–4, 152–3, 158–9, 259
communists, 3, 6, 152–4, 246–8
community, 261–3
competition, 132–3, *see also* the market
contract, *see* the market
co-operatives, workers', 121, 255–6

democracy, 155–6, 160, 253, 260–1
desert, 257–8
dialectical materialism, 1–2
difference principle (Rawls's), 87–8, 223–6

ecological crisis, 9–11, 127–8
efficiency, 259–60
egalitarianism
    complete, 39, 70, 106–7, 160, 165–6, 169–70, 229
    partial, 106–7, 121, 166, 170–1, 175, 229, *see also* left-wing libertarianism
    see also equal division, equality
equal division (of external resources), 94, 102–9, 120–1, 161, 169, 203–5
equality
    and communism, 122, 124–5, 127–30, 135–7
    and freedom, 28–32, 93–4, 97–102, 111–13
    and historical materialism, 5–11
    and joint ownership, 96, 104–5
    and Marxism, 5–11
    principle of, 3, 33, 69–71, 92, 115, 144, 151–2, 155, 253, 261

and self-ownership, 13–17, 259
and socialism, 94, 112
and taxation, 264
see also egalitarianism, equal division,
   justice
exchange-value, 147–9, 171–4, 179–80, *see
   also* labour theory of value
exploitation, 1–2, 12–13, 16–17, 119–21,
   144–64, 167–70, 172, 195–208, 253, 258
eye transplant lottery, 70, 243–4

force, *see* coercion
fraud, 39
freedom
   and capitalism, 30, 34, 36–7, 68, 94, 101–2
   and communism, 16, 137
   definitions of, 53–65
   and equality, 28–32, 93–4, 97–102, 111–13
   and joint ownership, 15, 98–102
   and justice, 12, 19, 38, 53, 65
   and libertarianism, 36–7, 60, 67, 80, 90
   and liberty, 61–2
   and the market, 34
   and ordinary language, 60–5
   and private property, 55–60, 65, 89
   rights definition of, 60–5
   and self-ownership, 18, 67, 93–4, 97–102,
      111, 230, 236–8
   and social self-direction, 260–2
   and socialism, 19–20, 28–31, 33, 56, 101

God, 188–9

harming and helping, 69, 117, 120, 130, 190,
   210, 215–17, 223–8
historical materialism, 1–11, 127
human nature, 28–9, 128, 134–5, 140–2,
   262–4

joint ownership
   and equality, 96, 104–5
   and freedom, 15, 98–102
   of persons, 98
   of the world, 14–15, 83–4, 93–106, 111, 115
justice
   in acquisition, 37, 72–91, 92–4, 108–10,
      113–15, 165, 176–7, 187–8, *see also*
      value/appropriation argument, labour
      mixture, provisos
   and capitalism, 15–17, 28, 34, 119–21, 123,
      125, 139, 160–2
   and communism, 138–9, 141, 143
   and end-state principles, 40
   and exploitation, 145–51, 157–8, 164,
      195–208
   and freedom, 12, 19, 28, 53, 65
   and historical materialism, 1–3, 11, 127

and infirmity, 130–1
and the market, 257, 259, 262–3
as moral virtue, 128–9, 136, 139–43
patterned principles of, 20, 24, 29, 33
and socialism, 19–20, 25
starting gate theory of, 107–11, *see also*
   equal division
in transfer, *see* the market
see also difference principle,
   egalitarianism, equality, rights

labour
   and communism, 126–7
   and desert, 257–8
   mixture, 74–5, 108–9, 165, 176–7, 187
   power, 16, 34, 53, 68, 86, 146–51, 167–8,
      195
   and socialism, 172
   theory of value, 17, 167, 169–74, 178–82
   time, 145–50, 152, 162, 197
   and utility, 95–6, 103
   see also rent, value/appropriation
      argument, value/inequality argument
laissez-faire, 19, 107–9, 214, 219, 224
land, *see* natural resources
law, 128–31, 193
law of nature (in Locke), 193
liberalism, 4, 17, 56–7, 70, 112, 120, 160–3
libertarianism
   and freedom, 36–7, 60, 67, 80, 90
   and justice in acquisition, 72–3
   and justice in transfer, 41–3
   left-wing, 15–17, 116–22, 127, 129–31, 197,
      see also partial egalitarianism
   and liberalism, 57
   Marxism and, 4, 12–13, 16–17, 144–5, 152,
      155, 163, 170, 172
   Marxists and, 4, 15–17, 119–21, 151–2,
      154, 159–60, 163
   and self-ownership, 12, 14–15, 38, 65–6,
      92–4, 97–8, 213, 229
   see also Nozick, rights, self-ownership,
      side constraints
liberty, *see* freedom
luck, 229

market, the
   and capitalism, 253–9
   and communism, 257–8
   and exchange-value, 171, 179–80
   and freedom, 34
   and harm, 120, 227–8
   and human nature, 29, 262–4
   and justice, 257, 259, 262–3
   and justice in transfer, 12, 19–28, 38–53,
      61, 72–4, 204
   see also competition, market socialism

Marxism
　　analytical, 15–17, 144, 152, 163
　　and equality, 5–11, *see also* communism
　　　and equality
　　and exploitation, 144–6, 166–7, 169–72,
　　　175, 195–208
　　and libertarianism, 4, 12–13, 15–17,
　　　119–21, 144–5, 151–2, 154–5, 159–60,
　　　163, 170, 172
　　and money fetishism, 59
　　and morality, 2–3, 8–11
　　and normative philosophy, 1–3, 8, 11, 156
　　and self-ownership, 4, 13, 141–3, 146–53,
　　　155, 158–63, 170, 196
　　self-perception of, 5–6
　　see also communism, dialectical
　　　materialism, historical materialism,
　　　labour theory of value, Marx
money, 57–9, 189
Morris Winchewsky School, 246–7

natural resources, 7, 165, 167–9, 172, 174–6,
　　178–80, 182–6, *see also* common
　　ownership, ecological crisis, equal
　　division, joint ownership, provisos,
　　scarcity, world-ownership
need, 153–9, 189–90
normative philosophy, 1–8, 11, 144, 156, 160

ownership, *see* joint ownership, private
　　property, self-ownership, world-
　　ownership

paternalism, 89–90
planning, central state, 259–61, 263
power, 25–6, 28
private property
　　and freedom, 55–60, 65, 89
　　and government, 189, 191–4
　　and paternalism, 89–90
　　and scarcity, 188
　　and self-ownership, definition of, 211-16,
　　　227–8
　　and utility, 85, 141–3, 187
　　see also equal division, justice in
　　　acquisition, world ownership
privatization, *see* justice in acquisition
producer surplus, 217–19
production, means of, 16–17, 122–3, 145–6,
　　149, 167, 195–204, 206, 258, *see also*
　　world-ownership
productive forces, development of, 6–7, 121,
　　131–3
proletarians, 3, 6–9, 14, 16–17, 34–7, 68,
　　85–6, 94, 100–4, 114, 119–20, 145–57,
　　159–63, 167–9, 173–4, 187, 195–200, 207,
　　237, 241, 243, 255

provisos (on acquisition)
　　Gauthier's, 222–3
　　Locke's, 74–5, 77–8, 82–3, 85, 87–8, 187
　　Nozick's, 74–87, 89–91, 114–15, 187–8

reflective equilibrium, 65
religion, 137
rent (as return to talent), 210, 217–23
revolution, 3, 8, 30, 125, 154–5
rights, 34–5, 68, 86–7, 119, 130, 150, 213–15,
　　221–3, 226, 232–3, 237–8, *see also* self-
　　ownership, side constraints
risk, 40, 48–51

scarcity, 7, 9–11, 78, 131–3, 140–1, 188
self-ownership
　　and autonomy, 18, 230, 236–8
　　and communism, 16, 122–6, 129–30,
　　　132–4, 152–3, 158–9, 259
　　and consent, 238–43
　　definition of, 67–72, 116–19, 209–16, 226–8
　　and equality, 13–17, 259
　　formal and effective, 97–102, 105
　　and freedom, 18, 67, 93–4, 97–102, 111,
　　　230, 236–8
　　and harming and helping, 68–9, 117, 120,
　　　130, 210, 215–17, 223–8
　　and libertarianism, 12, 14–15, 38, 65–6,
　　　92–4, 97–8, 213, 229
　　Marxists and, 4, 13, 141–3, 146–53, 155,
　　　158–63, 170, 196
　　and persons as ends, 18, 211–12, 230,
　　　238–43
　　and rent, 217–23
　　and slavery, 18, 230–6, 241–2
　　and socialism, 72, 123–5, 159, 166, 258–9
　　and world-ownership, 13–14, 16–17,
　　　69–72, 79, 92–107, 110–11, 113–15,
　　　165–6, 170, 188, 205, 209, 229
serfdom, 3, 117, 146–8, 159, 163
side constraints, 32–3
slavery, 3, 18, 21–2, 34, 47–9, 54, 68, 100, 113,
　　118, 147, 165, 167, 214, 230–6, 241–2
social democrats, 120
socialism
　　and appropriation, 82
　　arguments for, 3–5, 86–7, 156
　　and equality, 94, 112
　　and freedom, 19–20, 28–31, 33, 56, 101
　　and justice, 19–20, 25
　　and labour, 172
　　market, 86–7, 255–9, 263–4
　　movement for, 3, 10
　　and self-ownership, 72, 123–5, 159, 166,
　　　258–9
　　Soviet, 18, 245, 249–50, 252–4
　　utopian and scientific, 5–6

Soviet Union, 18, 245–7, 249–50, 252–5
state, the, 137–8, 234, *see also* welfare state,
    taxation
state of nature, 76, 86, 193, 218–23, *see also*
    common ownership
subtraction criterion (Locke's), 179, 181–6
superstructure, the, 138
surplus product, *see* exploitation

taxation, 18, 19, 25–6, 53–6, 65, 68, 89–90,
    113, 128, 152, 210, 216–21, 223, 230,
    234–5, 240–1, 263–4
technological fix, Marxist, 116, 125–6, 132
totalitarianism, 32

unemployed, the, 160–1
United Jewish People's Order, 246–7
use-value, 149, 171–2, 174–84, 186–7
utilitarianism, 33, 85–7, 142

value, *see* exchange-value, labour theory of
    value, use-value
value/appropriation argument (Locke's),
    176–8, 182, 186–8
value/inequality argument (Locke's), 176,
    178, 182–3, 186–8
vanity of vanities, 254

welfare state, 113, 117, 151–4, 160, 235,
    243
workers, *see* proletarians
world-ownership
    and appropriation, 69–91
    and equal division, 108–9
    and self-ownership, 13–14, 16–17, 69–72,
        79, 92–107, 110–11, 113–15, 165–6, 170,
        188, 205, 209, 229
    see also equal division, joint ownership,
        justice in acquisition, private property

Printed in the United Kingdom
by Lightning Source UK Ltd.
9526900001B